Law and Philosophy Library

Volume 137

The Law and Philosophy Library, which has been in existence since 1985, aims to publish cutting edge works in the philosophy of law, and has a special history of publishing books that focus on legal reasoning and argumentation, including those that may involve somewhat formal methodologies. The series has published numerous important books on law and logic, law and artificial intelligence, law and language, and law and rhetoric. While continuing to stress these areas, the series has more recently expanded to include books on the intersection between law and the Continental philosophical tradition, consistent with the traditional openness of the series to books in the Continental jurisprudential tradition. The series is proud of the geographic diversity of its authors, and many have come from Latin America, Spain, Italy, the Netherlands, Germany, and Eastern Europe, as well, more obviously for an English-language series, from the United Kingdom, the United States, Australia and Canada.

More information about this series at http://www.springer.com/series/6210

Jorge Luis Fabra-Zamora • Gonzalo Villa Rosas
Editors

Conceptual Jurisprudence

Methodological Issues, Classical Questions and New Approaches

Springer

Editors
Jorge Luis Fabra-Zamora
Faculty of Law
University of Toronto
Toronto, ON, Canada

Gonzalo Villa Rosas
Hermann Kantorowicz-Institute of
Fundamental Legal Research
University of Kiel
Kiel, Germany

ISSN 1572-4395 ISSN 2215-0315 (electronic)
Law and Philosophy Library
ISBN 978-3-030-78802-5 ISBN 978-3-030-78803-2 (eBook)
https://doi.org/10.1007/978-3-030-78803-2

This Springer imprint is published by the registered company Springer Nature Switzerland AG.
The registered company address is: Gewerbestrasse 11, 6330 Cham, Switzerland

Preface

This volume contains 15 cutting-edge essays by leading legal theorists on the central issues of conceptual jurisprudence: methodological questions about its aim and approaches, substantive questions about the legal system and its coercive character, law's relationship with morality, and law's normative character, as well as the discussion of new approaches to the field. The introduction sets the stage by explaining the goals of conceptual jurisprudence and providing a summary of the essays. We hope that this volume helps to shape the agenda for future research in this field.

Jorge Fabra-Zamora would like to thank the support of the Provost's Postdoctoral Fellowship at the University of Toronto. Gonzalo Villa Rosas would like to express his gratitude to Professor Robert Alexy and Professor Stanley L. Paulson for their encouragement and support. We together would like to thank Jorge Emilio Núñez for helping us to organize a meeting to discuss these papers. In addition to the contributors, Andrés Botero Bernal, Luka Burazin, Tomas Gizbert-Stuydnicki, Sergei Kasatkin, Cyndy Phillips, Jorge Portocarrero, Jorge Sanchéz-Pérez, Natalia Satokhina, Torben Spaak, Julieta Rábanos, and Juan Ruiz Manero participated in this meeting and contributed to the discussion of the papers.

We are grateful to the Springer Law team for their superb editorial support. Finally, special thanks are owed to all of the contributors for their patience and forbearance during the editorial process.

Hamilton, ON, Canada
Kiel, Germany
December 2019

Jorge Luis Fabra-Zamora
Gonzalo Villa Rosas

Contents

Contributors

Jason G. Allen Humboldt-Universität zu Berlin, Berlin, Germany

Pierluigi Chiassoni University of Genoa, Genoa, Italy

Juan B. Etcheverry National Research Council of Argentina (CONICET) – Universidad Austral, Buenos Aires, Argentina

Jorge Luis Fabra-Zamora Faculty of Law, University of Toronto, Toronto, ON, Canada

Paula Gaido National Research Council of Argentina (CONICET), National University of Córdoba (UNC), Córdoba, Argentina

Sari Kisilevsky Queens College CUNY, New York City, NY, USA

Massimo la Torre Universidad of Catanzaro, Catanzaro, Italy

Pau Luque Universidad Nacional Autonoma de México, México City, Mexico

Margaret Martin University of Western Ontario, London, ON, Canada

Lucas Miotto University of Maastricht University, Maastricht, Netherlands

Andres Molina-Ochoa South Texas College, McAllen, TX, USA

Jose Juan Moreso Universidad Pompeu Fabra, Barcelona, Spain

Matti Ilmari Niemi University of Eastern Finland, Eastern Finland, Finland

Enrique Cáceres Nieto Institute of Legal Research, Universidad Nacional Autónoma de Mexico, Mexico City, Mexico

Andrea Romeo University of Catanzaro, Catanzaro, Italy

Ismael Martínez Torres University of Edinburgh, Edinburgh, UK

Gonzalo Villa Rosas Christian Albrechts Universität zu Kiel, Kiel, Germany

Antonia M. Waltermann Department of Foundations and Methods of Law, Faculty of Law, Maastricht University, Maastricht, Netherlands

Introduction

Jorge Luis Fabra-Zamora and Gonzalo Villa Rosas

Abstract The introduction sets the stage by explaining the goals of conceptual jurisprudence and providing a summary of the essays.

This volume advances a systematic exploration of the field of *conceptual jurisprudence,* the theoretical enterprise concerned with elucidating the concept of law and foundational concepts that figure prominently in legal discourse and practice, including legal systems, legal obligation, legal rights, and legal powers.[1] As we conceive it, conceptual jurisprudence involves the analysis, construction, engineering, and refinement of individual concepts as well as the creation and development of comprehensive theoretical frameworks and languages to clarify the legal phenomenon and explain its relationships, similitudes, and differences with other phenomena.

Following Hart's *The Concept of Law*, conceptual jurisprudence has been the primary concern of legal philosophy.[2] Discussing methodology early in that text, Hart rejects the strategy common among previous jurisprudents of attempting to provide a "definition" of law—i.e., a linguistic formula that differentiates objects properly marked by the word "law" from phenomena marked by different words.[3] For Hart, not only do definitions fail to resolve the puzzlements that motivate the question, but law is not an object type that a definition can capture. "Law" features both central cases (i.e., modern state legal systems) and borderline cases (i.e.,

[1]Although we have derived this illustrative label from KE Himma, as explained in footnote 14, we do not follow his approach. See Himma (2015). For more information, see van der Burg (2020).

[2]Hart (2012).

[3]For the classical expression of this view, see Kantorowicz (1958).

J. L. Fabra-Zamora (✉)
Faculty of Law, University of Toronto, Toronto, ON, Canada
e-mail: jorge.fabrazamora@utoronto.ca

G. Villa Rosas
Hermann Kantorowicz-Institute of Fundamental Legal Research, University of Kiel, Kiel, Germany

J. L. Fabra-Zamora, G. Villa Rosas (eds.), *Conceptual Jurisprudence*, Law and Philosophy Library 137, https://doi.org/10.1007/978-3-030-78803-2_1

international and so-called "primitive" laws), and these are not united by the same characteristics, as required by *per genus et differentiam* definitions.[4]

Instead of a definitional project, Hart suggests that legal theorists should attempt to elucidate the concept of law as understood by "ordinary educated" citizens. To do that, we must identify and resolve "persistent questions" that have vexed the legal theorists that are divided on how best to elucidate such a concept despite being able to identify clear instances of law. The three questions are: "How does law differ from and how is it related to orders backed by threats? How does legal obligation differ from, and how is it related to, moral obligation? What are rules and to what extent is law an affair of rules?"[5] According to Hart, these puzzles "are not graciously chosen or invented for the pleasure of academic discussion... [but] concern aspects of law which seem naturally, at all times, to give rise to misunderstandings, so that confusion and a consequent need for greater clarity about them may coexist even in the minds of thoughtful men with a firm mastery of knowledge of the law."[6]

In this Hartian understanding, jurisprudence's theoretical task is to provide a rational reconstruction of the citizen-animated concept of law by examining certain influential attempts to capture it and their coherence with academic and folk beliefs about law and a range of related phenomena, including coercion and morality. Although Hart never explicitly mentions "conceptual analysis" nor does he thoroughly explain the title of his book, the philosophical context in which the book is positioned has been taken as sufficient reason for asserting that conceptual analysis is "the spirit" and "the implicit method," that animates his philosophical project.[7] Nonetheless, in a later work, he suggests that the task of jurisprudence is to provide a "general" theory of all instances of legal practices (as opposed to particular accounts of specific legal systems) that should be advanced in a "descriptive" or value-neutral manner (as opposed to value-committed or "normative" jurisprudence).[8] As this volume examines, these statements have been the focus of methodological discussions of conceptual jurisprudence.[9]

For Hart, what we are calling conceptual jurisprudence constitutes one of law's three main philosophical problems, along with normative jurisprudence and

---

[4]Hart (2012), pp. 13–14; Hart (1983a), pp. 33–35.

[5]Hart (2012), chap. 1.

[6]Ibid., p. 6.

[7]Mainly based on certain historical connections with the school of Oxford's ordinary language philosophy, Hart was taken "to be engaged in a familiar philosophical project of conceptual analysis"—that is, according to this interpretation, he was "doing the same kind of philosophical work that his peers in the philosophy of language, metaphysics, ethics and epistemology were doing." Coleman (2001), p. 175. Similarly, according to Nicos Stavropoulos, "Rather than seeking rules for using the key expressions, or setting out to list the situations in which users apply the expressions, Hart's method was usually called conceptual analysis." Stavropolous (2001), p. 69. Others, however, have rejected such a connection. See, for example, Green (2012); Marmor (2013).

[8]Hart (2012), pp. 239–40.

[9]Langlinais and Leiter (2016), p. 671.

adjudicative affairs.[10] Following the Hartian tradition, Joseph Raz further suggests that each of the three branches of practical philosophy—legal, political, and moral—comprise both a "substantive" or "evaluative" component and a "formal" component, which elucidates its basic concepts.[11] Thus, what we call here "conceptual jurisprudence," philosophy of law's formal element in Raz's terminology, has correlatives in both ethics ("conceptual ethics," which studies the basic notions of moral discourse)[12] and political philosophy ("conceptual political philosophy," which examines foundational concepts of political discourse).[13]

By using the label "conceptual jurisprudence," we do not mean to suggest that this philosophical project presupposes a specific methodology. Importantly, conceptual jurisprudence is not necessarily equivalent to the influential type of conceptual analysis qua elucidation of folk concepts that aims to explain the nature of law in terms of necessary and sufficient conditions.[14] As several of this volume's chapters recognize, there are numerous forms of "analysis" and "conceptual analysis" to be found in both general philosophy and jurisprudence.[15] Furthermore, as Michael Giudice has aptly indicated, there exist other devices different from the "analysis" of folk concepts that have dominated contemporary jurisprudence. For example, Giudice discusses "conceptual construction"; that is, the theorist's creation of novel concepts that aim to remedy the defects of insufficiently consistent folk concepts.[16] In a related project, some philosophers have introduced the notion of "conceptual engineering" to represent several initiatives that aim to design, create and improve conceptual devices for explanatory and normative purposes.[17] Furthermore, in addition to conceptual analysis tools—rational reconstruction, reflective equilibrium, thought experiments, etc.— philosophers use several other methodological devices. These include linguistic analysis and other forms of language clarification, the creation of terms, hermeneutic approaches, deconstruction, and the development of analogies, characters, models, and metaphors.[18]

While conceptual jurisprudence primarily constitutes a philosophical enterprise, we do not imply that it is the exclusive domain of legal philosophers. As some chapters in this volume illustrate, there are meaningful connections between conceptual jurisprudence and empirical and doctrinal inquiries that might provide new

[10]Hart (1983b).

[11]Raz (1999), pp. 10–1.

[12]See, e.g., Burgess and Plunkett (2013).

[13]See, e.g., Flathman (1973).

[14]The most influential approaches in this sense are found in Shapiro (2011), chap. 1, and Himma (2015).

[15]As an illustration of the richness of the notion analysis, see Beaney (2014). For the different understandings of "conceptual analysis" in jurisprudence, see the first Chapter by Pierluigi Chiassioni.

[16]Giudice (2015).

[17]Cappelen (2018); Burgess et al. (2020).

[18]William Twining offers a useful catalogue of the tools available to legal theory, with references to secondary literature. Twining (2009), pp. 40–1.

evidence regarding existing legal practices or highlight new pre-theoretical data that theoretical accounts should consider.[19] Furthermore, it is possible that empirical scholars and legal practitioners might more directly contribute to the conceptual jurisprudence project. Some writers have developed *ad hoc* accounts of law to pursue specific empirical or doctrinal inquiries. For example, representatives of the heterogeneous tradition of legal pluralism have developed different theories of the concept of law. These include approaches focused on bodies of justiciable procedures and standards[20] and self-generated discourses that both adopt the binary code legal/illegal and incorporate institutionalized secondary rulemaking processes.[21] While some of these theories might be disconnected from mainstream philosophical discourse, it would be a mistake for jurisprudents to entirely dismiss the analytical components of the proposals of anthropologists, sociologists, and jurists as non-philosophical. It would also be erroneous to assume the superiority of theories with philosophical pedigree. The analytical components of these *ad hoc* theories and theoretical fragments also contribute to conceptual jurisprudence insofar as they in some way answer the question of law, and it is possible to compare them with the standard accounts of jurisprudence—such as those advanced by Hart, Raz, and Kelsen—using the theoretical standards of simplicity, coherence, consilience, and generality.

Thus, we arrive at a broader understanding of conceptual jurisprudence that encourages philosophers to consider contributions to conceptual jurisprudence advanced outside of mainstream philosophical theory and empirical scholars and jurists to overcome their contrived attitude towards purely theoretical inquiries. "Conceptual jurisprudence" is not defined by a certain disciplinary pedigree, method, or form of evidence. Instead, it is characterized by its attempt to provide general answers to the conceptual questions about law and fundamental legal concepts that do not refer to any particular legal order or institution, a characterization that enables philosophers, empirical scholars, and doctrinal theorists alike to contribute to what is a collective enterprise.

The chapters are divided into five parts. Part I comprises three chapters concerning methodological issues of conceptual jurisprudence, including the scope and purposes of legal philosophy, its proper methodology, and theoretical criteria for adjudicating between competing theories of legal phenomena.

In the first chapter, Pierluigi Chiassoni provides a general exploration of the problem and methodology of conceptual jurisprudence. Despite the near consensus that conceptual jurisprudence aims to investigate "the concept of law," it is not clear what is meant by this expression nor what the proper methodology for accessing this concept might be. Furthermore, while many philosophers endorse the "conceptual analysis" methodology, there are multiple understandings of the requirements and process of such an analysis, including several skeptical and revisionist views.

[19] See, e.g., the chapters by Lucas Miotto and Andrés Molina-Ochoa.

[20] de Santos (2002), p. 86.

[21] Teubner (1997), p. 14.

Chiassioni's chapter provides a thorough investigation of the central methodological questions of conceptual jurisprudence, exploring the diverse understandings of conceptual analysis and discussing several criticisms about them.

Meanwhile, Juan B. Etcheverry focuses on Hart's proposal of advancing a "general" and "descriptive" legal theory, a proposal furthered by many of his followers, including Raz, but rejected by so-called "normative" jurisprudents of many sorts, including John Finnis and Ronald Dworkin. Etcheverry taxonomizes the main challenges to Hart's proposal: if legal theory takes as its object of study "our" concept of law, as Raz suggests, how could it be that a general theory merely studies a parochial concept? How is it possible to develop a theory of the nature of law in terms of necessary features of a practice that is often thought to be contingent? How is it possible to create a descriptive theory of a practice that, according to critics, does not merely describe empirical facts but necessarily requires descriptive judgement? How is it possible to describe, in morally neutral terms, a normative practice such as law? Can jurisprudence be both prescriptive and descriptive? Is there only one concept of law? Why do we need a concept of law in the first place? In turn, these questions promote the issue of the theoretical criteria for selecting among diverse theories of law. Ultimately, Etcheverry doubts the success of Hart's project, mainly on the basis of the absence of clarity surrounding its aim and its central terms.

In the closing chapter of Part I, Margaret Martin advances other critiques of the project of a descriptive jurisprudence developed by Hart and Raz. For Martin, Hart's endorsement of inclusive legal positivism[22] entails a dramatical transformation of his methodological approach: if morality were a condition of validity, as the inclusive theorist would maintain, we would be forced to revisit or abandon the descriptive project. Martin finds a similar defect in Raz's proposal, although he does attempt to accommodate the normative dimensions of law within the value-neutral Hartian conceptual analysis. Following Nigel Simmonds, Martin reframes the project of jurisprudence in terms of three questions, namely, the problem of fundamental law-making authority, the issue of law's justificatory force, and the problem of the "ideality" of law. The chapter aims not only to demonstrate the shortcomings of the descriptive project but also to emphasize the connection between substantive and methodological concerns.

Part II turns its attention to the primary tool created to explain the concept of law as an "affair of rules," i.e., the notion of a *legal system*.[23] According to numerous theorists, the central cases of law concern specific complex of norms that comprise criteria of validity and officials responsible for the creation, application, and identification of law, including those of paradigmatic nation-states and similar arrangements (e.g., the Greek *polis*, the Roman *civitas*, the Inca *tawantinsuyu*). Some theories have further argued that the *differentia specifica* of legal systems, compared to other normative arrangements that might share similar features (say, the normative

---

[22] This view is discussed in the chapters by José Juan Moreso and Sari Kisilevsky, among others.

[23] HLA Hart, for example, suggests that this notion is the "most powerful tool for the analysis of much that has puzzled both the jurist and the political theorist." Hart (2012), p. 98.

systems of universities or FIFA), is that legal systems distinctively employ forms of coercion—e.g., using force or intense social pressure (such as depriving citizens of honour, resources, or even their life)—that are unavailable in other arrangements. Part II questions the nature of legal systems and explores their main attributes.

Antonia M. Waltermann connects the question of the social foundation of legal systems with the notion of popular sovereignty, the idea that political power emanates from the people. However, despite popular sovereignty being a widely used notion in legal and political philosophy, constitutional law, and many empirical studies, it is far from clear what popular sovereignty is or how political power can be said to emanate from people. Responding to this issue, Waltermann develops a conception of popular sovereignty that connects legal theories of social rules and conventions with understandings of political sovereignty developed by political philosophers. The resulting account of popular sovereignty applies to state-law and non-state political communities (such as the European Union).

Then, Massimo La Torre criticizes a recent positivist approach, paradigmatically represented by Frederick Schauer,[24] which grounds law in the use of force and sanction. For La Torre, this law-as-coercion approach aims to offer a common-sense account of law in which the use of force is the central and distinctive feature of legal systems. Furthermore, to evade Hart's objection to Austin's coercion-based account of legality, the law-as-coercion approach adopts an anti-essentialist perspective which recognizes coercion as an explanatorily central element of legal practice but not a necessary or sufficient condition. However, La Torre argues, such alleged anti-essentialism is only superficial because force remains the core condition of the legal experience, and law is effectively reduced to some form of organized violence. Furthermore, *pace* the putative common-sense perspective heralded by its defenders, La Torre claims that the law-as-coercion approach fails to account for the complexity of the legal phenomenon as understood by those who practice it. Moreover, the law-as-coercion approach might not promote its desired anti-ideological assessment of legal practices but, on the contrary, intimate an authoritarian perspective potentially at odds with certain rule of law principles.

Finally, Lucas Miotto closes Part II with an examination of the role of coercion in the motivation of the agents who participate in the legal system. He argues against the view that citizens are motivated, at least partly, to comply with most legal mandates most of the time by their legal system's threats of sanctions and other unwelcome consequences. After providing several refined versions of this view, Miotto rejects all of them as not according with the best empirical evidence available. Consequently, he suggests that while coercion is a factor that motivates citizen conduct, it is not the only one, with other elements—i.e., social, cultural, and moral norms and beliefs—also demanding consideration.

[24]Schauer (2015).

Part III studies what has historically been considered the central question of conceptual jurisprudence: the relationship between law and morality.[25] According to contemporary legal theory, jurisprudents can be divided into two general camps. On the one hand, legal positivists that hold that there are no necessary connections between law and morality, thereby focusing their attention on the existence conditions of legal systems.[26] On the other hand, non-positivists, which include classical natural lawyers in this characterization, that claim that there are relevant explanatory connections between law and morality, devoting their theoretical efforts to elucidating them.[27] In addition to this traditional debate, defenders of Hartian positivism are divided into two camps, with "inclusive" legal positivists holding that morality can sometimes be a condition of validity or membership in a legal system,[28] and "exclusive" legal positivists holding that, for conceptual reasons (such as the service function that law should play), morality can never be a condition of validity.[29]

In the first chapter, José Juan Moreso explores the problem of law and morality in Hart's positivism, criticizing Hart's endorsement of the inclusive camp in his influential *Postscript* to *The Concept of Law*.[30] According to Moreso, Hart's particular defence creates a dilemma: either the thesis of moral objectivity is true and, thus, determining what the law requires depends on moral arguments, or the thesis is false and, thus, the law's references to morality only constitute recommendations to courts to create laws in accordance with morality. In this view, both approaches to the dilemma remain within the sphere of exclusive legal positivism, precluding any consideration of inclusive positivism.

Matti Ilmari Niemi establishes a novel approach to legal theory that captures the fundamental intuitions of both natural law and positivist theories of law while also resisting the core objections to them. Concerning classical natural law jurisprudence, Niemi argues that this approach adequately captures the ways legal systems share many common values and protect human goods. However, mainstream natural law theories are often problematic because they either presuppose a religious foundation or select principles of justice that appear arbitrary or unwarranted. Meanwhile,

---

[25]There are numerous statements from legal philosophers suggesting that this is the central question of jurisprudence. For example, as noted above, one of Hart's central questions concerns explaining how legal obligations differ from and are related to moral obligations. Hart (2012), pp. 7–8. Brian Leiter similarly diagnose legal philosophers as having "been preoccupied with specifying the differences between two systems of normative guidance that are omnipresent in all human societies: law and morality. In the last 100 years... the problem of how to distinguish these two normative systems has been *the* dominant problem in jurisprudence..." Leiter (2011), p. 664.

[26]Austin (1995), Kelsen (1992), and Hart (2012) are considered primary examples of legal positivism thus understood.

[27]Aquinas (1981), Finnis (2011), and Murphy (2003) are examples of classical natural lawyers, who generally endorse a specific conception of basic goods. In turn, Dworkin (1986) and Alexy (2002) are examples of self-styled "non-positivists," who differ from natural lawyers by not endorsing a classical conception of basic goods.

[28]See, e.g., Waluchow (1994).

[29]See, e.g., Raz (1994).

[30]Hart (2012), pp. 238–276.

although legal positivism captures the factual dimensions of law, it fails to adequately capture the role of principles of morality and justice in the interpretation of legal materials and the application of laws to specific cases. To overcome these issues, Niemi outlines the foundations of a theory of law as an "expression of adopted justice." In his view, this theory captures the factual dimension of legal materials emphasized by positivists and describes the role of principles and substantive reasoning in legal interpretation and the application of these materials.

Then, Andrés Molina-Ochoa's chapter examines what he calls "the Resistance argument," one of Hart's arguments for legal positivism. For Hart, a positivist concept of law that separates law from morality compares favourably with non-positivist concepts because it facilitates resistance against oppressive regimes.[31] According to this argument, given law is separable from morality, law loses part of its "aura of majesty," and, thereby, the legality of a norm is not a conclusive reason for citizen obedience. Molina-Ochoa argues that the evidence the Milgram experiments provides regarding obedience to authority figures offers empirical support for Hart's hypothesis. He also suggests that these experiments call non-positivist concepts of law into question, particularly those in which law claims moral correctness, such as that advanced by Robert Alexy.

In the next chapter, Andrea Romeo explores the problem of the concept of law in the domain of legal ethics, i.e., the study of the moral standards applicable to the legal profession. The chapter is framed as a dialectical reconstruction of the central jurisprudential debates in the domain of legal ethics. Romeo begins with the "standard view" in legal ethics—premised on certain forms of legal realism and certain positivist views—that portrays lawyers as "hired guns" that have to defend their client's causes to the best of their ability within the rules of the legal system. In response, some legal ethicists have utilized non-positivist theories of law to develop a second approach, according to which, given the connections between law and morality, lawyers must exercise their moral judgement on the client's goals, advancing their defence on the basis of the law's moral principles. Meanwhile, a third approach to legal ethics, based on Hart and Raz's positivist theories of law, maintains that, given law's goal is to remedy disagreements present in pluralist societies through forms of settlement, the function of lawyers is to enable these settlements by defending the causes of citizens without morally assessing them. Given objections to these views, Romeo sketches a new alternative that conceives of lawyers as "filters against legal abuse," arguing that this view compares favourably to the previous options by establishing a role for legal ethics not equal to pure moral discourse yet independent of the morality or values of the settled law.

Part IV focuses on questions on the law's normative character and its role in practical reason. While there are competing notions of what constitutes law's "normativity"—including its norm-based nature, its particular form of operation, and its moral value—many theorists have followed Raz by characterizing this problem as "protected" reasons for action: legal norms create reasons to act in a

[31]Ibid., p. 210.

certain way and to exclude other reasons in practical judgement.[32] Part IV explores several problems regarding these critical issues.

Sari Kisilevsky enters the debate between positivist and non-positivist approaches to conceptual jurisprudence with a discussion of the moral significance of law, particularly in the resolution of hard cases. She begins by considering the often-neglected Hartian claim that law is a system of rules rather than of orders backed by threats. According to Kisilevsky, Hart's conception of law as a system of rules involves a critical internal normative framework that provides law with its distinctive moral force. Moreover, she argues that the moral significance of this internal structure is distorted by theorists who develop external descriptions of legal practice. She illustrates these theses through discussion of hard cases, such as *Riggs v. Palmer*. While positivists often suggest that these cases concern the applicability of moral considerations external to law, Kisilevsky holds that the internal normative structure of law resolves these issues, helping positivists to answer the challenges non-positivists have levied against them.

Then, Pau Luque and Israel Martínez critically examine a recent attempt by David Plunkett and Scott Shapiro to reconstruct general jurisprudence as "a branch of meta-normative inquiry," i.e., as the project of explaining normative thought, talk, and reality.[33] While Plunkett and Shapiro hold that jurisprudence parallels metaethics, the other sector of meta-normative inquiry, they differ in their object of study. Whereas metaethics focuses on ethical talk, thought, and reality, jurisprudence is a meta-legal study that focuses on legal talk, thought, and reality. Luque and Martínez argue that this meta-normative approach to general jurisprudence is under-inclusive in two respects. On the one hand, the meta-normative approach might ultimately mischaracterize or exclude theories—traditionally considered parts of general jurisprudence—that deny the ways legal discourse is normative, particularly legal realism and imperativism. On the other hand, the meta-normative conception of jurisprudence ignores important sectors of legal discourse that are descriptive, including detached statements, i.e., statements about a normative system issued by a non-committed agent. According to Luque and Martínez, detached legal statements are legal thought and talk despite not being normative. They conclude that, *pace* Plunkett and Shapiro's goals, the meta-normative conception fails to capture both legal discourse and theory, and it is unable to illuminate the existing debate surrounding jurisprudence.

In the last chapter of Part IV, Paula Gaido critically evaluates the links between legal norms and reasons for action in Raz's theories of law, authority, and practical and legal reasoning. On the one hand, Raz's theory of law maintains that legal norms operate as protected reasons for action, including complex reasons that not only prescribe reasons to act but also exclude other considerations regarding the action required. In addition, Raz's conception of authority further holds that law's exclusionary powers are connected to the service that law provides, namely, identifying

---

[32]For the classical formulation, see Raz (1999).

[33]Plunkett and Shapiro (2017).

the right thing to do. However, on the other hand, Raz's theory of legal reasoning indicates that judges are required to make moral arguments while applying the law and that they are allowed to change it in some circumstances. Furthermore, Raz suggests that this feature persists even when the law is settled, potentially leading judges to change the law. Gaido argues that the judge's power to revise the underlying applicable moral reasons is incompatible with Raz's conception of law and its service function. Specifically, if the law is authoritative for judges, it is a protected reason and need not consult the underlying applicable reasons. Alternatively, if judges can change the law, it is not authoritative for them, at least not in the exclusionary sense developed by Raz.

Finally, Part V comprises two works that suggest novel approaches to conceptual jurisprudence. Their novelty derives from their attempts to break with the methodological approach and three vexing questions presented by Hart.

Jason Allen radically transforms the hackneyed analogy—employed by Hart and many of his followers—that compares law to games. While many jurisprudents and social philosophers have focused exclusively on simple games, such as chess,[34] Allen considers Massive Multiplayer Online Role-Playing Games (MMORPGs) such as World of Warcraft and Second Life. MMORPGs retain the rule-constituted nature of games that motivates the analogy; however, they include features that compare favourably to traditionally used games. According to Allen, whereas the mainstream examples are relatively simple—from a normative perspective—MMORPGs are complex normative phenomena intrinsically intertwining social, normative, and technical components. In these games, players commonly create avatars, act in a virtual environment, and, sometimes, perform economic-like transactions that resemble "real" life. Hence, MMORPGs not only constitute normative systems worthy of jurisprudential study but also significantly parallel the law in ways that might illuminate certain traditional questions of jurisprudence. These questions include issues of agency, personhood, acts-in-law, non-robust normativity, and the so-called fictional character of both games and law. Through this argument, Allen highlights connections between the work of general jurisprudence and the fields of social ontology, philosophy of language, and philosophy of games.

In this volume's final chapter, Enrique Cáceres Nieto outlines the foundations and main results of a novel approach to jurisprudence that he labels "Legal Constructivism," an epistemological, theoretical, and methodological approach that attempts to explain legal systems as complex social constructs that emerge from cognitive agents' consistent behaviour and attitudes. One distinctive feature of this approach is its explicit attempt to connect conceptual jurisprudence and social philosophy with scientific evidence. This specifically includes recent developments in the areas of cognitive science and complexity theory. Cáceres Nieto also suggests that this theory is an attempt to establish foundations for a truly naturalized jurisprudence, providing resources for addressing certain novel challenges of legal theory, including artificial

[34] For a classical formulation, see Marmor (2006).

intelligence, neuroscience, and complexity, that he considers incapable of proper explanation using extant legal theories.

References

Alexy R (2002) The argument from injustice: a reply to legal positivism. Clarendon Press, Oxford

Aquinas T (1981) The Summa Theologica of St. Thomas Aquinas. Christian Classics, New York

Austin J (1995) The province of jurisprudence determined. Cambridge University Press, Cambridge

Beaney M (2014) Analysis. In: Zalta EN (ed) Standford encyclopedia of philosophy

Burgess A, Plunkett D (2013) Conceptual ethics I. Philos Compass 8:1091–1101. https://doi.org/10.1111/phc3.12086

Burgess A, Cappelen H, Plunkett D (eds) (2020) Conceptual engineering and conceptual ethics. Oxford University Press, Oxford

Cappelen H (2018) Fixing language: an essay on conceptual engineering. Oxford University Press, Oxford

Coleman JL (2001) The practice of principle: in defense of a pragmatist approach to legal theory. Oxford University Press, New York

de Santos BS (2002) Toward a new legal common sense: law, globalization, and emancipation, 2nd edn. Cambridge University Press, Cambridge

Dworkin R (1986) Law's Empire. Harvard University Press, Cambridge

Finnis J (2011) Natural law and natural rights, 2nd edn. Oxford University Press, Oxford

Flathman RE (1973) Concepts in social & political philosophy. Macmillan, London

Giudice M (2015) Understanding the nature of law: a case for constructive conceptual explanation. Edward Elgar Publishing, Cheltenham

Green L (2012) Introduction. In: The concept of law, 3rd edn. Clarendon Press, Oxford, pp xv–lv

Hart HLA (1983a) Definition and theory in jurisprudence. In: Essays in jurisprudence and philosophy. Clarendon Press, Oxford, pp 21–48

Hart HLA (1983b) Problems of the philosophy of law. In: Essays in jurisprudence and philosophy. Clarendon Press, Oxford, pp 88–119

Hart HLA (2012) The concept of law, 3rd edn. Clarendon Press, Oxford

Himma KE (2015) Conceptual jurisprudence. An introduction to conceptual analysis and methodology in legal theory. Revus 26:65–92

Kantorowicz H (1958) The definition of law. Cambridge University Press, Cambridge

Kelsen H (1992) Introduction to the problems of legal theory: a translation of the first edition of the 'Reine Rechtslehre' or Pure Theory of Law. Clarendon Press, Oxford

Langlinais A, Leiter B (2016) In: Cappelen H, Gendler TS, Hawthorne J (eds) The methodology of legal philosophy. Oxford University Press, Oxford

Leiter B (2011) The demarcation problem in jurisprudence: a new case for scepticism. Oxf J Leg Stud 31:663–677

Marmor A (2006) How law is like chess. Legal Theory 12:347–371

Marmor A (2013) Farewell to conceptual analysis (in Jurisprudence). In: Waluchow W, Sciaraffa S (eds) Philosophical foundations of the nature of law. Oxford University Press, Oxford, pp 209–228

Murphy MC (2003) Natural law jurisprudence. Legal Theory 9:241–267

Plunkett D, Shapiro S (2017) Law, morality, and everything else: general jurisprudence as a branch of metanormative. Ethics 128:37–68

Raz J (1994) Authority, law, and morality. In: Ethics in the public domain. Clarendon Press, Oxford, pp 210–237

Raz J (1999) practical reason and norms, 2nd edn. Oxford University Press, Oxford

Schauer F (2015) The force of law. Harvard University Press, Cambridge

Shapiro SJ (2011) Legality. Harvard University Press, Cambridge
Stavropolous N (2001) Hart's semantics. In: Coleman JL (ed) Hart's postscript: essays on the postscript to the concept of law. Oxford University Press, New York, pp 59–98
Teubner G (1997) 'Global Bukowina': legal pluralism in the world society. In: Teubner G (ed) Global law without a state. Dartmouth, Aldershot, pp 3–30
Twining W (2009) General jurisprudence: understanding law from a global perspective. Cambridge University Press, Cambridge
van der Burg W (2020) Conceptual theories of law and the challenges of global legal pluralism: a legal interactionist approach. In: Berman PS (ed) The Oxford handbook on global legal pluralism. Oxford University Press, Oxford
Waluchow WJ (1994) Inclusive legal positivism. Clarendon Press, Oxford

Part I
Methodological Questions

On the Concept of the Concept of Law

Pierluigi Chiassoni

Abstract Jurisprudents often conceive their task as requiring investigating "the concept of law." What is, however, the concept of "(the) concept of law"? What do legal philosophers do when they investigate the concept of law? What do legal philosophers mean when they set for the concept of law? Is conceptual analysis—apparently, the primary tool for any search about the concept of law—a useful instrument for jurisprudential enquiries? The chapter purports to cast some light on these issues by way of a meta-philosophical investigation.

1 Foreword

Meta-philosophy of law is critical reflection upon legal philosophy. It may be conceived either as a prescriptive or as a descriptive enterprise.

Prescriptive meta-philosophy of law purports to provide recommendations about the philosophically proper (fruitful, useful, worthwhile) way of devising the matter, purpose, and method of legal philosophy.

Descriptive meta-philosophy of law, contrariwise, is about legal philosophy as it is carried out in fact by legal philosophers at a certain time and place.

Assuming the perspective of descriptive meta-philosophy, I will pursue two—very modest—aims in this chapter.

First, I will draw a (tentative) map of a few different ways in which legal philosophers conceive (and proceed to) an enquiry about the concept of law. The map, as we shall see, will provide an opportunity for setting forth a few arguments in favour of analytical enquiries, and against essentialist or synthetic ones.

Second, taking stock of an influential critique to conceptual analysis as a useful tool for worthwhile jurisprudential investigations, I will consider three varieties in turn and defend one of them as adequate for an analytical and realistic legal philosophy.

P. Chiassoni (✉)
Tarello Institute for Legal Philosophy, Department of Law, University of Genoa, Genova, Italy
e-mail: pierluigi.chiassoni@unige.it

J. L. Fabra-Zamora, G. Villa Rosas (eds.), *Conceptual Jurisprudence*, Law and Philosophy Library 137, https://doi.org/10.1007/978-3-030-78803-2_2

2 The Diversified Quest for the Concept of Law

Jurisprudents often regard their task as requiring some investigation about "the concept of law."[1] When they do so, however, it quite frequently happens that they understand such an investigation differently. Four different ways of inquiring upon the concept of law seem worthwhile considering.[2]

To begin with, an investigation upon "the concept of law" can be conceived as a lexicographic enquiry upon the actual meaning(s) (communicative content(s)) of the word "law" and the corresponding expressions in other modern languages, like, e.g., *derecho*, *direito*, *diritto*, *droit*, *Recht*, *prawo*, etc.[3]

Secondly, an investigation upon "the concept of law" can be conceived as an enquiry aimed at the elucidation—clarification, rational reconstruction—of the meaning(s) associated to the word "law" in a certain legal culture, in such a way as to furthering jurists' and people-at-large's understanding about it and the phenomena it refers to.[4]

Thirdly, an investigation upon "the concept of law" can be conceived as an enquiry geared to providing a proper (adequate, accurate, useful) definition of one or more meanings of the word "law", according to what the legal philosopher

---

[1]In the words of Uberto Scarpelli (1955), p. 35: "the definition of law, and the analysis of the relationships between the concept of law and the concepts of justice, morality, economics, politics, etc., are the matter of an ancient and always renewed dispute. " (my translation from the original text in Italian, ndr). Likewise, according to Robert Alexy (2006), p. 281: "The debate over the concept and the nature of law is both venerable and lively. Reaching back more than two millennia, it has acquired in our day a degree of sophistication hitherto unknown."

[2]Throughout this paper, I will deal with the concept or concepts of law conceiving them as linguistic entities: as the meaning(s) or communicative content(s) associated to the word "law" and corresponding expressions in other natural languages. In so doing, I do not wish to enter into the ontological dispute about the nature of concepts (whether, in particular, they are psychological entities or something else)—which, by the way, is often loaded with obscurity, baffling definitions, metaphors, and mental cramps. I will assume that, whatever conception we take, concepts always have a linguistic side: whatever they are, they are, and work as, the meaning(s) or communicative content(s) of "descriptive", "predicative", "categorical", or "class" terms. On the ontologies of concepts, see e.g. Carnap (1932), pp. 60–81; Margolis and Laurence (2011), para 1; Lalumera (2009), pp. 29–95; Moreso (2017), pp. 63–99, drawing on Margolis and Laurence (2011), and referring to the conceptual pluralism about the law advocated by Carlos Santiago Nino (Nino (1994a), Nino (1994b)) and Ronald Dworkin (Dworkin (2006) and Dworkin (2011)). In passing, Gottlob Frege appears to dismiss the ontological issue in the turn of a few, crystal-clear, lines: "The word 'concept' is used in various ways; its sense is sometimes psychological, sometimes logical, and sometimes perhaps a confused mixture of both. Since license exists, it is natural to restrict it by requiring that when once a usage is adopted it shall be maintained." Frege (1892), p. 42. In my enquiry I also considered Alexy and Bulygin (2001), Austin (1961), Bernal Pulido (2011), Burazin et al. (2018), Carnap (1956), Castignone et al. (1994), D'Almeida et al. (2013), Farrell (2006), Hart (1983), Jori and Pintore (2014b), Laslett (1956), Quine (1981), Raz (1983), Raz (1994), Raz (2007), Raz (2009a), Schilpp (1963).

[3]See e.g. Tarello (1993a), pp. 5–10.

[4]See e.g. Hart (1954), pp. 21–26; Hart (1961) pp. vi–vii, 213–237; Scarpelli (1955), pp. 36–38, 67–119; Tarello (1993a), pp. 10–12; Tarello (1993b), pp. 109–119; Jori and Pintore (2014a), pp. 41–56.

considers to be needed in view of certain legal theory's or legal policy's purposes.[5]

Fourthly, and finally, an investigation upon "the concept of law" can be conceived as an enquiry aimed at identifying the concept of law (the meaning of "law") that is adequate to the very nature or essence of law.[6]

The four lines of investigations understand "the concept of law" differently.

From the standpoint of *lexicographic enquires*, "the concept of law" is tantamount to the meaning(s) corresponding to the actual uses of the word "law" or homologous words in other modern languages. The correctness of the concept of law is a matter of empirical truth. A lexicographic concept of law is true, if, and only if, the word "law," as a matter of fact, is being used in that meaning within the relevant linguistic community.[7] Though they may appear idle, lexicographic enquiries are the bedrock of analytical legal philosophy. Usually, they provide the empirical data making up the starting point for conceptual investigations of the second (clarification) or third (stipulative) kind.[8]

---

[5]See e.g. Williams (1945), pp. 134–156; Kantorowicz (1958), pp. 37–49; Hart (1961), pp. 209–212; Nino (1994a, b), pp. 17–42; Jori and Pintore (2014a), pp. 45–46, where they deal with the stipulative approach as "idiosyncratic conceptual manipulation", leading to "idiosyncratic concepts of law", as opposed to the "minimal", "common sense" concept that can be identified by means of lexicographic enquiry. A stipulative approach, based on sound empirical knowledge about legal experience, is apparently endorsed also by Frederick Schauer in his crusade for considering coercion "not strictly necessary but so ubiquitous that a full understanding of the phenomenon [of law, ndr] requires that we consider it" (Schauer (2015), p. 40; see also Schauer (2018), para 1: "humans can remake or modify the very concept of law that exists within some community").

[6]See e.g. Alexy (2006), pp. 281–299; Alexy (2001); Alexy (2017) pp. 314–341.

[7]In perhaps more precise terms, a lexicographic concept of law is true of the word "law" when the corresponding lexicographic sentence is true: namely, when a sentence of the form "According to the linguistic uses of 'law' in time t_i and place p_i, 'law' means l_i" is empirically true.

[8]Acting as legal lexicographer, and using the (Benthamite) technique of contextual definition or definition in use, Tarello (1993a, b), pp. 5–10 identifies four different meanings of "*diritto*" in contemporary Italian legal experience. When it occurs in sentences like "Il diritto è dalla mia" ("The law is on my side"), "diritto" ("law") means law in an objective sense: i.e., it refers to a set of social norms having, as we shall see, a certain typical social function. When it occurs in sentences like "Ho diritto di fare *f*" ("I have the legal right to do *f*"), "diritto" refers, contrariwise, to a subjective, favourable, legal position. When it occurs in sentences like "Il diritto di proprietà è riconosciuto in Freedonia" ("The law of property is recognized in Freedonia"), "diritto" refers to a legal institute, i.e., to a certain sub-set of positive legal norms. Finally, when it occurs in sentences like "In caso di morte del Presidente il Vicepresidente subentra di diritto" ("In the event of the President's death, the Vice-President steps in by law"), "diritto" ("law") refers to some legal automatism. It must be emphasized that, according to Tarello, the identification of lexicographic concepts of law is to be considered as the first, sound step in a virtuous analytical enquiry. The second step, which already belongs to conceptual analysis in a reconstructive function, consists in bringing to the fore the conceptual connexions between the four actual meanings of "law" previously identified. These connexions allow for regarding the concept of law as a set of social norms (the law in an objective sense) as the basic concept, which the other three concepts presuppose. A legal right ("diritto in senso soggettivo") is a right conferred by some norm of objective law. A legal institute, like property or contract, is nothing else but a sub-set of norms of an objective law. A legal automatism is necessarily established, again, by some set of norms of objective law. The third and last step of

From the standpoint of *clarification enquiries*, "the concept of law" is the result, in terms of the analytical theory of definition, of a so-called explanatory definition, or re-definition, or, in logical positivism's terminology, rational reconstruction. This is a way of defining the concept of law that aims at replacing a clearer, more precise, more refined *explicatum*-concept of law to the extant, less clear, less precise, less refined *explicandum*-concept, taking into account the complex of ideas usually associated to the actual uses of the word "law". The correctness of an explanatory concept of law is not a matter of empirical truth. To be sure, it must get adequate empirical support from the relevant legal experience; it must be tightly fastened, so to speak, to a certain set of sound empirical linguistic and cultural data. Nonetheless, its theoretical correctness depends on such theoretical virtues as precision, simplicity and explanatory power. Precision requires the narrowing down, so far as possible, of any unnecessary indeterminacy in the extant concept of law. Simplicity rules out any unnecessarily complex concept of law. Explanatory power requires the concept of law to consist in a concise discourse bringing to the fore the theoretically paramount properties of the law. To be sure, from the standpoint of clarification enquiries about the concept of law, which properties, in a complex social phenomenon like "the law," are to be regarded as theoretically paramount is not, and cannot be, a matter for objective cognitive judgments (meaning by that judgements not depending on the jurisprudent's own beliefs, attitudes, and purposes). It is, rather, a matter for judgements by means of which the legal philosopher sets forth what, in her or his view, should be regarded as the theoretically paramount properties of law, taking into account legal experience and public jurisprudential opinion.[9] Explanatory concepts

---

Tarello's conceptual investigation belongs to a clarification or elucidation approach to the concept of law. Here, by way of clarification of the concept of law in use in actual Western legal culture, he sets forth a functional definition of "law" in the objective sense of the word. In his own terms: "the object or phenomenon to which the word law (and the corresponding words in other modern languages) refers" consists of "the set of rules that, in any society whatever, regulate (a) *the repression of the behaviours considered as socially dangerous* [...]; (b) *the allocation of goods and services to individuals and communities*; (c) *the institution and ascription of public powers*" (italics in the text, ndr). Tarello also adopts the same approach, binding lexicographic research to clarification enquiry, in relation to the notion of "positive law" in the Italian legal culture of the 1950s and 1960s (see Tarello (1993b), pp. 109–119).

[9]One of the prominent torchbearers of the clarification approach to the concept of law has been, to be sure, Herbert Hart. As it is well known, Hart insists that the purpose of clarifying or elucidating the concept of law ("our" concept of law) should not be meant as requiring to provide a definition of law: i.e., a set of rigid rules about the correct use of "law", to be adopted for regulating people's linguistic behaviours. He thinks, indeed, that people do already know how to use "law" (and related legal words), but also that, as it often occurs, they do not (fully) understand the phenomenon it refers to ("In law as elsewhere, we can know and yet not understand": Hart (1954), p. 21). That is the reason why, in *The Concept of Law*, he sets to "further the understanding of law, coercion, and morality as different but related social phenomena." Hart (1961), p. vi. That is the reason why, always in *The Concept of Law*, while dealing with international law, he rejects the definitional approach and stands for an analysis that purports to bring to the fore (make "explicit") "the principles that have in fact guided the existing usage" of "law" and "inspect" their "credentials." Hart (1961), pp. 214–215. These ideas of Hart, as it is well known, were developed in a direction conceiving of legal philosophy as an enquiry not (solely) on the concept of law, but rather on the

of law are, accordingly, something legal philosophers propose to other legal philosophers, and the legal community at large, hoping for approval. Sometimes the proposal succeeds.[10] But it may also fail. The Jurisprudence bookshelves of university libraries are replete with ambitious but forever forgotten explanatory concepts of law.

From the standpoint of *stipulative enquiries*, "the concept of law" is conceived as a pragmatic entity. It is a notion the value thereof depends on its adequacy to the specific theoretical or practical goals the legal philosopher happens to pursue. As I said, the output of a stipulative approach may even be not just one concept, but a set of several concepts, according to the several different needs being pursued at once by the legal philosopher. Furthermore, the need may be strictly theoretical. In such a case, the concept(s) of law will serve some explanatory goal. Accordingly, clarification enquiries can be regarded as a variety of stipulative enquiries as presently defined. It may also be of a practical character, though. In such a case, the concept will serve some ideological purpose. For instance, the goal may be that of providing the conceptual ground for a certain doctrine about the moral duty of obedience to positive laws. In any case, the correctness of stipulative concepts of law is a matter of instrumental rationality: they are correct, if, and insofar as, they serve the purpose (s) they are meant to serve in a satisfactory way.[11]

---

nature or essential or necessary properties of law. See e.g. Raz (2009b), pp. 17–46, 91–106; Shapiro (2011), pp. 9–32. The position of Raz, however, looks close to the idea of a rational reconstruction of the structure of legal thought as advocated by Hart. For instance, he insists that an enquiry upon the nature of law consists in "inquiring into the typology of social institutions, not into the semantics of terms. We build a typology of social institutions by reference to *properties we regard, or come to regard, as essential* to the type of institution in question." Raz (2009b), p. 29, italics added, ndr. Furthermore, he makes clear that an enquiry upon the nature of law is an enquiry about "the nature of our self-understanding [. . .] It is part of the self-consciousness of our society to see certain institutions as legal. And that consciousness is part of what we study when we inquiry into the nature of law." Raz (2009b), p. 31. Raz leaves "the question of the *kind of necessity involved* unexplored" ((Raz (2009b), p. 91, italics added, ndr). Apparently, however, the "necessary truths" about the law that, in his view, legal theory should be looking for are the truths about the law that *appear to be so* upon an inquiry on societies' legal self-consciousness (Raz (2009b), p. 98: "legal theory attempts to capture the essential features of law, as encapsulated in the self-understanding of a culture"). On the same footing, in view of getting to law's "necessary and interesting properties", Shapiro adopts a conceptual analysis approach, the starting point of which is provided by a set of legal "truisms." Shapiro (2011), pp.13–22. On Hart's and Raz's approach to the concept of law, see also, in the present book, Etcheverry (2020) and Martin (2020).

[10] For instance, Hart's proposal of conceiving the law of municipal legal systems as the union of primary rules of conduct and secondary rules of change, adjudication, and recognition (Hart (1961), chs. V and VI), can be counted among jurisprudential successes, at least so far as contemporary common law legal culture is considered.

[11] In his posthumous work *The Definition of Law* (Kantorowicz (1958), pp. 37–49), Hermann U. Kantorowicz advocates "conceptual pragmatism", "conceptual relativism", or Carnap's "tolerance principle", against "verbal realism." The latter he sees as a mysterious quest for the essence of the things the concept of which is to be defined: "Nobody [. . .] has [ever] been able to explain what the metaphysical term '*Wesen*' or 'essence' means, and nobody has [ever] been able to point to a method for teaching the intuition necessary to grasp it" (Kantorowicz (1958), p. 41). Conceptual

Finally, from the standpoint of *essentialist enquiries*, "the concept of law" is conceived as liable to objective, truth-like, correctness. A concept of law is correct, if, and only if, it is adequate to the essence or nature of law: that is to say, if, and only if, it captures the set of properties, the presence of which makes some social phenomenon to be (really) *law*, and not something else.[12] In perhaps more precise terms, an essentialist concept of law is true of the word "law" when the corresponding essentialist sentence is true: i.e., when a sentence of the form "According to the very nature or essence of law, the word 'law' means L_i," is true, whatever we take the conditions of the essentialist truth of a concept to be.

Of the four different ways of investigating the concept of law, the former may appear totally un-philosophical. Indeed, one may say, it is just a dull exercise in legal lexicography. A couple of arrows can be shot in its favour, though. To begin with, it is worthwhile emphasizing its salutary, demystifying import. The lexicographic approach to the concept of law is in fact the tip of that powerful philosophical iceberg that is the analytical way of philosophizing. Now, such a way considers (what I shall call) the principle of conversion as paramount. The principle of conversion requires converting (obscure, overwhelming, puzzling, paralyzing) metaphysical issues ("What is law?") into (manageable) conceptual issues ("What do we (they) mean by the word "law"?"). To be sure, as I said before, the lexicographic approach does not usually exhaust the enquiries about the concept of law. Usually, it is the first step in the process of investigation that is geared either to the clarification of the on-going concept of law in a given legal culture, or to the stipulation of some theoretical or practical concept, to some corresponding theoretical or practical purpose.

The second and the third ways of investigating the concept of law belong, too, to the analytical way of philosophizing. In fact, the clarification approach can be regarded, as I said, as nothing else but a specific variety of the stipulative approach, where the aim the re-defined, rationally reconstructed, elucidated concept of law must serve consists in providing a notion, at the same time, as much precise and simple as possible, and as much ripe with explanatory (understanding-furthering) power as to the corresponding social phenomenon of law.

The fourth way of investigating the concept of law, the essentialist approach, is to be sure the more ambitious and, on its face, promising. It rejects any dwelling in dull

pragmatism, contrariwise, is to be regarded as the only approach compatible with truly rational enquiries. Following it, Kantorowicz comes to stipulating a concept of law suitable to identify the matter of "legal science", from classical antiquity to modern times, from China and India to Europe (Kantorowicz (1958), pp. 64–66, 106–157). Hart considers a stipulative, pragmatic, approach to the concept of law as the only sensible approach, when he comes to analysing Gustav Radbruch's critique to the positivist concept of law (see Hart (1961), pp. 209–212). Another instance of pragmatic conceptualism about the concept of law can be found in Carlos Santiago Nino's *Derecho, moral y política. Una revisión de la teoría general del derecho*, where he advocates conceptual pluralism as the sole adequate answer to the variety of problems besetting legal theory. See Nino (1994b), pp. 17–42.

[12]Alexy (2001); Alexy (2017), pp. 314–341.

lexicography.[13] It likewise turns down, as fatally subjective, and therefore philosophically inadequate, the rational reconstructions or stipulations about the concept (s) of law that characterize the second and third approach. It claims, as we have seen, to be able to get to the very, the true, essence of law, and capture it in its concept.

It must be emphasized however that, from the standpoint of the analytical way of philosophizing, any (purportedly) essentialist concept of law whatsoever is fool's gold.

I have already recalled the analytical way of thinking about concepts, which is resumed in the idea of pragmatic conceptualism. Pragmatic conceptualism sounds sensible from the vantage point of experience. Phenomena have properties, to be sure. They have not, however, intrinsically essential properties. The essential character of any property whatsoever is, fatally, in the eye of the beholder. Coming to the matter of the present paper, it is in the eye of the legal philosopher who looks after the essence of law. What such an essence is depends, necessarily (as a matter of empirical, psychological necessity), on the theoretical or practical purpose(s) the philosopher happens to pursue.[14] As a consequence, essentialist investigations about the concept (and the nature of) law either are preposterous, or, if they have any useful sense at all, are reducible to investigations of the clarification or stipulative sort, though couched in the pre-analytical, or anti-analytical, pseudo-objective mode of speech dear to "synthetic," "hard," philosophical outlooks.[15]

This conclusion of mine—delusive and disappointing as it may appear—is not a piece of analytically biased wishful thinking. It looks sound, for instance, as soon as we cast an analytical glance upon what is perhaps the most powerful and influential essentialist approach to the concept of law in recent times: I mean the one defended by Robert Alexy.

The core of Alexy's essentialist approach to the concept (and nature) of law can be recounted as follows.

---

[13]Essentialist legal philosophers reject dwelling in lexicographic enquiries. Nonetheless, they may consider such enquiries as a necessary, preliminary step to capturing the essence of law and formulating its proper concept. Starting from the statement that "Concepts, as always on the path to the nature of those things to which they refer, are in part parochial or conventional and in part universal", i.e., "non-conventional", or endowed with an "ideal dimension", Robert Alexy concedes that "concepts as conventional rules of meaning" play an "indispensable" role in "philosophical analysis", since they make possible the very "identification of the object of analysis. Without a concept of law *qua* conventional rule, we would not know what we are referring to when we undertake an analysis of the nature of law."

[14]Unless, of course, the legal philosopher aims at bringing to the fore the properties of the phenomenon "law" which are in fact *regarded as* essential in a certain legal culture at a certain time. In which case the enquiry is a piece of cultural sociology, usually in view of ideologies' critique and *Weltanschauungen* analysis.

[15]The pseudo-objective, or "material", mode of speech consists in presenting verbal or conceptual issues (i.e., issues about the meaning or communicative content of words) in the form of objective issues (i.e., issues dealing with the properties of non-linguistic objects). The material mode of speech resorts to "pseudo-object-sentences", while genuine objective speech (i.e., speech about non-linguistic objects) is made of "object-sentences." Carnap (1959), pp. 284–292.

1. The debate about the concept (and nature) of law is endowed not only with practical relevance ("significance"), one that would turn it "simply" in "one more dispute in law" among jurists, but also with a theoretical relevance. It is, in fact, a debate "over necessary truths about law."
2. An enquiry concerning necessary truths about law is not an empirical enquiry. It is, rather, a philosophical enquiry. The debate concerning the concept and the nature of law is, accordingly, a "genuine philosophical debate."
3. Necessary truths about law are truths about the "necessary or essential properties of law":

   Necessary properties that are specific to the law are essential properties of law [. . .] Essential or necessary properties of law are those properties without which law would not be law. They must be there, quite apart from space and time, wherever and whenever law exists.
4. The necessary or essential properties of law are the objective benchmark for telling the adequate concept of law (for there is one, and only one, adequate concept of law), from those concepts that, contrariwise, are inadequate.[16] A concept of law is philosophically adequate, if, and only if, it is adequate to the object to which it refers. And it is adequate to its object, if, and only if, it captures, it accounts for, the necessary or essential properties of the object.
5. The method of a philosophical enquiry on the concept and the nature of law, properly conceived, is not intuition, but rational argumentation. Accordingly, a set of properties we find in legal phenomena is the set of the necessary or essential properties of law, if, and only if, the claim that it is the set of the necessary or essential properties of law can be supported by rational argument.
6. Rational argument supports the following necessary truths about law:

   law necessarily comprises a real or factual and an ideal or critical dimension. This might be termed the dual-nature thesis. A central element of the real dimension of law is coercion or force. A central element of its ideal dimension is a claim to correctness, which includes a claim to moral correctness and which, if violated, implies legal defectiveness in normal cases and legal invalidity in extreme cases.[17]
7. The necessary character of coercion depends on the fact that coercion is a necessary means (a *sine qua non* condition) to achieve the goals ("the basic

[16]As it is well known, according to Alexy the necessary or essential properties of law would allow discriminating the sole adequate concept of law—that happens to be his own inclusive non-positivist concept—from four inadequate concepts: namely, the inclusive positivist concept (proposed by inclusive legal positivism), the exclusive positivist concept (proposed by exclusive legal positivism), the exclusive non-positivist concept, and, finally, the super-inclusive non-positivist concept.

[17]Alexy "the single most essential feature of law is its dual nature. The thesis of the dual nature of law presupposes that there exist necessary properties of law belonging to its factual or real dimension, as well necessary properties belonging to its ideal or critical dimension. Coercion is an essential feature found on the factual side, whereas the claim to correctness is constitutive of the ideal dimension."

formal purposes") of legal certainty and efficiency. The necessary character of the goals of legal certainty and efficiency, in turn, depends on their necessary connection to justice. Justice, in its broader scope, requires the law to be certain and efficient, besides having contents that must keep below the threshold of extreme (substantive) injustice. The necessary character of law's connection to justice depends, in turn, on law's necessary claim to correctness, which is also a claim to moral correctness. The necessary character of law's claim to justice can be argued for, finally, by appealing to the argument from pragmatic contradiction ("performative contradiction"). A constitutional provision claiming, for instance, that "*X* is a sovereign, federal, and unjust republic" would be evidently absurd.[18] Such an evident absurdity is—and cannot be but—the index of a contradiction between what the constitution expressly says (i.e., to be unjust), on the one hand, and what the constitution—indeed, any constitution *qua* constitution—tacitly but necessarily claims (i.e., to be just), on the other hand.

So much for Alexy's argument on behalf of the essentialist concept of law he stands for. It should be evident, by now, why the essentialist approach to the concept of law, even one as sophisticated as Alexy's, is pretence. The necessary or essential properties on which the objective adequacy of the concept of law depends, as Alexy avows, neither are the matter of a purely empirical enquiry (therefore, statements about them are not empirically true or false propositions), nor are the matter of incontrovertible, indisputable, rational arguments. Indeed, as we have seen, the rational arguments Alexy provides boil down, finally, to the argument from pragmatic contradiction. Such an argument, however, is too weak to bear the heavy burden of the necessary truths about law Alexy wishes it to carry. Absurdity is, fatally, in the eye of the beholder.[19] Furthermore, the argument appears to be flawed by a *petitio principii*. It assumes what it is meant to prove: i.e., the necessary implicit claim to justice every constitution would make, *qua* constitution. Indeed, the sheer fact of a constitution that includes a clause such as the one Alexy considers ("*X* is a sovereign, federal, and unjust republic"), by itself, can also be read as evidence that *no* claim to moral correctness, *no* claim to justice, is necessarily connected to the making of a constitution. These remarks bring us back to the conclusion I adumbrated before. Though dressing his theory in the language of "essences" and "necessary truths," Alexy is in fact (a) stipulating a concept of law in view of certain theoretical and, above all, practical goals, and (b) providing rational (but, as we have seen, disputable) arguments in its favour.

So, to sum up, if we cast a cool, discriminating, glance on Alexy's way of proceeding as a searcher for the (truly) adequate concept of law, it turns out that Alexy is doing nothing else but adopting and recommending a concept of law in tune

[18]Alexy "It is scarcely possible to deny that this article is somewhat absurd."

[19]See e.g. Bulygin (1993), pp. 41–51; Bulygin (2000), pp. 85–93; Chiassoni (2011), pp. 127–142.

with the (noble) ideals enshrined in Radbruch's Formula and Radbruch's human dignity and human rights geared conception of justice.[20]

3 Varieties of Conceptual Analysis

In a well-known collection of essays, Brian Leiter makes a pressing call for a "naturalized jurisprudence." This aims "to describe the reality of legal phenomena," posing as the heiress to American Legal Realism and Quine's empiricist philosophy of science.[21]

In his advocacy of naturalized jurisprudence, Leiter also urges the abandonment of the "method of conceptual analysis via an appeal to folk intuitions."[22] He claims such a method to be doomed to failure, if one is looking for a philosophically valuable explanation of the "nature" or "essence" of law: that is to say, if one wishes to get at "necessary truths" about the law, as many *soi-disants* analytical jurisprudents, in recent times, seem fond to do.[23]

---

[20]In a classical statement of the analytical theory of definition, Richard Robinson (Robinson (1954), pp. 149–192) identifies twelve different paths actually followed by philosophers in their search for the "real definition" of something: i.e., for definitions of the essence of the object to which a certain concept refers. Among them, the "betterment of existing concepts" and the "adoption and recommendation of ideals" represent useful activities actually consisting in proposing some stipulative or explanatory definition of some key-term. See also Scarpelli (1955), pp. 62–67, and, so far as the concept of law is concerned, pp. 71–86.

[21]Leiter (2007), pp. 183 ff.; Leiter (2012). On conceptual analysis in (and) jurisprudence, see also Endicott (2002), para 3.1; Bix (2007), pp. 1–7; Marmor (2012), pp. 1–26.

[22]Leiter (2007), pp. 1–2: "the method of conceptual analysis via appeal to folk intuitions (as manifest, for example, in ordinary language), a method that was itself at risk of becoming an item of antiquarian interest in the context of the naturalistic revolution of late 20th century philosophy"; Leiter (2012), para 2: "The question that plagues conceptual analysis, post-Quine, is what kind of knowledge such a procedure actually yields? Why should ordinary intuitions about the extension of a concept be deemed reliable or informative? Why think the "folk" are right?."

[23]Leiter (2007), pp. 177–178, 196–197, where, discussing Ian P. Farrell's defence of the Hartian search for "the concept of law" as a worthwhile piece of "modest conceptual analysis", retorts: "But on Farrell's (more plausible) rendering of conceptual analysis, we do not illuminate the reality, i.e., the nature of law, we illuminate, rather, the nature of our "talk" about law [. . .] *Modest* conceptual analysis illuminates our concepts – our *talk*, as it were – not the referent we might have intended to understand" (italics in the text, ndr). See also Leiter (2012), para 2. Leiter's criticism is acceptable when, by "modest conceptual analysis", necessary truths about aspects of reality are looked for. It is disputable, contrariwise, when, following J. L. Austin's suggestion (Austin (1956–1957), pp. 129–130), such an ambitious, mysterious, and (as I have argued in the previous section of this essay) misleading, task is put down, and a "sharpened awareness of words" is looked for in order to "sharpen our perception of the phenomena", though "*not as the final arbiter of*" (italics added; the passage, without this last, quite relevant, qualification, is quoted by Hart in the opening page of the "Preface" to *The Concept of Law*: Hart (1961), p. vii). For a defence of "traditional conceptual analysis" in jurisprudence, like the one performed by Hart (1961), against Leiter's naturalistic attack, see Himma (2007), pp. 1–23; Himma (2015), pp. 65–92. Himma's defence,

Leiter's case for a naturalized jurisprudence, and against conceptual analysis, casts a sinister light on the very possibility of carrying out fruitful conceptual investigations on legal issues—and, to begin with, on the concept(s) of law.

Upon consideration, however, it seems clear that Leiter's darts aim at a quite specific variety of conceptual analysis, though one that represents by now the *par excellence* instance: namely, folk conceptual analysis.[24] They do not aim, accordingly, at any form of conceptual analysis whatsoever.

Very roughly speaking, three basic forms of conceptual analysis seem worthwhile distinguishing to the present purpose. These are essentialist conceptual analysis, folk conceptual analysis (which I have just mentioned), and empiricist conceptual analysis.[25]

Essentialist conceptual analysis is a Platonist-flavoured enterprise. By way of intuitions aimed at discovering the concepts that are truly adequate to the very nature of things, it presumes to be capable to "reveal" the "a priori," "necessary," "conceptual truths" about "the way things are and the way the mind works."[26]

Folk conceptual analysis investigates current conceptual and terminological apparatuses in the light of the "intuitions" of those who make daily use of them ("the (mythical) folks"), whatever such intuitions may be, in order to get at the very nature or essence of the phenomena the apparatuses are about.[27] People's intuitions—their methodologically unaccountable "sense" about objects and concepts—

however, looks troublesome. It sets forth an apparently inconsistent view of "traditional conceptual analysis." On the one hand, it would be just about "our" concept of law, and hence would be tied, and limited, to a contingent, changeable, local, experience. On the other hand, it would lead, mysteriously, to making metaphysical claims about the nature or essence of law in general, telling us metaphysical, necessary, truths "about not just all *existing* legal systems, but all *conceptually possible* legal systems. Thus conceived, a conceptual analysis of law consists in a set of conceptually (or metaphysically) necessary truths and thus constitutes a piece of metaphysical theorizing—just as an analysis of the concept of free will is a piece of metaphysics" (Himma (2015), para 5). In the same passage, Himma also presents Hart as a torchbearer of such a metaphysical conceptual analysis. This view, nowadays common among jurisprudents, is disputable. See, for instance, Marmor (2012), who advocates that the basic thrust of Hart's jurisprudence was not conceptual analysis, but theoretical reductionism. I have argued against the essentialist reading of Hart's conception of conceptual analysis in Chiassoni (2013), para 2.2, and Chiassoni (2016), pp. 61–71.

[24]See, e.g., Margolis and Laurence (2011), para 5. Among jurisprudents, folk conceptual analysis is also the target, e.g., of Priel (2007), pp. 175–176.

[25]Leaving aside the essentialist variety, I take the folk and empiricist varieties as instances of *external* or *detached* conceptual analysis: i.e., of a conceptual analysis calling for an external observer's attitude, and aiming at furthering the understanding of extant conceptual frameworks ("conceptual structures") and the phenomena they are about. Therefore, I take them not to be samples of *internal* or *committed* conceptual analysis: i.e., of a conceptual analysis calling for an internal participant's attitude, and aiming at some justificatory practical purpose. On the distinction between external and internal conceptual analysis, see e.g. Perry (2001), pp. 331–353.

[26]These words, by which I characterize essentialist conceptual analysis, are from Smith Churchland (2013), pp. xi–xii.

[27]See Leiter (2007), pp. 1–2, 183–199; the basic source for folk conceptual analysis is Jackson (1998), especially ch. 2.

are paramount: they both delimitate the ground, and determine the output, of the inquiry.[28]

Empiricist conceptual analysis, finally, conceives of linguistic-conceptual enquiries mainly as a way to bring to the fore the ways of thinking, the sets of beliefs and attitudes, that are embodied in on-going conceptual and terminological apparatuses; grants to on-going apparatuses only a presumptive epistemic value, since it assumes that the intuitions (beliefs, attitudes) they mirror may be inchoate, confused, contradictory, idle, superstition-laden, wrong as a matter of fact, etc., so that such apparatuses may provide a misleading way to look at natural or social phenomena; adopts an uncompromising conventionalist and pragmatist conception of conceptual sets;[29] does not look for "necessary," "a priori," "conceptual truths" about reality, but for the innocent, tautological, a posteriori ones that are relative to contingent, on-going, sets of concepts.[30]

Empiricist conceptual analysis comes, in turn, in two varieties: these are the (purely) descriptive and the reconstructive ones.

Descriptive conceptual analysis inquires on current conceptual and terminological apparatuses in view of providing them with as much clear and precise account as

[28]According to Jackson, (folk) "conceptual analysis" is needed, if we want to "have much of an audience", and do not want turning "interesting philosophical debates into easy exercises in deduction from stipulative definitions together with accepted facts." If, for instance, our problem is about free action and determinism, the only fruitful way to proceed is by asking "whether free action *according to our ordinary conception*, or something suitably close to our ordinary conception, exists and is compatible with determinism" (Jackson (1998), pp. 30–31, italics in the text). The ascertainment of our (or folks') conception of free action, in turn, requires appealing to ordinary, shared, intuitions, which reveal "our shared theory" (Jackson (1998), pp. 31–32, 46 ff.). This can be carried out by means of introspection and, above all, socio-psychological enquiries. It is worthwhile stressing that, according to Jackson, "in practice", "the role" he is "recommending for conceptual analysis will often be *very* like the role Quine gives to the [Benthamite] notion of paraphrase" (Jackson 1998, p. 46). In the light of such remark, the case against "conceptual analysis" *à la* Jackson from Quinean perspectives seems, at least partly, the fruit of an uncharitable exaggeration.

[29]Among the supporters of such a conception of "linguistic frameworks" there is, for instance, Rudolf Carnap. In his view, many questions which are presented as "*theoretical* questions" (like, e.g., the question ""are there natural numbers?""), should be interpreted as "*practical* questions, i.e., as questions about the *decision* whether or not *to accept a language* containing expressions for the particular kind of entities" at stake (italics added, ndr). In his view, "whether or not" a "linguistic framework" should be introduced depends on the purposes one is aiming at, and "is a practical question of language engineering, to be decided on the basis of convenience, fruitfulness, simplicity, and the like" (Carnap (1963), p. 66; see also Carnap (1950), pp. 205–221).

[30]Smith Churchland (2013), pp. xi–xiv; "So what is a philosopher to do, if not troll his mind for conceptual truths? The Quinean answer is this: *many* things, including synthesizing across various subfields and theorizing while immersed in and constrained by available facts. Despite much hand-wringing by overwrought philosophers, Quine did not aim to put an end to philosophy, but to remind us of what the older philosophical tradition had always been: broad, encompassing, knowledgeable of everything relevant, and imaginative" (xiv, italics in the text). For a condensed account by Quine himself, see e.g. Quine (1960), pp. 275–276.

possible. It roughly amounts to lexicographic or linguistic phenomenology enquiries.[31]

Reconstructive conceptual analysis, contrariwise, investigates current conceptual and terminological apparatuses with the aim of eventually and ultimately replacing them with better ones, from the standpoint of the rational values of clarity, precision, simplicity, empirical adequacy, consistency, coherence, comprehensiveness, explanatory force, and adequacy to the (presumed) purposes of the "game(s)" they are played in. The reconstructive conceptual analysis takes into account folks' intuitions, as they are fatally embodied in, and mirrored by, linguistic practices. In doing so, however, it assumes such intuitions may back a conceptual and terminological apparatus in need of rational repair (rational reconstruction, rational revision). Accordingly, reconstructive conceptual analysis is something different from a "glorification" of lexicography, though it may walk some way along with it. It does not aim at "teaching the use of sentences"; it does not wish to make its readers "profit by the sentences" that they "see or hear," or helping them "react to" sentences "in expected ways" and "emit sentences usefully."[32] Rather, it aims at providing its readers with improved, better, ways of thinking about some natural phenomenon or human undertaking, as observers and participants alike.

It goes without saying that, from an analytical standpoint, essentialist and folk conceptual analysis should both be put down.[33]

Essentialist conceptual analysis—even when it assumes a rationalistic posture like the one advocated by Robert Alexy (see § Sect. 2 above)—remains a pseudo-objective enterprise, where the (often quite disputable) theoretical or normative attitudes, beliefs, and preferences of the inquirer are presented as grounded on the very nature of things.

---

[31]On the notion of "linguistic phenomenology" I will come back in a moment.

[32]See Quine (1992), pp. 56–57.

[33]Leiter criticizes, apparently, both folk conceptual analysis and (what I regard as) the purely descriptive variety of empiricist conceptual analysis. At the same time, however, following Larry Laudan, he recognizes the usefulness of something like the reconstructive variety of empiricist conceptual analysis I stand for here (see Leiter (2007), p. 183 footnote 3; see also Leiter (2007), p. 133 footnote 45, and pp. 168 ff., 179–181, where, in line with a central tenet of Logical Positivism, he regards philosophy as "the abstract branch of successful scientific theory [...] the abstract and reflective part of empirical science"; Leiter (2008). In a book of some years ago, Michael Giudice opposes "conceptual analysis" to "constructive conceptual explanation". The former corresponds, roughly, to folk conceptual analysis. The latter presents itself as something like reconstructive empiricist conceptual analysis. "Conceptual analysis" is "a common philosophical technique of discerning necessary and sufficient conditions of some concept by a priori reflection on possible instances to see where our linguistic intuitions lie [...] While conceptual analysis concerns itself with elucidating or making explicit what is already implicit in some particular culture's self-understanding of law, constructive conceptual explanation attempts to correct, revise or improve on what might be mistaken, distorting or parochial in that self-understanding when tested against observable social reality" (Giudice (2015), pp. vi, 43–66, 75 ff.).

Folk conceptual analysis is flawed insofar as it claims that reflection on the people's intuitions, as embodied in a contingent conceptual apparatus, can lead to necessary, universal truths about the very phenomena the apparatus is about.[34]

From an analytical standpoint, therefore, the only viable form of conceptual analysis is the empiricist variety. This, as I have said, comes in a purely descriptive or in a (also) reconstructive variety. The latter includes the former and, to theoretical purposes, should all-things-considered be preferred. It deserves therefore a few lines more, if only for clarity's sake.

Empiricist reconstructive conceptual analysis, as I see it, proceeds by means of investigations that typically encompass three stages: conceptual detection, conceptual reconstruction, and conceptual therapy.

The first stage is devoted to *conceptual detection*, or conceptual analysis in a narrow sense: what JL Austin proposes to call "linguistic phenomenology."[35] Here, the on-going terminological and conceptual apparatus that is the subject matter of the enquiry is identified, analysed, and its rational virtues and flaws dispassionately brought to the fore.

The second stage is devoted to *conceptual reconstruction* or rational reconstruction. Here, the on-going terminological and conceptual apparatus is modified into a new one. This is presented as capable of replacing the old one, while doing roughly the same job it did, though in a better, more rational way. For instance, due to its finer articulation in a larger, more comprehensive, set of terminologically distinct and semantically clearer and more exact concepts.

The third, and final, stage is devoted to *conceptual therapy*. Here, the use of the reconstructed and replacing conceptual and terminological apparatus set forth in the second stage is recommended, and carried out, as a way-out from the (supposed) rational flaws of the on-going one.[36]

Sociological inquiries about legal practice, even the armchair ones so typical in jurisprudential literature, bring to the fore and isolate terminologies, linguistic uses,

---

[34]Leiter (2007), pp. 1–2, 177–178, 183–199; Priel (2007), pp. 175–176. It must be remembered, however, as I suggest in footnote 36 above, that folk conceptual analysis may also have a less questionable variety, which is in fact close to the empiricist one.

[35]Austin (1956–1957), p. 130.

[36]A more encompassing view of reconstructive conceptual analysis is propounded, as it is well known, by P. F. Strawson. Strawson (1962), pp. 112–118, identifies five intertwining ways ("strands") of philosophical analysis: (1) conceptual therapy, to be used for solving paradoxes and perplexities; (2) descriptive analysis, which is about the actual working of "our" conceptual and logical apparatus; (3) explanatory analysis, which puts to work philosophical imagination in order to bring to the fore the "natural foundations" of our conceptual and logical apparatus; (4) reformist metaphysics, which puts to work philosophical imagination in view of providing a new and different conceptual framework for "our" same old world; and, finally, (5) descriptive metaphysics, which purports to clarify the "general structure" of "our" conceptual apparatus. My view of conceptual analysis may look a piece of eclecticism, where suggestions from Bentham, Russell, Carnap, Quine and Strawson, among others, are put together in a sort of mental patchwork. It is indeed. In fact, I do not care for strict philosophical allegiance. I care for (hopefully) smoothly working tools for (hopefully) fruitful jurisprudential investigations.

working conceptual apparatuses, and "theories" behind them, that are fatally in need of clarification, rational reconstruction, and therapy.[37]

It must be considered, furthermore, that the reality of law is largely linguistic in character. What are "legal norms", unless linguistic entities, in the form either of authoritative legal provisions, or of the explicit or implicit meanings thereof? What is a legal argument, unless a string of sentences in a natural language? What are interpretive rules and interpretive codes, unless, again, linguistic entities?

If we adopt an analytical and realistic approach to the study of law, and reject firmly, as a delusive pretence, any pursuit of the very nature, essence or necessary truths about the law, conceptual analysis—in the empiricist, reconstructive, and, if you like, modest, three-stages, variety I presented above—appears, therefore, to be a tool of enquiry that cannot be dispensed with.

Willard Quine depicts the naturalization of epistemology as a course of action that transforms "theoretical epistemology," i.e., a philosophical enterprise above, and outside, of science, into "a chapter of theoretical science."[38] Rejecting any "a priori" conception of philosophizing, he sees the "naturalistic philosopher" as an inquirer who:

> begins his reasoning within the inherited *world theory* as a going concern. He tentatively believes all of it, but also believes that some unidentified portions are wrong. He tries to *improve*, *clarify*, and *understand* the system *from within*. He is the busy sailor adrift on Neurath's boat.[39]

Likewise, we can see the realistic, skeptical, analytical jurisprudent, armed with empiricist and reconstructive conceptual analysis, as the busy sailor adrift on the norm-hulled, material-and-immaterial-interests propelled, juristic constructions-laden, boat of legal thinking.

References

Alexy R (2001) The argument from injustice. A reply to legal positivism. Oxford University Press, Oxford

Alexy R (2006) On the concept and the nature of law. Ratio Juris 21(3):281–299

Alexy R (2017) The ideal dimension of law. In Duke, George (eds.) (2017), pp 314–341

Alexy R, Bulygin E (2001) In: Gaido P (ed) La pretensión de corrección del derecho. La polémica Alexy/Bulygin sobre la conexión necesaria entre derecho y moral. Externado de Colombia, Bogotá

Austin JL (1956–1957) A plea for excuses. In Austin (1961), pp 123–152

[37] A still valuable overview of the several, often intertwining, forms of philosophical analysis is offered by Urmson (1962), pp. 11–22; see also Strawson (1962), pp. 105–118; Strawson (1985), pp. 7–60.

[38] Quine (1992), p. 19, italics added. See also Quine (1969), pp. 69–90, where epistemology, as an enquiry on the way empirical knowledge is acquired and processed, is presented as merging "with psychology, as well as with linguistics."

[39] Quine (1975), p. 72, italics added.

Austin JL (1961) Philosophical papers. Clarendon Press, Oxford
Bernal Pulido C (ed) (2011) La doble dimensión del derecho. Autoridad y razón en la obra de Robert Alexy. Palestra, Lima
Bix B (2007) Joseph Raz and conceptual analysis. APA Newsletter 6(2):1–7
Bulygin E (1993) Alexy y el argumento de la corrección. In Alexy, Bulygin (2001), pp 41–51
Bulygin E (2000) La tesis de Alexy sobre la conexión necesaria entre el derecho y la moral. In Alexy, Bulygin (2001), pp 85–93
Burazin L, Himma KE, Roversi C (eds) (2018) Law as an artifact. Oxford University Press, Oxford
Carnap R (1932) The elimination of metaphysics through logical analysis of language. In: Ayer AJ (ed) Logical positivism. The Free Press, New York, pp 60–81, 1959
Carnap R (1950) Empiricism, semantics, and ontology. In Carnap (1956), pp 205–221
Carnap R (1956) Meaning and necessity. a study in semantics and modal logic. Enlarged edition. The University of Chicago Press, Chicago
Carnap R (1959) The logical syntax of language. Littlefield, Adams & Co., Paterson
Carnap R (1963) Intellectual autobiography. In Schilpp, (ed.) (1963), pp 1–84
Castignone S, Guastini R, Tarello G (1994) Introduzione teorica allo studio del diritto. Prime lezioni. Ecig, Genova
Chiassoni P (2011) Alexy y la doble naturaleza del derecho: comentarios escépticos. In Bernal Pulido (ed.) (2011), pp 127–142
Chiassoni P (2013) The model of ordinary analysis. In D'Almeida, Edwards, Dolcetti (eds.) (2013), pp 247–267
Chiassoni P (2016) El discreto placer del positivismo jurídico. Externado de Colombia, Bogotá
D'Almeida D, Edwards J, Dolcetti A (eds) (2013) Reading H. L. A. Hart's the concept of law. Hart, Oxford
Dworkin R (2006) Justice in Robes. The Belknap Press of Harvard University Press, Cambridge
Dworkin R (2011) Justice for Hedgehogs. The Belknap Press of Harvard University Press, Cambridge
Endicott T (2002) Law and language. In Stanford Encyclopedia of Philosophy. First published Thu Dec 5, 2002; substantive revision Fri Apr 15, 2016
Etcheverry JB (2020) Scope and limits of general and descriptive legal theories. In: Fabra-Zamora J, Villa G (eds) Conceptual jurisprudence. Springer, Berlin, chapter 3
Farrell IP (2006) H.L.A. Hart and the methodology of jurisprudence. Texas Law Rev 84:983–1011
Frege G (1892) On concept and object. In: Geach P, Black M (eds) Translations from the philosophical writings of Gottlob Frege, vol 1970. Basil Blackwell, Oxford, pp 42–55
Giudice M (2015) Understanding the nature of law: a case for constructive conceptual explanation. Edward Elgar Publishing, Cheltenham
Hart HLA (1954) Theory and definition in jurisprudence. In Hart (1983), pp 21–48
Hart HLA (1961) The concept of law, 3rd edn. Oxford University Press, Oxford
Hart HLA (1983) Essays in jurisprudence and philosophy. Clarendon Press, Oxford
Himma KE (2007) Reconsidering a Dogma: conceptual analysis, the naturalistic turn, and legal philosophy. Law Philos:1–23
Himma KE (2015) Conceptual jurisprudence. An introduction to conceptual analysis and methodology in legal theory. Revus 26:65–92
Jackson F (1998) From metaphysics to ethics. A defence of conceptual analysis. Clarendon Press, Oxford
Jori M, Pintore A (2014a) Concetto di diritto. In Jori, Pintore (2014), pp 41-56.
Jori M, Pintore A (2014b) Introduzione alla filosofia del diritto. Giappichelli, Torino
Kantorowicz H (1958) The definition of law. Cambridge University Press, Cambridge
Lalumera E (2009) Cosa sono i concetti. Laterza, Roma-Bari
Laslett (ed) (1956) Philosophy, politics and society. Blackwell, Oxford
Leiter B (2007) Naturalizing jurisprudence. Essays on American legal realism and naturalism in legal philosophy. Oxford University Press, Oxford

Leiter B (2008) Naturalizing jurisprudence: three approaches. The University of Chicago Law School, Public Law and Legal Theory Working Paper n. 246, http://www.law.uchicago.edu/academics/publiclaw/index.html
Leiter B (2012) Naturalism in legal philosophy. Stanford Encyclopedia of Philosophy, https://plato.stanford.edu/entries/lawphil-naturalism/
Margolis E, Laurence S (2011) Concepts. Stanford encyclopedia of philosophy, https://plato.stanford.edu/entries/concepts/
Marmor A (2012) Farewell to conceptual analysis (in jurisprudence). University of Southern California Law School, Los Angeles, CA 90089-0071, USC Legal Studies Research Paper No. 12-2, pp 1–26
Martin, M. (2020) Method matters: non-normative jurisprudence and the re-mystification of the law. Jorge Fabra-Zamora, Gonzalo Villa (eds.) Conceptual jurisprudence, Springer, Berlin., chapter 4.
Moreso JJ (2017) El derecho: diagramas conceptuales. Universidad Externado de Colombia, Bogotá
Nino CS (1994a) La validez del derecho. Astrea, Buenos Aires
Nino CS (1994b) Derecho, moral y política. Una revision de la teoría general del derecho. Ariel, Barcelona
Perry SR (2001) Hart's methodological positivism. In: Coleman J (ed) Hart's postscript. Essays on the postscript to the concept of law. Oxford University Press, Oxford, pp 311–354
Priel D (2007) Jurisprudence and necessity. Can J Law Jurisprud 20(1):173–200
Quine WVO (1960) Word and object. The M.I.T. Press, Cambridge
Quine WVO (1969) Ontological relativity and other essays. Columbia University Press, New York
Quine, WVO (1975) Five milestones of empiricism. In Quine (1981), pp 67–72
Quine WVO (1981) Theories and things. The Belknap Press of Harvard University Press, Cambridge
Quine WVO (1992) Pursuit of truth. Revised Edition. Harvard University Press, Cambridge
Raz J (1983) The problem about the nature of law. In Raz (1994), pp 195–209
Raz J (1994) Ethics in the public domain. Essays in the morality of law and politics. Clarendon Press, Oxford
Raz J (2007) The argument from justice, or how not to reply to legal positivism. In Raz (2009b), pp 313–335
Raz J (2009a) Between authority and interpretation. On the theory of law and practical reason. Oxford University Press, Oxford
Raz J (2009b) The authority of law. Essays on law and morality, 2nd edn. Oxford University Press, Oxford
Robinson R (1954) Definition. Oxford University Press, Oxford
Scarpelli U (1955) Il problema della definizione e il concetto di diritto. Nuvoletti, Milano
Schauer F (2015) The force of law. Harvard University Press, Cambridge
Schauer F (2018) Law as a malleable artifact. In Burazin, Himma, Roversi (eds.) (2018). Available at SSRN: https://ssrn.com/abstract=3183928
Schilpp PA (ed) (1963) The philosophy of Rudolf Carnap. Cambridge University Press, London, La Salle, Ill., Open Court
Shapiro S (2011) Legality. The Belknap Press of Harvard University Press, Cambridge
Smith Churchland P (2013) Foreword. In: Quine WVO (ed) Word and object. New Edition. The MIT Press, Boston, pp xi–xiv
Strawson PF (1962) Analyse, Science et Métaphysique. In: La philosophie analytique. Les Éditions de Minuit, Paris, pp 105–118
Strawson PF (1985) Analyse et Métaphysique. Librairie Philosophique J. Vrin, Paris

Tarello G (1993a) Organizzazione giuridica e società moderna. In Castignone, Guastini, Tarello (1994), pp 5–29
Tarello G (1993b) Il diritto positivo. In Castignone, Guastini, Tarello (1994), pp 109–11
Urmson JO (1962) L'histoire de l'analyse. In: La philosophie analytique, Les Éditions de Minuit, Paris
Williams G (1945) The controversy concerning the word "Law." In Laslett (ed.) (1956), pp 134–156

Scope and Limits of General and Descriptive Legal Theories

Juan B. Etcheverry

Abstract The purpose of this essay is to shed some light on general and descriptive legal theories—as proposed by H.L.A. Hart. To achieve such a goal, we will highlight some of the hurdles that these theories face by: (i) trying to identify and explain the *necessary* features of a practice that is considered to be absolutely *contingent*; (ii) proposing a *general* theory that explains only *our* concept of law; (iii) developing a descriptive or non-evaluative theory that does not describe empirical facts but instead uses evaluative judgments; (iv) describing a normative practice; *etc.* Finally, this essay concentrates on the debate over the criteria that determine which theory or when a theory of law is better than another in order to determine if general and descriptive legal theories depend on a normative thesis to get started.

1 Introduction

The aim of this chapter is to present some challenges for general and descriptive legal theories—as proposed by H. L. A. Hart. For this, we will start (Sect. 2) by providing a brief outline of the kind of analytical jurisprudence proposed by Hart, which many authors adhere to. We will present it as a *general* and *descriptive* theory of our legal practices. Then, (Sect. 3) we will focus our attention on some of the difficulties that arise when attempting to establish this type of theory of law. After making these observations, we will focus (Sect. 4) on the debate over the criteria that determine which theory or when a theory of law is better than another. We will also consider why Hart and other authors prefer the theoretical framework which they propose in order to analyze the law. Finally, this paper will conclude (Sect. 5) by making an assessment and summary of some of the aforementioned claims.

J. B. Etcheverry (✉)
CONICET - Universidad Austral, Pilar, Argentina
e-mail: jbetcheverry@austral.edu.ar

J. L. Fabra-Zamora, G. Villa Rosas (eds.), *Conceptual Jurisprudence*, Law and Philosophy Library 137, https://doi.org/10.1007/978-3-030-78803-2_3

2 A *General* and *Descriptive* Theory of Our Concept of Law

The importance and influence of Hart's work on Anglo-American contemporary philosophy of law go without saying. One needs only to take note of the number of philosophical debates of law which focus on his proposals and innovative method of analysis of law.

From his first essays on jurisprudence, Hart seemed to have been clear about the central purpose of his research—to provide an answer to the recurring question of "what is the law?" by explaining its core or essence—and the method to obtain it—by examining the relevant concepts in order to make our perception of the phenomena more acute.[1] This effort is made in the hope that the change of focus to the different and complex ways in which language is used may serve to allay common misconceptions.[2] However, it should be noted that he made no particular effort to specify or, more importantly, justify the singularity of his analytical method.[3]

Many years after choosing conceptual analysis[4] as the method of approach to legal phenomena, and after defending his theory of law from criticisms raised by Dworkin for a quarter of a century, Hart comes back to his first methodological assertions, believing that they have been misconstrued or misunderstood. In order to eliminate any doubts, he clarifies that his theory of law is general and descriptive. He explains that his theory of law is general because it is not tied to any particular legal system or legal culture.[5] More specifically, he states that his theory of law seeks to describe a kind of social institution that exhibits many common characteristics of form, structure and content throughout its perpetual existence in various societies and periods.[6] Hart's proposal is also descriptive, meaning "morally neutral" and "without any justificative purpose": it does not attempt to justify or suggest forms or structures that appear in his description of law on the basis of morality or otherwise.[7]

Besides these observations, Hart notices that Dworkin rejects theories of law that are merely descriptive because they fail to fully take into consideration an internal perspective of the law—the viewpoint of a participant in a legal system. In sum, Dworkin's criticism suggests that an accurate explanation of the internal viewpoint

[1]Hart (2012), pp. v and chap. I. He also clarifies that this book may also be considered an essay on descriptive sociology, apart from its concern on analysis. See Hart (2012), pp v–vi. Green explained the scope of this claim. Green (2012), pp. xlv–xlviii.

[2]Hart (1983), pp. 2–3.

[3]Green (2004), p. 575.

[4]Recently, Michael Guidice attempted to show that while analytical jurisprudence and conceptual analysis of law have often been identified as one and the same proyect, the identification is false. Guidice claimed that conceptual analysis is not the most important part of analytical jurisrpudence. Guidice (2015), p. 17.

[5]Hart (2012), p. 239.

[6]Hart (1987), p. 36.

[7]Hart (2012), p. 240.

cannot be given from a merely descriptive theory.[8] Nevertheless, Hart proposes that a descriptive legal theory may include and describe the internal perspective of those who are subject to the law without adopting or sharing it.[9] In fact, according to Hart, even when what is described is an evaluation, descriptions of evaluations will continue to be descriptions.[10]

Hart also clarifies that his theory is not purely semantic—or, as some authors have named it, "criteriological"[11]—in the sense that Dworkin has interpreted it. More specifically, he denies that his position attempts to reveal the linguistic criteria that determine the meaning of the word "law."[12]

Finally, Hart focuses on Dworkin's criticisms that suggest that his theory of law—insofar positivist—can be related to a kind of conventionalism capable of justifying coercion by the state. This interpretation of legal positivism suggests that the criteria to identify the law must be purely factual, because this guarantees the ideal of protected expectations and the potential for everyone to be able to know in advance when law can be coercive. In response to this critique, Hart argues against Dworkin's thesis, which states that the purpose of law is to justify the state's coercion; and points out that his version of positivism does not make any assertion that identifies the purpose or the function of law.[13]

Hart concludes this argument by saying that his theory of law is radically different from Dworkin's—which is justificative and designed for a specific legal culture.[14]

Many authors[15] have criticized the lack of coherence of some of Hart's theses with his own methodological proposal. In fact, Hart himself seems to admit that at least on a few occasions—e.g., in "Positivism and the Separation of Law and Morals"—he would have opted for a causal-moral argument to support his positivism.[16] However, we are not particularly interested in whether Hart was or was not consistent with his methodological proposal, but whether or not it is *possible* to be consistent in this regard. For this, in the following section, we will attempt to address the challenges that a theory like Hart's must face. It should be noted that this effort is not made in order to highlight the impracticality of his theory, but simply to identify such difficulties.

---

[8] Hart (2012), p. 242.

[9] Hart (2012), p. 243.

[10] Hart (2012), p. 244.

[11] Endicott (1998), pp. 283–300, Bix (1993), p. 9.

[12] Hart (2012), pp. 244–248.

[13] Hart (2012), pp. 248–250.

[14] Hart (2012), p. 243. In fact, some authors propose to construe—or to mitigate—the characterization that Hart creates with his theory in light of the context of Hart's debate with Dworkin, bearing in mind his intent to contrast his theory with that of Dworkin. See Dickson (2004), p. 120.

[15] Most notably: Dworkin (1983), p. 255, MacCormick (1981), pp. 160 and Lyons (1993), pp. 96–101.

[16] Waluchow revealed that in a private communication Hart admitted that "Positivism and the Seperation of Law and Morals" contained a causal-moral argument for positivism. Waluchow (1998), pp. 411, 66fn.

3 Difficulties of General and Descriptive Legal Theories

3.1 Could It Be General *a Theory That Merely Analyzes* Our *Concept of Law?*

The possibility of a *general* or universal theory of *our* concept of law may seem paradoxical at first glance. The purpose of constructing a theory capable of explaining the attributes that each and every phenomenon must display, at any given time and place, to be considered law, may not seem altogether compatible with the means utilized to obtain such a result: the analysis of *our* exclusive concept of law. In Hart's case, the concept of law he proposes seems to derive from British language and legal practices. Thus, the true purpose is to investigate if other cultures have law in the sense of what the English society of his time understood as law. This indicates that Hart's theory may be more parochial than it had appeared.

In response to this argument, authors have contended that if we are seeking to compare institutions such as the law in different cultures, we must first have an idea of what law is; its core components, etc. Thus, it is necessary to have at least some provisional notions of the nature of law in order to decide what we are trying to compare.[17]

Although the assertion that this theory is general in the sense that could be used to apply to other cultures may seem irrefutable,[18] we must clarify some matters that could lead to confusion. Firstly, Hart's theory allows us only to understand *our* concept of law, which is local, and to employ it as a means to investigate if other societies—that might or might not share our concept of law—share the phenomenon that we conceptualized as law. Secondly, Hart's theory of law does not seek to describe a reality that transcends *our* understanding of law—which different societies may take part in—nor does it seek to explain the way in which other societies understand their own practices and organizations. Thirdly, Hart's theory rejects the premise that the essence of law can be analyzed across cultures, because his theory suggests that this very nature is itself defined by our autochthones concept of law. Fourthly, the manner in which Hart suggests that his theory is general supposes that our concept of law is capable of revealing something significant about other cultures; that lets us begin to understand them. This idea seems to be based on the assumption that we share some aspect of our legal practices with other cultures.[19] However, this is contrary to Hart's standpoint that law is a socially contingent practice, whose characteristics and content depend purely on institutions and facts.

---

[17]Raz (1996), pp. 1–7.

[18]I appreciate the valuable comments offered by Professor Michael Moore on this subject. His opinion about this matter can be found in Moore (1998), pp. 302–303.

[19]Bix (1999b), p. 191 and Moore (1992), pp. 188–242.

3.2 *Is It Possible for a Theory to Seek the Nature or Essence of a Purely Contingent Practice?*

The preceding statements let us move on from the matter of the broadness of Hart's theory to a different but closely related topic.[20] There seems to be a contradiction between the thought that legal practices have their own essence—or nature—and, at the same time, considering that legal practices are a purely contingent phenomenon. At first glance, such statements need clarification at the very least. Several supporters of Hart's theory have realized this and attempted to provide an explanation. Some suggest that the search of these kinds of necessary properties of law neither presume nor support its existence. They simply state that if such properties exist, then a successful legal theory of the kind we are examining must discover them.[21] This issue does not, however, tell us whether any essential or necessary attributes of law exist. Furthermore, it suggests that the type of theory it defends will be pointless once it is proved that such attributes do not exist. This response may come across as surprising because the idea of the *nature* (as a reference to essential or necessary elements) of law and the claim that law is a purely contingent social artifact continue to result difficult to reconcile.

Raz, one of the most noteworthy Hart followers, recognizes that there is a discord between the studies of the nature of law and our own self-understanding contained in such a concept.[22] Contrary to Hart's viewpoint, Raz suggests that there is a difference between the explanation of the concept of something and the explanation of the *nature* of something. For Raz, Hart believed that the complete understanding of a concept consists of the knowledge and comprehension of all its essential properties.[23] Raz believes that the explanation of a concept, in addition to the complete understanding of the concept, also seeks to describe the minimum conditions necessary to master a concept. In fact, he states that the majority of the concepts

[20]On this matter we share the distinction made by Raz (1998), p. 273, n. 38 between general and essential aspects of law. For the Oxford professor, the general aspects of law are those that are shared by all legal systems, whereas the essential aspects are those attributes without which a social phenomenon could not be considered law. Based on this distinction it can be said that the issue of the essential properties of law is related to the issue of its general aspects because every essential property is also a general feature of law, however, not every general property is an essential property of law—this is the purpose of the distinction.

[21]Dickson (2001), pp. 18–19.

[22]Raz (2004), pp. 13, 19.

[23]Langlinais and Leiter consider that Hart is a modest essencialist and summerized his method in the following way: "(1) a theory of law should be an account of the essential properties of modern legal systems in general; (2) a theoretical account of law's essential properties can proceed without consideration of its value or reason-giving force; (3) legal systems are socially constructed, and a theory of law is therefore a theory of the social facts about beliefs, attitudes and actions that constitute a legal system; (4) this social construct is amenable to linguistic analysis, given that it is constituted by language; and (5) given that law is socially constructed, a general theory of law is just an attempt to elucidate the folk concept of law, that is, the concept manifest in the language we use to think and talk about it." Langlinais and Leiter (2016), p. 679.

we understand and master are done so only partially. This explains why people may make mistakes on concepts that they have grasped only partially, and it also sheds light on the idea that explaining a concept is similar to explaining the nature of what a concept is, and yet the two tasks differ.[24] From these statements, Raz concludes (contrarily to Hart) that the primary objective of the theory of law is to explain the nature of law and the concept of law is merely secondary. Therefore, in a country where law exists, it is only when the people understand the concept of law that it is relevant to know if law is affected by its concept.[25] In addition, Raz supports the idea that the nature of law can be universal in spite of legal institutions and concepts of law changing over time and in different regions.

Raz approach is somewhat confusing. In fact, authors as Dworkin, Bix and Bulygin doubt and question the scope of his statements. There are essentially two different interpretations. One considers that this response to the issue of the nature of law shifts to a type of referential and semantic theory, such as the one held by Kripke-Putnam or Moore.[26] The other clarifies that no Platonic theories on natural types are sought but rather a notion of necessity that is relative to a specific community, a given time or way of life.[27]

Raz proposes to distinguish between explaining the nature of something and explaining the concept of something, and defends this distinction by observing that the physical reality does not change if the concept we use to designate it changes. Of course, Raz recognized that it is possible to suggest that some social things—for example, the institution of marriage—could not exist if their concept did not exist, but he claims that that is not a general truth, nor it is something that can be said of law. At the same time, Raz claims that law is not simply a noun determined by the way in which reality is divided, independently of its speakers—as could be said of terms of nature. This is manifest in the way Raz considers that the concept of law could be changeable.[28] The issue here is that, although it is clearly stated that the properties of law do not completely depend on its concept and that law is not completely independent of us, insofar it does not depend solely on how things are

---

[24]Raz (2004), pp. 4–7.

[25]Raz (2004), p. 8.

[26]Dworkin (2006), p. 229 and Bulygin (2007), pp. 99–110 support this option. With a similar approach, Moore argues the possibility that Hart may have believed that law has an essence that is related to the social world in a manner similar to the one in which natural phenomena are related to physics and natural sciences. In sum, it is said that instead of referring to "natural types" one could refer to "social types". Moore (1998), pp. 312–313.

[27]Bix (2003), pp. 555–556. See also Raz (1996), p. 7. In fact, Raz (2007), pp. 117–118 clarifies that his viewpoint does not adhere to the idea that law is a noun that is determined by the way in which reality is divided independently of the speakers and maintains that his position on how the concept of law changes is proof of this. Nevertheless, he maintains that in most cases things have their own nature independent of whether or not we have concepts that allow us to refer to them. In order to clarify this, he questions if the physical reality changes when we acquire the concept of a molecule. With this observation he suggests that things have a nature that differs from the concepts that are cultural products.

[28]Raz (2007), pp. 117–118.

by their nature, nevertheless, it is not clearly specified how law is to be understood and to what extent its properties depend on *our* concept of law.

In short, both the explanation which identifies the concept of law by its nature (Hart), and that which proposes to distinguish between one explanation and the other (Raz) need to be clarified in order to truly understand the scope of their claims. As to this first explanation (Hart), the challenge is to reconcile the idea that law is a combination of unchanging and contingent features.[29] If we concede that law is a completely contingent and potentially unstable social institution, essence or nature seems only to be applicable to a particular concept of law—e.g., one that arises from contemporary British language. By identifying the nature of law by its concept such a theory ends up being able to explain only the law of those societies which have shared or will share *our* concept of law—not offering the possibility that another society has had or will have law if it does not share our concept of law.[30] Given that the notion of law is considered local and contingent—i.e. that it can change throughout time and various societies—Hart's methodological proposal is more local than universal and has a purely contingent and local analysis of the nature of law.[31] These explanations where ideas like essence are used, lead us to question the benefits that may be derived—for the sake of clarity—from applying this metaphysical language to practices that are considered purely contingent.

Two observations can be made regarding the explanation that distinguishes between the concept of law—local—and its nature—universal (Raz). Firstly, if this theory involves a shift to a referential and semantic approach (such as the one held by Kripke-Putnam or Moore), the idea that law is purely contingent and potentially unstable must be abandoned. Secondly, if the idea of "necessity" that handles this theory is relative to a society, a moment or a way of life, although this explanation provides a distinction between the nature of law and its concept, conceding that law can exist in a society without a concept of law, ultimately, what determines if institutions are or not legal is nothing more than *our* perception of law. Thus, a society that does not share our same concept of law—even one that has no concept of law[32]—can have institutions that our approach to law considers juridical institutions; that is to say, such a society can have law.[33] This theory is universal or general in that it applies to all legal institutions, of any time and place, as long as they are accepted as such by *our* concept of law—even if in the society in which such institutions exist they do not have a concept of law.[34]

---

[29]Bix (2006), p. 15.

[30]For example, it should be stated that a society such as the Egyptians of the IV century B.C., did not have law because it did not share our concept of law. See Raz (2004), p. 19.

[31]Bix (2009), Raz (1996), p. 7.

[32]Jewish Theocratic societies are cited as examples of societies that did not have a concept of law but had legal institutions.

[33]Raz (2004), pp. 23–27.

[34]Raz (2004), p. 74.

This statement can be challenged because it appears unsuited to explain legal systems—understanding such terms in a primitive and non-philosophical sense[35]—such as that of the Mayan or Roman Empire, *etc.* because they do not share the characteristics of the modern concept of law. The response to this challenge has highlighted how our concept of law is increasingly more inclusive and less parochial—in part because of the expansion of our knowledge of history and the world.[36] On this matter, I will just pose a question that may help us understand some obstacles that have not been fully resolved. If the so-called expansion process undergone by the western concept of law in the last centuries is at least partly due to the expansion of our knowledge, it is unclear what the relation that may exist between this increased knowledge and the expansion of the concept of law is. In other words, if we consider that the concept of law that is produced from specific practices determines what law is and it is not, it would seem that learning of different practices that are not legal for this concept of law would not necessarily help to expand such a concept of law.

Although Hart makes it clear that his theoretical proposal refers to the "general nature of law,"[37] such a claim does not necessarily deny the viability or utility of theories of law addressing a particular legal culture.[38] Thus, in his *Postscript* Hart suggests that it is not necessarily obvious that theories with such different approaches as his—general and descriptive—and Dworkin's—evaluative, justificative and parochial—are incompatible.[39] Moreover, there are some authors—who share Hart's methodological proposal—who support theories addressing a particular legal culture because they are feasible and can be useful.[40]

3.3 Could a Theory That Uses Evaluative Judgments Be Descriptive?

Hart's methodological approach has to face other challenges related to its characterization as a descriptive theory. Not only Hart and his followers have to clarify what

[35]This distinction proposed by Raz suggests that we must not identify the concept with the definitions of words. In fact, it is said that the meanings are somewhere between the words and the world. This distinction is exemplified by saying that the theories of law do not aim to explain the meaning (total or partial) of the word law, but the concept of law. It is considered that the context (linguistic and non-linguistic) is what establishes that the concepts do not need to be identified by the use of the specific words. However, the conditions that establish the identity of the particular concepts are idealizations built from our conceptual practices, that is to say, from the usage of those concepts in general. See Raz (2004), pp. 49–51, 55, 63.

[36]Raz (2004), p. 68.

[37]Hart (2012), p. 240.

[38]Moore (1998), pp. 324–327.

[39]Hart (2012), p. 241.

[40]Dickson (2001), pp. 21–25 and Schauer (2005), p. 495, 10fn.

they mean when they say that they propose a "general" theory that aims to explain its "essence" or "nature" of law, but also they need to do that when they say that the theory they endorse is "descriptive."

In this section we will analyze whether Hart's theory is descriptive in that its purpose is to describe something—in this case, a phenomenon—without resorting to a value judgment of the item being described. Some theories of law may have this goal, but that is not the kind of theory that Hart proposes. As described earlier, Hart's theory of law claims to be conceptual or analytical because it attempts to provide the "central elements in the concept of law" to find its general nature by way of conceptual analysis.[41] Consequently, it can be stated that Hart's theory is not merely descriptive, in that it does attempt to provide more than a mere report of data or local observations.[42] Hart's followers and Hart himself recognize that in order to fulfill their methodological proposal—to be both general and descriptive—it is necessary to make selections and evaluative judgments that will allow organizing the data; rejecting some aspects of the practice and emphasizing others.[43] Nevertheless, they aim to prove that Hart's theory is not justificative, since the kind of evaluative judgment necessary refers to the importance of the varying characteristics of social organizations and is therefore considered non-moral.[44] This kind of evaluation is currently called "indirect evaluation" to distinguish it from a direct or moral evaluation.[45] This proposal attempts to provide an intermediate category between the merely descriptive and normative theories. This also involves criticizing the use of a descriptive/normative dichotomy to characterize the methodological debates of the legal theory on the grounds that it is too simplistic.[46]

It is clear that for an evaluative and morally neutral theory of law to be successful, the distinction between non-moral and moral values must be consistent. Thus, those who endorse such a distinction have dedicated effort to describe it.[47] More specifically, they claim that although evaluating involves assigning value to something, there are different categories of value judgments. Thus, a basic category of values may exist, for example, the quality of being "good." This falls within the evaluations category or simply, moral evaluations. However, they consider that this kind of evaluation is one possible category among many. In fact, they claim that many of the propositions considered evaluative do not fit into this category. For example, the category that labels something as important does not involve categorizing such an item as "good."[48]

---

[41]Hart (2012), p. 14.

[42]Coleman and Leiter (1995), p. 207.

[43]Hart (1987), p. 39.

[44]Raz (1994), pp. 208–209.

[45]Dickson (2001) *passim*. See also Hart's distinction (1965), p. 1286 between purposive activity (as poisoning) and moral activity.

[46]Coleman (2001), pp. 3, 175.

[47]Dickson (2001) *passim* and Waluchow (1994), pp. 19–29.

[48]Dickson (2001), p. 66.

Next, they explain the relationship between moral—or direct—evaluations and non-moral—indirect. With this issue they attempt to evidence that although a relation—or more than one—exists with these value judgments, such a relation does not necessarily imply that all non-moral—indirect—evaluations must be based on a moral—direct—one.[49] A way of supporting indirect evaluative judgements on law can be found in the fact that a feature that has been evaluated as important is something that any law invariably exhibits. Another method of supporting an indirect evaluative judgment on law can be to consider the consequences that emerge from certain beliefs that people (being subject to law) have on some aspect of law. Because the concept of law is something that people use in order to understand themselves, the aspects of law that people consider important reveal a substantial facet of their own self-understanding.[50] Finally, indirect evaluative judgments are supported by the idea that sometimes they are necessary to make direct judgments possible. In other words, it is necessary to first isolate and explain—by means of indirect evaluative judgments—the pertinent characteristics that will then be judged in a direct way.[51] According to this idea, the formulation of descriptive theories of law amounts to the first necessary step, that should be taken in order to be able, then, to proceed with a direct evaluation of law.[52]

In regards to the possibility that the theory of law can be evaluative and remain descriptive—not justificative or morally evaluative—we can make two observations. First, any statement suggesting that something holds importance, it should specify for whom it holds importance, why and to what end. To address these concerns, there are several defensible theories that suggest different characteristics that seem to be important elements of our practice. This is problematic because we no longer have any non-moral elements to select. Also, it is necessary to justify that only one concept of law exists in our practice, since there are some authors who believe there is more than one sustainable theory about the nature of law and that the selection can only be made with moral reasoning.[53] Furthermore, it is necessary to clarify what it means that a characteristic of law can be important but not necessarily "good." When we discuss human constructs such as law, things considered important and good are interdependent. What may appear contrary is that what the practice establishes as important may differ from what an observer of this practice considers good. This brings us to the following question: when an observer is trying to understand what a practice has established as a significant characteristic of itself, is the observer truly making an evaluative judgment or is he describing an evaluative practice? This returns us to the beginning of the problem that we were initially trying to solve: if we develop a general theory of law that aims to be universally valid, then when we judge the characteristics of law that are universally important, such an

[49]Dickson (2001), p. 54.

[50]Dickson (2001), pp. 58–60.

[51]Waluchow (1994), pp. 19–29.

[52]Dickson (2001), p. 181.

[53]Bix (1993), pp. 194–197.

evaluation will combine what is considered important about law to what is considered good for law. Now, if we develop a general theory that explains only our concept of law—and the characteristics by which this concept deems other practices as juridical—the prospective evaluation of what holds importance is simply what is important only for our concept of law. Therefore, a theory cannot be descriptive and also general, nor can it explain the nature of law in universal terms.[54]

3.4 *Is It Possible to Describe a Normative Practice Such as Law, in Morally Neutral Terms?*

The acceptance by current analytical jurisprudence that theories of law must use evaluative judgements[55] and the debate over Hart's theory as descriptive have brought up several related questions. We described one of those issues earlier. Another issue is the inherent difficulty in providing a neutral description of a *normative* phenomenon such as law.

In order to overcome the shortcomings of traditional legal positivism regarding this issue, Hart suggests explaining law from an internal point of view.[56] In other words, to approach the law from the standpoint of a participant who accepts law as a guide for her or his behavior and for the critique of others' behavior.[57] Hart clarifies this by saying that an internal point of view does not require accepting the law as if it were morally binding.[58] Rather, it is a question of observing the reality of the law from an internal perspective, as a set of rules for guiding human conduct.[59] Some suggest that what Hart proposes for his descriptive theory is a hermeneutic shift.[60]

Hart proposes to shift the attention to the internal point of view because it does not involve giving up his descriptive explanation of law—morally neutral and non-justificative. In his opinion,[61] a descriptive legal theory can both understand and describe the internal perspective of those subjected to law without needing to adopt it. If the phenomenon that must be described is made of evaluations, "descriptions will still be descriptions, even if what is described is an evaluation."[62]

[54]Finnis 2003, p. 116.

[55]Hart 1987, p. 39, Raz (1994), pp. 208, Dickson (2001) *passim* and Waluchow (1994), pp. 19–29; etc.

[56]Hart (2012), p. 89.

[57]Hart (2012), pp. 89–91.

[58]Hart (2012), pp. 202–203.

[59]Hart (2012), p. 94.

[60]MacCormick (1981, p. 29) and Bix (1999a). In fact, Hart (1983), p. 14 himself categorizes his theory this way.

[61]Hart (2012), p. 243.

[62]Hart (2012), p. 244.

At this stage of Hart's methodological proposal, it is clear that his shift towards the analysis of language as the means to approach the study of law is searching for a middle ground between a position compromised by morals and one that tries to pare down the entire legal phenomenon to empirical data.[63] In the words of some of Hart's followers, he tries to develop a descriptive theory, albeit impure and without a scientific aim.[64]

The issue is now whether this intermediate position is actually possible. The criticisms can be structured around two arguments. The first suggests that many internal points of view exist;[65] that there are various reasons why someone accepts law as a reason for action. Hart concedes this point and suggests some of these possible explanations: estimation of interests, selfless interest in others, a non-reflexive attitude or desires to behave as others do.[66] The issue is that in order to explain law—and its normativity—it is necessary to choose or evaluate which of these internal points of view to base upon and for that is necessary to resort to moral arguments or reasons.[67]

The second argument suggests that if the rules cannot be conceived of as objective moral reasons for action, they are not reasons at all, and whoever asks "why do I have to obey?" will find a will that is being imposed on him.[68] This ultimately prevents Hart from achieving the goal with which he introduced the notion of the internal point of view: to explain the normativity of law and to distinguish it from a mere band of thieves.

3.5 *What Is the Interest in Developing a Descriptive Theory of a Highly Normative Phenomenon?*

Hart's attempt to provide a general and descriptive theory of law must overcome another objection that does not concern its viability but its ultimate goal. Hart already outlined the importance of a description of law as a substantial first step for any useful moral evaluation thereof. Other authors admit that although a general and descriptive theory like Hart's can seem to amount to a purely theoretical achievement of no practical importance, such a theory requires no further justification than

---

[63]Hart (1983), pp. 31–35.

[64]Waluchow (1994), p. 30 and Marmor 2001, p. 154.

[65]To see how confused the division that Hart makes between the internal and external points of view can be: Postema (1998), p. 226.

[66]Hart (2012), p. 203.

[67]Finnis (1980), pp. 9–19; Perry (1995), pp. 107–135.

[68]Orrego (1997), p. 342.

any theory that aims to describe a phenomenon.[69] Knowledge needs no instrumental justification, because it has intrinsic value.[70]

Although it may be accepted that the factual analysis of a particular legal system can a have purpose in understanding law and its normativity, this analysis constitutes a small part of the general observation of why law is obeyed and why law binds. If we take a wider look, we can also consider why legal practices have been invented, what the reasons to establish it, accept it and maintain it are. In short, a purely descriptive theory of what judges, officials and common people bound by law do can seem superfluous,[71] because it leaves the aforementioned core questions about the normativity of law unanswered.

This lack of interest for the reasons—not merely the motivations—of why law is a binding practice can be the cause of the growing sense of dissatisfaction in the last few years with the domineering approach in analytical legal philosophy from both inside and outside its somewhat closed circles.[72] Some authors describe this philosophy of law as narrow-minded, austere and similar to scholastic philosophy.[73] That is to say, it is a sterile and naive activity, illustrative of the depletion of the traditional theory of law.[74]

3.6 Apart from Being Descriptive, Can Analytical Jurisprudence Also Be Prescriptive?

A theory that only describes how a practice conceptualizes law without explaining why it binds and produces practical consequences invites further inquiry: apart from being descriptive, can analytical jurisprudence be prescriptive?

The current analytical jurisprudence offers two answers to this question. Firstly, there are those who endorse Hart's theory by suggesting that a theoretical analysis of law that aims to discover its nature or essence is only descriptive. However, they claim that this does not imply barring any other concept of law. In fact, they suggest that their theory can serve as the first step towards a critical or prescriptive analysis of law. On the other hand, even if their theoretical proposal is only descriptive, they are aware that it can have an indirect influence on the legal practice. By recognizing that our concept of law fluctuates, and that the theory of law is part of our concept of law,

---

69 Moore (1998), p. 326.

70 Himma (2002), p. 1224.

71 Some authors believe that these questions can find their origin in the question "what should I do?". See Finnis (2003), pp. 107–108 and 115–116. A clear example of how an extensive debate between two viewpoints within the current analytical jurisprudence finishes without offering any kind of practical difference when trying to be applied can be seen in Etcheverry (2005).

72 Twining (2005), p. 577.

73 Dworkin (2002), pp. 1678–1679.

74 Posner (1996), p. vii.

they acknowledge that it is inevitable for the theory of law not to be merely a passive observer of the concepts of a given culture. This influence of theory over practice does not result in the identification of theory and normative proposal, as theory only strives to understand. Such authors claim that only "bad" theories can lead to a change. In spite of the previous, they recognize that in some cases it is difficult to draw clear-cut delineations, for example in the cases in which our culture's self-comprehension is diverse or inconsistent.[75]

The second response is derived from ethical or prescriptive positivism which employs a methodological approach that is somewhat different from Hart's but tries to respect his positivist tradition.[76] This approach does not aim to discover the nature of law, but rather tries to defend a concept of law based on moral arguments—in other words, they attempt to create a political theory. It does not suggest that the law in our legal practices is based purely on social sources, but they suggest that this is ultimately the best-case scenario. Usually, the reason to adopt this kind of approach is that the concept of law is normative and it is not possible to understand it without considering morals. Authors adopting such an approach tend to defend the thesis that the positivist tradition—including Hart—has always created a normative theory, or to suggest that legal positivism can only be defended with normative arguments.

Thirdly, situated between both viewpoints, are those who claim that analytical jurisprudence is only descriptive and therefore fails to cover the many facets of the theory of law. This response does not hold that a descriptive analysis of law is impossible or completely useless, however, it does insist that law is a socially constructed institution that evolves over time and is better understood as a process of continuous construction and reconstruction—a process without a beginning or end. This does not mean we cannot stop and analyze the concept of law as it exists now. The issue arises when we start to believe that this is the only way of viewing things. The authors who endorse such a view suggest that the theory of law has multiple expressions and, therefore, can be descriptive as well as prescriptive.[77] In short, they highlight that Hart himself defended his theory of law with prescriptive arguments.[78] This viewpoint obviously assumes that there is no reason why normative and descriptive views should be incompatible.

---

[75] Raz (1996), p. 7.

[76] Authors like MacCormick, Waldron, Schauer and Campbell are part of this movement. See MacCormick (1985), pp. 1–41, Waldron (2001), pp. 411–433, Schauer (1998), 65–78 and Campbell (1996). See also Goldsworthy (1990), pp. 449–486 and Postema (1998), pp. 329–357. An interesting critical study of this version of legal positivism can be seen in Rivas (2007) *passim*.

[77] Schauer (2005), pp. 495–501.

[78] Hart discusses with Fuller about what kind of theory (defended by positivism or natural law) favors the civil disobedience to evil law. See Schauer (2005), pp. 493–495.

3.7 *Does Only a Unique Concept of Law Exist in Our Practice?*

Another possible argument against the idea that law can be described in a morally neutral way is that law is inherently controversial, to such an extent that it is possible to choose among the options only by using moral arguments.[79] In opposition, supporters of Hart's theory have suggested that what is truly controversial is the concept of legitimacy or justification that people consider in order to accept law, but not the concept of law itself.[80] This response is complicated, as noted above, because in order to be able to explain law and its normativity it is necessary to choose one of the interpretations of legitimacy or justification and one internal point of view. To do so, one must resort to moral arguments or moral reasons, that is to say, value judgments.[81]

Essentially the question is whether our practice contains more than one specific concept of law and, if so, if the evaluation or selection of these concepts can only be made by means of moral arguments,[82] or if the meta-theoretical values would suffice.[83] For this to be feasible, these values cannot be equated to moral or direct values (as observed *supra*, paragraph 3.3).

3.8 *Why Should We Analyze the Concepts of our Practice and Not Just the Practice Itself?*

In the beginning of this paper we noticed how Hart takes advantage of the shift made in philosophy towards the analysis of language to apply such methodology to the study of law. In particular we observed that Hart uses analysis of concepts to explain the nature or essence of law, because examining the significant legal concepts can sharpen our perception of these phenomena. We explained also why Hart considers that the conceptual approach to law is superior to one that is purely empirical.

Other arguments have been included throughout the years to defend a conceptual approach against purely empirical ones. For example, it has been claimed that a purely empirical theory is incapable of becoming a general theory of law or of explaining the nature of law. Furthermore, conceptual analysis has been considered of high priority because law can only be studied once we know what we mean by the

---

[79]Dworkin (2004), pp. 9–12.

[80]Marmor (2006), pp. 395–704.

[81]Murphy (2001), pp. 371–409.

[82]Perry (1995), pp. 197–135, Leiter (2001), pp. 355–370, Nino (1995), pp. 12–50 and Scarpelli (1955), p. 5.

[83]Coleman (2001), p. 197.

term “law”[84] or because it allows us to maintain a structure in which discussions can have logic.[85] Finally, others suggest that the virtue of the conceptual analysis is its capacity to identify and explain the important elements of law without prejudging them, serving as a precedent for direct judgments.[86]

4 Which Criteria Dictate That One Theory of Law Is Better Than Another?

Apart from all the aforementioned reasons to adopt an analytical theory of law, there is a question that must be answered: what criteria must be taken into account in order to evaluate the different analytical theories that try to explain law? Within the current analytical jurisprudence there are those who claim that non-moral or meta-theoretical evaluation criteria exists—e.g., simplicity, clarity, elegance, generality or coherence—and any legal theory must consider them in order to be successful. Such criteria determine the questions that any legal theory must answer.[87]

Others consider that the success of a conceptual analysis of law can be evaluated on the basis of the beneficial consequences that can be obtained from it. The success of an analysis of the concept of law should be evaluated by taking into account its beneficial theoretical-sociological results,[88] or its beneficial moral consequences.[89]

Finally, there are some who recently claim that different kinds of conceptual assertions exist, and that the differences between them derive from their differing purposes. For example, an assertion that appears as an arbitrary stipulation is not the same as one that simply tracks linguistic uses, or one that attempts to explain something important about a problem—a hidden meaning behind a practice–, or one that establishes evaluative criteria to describe something in a particular way—on the basis that such criteria are deeply rooted in the practice. We can derive from this that there may be more than one correct theory on a specific conceptual question because, often, such theories approach the same subject, but with different purposes. In sum, these authors attempt to explain why the conceptual debates on law seem tangled up in mere verbal controversies.[90]

In opposition to these theses, it has been upheld that the concept of law is not something that can be chosen on the basis of meta-theoretical criteria, by its moral or empirical results, or based on the purposes we may ourselves have. The concept of

[84]Coleman (2002), p. 347.

[85]Bix (2004), p. 18.

[86]Dickson (2001), p. 144.

[87]Coleman (2001), p. 3, Waluchow (1994), pp. 19–29 and Guidice (2015), pp. 88–89.

[88]Lyons (1983), pp. 104–109.

[89]Schauer (2005), pp. 65–78 and Schauer (1996), pp. 31–35.

[90]Bix (2004), pp. 18–23, 28. Using a similar idea, Nino (1985), p. 191 attempts to solve the controversy between positivism and the natural law theory.

law exists, it is unique, and it is part of our own self-understanding, and can be described correctly or incorrectly. In synthesis, the concept of law is independent from the theories that try to formulate it.[91]

All these results in an argument of whether a concept of law really exists in the manner described in the above paragraph—unique, *etc.*–[92]or if it is possible to choose a concept of law—in addition to describing the existing one—in a normative way, assuming that it is a concept that evolves.[93]

We will go no further on this subject, and will only highlight two matters. The first is the lack of discussion and clear agreement about why the conceptual analysis is chosen as the more appropriate method to study law—e. g., it is unclear if these reasons are compatible or complementary. This basic question is taken for granted or simply ignored. The second matter is that the theory that suggests law must be explained or studied using conceptual analysis, is an approach based on normative reasons. In short, we are suggesting that the legal theory depends on a normative thesis to get started.[94]

5 Conclusion

From the above passages one can see that the current claim of analytical jurisprudence suggesting that its theory of law is general and descriptive and that its aim is to explain the nature of law needs, in the very least, to be explained with great precision.

This theory of law attempts to be general and ends up being able to explain only specific practices. This theory is also intended to be descriptive although it does not describe empirical facts and is not necessarily non-evaluative. In addition, it is a theory of the essence or the nature of law, that is considered purely contingent. Finally, the purpose is to formulate such a theory by means of a conceptual analysis but, as we have seen, those means have not been justified in an absolute and precise way, and may depend from the beginning on normative arguments.

In sum, the challenges that analytical jurisprudence still encounters and the need to clarify the way it uses the terms such as "essence", "nature", "general" and "descriptive" seem to reflect the internal tension that exists in its endeavor to find theoretical roads (e.g., between the purely descriptive theories and normative ones) that can be followed.

[91]Raz (1996), pp. 4–7, (1998), pp. 280–281 and Dickson (2001), p. 93.

[92]Bix (2003), p. 546.

[93]Schauer (2005), pp. 493–501.

[94]Orrego (1997), p. 129.

References

Bix B (1993) Law, language, and legal determinacy. Oxford University Press, Oxford

Bix B (1999a) H.L.A. Hart and the hermeneutic turn in legal theory. South Methodist Univ Law Rev 52:167–199

Bix B (1999b) On description and legal reasoning. In: Meyer L (ed) Rules and reasoning. Essays in honour of Fred Schauer. Hart, Oxford, pp 7–28

Bix B (2003) Raz on necessity. Law Philos 22(6):537–559

Bix B (2004) Conceptual questions and Jurisprudence. In: Bix B (ed) Jurisprudence. Theory and context, 3rd edn. Carolina Academic Press, Durham, pp 15–32

Bix B (2006) Palabras previas. In: Bix B (ed) Teoría del derecho. Ambición y límites. Marcial Pons, Madrid, pp 13–15

Bix B (2009) Legal Theory: Kinds and Purposes. In: IVR Encyclopedia of Legal Theory. http://ivr-enc.info/index.php?title=Legal_Theory:_Types_and_Purposes. Accessed 10 Oct 2013

Bulygin E (2007) Raz on legal theory. In Raz J, Alexy R, Bulygin E (eds) Una discusión sobre la teoría del derecho. Marcial Pons, Madrid, pp 99–110

Campbell T (1996) The legal theory of ethical positivism. Darmouth, Aldershot

Coleman JL (2001) The practice of principle. In defence of a pragmatist approach to legal theory. Oxford University Press, Oxford

Coleman JL (2002) Methodology. In: Coleman JL, Shapiro SJ (eds) The Oxford handbook of jurisprudence and philosophy of law. Oxford University Press, Oxford, pp 311–351

Coleman JL, Leiter B (1995) Determinacy, objectivity, and authority. In: Marmor A (ed) Law and interpretation. Essays in legal philosophy. Clarendon Press, Oxford, pp 203–278

Dickson J (2001) Evaluation and legal theory. Hart, Oxford

Dickson J (2004) Methodology in jurisprudence: a critical survey. Legal Theory 10(3):117–156

Dworkin R (1983) A reply. In: Cohen M (ed) Ronald Dworkin and contemporary jurisprudence. Duckworth, London

Dworkin R (2002) Thirty years on. Harv Law Rev 115(6):1655–1687

Dworkin R (2004) Hart's postscript and the character of political philosophy. Oxf J Leg Stud 24 (1):1–37

Dworkin R (2006) The concepts of law. In: Dworkin R (ed) Justice in Robes. Harvard University Press, Cambridge

Endicott T (1998) Herbert Hart and the semantic sting. Legal Theory 4(3):283–300

Etcheverry JB (2005) What has been the outcome of the ILP/ELP debate? Archiv für Rechts- und Sozialphilosophie 106:53–65

Finnis J (1980) Natural law and natural rights. Clarendon Press, Oxford

Finnis J (2003) Law and what I truly should decide. Am J Jurisprud 48(1):107–129

Goldsworthy JD (1990) The self-destruction of legal positivism. Oxf J Leg Stud 10(4):449–486

Green L (2004) General jurisprudence: a 25th anniversary essay. Oxf J Leg Stud 25(4):565–580

Green L (2012) Introduction. In Hart HLA the concept of law, 3rd edn. Clarendon Press, Oxford

Guidice M (2015) Understanding the nature of law. A case for constructive conceptual explanation. Elgar Publishing, Cheltenham

Hart HLA (1965) Review of the morality of law, by Lon L. Fuller. Harv Law Rev 78(6):1281–1296

Hart HLA (1983) Essays in jurisprudence and philosophy. Oxford University Press, Oxford

Hart HLA (1987) Comment on Dworkin 'legal theory and the problem of sense'. In Gavison R (ed) Issues in contemporary legal philosophy. The influence of H.L.A. Hart, Clarendon Press, Oxford, pp 35–42

Hart HLA (2012) The concept of law, 3rd edn. Clarendon Press, Oxford

Himma KE (2002) Substance and method in conceptual jurisprudence and legal theory. Va Law Rev 88(5):1119–1228

Langlinais A, Leiter B (2016) The methodology of legal philosophy. In: Cappelen H, Szabó Gendler T, Hawthorne J (eds) The Oxford handbook of philosophical methodology. Oxford University Press, Oxford, pp 671–689

Leiter B (2001) Legal realism, hard positivism, and the limits of conceptual analysis. In: Coleman J (ed) Hart's postscript. Essays on the postscript to the concept of law. Oxford University Press, Oxford, pp 355–370
Lyons D (1983) Ethics and the rule of law. Cambridge University Press, Cambridge
Lyons D (1993) Moral aspects of legal theory. Cambridge University Press, Cambridge
MacCormick N (1981) H.L.A. Hart. Arnold, London
MacCormick N (1985) A moralistic case for A-moralistic law? Valparaiso Law Rev 20(1):1–41
Marmor A (2001) Positive law and objective values. Clarendon Press, Oxford
Marmor A (2006) Legal positivism: still descriptive and morally neutral. Oxf J Leg Stud 26 (4):683–704
Moore M (1992) Law as a functional kind. In: George RP (ed) Natural law theory. Oxford University Press, Oxford, pp 188–242
Moore M (1998) Hart's concluding scientific postscript. Legal Theory 4(3):301–328
Murphy LB (2001) The political question of the concept of law. In: Coleman J (ed) Hart's postscript. Essays on the postscript to the concept of law. Oxford University Press, Oxford, pp 371–409
Nino CS (1985) El enfoque esencialista del concepto de derecho. In Nino CS (ed) La validez del Derecho. Astrea, Buenos Aires, pp 176–195
Nino CS (1995) Introducción al análisis del Derecho, 6th edn. Ariel, Barcelona
Orrego C (1997) H.L.A. Hart. Abogado del positivismo jurídico. Pamplona, Eunsa
Perry SR (1995) Interpretation and methodology in law. In: Marmor A (ed) Law and interpretation. Oxford University Press, Oxford, pp 97–135
Posner R (1996) Law and legal theory in the UK and the US. Clarendon Press, Oxford
Postema GJ (1998) Jurisprudence as practical philosophy. Legal Theory 4(3):329–357
Raz J (1994) The problem about the nature of law. In: Raz J (ed) Ethics in the Public Domain. Oxford University Press, Oxford, pp 195–209
Raz J (1996) On the nature of law. Archiv fur Rechts- und Sozialphilosophie 82:1–25
Raz J (1998) Two views of the nature of the theory of law: a partial comparison. Legal Theory 4 (3):249–282
Raz J (2004) Can there be a theory of law. In: Golding MP, Edmundson WA (eds) The Blackwell guide to the philosophy of law and legal theory. Blackwell, Malden, pp 324–342
Raz J (2007) Teoría y conceptos. Réplica a Alexy y Bulygin. In: Raz J, Alexy R, Bulygin E (eds) Una discusión sobre la teoría del derecho. Marcial Pons, Madrid, pp 111–120
Rivas P (2007) El retorno a los orígenes de la tradición positivista. Una aproximación a la filosofía jurídica del positivismo ético contemporáneo. Civitas, Madrid
Scarpelli U (1955) Il problema della definizione e il concetto di diritto. Instituto Editoriale Cisalpino, Milano
Schauer F (1996) Positivism as Pariah. In: George RP (ed) The autonomy of law. Essays on legal positivism. Clarendon Press, Oxford, pp 31–56
Schauer F (1998) Positivism through thick and thin. In: Bix B (ed) Analyzing law. New essays in legal theory. Clarendon Press, Oxford, pp 65–78
Schauer F (2005) The social construction of the concept of law: a reply to Julie Dickson. Oxf J Leg Stud 25(3):493–501
Twining W (2005) General theory of law. Anales de la Cátedra de Francisco Suárez 39:597–644
Waldron J (2001) Normative (or ethical) positivism. In: Coleman J (ed) Hart's postscript. Essays on the postscript to the concept of law. Oxford University Press, Oxford, pp 411–433
Waluchow WJ (1994) Inclusive legal positivism. Clarendon Press, Oxford
Waluchow WJ (1998) The many faces of legal positivism. Univ Toronto Law J 48(3):387–449

Method Matters: Non-normative Jurisprudence and the Re-mystification of the Law

Margaret Martin

Abstract By exploring HLA Hart's *The Concept of Law*, and the trajectory of the debate following Hart's contribution, it quickly becomes apparent that value-neutral "conceptual analysis" is a more tenuous methodological approach than its proponents assume. Once Hart becomes an inclusive positivist, many of the ideas and aims that were once central to his project are either wholly abandoned or dramatically transformed. Even the "idea of a rule" is re-conceived in a manner that is antithetical to both the letter and the spirit of his canonical work. The value of the value-neutral method is called into question once the limits of this approach come into view: many seemingly central questions—including questions that Hart explored—must never be answered if this commitment is to be kept. While much of this paper addresses the shortcomings of inclusive positivism, I will also argue that exclusive positivism does not solve Hart's problems. Following Nigel Simmonds, I re-frame Hart's project around the distinction between law and the gunman writ large. Not only are the shortcomings in Hart's substantial theses illuminated, but the close connection between substance and method is exposed. Raz, unlike Hart, appears to account for the normative dimensions of law without sacrificing Hartian conceptual analysis. This, I will argue, is an illusion. Value-neutrality is more difficult to adhere to than its proponents assume.

1 Conceptual Clarity and Hartian Jurisprudence

"What then is time? Provided that no one asks me, I know. If I want to explain it to an inquirer, I do not know."[1] Like time, law has a double existence—at once remarkably familiar and frustratingly elusive. HLA Hart is surely correct to observe that it

I wish to thank Jorge Fabra-Zamora, Gonzalo Villa-Rosas, and Nigel Simmonds for their excellent comments. All errors are my own.

[1]Saint Augustine (1992), p. 230. Famously cited by HLA Hart in (2012), p. 14.

M. Martin (✉)
Western University, Faculty of Law, London, ON, Canada
e-mail: mmart2@uwo.ca

J. L. Fabra-Zamora, G. Villa Rosas (eds.), *Conceptual Jurisprudence*, Law and Philosophy Library 137, https://doi.org/10.1007/978-3-030-78803-2_4

"is in this way that even skilled lawyers have felt that, though they know the law, there is much about law and its relations to other things that they cannot explain and do not understand."[2] This is presumably because law has a double life of sorts. It has an institutional dimension that is visible and familiar. We have the courts and the legislature. There are also jails and police officers. Its manifestations are similar to the familiar characteristics of time. We rely on clocks and calendars. We celebrate birthdays and the new year. But time has another, less tangible life that cannot be easily explained—a life that is irreducible to its more physical manifestations. Law is similar. It exists as a body of knowledge but is irreducible to it. Despite our familiarity with both phenomena, they are also sources of bewilderment.

Hart's proposed solution to the confusion that confronts lawyers, and others, is to turn our attention to the "idea of a rule."[3] Hart admits that "the concept of a rule . . . is as perplexing as that of law itself."[4] Presumably, because legal rules often enjoy a physical existence as written rules, but they also have a normative existence insofar as they instruct people about how they ought to behave. Hart's proposed solution places a great deal of emphasis on the former, more tangible aspect of legality. The ideal dimension of legality is famously excluded from the reach of his concept of law. Hart is not interested in grasping what law ought to be, as that, he insists, is a job for the moral philosopher, not the legal philosopher.[5] The job of the legal philosopher is to tell us what law *is*. The method Hart offers us is supposed to bring much-sought-after clarity to the debate, in part, by securing this particular division of labour within philosophy. The legal philosopher must be a careful observer of the world. She must discard the "contingent" features that change from society to society and focus only on those "necessary" features that are present in all existing legal systems.

It is unclear, however, that the mystery and confusion that surrounds law can be addressed with such ease. If the "idea of a rule" is the key to jurisprudence, then one might expect that this simple insight would provide a sturdy bedrock for the debate going forward. Instead, the jurisprudential debate has become remarkably complex, leading to a certain level of confusion, rather than the hoped-for consensus.[6] In what follows, I will not rehearse the various debates between Hart and his adversaries in full; rather, I will suggest that the power of certain criticisms can be discerned by tracking the trajectory of the debate. After Ronald Dworkin's intervention, for instance, Hart re-orients his account around a single idea: the claim that law and morality are conceptually separable.[7] The price Hart pays for this explicit endorsement of inclusive positivism is notable. Many of the ideas and aims that were once central to his project are either wholly abandoned or dramatically transformed. Even

[2]Hart (2012), p. 14.

[3]Hart (2012), p. 80.

[4]Hart (2012), p. 15.

[5]Hart (2012), ch. VIII.

[6]Bix (2011), pp. 431–440.

[7]Hart (2012), p. 250.

the "idea of a rule" is re-conceived in a manner that is antithetical to both the letter and the spirit of his canonical work.

From the perspective of the modern debate, this seems to matter little. Legal philosophers insist that their points are interesting, even if others do not find them so.[8] The distinctions drawn are meant to cast light on *our* concept of law (although we can wonder whether the word "our" refers only to the members of the philosophical community who defend such accounts). Even the puzzles that engross many legal philosophers are often generated by the theories themselves; any connection to real-world problems is barely intelligible.[9] Insofar as we view legality through the prism of the current debate, the stakes appear to be remarkably low. But the current debate obscures much. This becomes clearer once we see what is required for a value-neutral approach to be sustained: there are a limited number of questions that can be asked and a limited number of answers that can be offered.

After Hart's practical arguments are severed from his concept of law, the methodological presuppositions underpinning his position are assumed to be correct—Hartians simply assume that value-neutral conceptual analysis illuminates more than it obscures. This is the assumption that I wish to challenge throughout, initially by underscoring the elements of Hart's conception of law that are lost once *conceptual possibilities* displace real-world actualities as the touchstone for jurisprudential inquiry. My worry about the turn to the "conceptually possible" is underscored when John Gardner's re-casting of a portion of Hart's *The Concept of Law* is scrutinized. Gardner attempts to remove value assumptions from Hart's well-known fable about the shift from a pre-legal society to a full-fledged legal regime, but ultimately, he strips this narrative of its meaning as well. The value of value-neutral analysis remains unclear.

In the closing section, I follow Nigel Simmonds and re-frame Hart's project around problems related to law's authority and its justificatory force. Once Hart's project is seen through this lens, not only are the shortcomings in Hart's substantial positions illuminated, but the close relationship between his substantive positions and his methodological commitments are accentuated. While much of the paper casts suspicion on the value of Hart's inclusive positivist turn, the final section raises doubts about the viability of the second pathway charted by Joseph Raz. Unlike Hart, Raz offers an account of law's normativity, but it is far from clear that he can do so without sacrificing conceptual neutrality. Hart understood the boundaries of value-neutral concept analysis and worked to steer his substantive account away from value-laden commitments (albeit, without complete success, or so I shall argue). Raz, in an attempt to address the weaknesses in Hart's account, seeks to walk a conceptual tightrope, but it is not a path that is easily traversed. It is not even clear that this pathway exists. What becomes apparent, however, is that Hartian conceptual analysis is not the jurisprudential elixir that so many believe it to be.

---

[8]Gardner (2012), p. 280.

[9]Shapiro (2011), pp. 39ff.

2 Demystification and Hart's "Double Ground"

In an attempt to demystify the law, Hart famously distils the concept of law down to what he sees as the essential, "universal" elements that are "necessary and sufficient" for the existence of a legal system.[10] He tilts our collective gaze towards the more tangible elements of legality, intentionally leaving out any appeal to justice or morality; such an appeal would exacerbate disagreement about the nature of law. Understanding the nature of law requires careful observation about common features of legal systems. What is not required is the careful study of moral values, or any theory that places such values at its centre. Hart famously maintains that every legal system must include the union of primary and secondary rules (including a rule of recognition). The rule of recognition distinguishes "valid" legal norms from other norms that do not spring from the correct source.[11] In order for a legal system to exist, Hart adds that the primary rules that are validated by the system's rule of recognition must be "generally obeyed" by the populace.[12]

While Hart ushered in the current jurisprudential tradition, his work is part of the tradition of political philosophy from which he sought to make a clean break. Hart defends his predecessors, Jeremy Bentham and John Austin, insisting that they "were not dry analysts fiddling with verbal distinctions while cities burned, but were the vanguard of a movement which laboured with passionate intensity and much success to bring about a better society and better laws."[13] The project of demystification, which traces back to Bentham and Austin, is one where the stated aim is to strip away the law's moral aura. Instead of thinking about law as some kind of divine ordinance, it must be seen for what it is: law is a set of posited norms created by humans and humans are fallible. Hart, in an important respect, aimed to carry forward the spirit of reform. His jurisprudential project was not born out of an interest in conceptual analysis for its own sake. Rather, like legal positivists before him, Hart has a vision of the good in mind.

This vision places him in a certain relationship with other thinkers in the history of political thought. Jean-Jacques Rousseau, for instance, takes "men as they are and laws as they might be" in the hopes of determining if there can be "any legitimate and sure principle of government."[14] Hart wants us to see law as it *is* in the hopes that this will bring about the betterment of humankind:

> What surely is most needed in order to make men clear-sighted in confronting the official abuse of power, is that they should preserve the sense that the certification of something as legally valid is not conclusive of the question of obedience, and that, however great the aura

[10]Hart (2012), p. 116.

[11]Hart (2012), p. 107.

[12]Hart (2012), p. 116. Hart's official second condition is that officials must adopt the critical reflective attitude towards the norms that govern their behaviour.

[13]Hart (1957), p. 596.

[14]Rousseau (2004), p. 1.

> of majesty or authority which the official system may have, its demands must in the end be submitted to a moral scrutiny.[15]

Hart wants us to see law as a mundane institution so that humans can realize their potential to think critically. When faced with legal norms that have morally questionable content, he urges us to turn inwards and explore the dictates of conscience in the hopes that resistance, not obedience, will ensue. Writing in the shadows of the rise and fall of National Socialism, Hart endeavours to help ensure that individuals will not assume the posture of unquestioning obedience in the face of unconscionable demands. His real-world concerns infuse his writings with a sense of urgency.

Hart does not envision a clean separation between jurisprudential insight and the foreseen practical benefits. He commends Austin and Bentham for offering "simple truths" that are the foundation of their programs for reform: "No one has ever combined, with such even-minded sanity as the Utilitarians, the passion for reform with respect for law together with a due recognition of the need to control the abuse of power even when power is in the hands of reformers."[16] Philosophical clarity can bring with it certain practical benefits. It is upon this "double ground"[17] that Hart erects his theory. Only when philosophers eliminate value judgments can we hope to identify a few certainties upon which further jurisprudential reflections can spring.[18]

The manner in which the practical and conceptual are united in Hart's work is placed in relief when he comments on the problem of obedience. In *Leviathan*, for instance, Thomas Hobbes forcefully argues that our fundamental desire for survival justifies our submission to authority. Hobbes wants subjects to acquiesce to the sovereign and his laws, both in action and in speech, for the sake of peace.[19] Bentham famously advises us to "obey punctually" and "censure freely."[20] For him, political speech can alter laws for the better, but obedience remains important for the sake of the preservation of order. Hart distinguishes himself from these thinkers, insisting that the "danger of anarchy" may have been "overrated."[21] Citizens can both *criticize* existing laws and *act* contrary to the law when conscience demands. Unlike his predecessors, Hart assumes they can do so without threatening the social order. The central point is that Hart's theory is underpinned by an ideal that

---

[15]Hart (2012), p. 210. After admitting that there is no knock-down argument available to the positivist over the natural lawyer, he nevertheless believes that his view promotes a clear-sighted view of legality: "A concept of law which allows the invalidity of law to be distinguished from its immorality, enables us to see the complexity and variety of these separate issues; whereas a narrow concept of law which denies legal validity to iniquitous rules may blind us to them" Hart (1961), p. 211.

[16]Hart (1957), p. 596. Hart also states: "Both thinkers' prime reason for this insistence was to enable men to see steadily the precise issues posed by the existence of morally bad laws, and to understand the specific character of the authority of a legal order."

[17]Fuller (1957), p. 631.

[18]Hart (2012), pp. 186–187.

[19]Hobbes (1994), pp. XIV [5]–[7].

[20]Bentham (1998), p. 10.

[21]Hart (2012), p. 211.

he hopes to realize in the world—an ideal that he believes is best realized by way of a non-ideal conception of law.

This vision of the good has long since been abandoned. Hart's fellow positivists quickly discarded Hart's practical arguments. It is unclear, after all, if legal positivism would be able to bring about the desired practical result.[22] Conceptual clarity must be the lodestar that guides jurisprudential inquiry. When positivists after Hart leave behind the practical arguments that animate Hart's thought, there are a number of implications. The practical dimension of Hart's work, which connected his account both to the history of philosophy and to real-world concerns, is no longer present. Once this tether to worldly issues is severed, the positivist project becomes a free-standing, self-justifying enterprise. The value of value-neutral analysis is now simply presupposed.[23] If arguments are offered in defence of such methodological presuppositions, the viability of the value-neutral project will be revealed to rest on a contestable, value-laden foundation. It is, after all, impossible to offer a value-neutral defence of value-neutral analysis: why recommend a method of analysis if one does not suppose that it is a good method in some way? It is at this point that Hart's methodological assumptions harden into tenets of a new faith. It is this faith that I am questioning.

3 Exposing Vulnerabilities: Descriptive Jurisprudence and the Problem of Counterexamples

While Hart's theory has a clear empirical bent—he places great emphasis on institutional realities and posited rules. Hart, nevertheless, offers some important insights into certain less tangible dimensions of law. Consider his discussion of the "*internal aspect* of rules," whereby people who have this perspective "look upon the behaviour in question as a general standard to be followed by the group as a whole."[24] The internalization of norms is one of the ways that law shapes the self and, thus, it is one of the dimensions of law's existence that transcends the empirical world. Hart initially introduces this idea in order to cast doubt on the viability of Austin's command theory of law. Contra Austin, Hart argues that we do not simply obey the law out of habit, we also hold it up as a standard by which to judge our own behaviour and that of others.[25]

Instead of developing his point about the internalization of rules, Hart marginalizes it. Recall that when he finally articulates the components of his concept of law, only officials must adopt this attitude toward the secondary rules that govern their

[22] Waluchow (1994), pp. 86–98.

[23] For a powerful critique of Hartian jurisprudence on this point, see Stone (2010).

[24] Hart (2012), p. 56.

[25] Ibid., 56–57.

behaviour. Citizens must simply obey, but they can do so for any reason.[26] Hart aims to make sense of all types of legal systems, including wicked ones. The internal attitude is but one kind of relationship that citizens can have with rules. Hart correctly observes that, in some systems, fear is the central mechanism by which obedience is secured.[27] In other words, the adoption of the attitude of acceptance on the part of the populace is a contingent feature that is present in some, but not all, existing legal systems. In sum, Hart's introduction of the idea of the critical reflective attitude reveals that Austin's theory is too simple. Austin has failed to account for this particular feature of our lived experience and hence his command theory distorts, rather than illuminates, the nature of law. While simplicity may be a virtue, theories can be too simple.

At this juncture, Hart presupposes that an adequate theory of law must account for familiar features of our experience of legality. Notice the form of Hart's argument against Austin: Hart points to a feature of our practice for which Austin does not account for in his non-normative theory of law. A single counterexample can cast an entire theory in doubt *if* that theory is the product of an attempt to identify features shared by *all* existing legal systems. Like Austin before him, Hart's "descriptive" account is vulnerable in precisely the same way. Hart points to the existence of the critical reflective attitude to demonstrate that Austin's theory is too simplistic; Dworkin points to the value-laden argumentative nature of adjudication in order to demonstrate that Hart's theory is flawed.

Dworkin claims that principles fundamentally differ from rules: principles are a matter of weight, whereby rules have an "all-or-nothing quality."[28] Principles are by nature rather elusive and hence they cannot easily be traced back to a single source, and consequently, they resist being captured in a meaningful way by Hart's rule of recognition. Recall that Hart states that we can identify legal norms from other norms by tracing them back to their source—"the Queen in Parliament."[29] Validity is presented as a matter of correct pedigree. While it is far from clear that the distinction between rules and principles is as clear as Dworkin assumes it is, this is not the essential point: the point is adjudication is a morally robust practice that resists conceptualization in a value-neutral way. Dworkin is suggesting that moral argumentation displaces the idea of "source," at least in part.[30] Contra Hart, Dworkin insists that determining what law is, always inevitably involves determining what it ought to be.[31]

---

[26]Hart (2012), p. 116. If he had given priority to internal aspect of rules, he would likely arrive at an account of law that is ideal based, not descriptive. For a critique of this point, see Finnis (1980), pp. 11–18. For my development of this point, see Martin (2020b).

[27]Hart (2012), p. 116.

[28]Dworkin (1978), p. 24.

[29]Hart (2012), p. 102.

[30]Dworkin (1986), pp. 11–35.

[31]Dworkin (1986), p. 90.

One might be tempted to respond by noting that we are capable of describing value-neutral practices without making value commitments.[32] But this response misses the point in one key respect. It is the reflexive and deliberative nature of legal argumentation that prevents Hart's rule of recognition from acting as a stopping point—a factual ground upon which an account of law is supposed to rest. Pavlos Eleftheriadis maintains that "if the question about what the law is on any particular matter is an irreducibly deliberative question, then the authority of law cannot be settled by any factual, causal chain of events."[33] If this is the case, then Hart's rule of recognition cannot act as a backstop for jurisprudential reflection, as he had hoped. And, if this criticism is correct, this means that the dream of non-normative jurisprudence is unrealizable.[34] It is not my immediate aim to directly argue for this conclusion (although I will say more about this point in the concluding section). By tracing the trajectory of the modern debate after Dworkin's intervention, the force of Dworkin's point is visible: Hart must reshape his account in ways that undermine the project as once imagined.

Hart begins with a desire to identify fundamental tangible aspects of legality that both the laymen and the lawyer can concede are central to their experience of law. After Dworkin, Hart ends up in a world of imagined spaces that are foreign to the lived experience of laymen and lawyer alike. Hart begins with an account that is overly vulnerable to empirical counterexamples, but he ends up with an account that is virtually invulnerable. But value-neutrality, and seeming invulnerability of this methodological approach, is secured at a significant cost.

4 The Idea of a Rule: After Dworkin

Hart's response to Dworkin, articulated in the postscript to *The Concept of Law*, involves two strategies: Hart begins by deflecting Dworkin's value-laden interpretive account before proceeding to absorb it into his own account. Consider his first strategy. Hart insists that his own enterprise is radically different from Dworkin's: Dworkin views legal theory as "evaluative" and "justificatory" in addition to being oriented toward a "particular legal culture."[35] Dworkin, Hart maintains, offers us a theory about how judges *should* decide cases, which is directed primarily at the American system. Contrariwise, Hart is not offering a theory of adjudication, but rather he is constructing a theory of law that is general insofar as it is meant to explain the existence conditions for all legal systems. Dworkin urges us to view law as his ideal judge, Hercules, would see it: through the lens of the moral ideal of

[32] See Hart (2012), p. 244.

[33] Eleftheriadis (2013), p. 74. Also See Dworkin (2002), pp. 1658–1665.

[34] Raz tries to separate theories of adjudication from theories of law. I discuss this move below.

[35] Hart (2012), p. 240.

"integrity."[36] This project is at odds with Hart's account—Hart's conceptualization of law is meant to be "*descriptive* in that it is morally neutral and has no justificatory aims."[37] Dworkin, Hart argues, has fundamentally misunderstood the difference between the two projects. According to Hart, both projects can happily co-exist in distinct intellectual spaces.

If these two theories do not intersect, why does Hart employ his second strategy? When Hart absorbs Dworkin's theory into his own, he quietly concedes that Dworkin's criticisms have hit their mark. Hart argues that "the rule of recognition may incorporate as criteria of legal validity conformity with moral principles or substantive values."[38] It is at this juncture where he officially declares his allegiance to "soft" or "inclusive" positivism.[39] In so doing, Hart opts to champion the *separation thesis* over the *sources thesis*. That is, he commits himself to the view that the rule of recognition of a given legal system may, but need not, contain moral criteria. Hart abandons the view that ascertaining the content of law is always a factual exercise (the *sources thesis*). He now must concede that identifying valid law may require more than simply tracing a rule back to its source (i.e., the Queen): in legal systems where moral criteria are incorporated into the rule of recognition, moral arguments will be required in order to determine the content of legally valid norms.

What, then, is the dividing line between Dworkin and the inclusive positivists? The answer to this question proffered by the inclusive positivists is that it is *possible* for the criteria of validity contained in the rule of recognition to be purely factual. Dworkin's theory is, once again, relegated to the world of mere contingencies. Moral arguments *may* be required to establish legal validity, but this is not a *necessary* feature shared by all legal systems. This response raises a further question: what if officials in all existing legal systems rely on moral arguments, either implicitly or explicitly, in order to determine what the law *is*? In other words, what if all existing legal systems have a rule of recognition that includes moral criteria?

Extensive empirical research would be needed to determine whether Dworkin or the inclusive positivists emerge victorious. Instead of setting off on a potentially fruitless hunt for such a system, the inclusive positivist sidesteps the question. She maintains that it simply does not matter: it is *conceptually possible* that the rule of recognition contains only fact-based criteria. It does not matter if this possibility is realized in the world that we inhabit. According to this formulation of the positivist position, conceptual possibilities take priority over real-world actualities. We can separate two things in thought, even if they are always conjoined in the real world. Once this move is made, the actual features of existing systems cease to hold as much relevance for the debate in jurisprudence. While this means that empirical counterexamples pose little danger to Hart's account, the implications for his

---

[36]Dworkin (1986), p. 239.

[37]Hart (2012), p. 240.

[38]Hart (2012), p. 250.

[39]Hart (2012), p. 250.

concept of law are far-reaching. Recall that much of Hart's theory springs from empirical observations about the world, thus this move marks a radical shift for Hart.

Hart's adoption of inclusive positivism amounts to a quiet concession that the "idea of a rule" does not hold the key to jurisprudence. The idea of a valid legal rule has been transformed into a morally contestable idea that hovers above, and displaces, the tangible representation of rules. It is, after all, one of the upshots of inclusive positivism that "valid" law may not capture the set of norms as they are currently articulated. Any given law may fail to meet the moral criteria set out in that society's rule of recognition, and of course, people can disagree about which norms do and which do not. If we adopt this view, it means that a *legally valid rule* is an idea that is accessible via thought and not through the rather pedestrian exercise of tracing a given norm back to the Queen.[40] Moreover, the very thing that Hart hoped to excise from the realm of jurisprudence—contestable moral argumentation—now infects his account at the very centre. As the old adage goes, choose your enemies carefully.

The idea of a rule is not the only casualty. Many of Hart's other commitments must also be discarded or significantly revised. Hart initially assumes that rules are important because they directly guide the behaviour of the populace.[41] He also assumes citizens are able to ascertain the content of the law with relative ease. Hart can longer assume that "valid" legal rules are ascertainable with ease in legal systems that incorporate moral criteria into the rule of recognition; nor can he assume that they guide conduct in the manner he had once supposed in such systems. The idea of a rule, as it turns out, has limited explanatory power. Again, once Hart champions inclusive positivism, the idea of a "rule" has become a rather mysterious entity that lives primarily, if not exclusively, in the mind of each official.

The introduction of inclusive positivism also shapes the way in which the debate in jurisprudence transpires. The posture of the committed inclusive positivist is often quite defensive: any perceived connections between law and morality are dealt with by turning to the world of conceptual possibilities. The inclusive positivist transports us to imagined places where we encounter wicked gods who happen to be frogs,[42] a society of angels who need laws but not the enforcement of them,[43] and "the Swede" who is able to tell us what the law requires if we are uncertain.[44] What began as an attempt to view the law through a mundane lens that conceptualizes certain aspects of our shared experience of legality has become a theoretical project that is remarkably otherworldly.

[40] Hart (2012), p. 102.

[41] Hart (2012), p. 124. "If it were not possible to communicate general standards of conduct, which multitudes of individuals could understand, without further direction, as requiring them certain conduct when occasion arose, nothing that we now recognize as law could exist."

[42] Kramer (1999) ch. 6.

[43] This particular argument is championed by many positivists of various persuasions (and some non-positivists). See Raz (2002), p. 159.

[44] Coleman (2000), p. 141.

5 Faith in Method

If one faithfully adheres to the Hartian method, other key arguments in Hart's *The Concept of Law* may need to be revised. For instance, John Gardner worries that Hart's fable about the move from pre-legal to legal is not value-neutral. Hart argues that the move from a pre-legal society to a full-fledged legal regime is marked by the introduction of secondary rules: the secondary rules of recognition, change, and adjudication enable officials to respond to the demands of a growing, and increasingly complex, society.[45] According to Hart, the creation of a modern legal regime brings with it the benefits of certainty, efficiency, and flexibility, thereby fixing all three problems that were plaguing Hart's imagined society.[46]

Hart's critics suggest that this argument contains an implicit value assumption in contravention of Hart's purported methodological commitments. Gardner worries about the possibility that Hart's critics are correct. Gardner notes that we may be tempted to place Hart in the same camp as Lon L. Fuller, who, in Gardner's words, holds that "no legal system exists without the rule of law."[47] If so, Hart would be offering an ideal of law and not the value-neutral account he purports to be championing. One way in which any value assumptions can be eliminated, Gardner maintains, is by re-articulating the tale.

He argues that Hart would be wise to adjust his account so that it becomes one about the *beliefs* of the participants experiencing the transition out of a primitive society. That is, Gardner maintains that Hart should have stated that the citizens in the fictitious primitive community "should regard or experience their existing arrangements as defective" and view the introduction of secondary rules as a solution to the problems that they had identified.[48] He insists, however, that "it is not necessary that they should be right to do so; there may be no such defects."[49] The claim that such defects exist, and are fixed by the move to legality, must be *intelligible*; it need not be *defensible*.[50] It must be intelligible that participants might *believe* that law brings certain advantages, but Hart should not defend this claim. Hart must remain agnostic on this point, at least if he hopes to avoid importing value judgments into his concept of law.

If we focus on this particular re-casting of Hart's fable, we can see the way that Hart's method, when stringently adhered to, requires us to say as little as possible about the nature of law. The legal philosopher who is attempting to offer a value-neutral analysis must be silent on this issue. She must be silent on all issues that threaten to bring values in. In this instance, we are told by Gardner that we should *not* inquire into the benefits of the move to a full-fledged legal system. We are instructed

[45]Hart (2012), pp. 92–99.
[46]Hart (2012), pp. 92–93.
[47]Gardner (2013), p. 87.
[48]Gardner (2013), p. 88.
[49]Gardner (2013), p. 88.
[50]Gardner (2013), p. 89.

to defer to the imaginary views of this imaginary community in order to preserve the substantive elements that emerge from Hart's story, in addition, of course, to Hart's methodological commitments.

This approach is not only a departure from the tradition in political philosophy but a wholesale reversal. Traditionally, philosophers subjected conventional views—views held by members of actual communities—to extensive critique. They work to expose the fragile foundations of such claims, inviting a reconsideration of any views that cannot withstand critical scrutiny.[51] If Gardner's approach is followed, what emerges is a set of reflections about law that are forever suspended in time as "plausible candidates" for a viable account of legality. Given that an evaluation of these candidates will involve normative arguments of the kind that Hart's method prohibits, Gardner halts the inquiry instead of abandoning the method. But it is precisely the truncated—the artificially truncated—nature of Gardner's reflections that should give us pause. If this is the road that a commitment to Hart's method takes us down, then surely the real lesson here is that it is highly likely that value commitments are necessary if we hope to improve our understanding of law. Gardner is assuming that there is value in value-neutral analysis, but it is hard to grasp precisely what that is.

Hart's fable was originally meant to take us to an imagined world only to lead us back to our shared world, highlighting certain features to which he considers important. Gardner, in an attempt to be true to Hart's methodological commitments, invites readers to ascend into the imagined space only to leave us there. The content of the fable remains untouched and untested. If conceptual clarity is the aim, then surely, we would be impelled to reflect further on Hart's account. Does law bring with it the benefits that Hart mentions in his fable? Are there other benefits that accompany the emergence of modern legal systems that Hart does not mention? Are there any drawbacks?[52] Is it useful to rely on such fables? Again, if the aim is to elucidate law and clarify our understanding of the features of legality that confront us, these and other questions should be continually revisited, regardless of whether the answers necessitate an abandonment of Hart's methodological presuppositions. Hart's project, born out of the desire to be clear minded about law as it is encountered every day in the world, is wholly unrecognizable in this new guise.

---

[51]The quintessential example of this approach is found in Plato's dialogues. I discuss this theme in Martin (2020a). Philosophers also work to deconstruct the idea of truth. But this is not on offer in Gardner's text either.

[52]It is implied in my argument that I do not view *The Concept of Law* as an exercise in what Gardner calls the "generic-analytic method." Also see Priel (2013), pp. 404–411. In short, Priel argues that this is an important question to ask given that Hart does not provide sufficient reasons for us to accept his account over any other.

6 Normativity and Value-Neutrality: Drawing the Battle Lines

Hartians may protest that the weaknesses I have identified may indeed be weaknesses, but this does not mean that conceptual analysis, as Hart conceived of it, is a failed project. Those who rely on this method see value in identifying shared features of legality in order to clarify the content of "our" concept of law. According to this view, Hart may not have gotten everything right, but he introduced thinkers to a method that still holds promise. In what follows, I will suggest that it is very difficult to untangle Hart's methodological commitments from his substantive ones. Once these connections come into view, the significant limitations of Hart's value-neutral method become visible.

Simmonds's critique of Hart is invaluable at this juncture. In "The Nature of Law: Three Problems with One Solution," Simmonds argues that legal philosophers continually grapple with three interrelated problems: the problem of fundamental law-making authority, the problem of law's justificatory force, and the problem of "ideality" of law.[53] I will focus primarily on the first two problems, which will be elaborated on below. The third problem refers to the need to provide an explanation for the persistence of disagreement amongst legal experts, despite a shared set of legal materials: lawyers "therefore seem to be working with a conception of law that cannot straightforwardly be equated with the totality of rules explicitly established in statutes and cases."[54] All three problems require legal philosophers to think about aspects of the normative dimension of legality. Hart, Simmonds persuasively argues, cannot satisfactorily account for law's normative dimensions, and thus, even on his own terms, the Hartian project fails.

Consider the first problem: the source of law's authority. If we assume, as Hart does, that law is made by humans for humans, the question then arises: how is an infinite regress avoided when legal philosophers attempt to locate the authority of the law-maker? As Simmonds notes, Hart famously rejects Austin's answer, i.e., that the law-maker is outside of the system and hence not bound by "legal authority."[55] Instead, he argues that secondary rules govern the work of officials, the content of which is discernible when we come to understand the criteria for valid law contained within the rule of recognition. It is unclear if Hart can solve the problem of "infinite regress," without making value-judgments about law—again, if Eleftheriadis is correct, values, not facts, underpin the adjudicative process. Even if Hart is able to convincingly address this concern, another a key problem remains: can Hart distinguish living under the sway of law from living under the sway of the gunman writ large? In other words, does Hart have the resources to address the second problem—can he account for law's justificatory force?

---

[53] Simmonds (2011), pp. 603–605.

[54] Simmonds (2011), p. 605.

[55] Simmonds (2011), p. 606.

Critics might quickly interject, pointing out that it is Dworkin, not Hart, who states that a theory of law must make sense of judges' attempt to justify the use of coercive force.[56] While this is undoubtedly true, this response is too quick. Simmonds is correct to argue that Hart quietly concedes the centrality of the problem of law's justificatory force early on in *The Concept of Law*. Simmonds explains:

> Laws are typically invoked by judges as a reason or justification for imposing a sanction. Any theory of law needs to accommodate this fact. For example, one of Hart's numerous reasons for rejecting Austin's theory of law concerns Austin's analysis of "legal obligation." Seeking clearly to distinguish law from morality (the latter being, for Austin, embodied in the principle of utility) Austin viewed statements of legal obligation as statements concerning the likelihood of suffering a sanction in certain circumstances. Hart rejected this analysis on the ground that it would render unintelligible the judge's invocation of legal obligations as a *reason for imposing* a sanction. Hart thereby acknowledges that a theory of law must explain how laws can intelligibly be invoked as a justification for imposing sanctions.[57]

Once we see this problem, the question becomes: what kind of justification is required? Is it necessarily moral, or can the justification be merely "technical" or "confined"?[58] Hart, after all, can only draw upon the resources found within the rule of recognition and these resources are devoid of necessary moral content.

It is for this reason that Simmonds raises serious doubts about the possibility that Hart's account of the rule of recognition can distinguish law from the gunman writ large. If an accused asks the judge for a justification for the decision to convict him, a Hartian judge will have limited resources from which to draw to construct a justification. The Hartian judge's answer—that he accepts the rule of recognition for self-interested reasons—is inadequate. Simmonds is correct to argue that a judge must be able to say more than "this is how we do it here" if there is going to be a normative difference between the law and the gunman.[59]

Hart's reliance on a metaphor—the core and the penumbra—papers over this point. It is well-known that Hart assumes that, in most cases, the job of the judge is fairly straightforward: judges can apply the settled law with relative ease. In these cases, judges rely on what Hart calls the "core" of settled meaning.[60] According to Hart, it is in the "penumbra of uncertainty" where interpretive disagreements arise; it is only here where explicit appeals to norms, not fact-based laws, must be made. Hart concedes that, in the penumbra, judges must operate with a view of what *ought* to be in such cases; but this concession does not mean that law and morality are necessarily connected. Hart rejects the suggestion that the "ought" is always going to be "moral" in nature.[61] Judges may opt to do what they believe is best from a prudential perspective, for instance. Hart works hard to keep moral norms out of his account,

[56]Dworkin (1986), p. 98.

[57]Simmonds (2011), pp. 604–605. Footnotes omitted.

[58]Simmonds (2011), p. 610. The terms are Hart's own. See Hart (1982), p. 266.

[59]Simmonds (2011), p. 610.

[60]Hart (1957), p. 607.

[61]Hart (1957), p. 608.

but again, this leaves him with few resources to distinguish a legal system from the gunman writ large.[62]

Notice that Hart's account of adjudication also provides an answer to the third problem—what Simmonds calls the problem of law's ideality. Judicial disagreements, according to Hart, emerge in the penumbra because of the nature of language: language is open-textured, thereby allowing for multiple interpretations of the same rule.[63] Given Hart's insistence that morality does not enter into the courtroom as a necessary component of judicial argumentation, his claims about legal language bear a lot of weight. While, no doubt, Hart is right about the open-textured nature of language, this does not mean that he is correct that this point explains the persistence of disagreement in the courtroom. As mentioned above, Dworkin challenges this picture, arguing that the disagreement between judges is moral in nature: language, even clear language, is not determinative.[64] The power of Dworkin's critique is underscored when an attempt is made to construct a Hartian answer about the possibility of offering a justification for a particular decision.

Hart's discussion of the core of settled meaning offers a picture of adjudication that presents rules as self-justifying (i.e. judges apply the law because it is their job to apply the law). But if a normative justification for applying positive law is to be given, we quickly see that it is a familiar one (but not one that Hart offers). The missing argument is one that Dworkin supplies on behalf of the positivist ("conventionalist") judge: judges who apply the law as written defend that decision by appealing to the moral ideal of "protected expectations."[65] Through the preservation of settled law, people know what is expected of them going forward. Without this argument, the positivist judge relies on the worst possible version of "law is law" formalism—an appeal to the law for no reason other than it is the law. The desire to protect expectations is, of course, a desire to realize a certain moral vision of the rule of law. Thus, contra the positivists, their non-normative vision of law is extremely hard (or impossible) to disconnect from a normative vision of the rule of law. Once this connection is made, positivism becomes a normative theory that must compete with other normative theories, both within and outside of the courtroom (which, of course, is Dworkin's point).[66]

Another sign that Hart's account of adjudication is a significant weak point in his argument can be located in the debate itself: the distinction between the core and the penumbra has been largely (if not completely) abandoned by Hart's predecessors. Although I am not convinced that positivists can shed this distinction with ease given the role it plays in Hart's account, the desire to do so is understandable. Of course, many believe that Hart's shortcomings have been dealt with by one of his leading torchbearers: Raz.

---

[62]See also Priel (2013), p. 407.

[63]Hart (1957), p. 615.

[64]Dworkin (1986), p. 114.

[65]Dworkin (1986), p. 117.

[66]Dworkin (1986), p. 90.

Tellingly, Raz does not reject the set of questions identified by Simmonds, he simply offers a new set of answers. Raz boldly declares that judges are moral reasoners and that any theory of adjudication is a moral theory: "[l]egal doctrines are justified only if they are morally justified, and they should be followed only if it is morally right to follow them."[67] Theories of adjudication are moral theories and they are fundamentally different from theories about the nature of law, which are conceptual.[68] Raz relegates Dworkin to a domain beyond the reach of jurisprudence as he defines it. Problems about this strategy are, yet again, perceptible. If Simmonds is right—if Raz and Hart are grappling with the same questions as Dworkin—then Dworkin cannot be easily exiled.

Notice that the entire Hartian project now rests on the tenability of this sharp distinction between a theory of law and a theory of adjudication. Elsewhere, I have argued at length that this distinction is deeply unstable, and ultimately, untenable.[69] While I will not rehearse my argument here, notice one of the uncomfortable implications with which Raz must live: given that adjudication falls outside the reach of conceptual analysis, the idea of "legal obligation" relied on by judges in the courtroom is not the same as the idea of "legal obligation" that is conceptualized by philosophers. Again, it is apparent just how far a Hartian positivist must move away from the task of explaining familiar features of our experience in order to ensure that value-neutrality is maintained. For present purposes, it is Raz's other move—the introduction of a morally robust theory of authority—that is of greatest interest given that it will allow for an exploration of the law's normativity more generally. With the addition of his theory of law's moral authority, Raz, unlike Hart, seeks to account for law's normative authority. Raz offers readers a normative account of law's authority that is meant to co-exist with his non-normative concept of law.

Raz argues that any given law or a set of laws will enjoy the moral authority it necessarily claims to have insofar as it reproduces the requirements of "right reason."[70] To do so, legal norms must reproduce reasons that law's subjects have independently of the law.[71] His concept of law remains value-neutral given that the conceptually necessary portion of the concept is the *claim* to moral legitimacy, not its realization. Raz appears to offer Hartian positivists the possibility of engaging in value-neutral conceptual analysis about the nature of law, while simultaneously endorsing a morally robust account of law's normative force. Most assume that this space is available precisely because of this particular argument, but it is not clear that it is. It is not clear that the claim to authority is a thesis that bridges Raz's theory of law with his morally robust account of authority in a manner that allows Raz to maintain a value-neutral account of law.

---

[67] Raz (1994), p. 113.

[68] Raz (1994), p. 209.

[69] Martin (2014), ch. 3.

[70] Raz (1986), p. 61.

[71] Raz (1986), p. 47.

Herein lies the problem: instead of successfully distinguishing law from the gunman writ large, Raz finds himself on the horns of the dilemma. Consider the first possibility: the law's claim to authority may not be realized *at all* in a given system. This means that law's claim to authority can, at least potentially, be completely empty. In this case, law's claim to legitimate authority operates as a cloak to the exercise of morally illegitimate power. This option is even more worrying if we combine it with Raz's tendency to urge individuals to treat legal norms as authoritative reasons for action. Specifically, he argues that individuals ought to treat legal norms as content-independent reasons for action because we should assume that the officials get it right more often than we do,[72] or because deference to authority simplifies our reasoning processes.[73] Given that legal obligations are potentially empty of normative force, such arguments are troubling. Hart, recall, is far more cautious. As mentioned above, Hart separates legal validity from moral legitimacy in order to encourage critical thought when faced of the exercise of legal power. If this is the path Raz takes, "law is law" formalism is not a specious charge launched against positivists; rather, it surfaces in a particularly dangerous form. It is not only the gunman who disguises the nature of his orders; he now has help from Raz.[74]

This path is not going to be attractive for Raz. He explicitly asserts that officials cannot be "systematically confused" about the nature of the practice of which they are a part.[75] If this is so, then the law's claim to moral authority is *necessarily* realized, to some degree, in every system. Setting aside the complexities that arise from this argument,[76] Raz can now distinguish his account from the gunman: unlike the gunman's dictates, some legal obligations will enjoy moral authority. If this is true, law's claim to authority is a normative thesis about the *moral content* that all existing legal systems *necessarily* have. The claim to authority is a morally robust thesis that can help us to distinguish legal systems from imposters. Given that the claim to authority is treated as a conceptually necessary component of his concept of law, Raz's concept of law has necessary moral content. But if this is so, then the claim to authority is not only about law's potential, but the requisite actualization of that potential, at least in part. Raz has quietly departed from Hart's methodical commitments. He has entered into the territory of the natural lawyer.

---

[72]Raz (1986), p. 61.

[73]Raz (1986), p. 58.

[74]It is worth pointing out that Hart's practical argument for positivism is relevant again, even though it was once thought that it could be abandoned.

[75]Raz (1994), p. 217.

[76]Given that the authority of law turns, in part, on the expertise of individual citizens, it is unclear how he can guarantee that law will enjoy legitimate authority. Focusing on law's co-ordination function (instead of on expertise) is one possible way that Raz could explain how legal systems must enjoy some of the moral authority they claim, but Raz downplays this point in his exchange with Gerald Postema. See Raz (1998), p. 2. For a detailed discussion of this exchange, see Martin (2014), pp. 156–158, 167.

Raz explicitly states that his concept of authority refers to the "ideal exercise of authority," which is used to explain the difference between deviant cases and normal cases.[77] Raz explains via the example of advice:

> The normal reason for accepting a piece of advice is that it is likely to be sound advice. The normal reason to offer advice is the same. It will be clear that these judgments of normality are normative. But the very nature of advice can only be understood if we understand in what spirit it is meant to be offered and for what reason it is meant to be taken. The explanation must leave room for deviant cases, for their existence is undeniable. But it must also draw the distinction between the deviant and the normal, for otherwise the very reason why the 'institution' exists and why deviant cases take the special form they do remains inexplicable.[78]

Instead of identifying shared features of all instances of the practice of advice-giving, Raz begins with a moral judgment about the central case, before moving on to identify deviant instances of the practice. Once Raz concedes that all systems enjoy moral legitimacy to some degree, he cannot isolate his normatively robust theses about the nature of authority in a way that allows the Hartian method to endure: every legal system must live up to the ideal to some extent. Significantly, there is a necessary connection between Raz's morally robust account of authority and his positivistic concept of law, which renders that latter normative from the outset. In sum, Raz presents the claim to authority as a normatively inert thesis that is meant to bridge his morally robust, content-dependent account of authority with his conceptual, content-independent concept of law. It is now clear that the middle position between Austin and the natural lawyers—a position that Hart had hoped to carve out a space for—is not a space that Hart or Raz have successfully occupied. It is doubtful that such a space exists.

If Raz is right about the nature of authority, we must begin with a moral judgment. Notice that it is not a moral judgment about what Raz thinks law *ought* to be; rather, it is a judgement about the *moral content of law* that explains how law is different from the gunman.[79] And if one does not believe that there is a difference, this is not a bare fact, but a deeply political account of legality and authority. In other words, a sceptical account is *not* simply tethered to a set of observations: it is a set of value-laden judgments about such observations. Recall that Hart initially invited us to look at the world to investigate the nature of law, thereby suggesting that the approach adopted by the philosophers before him in the history of political thought, had been mistaken. But it is now hard to avoid the conclusion that the project of dymystification was, itself, based on an error.

---

[77]Raz (1986), p. 47.

[78]Raz (1986), p. 54. I also discuss this quotation at Martin (2014), p. 90.

[79]Again, it is unclear how Raz is able to make this commitment: if the moral authority of law is piecemeal, and it turns on the expertise of individuals, then it is far from clear that Raz can guarantee that the law has moral content. Conversely, Hart famously defends the thesis that law has a minimum moral content. See Hart (2012), ch. IX. I claim that Hart's discussion places him in the world of natural law. See Martin (2020b), pp. 203–211.

Hart is unable hold our gaze on the very things that we were supposed to (finally) see clearly. But a retreat to the world of conceptual possibilities is surely an over-correction. The "real" tangible elements of legality find their place within the ideal. If we begin here, an easy answer to the question as to whether law distinguishable from the gunman, is available, as Dan Priel elegantly notes:

> One answer that as a historical matter many philosophers found persuasive is that law is, at least potentially, committed to justice. As Augustine famously put it: "Remove justice, and what are kingdoms but gangs of criminals on a large scale?" A putative legal system flourishes when it succeeds in promoting justice; when it utterly fails in doing so, or worse, when it subverts it, it no longer counts as a legal system at all: it becomes something that bears some superficial semblance to law, but really is not different from the acts of the gunman, only writ large.[80]

This is not an answer that Hart can offer us, but this very old starting point is nevertheless more promising than the new one offered by Hart in *The Concept of Law*.

I have argued that the pieces of Hart's *The Concept of Law* do not fit together as cleanly as Hart had hoped. Nevertheless, his writings reveal his astute awareness of the limits of his project, its historical roots, and his concern with real-world problems. Initially, Hart focused on the more tangible elements of legality, but perhaps the lesson is that the ideal, normative dimension should have been given a starring role. If legal philosophers are going to continue to explore law as it is encountered in the world, with the urgency and passion that Hart once did, they would be wise to abandon Hart's dream of value-neutrality. The dream, I suspect, is little more than that.

References

Bentham J (1998) A fragment of government. In: Guess R, Skinner Q (eds) Cambridge texts in the history of political thought. CUP, Cambridge

Bix BH (2011) John Austin and constructing theories of law. Can J Law Jurisprud 24(2):431–440

Coleman J (2000) The practice of principle: in defence of a pragmatist approach to legal theory. Oxford University Press, Oxford

Dworkin R (1978) Taking rights seriously. HUP, Cambridge

Dworkin R (1986) Law's empire. HUP, Cambridge

Dworkin R (2002) Thirty years on. Harv Law Rev 115:1655–1687

Eleftheriadis P (2013) Hart on sovereignty. In: Duarte L, Edwards J, Dolcetti A (eds) Reading HLA Hart's the concept of law. Hart Publishing, Oxford

Finnis J (1980) Natural law and natural right. OUP, Oxford

Fuller L (1957) Positivism and fidelity to law – a reply to Professor Hart. Harv Law Rev 71 (4):630–672

Gardner J (2012) Law as a leap of faith. OUP, Oxford

Gardner J (2013) Why law might emerge: Hart's problematic fable. In: Duarte L, Edwards J, Dolcetti A (eds) Reading HLA Hart's the concept of law. Hart Publishing, Oxford

80 Priel (2013), p. 407. Footnote omitted.

Hart HLA (1957) Positivism and the separation of law and morals. Harv Law Rev 71(4):593–629
Hart HLA (1961) The concept of law. Clarendon Press, Oxford
Hart HLA (1982) Essays on Bentham: studies in jurisprudence and political theory. OUP, Oxford
Hart HLA (2012) The concept of law, 3rd edn. OUP, Oxford
Hobbes T (1994[1668]) In: Curley E (ed) Leviathan. Hackett Publishing Company, Inc., Indianapolis
Kramer M (1999) In defense of legal positivism. OUP, Oxford
Martin M (2014) Judging positivism. Hart Publishing, Oxford
Martin M (2020a) Persuade or obey: Crito and the preconditions for justice. In: Bertea S (ed) In contemporary perspectives on legal obligations. Routledge, London
Martin M (2020b) Postema on Hart: the illusion of value-neutrality. In: Bustamante T, Decate T (eds) Philosophy of law as an integral part of philosophy: essay on the jurisprudence of Gerald J. Postema. Hart Publishing, Oxford
Priel D (2013) Reconstructing Fuller's argument against legal positivism. Can J Law Jurisprud 26 (2):399–413
Raz J (1986) The morality of freedom. OUP, Oxford
Raz J (1994) Ethics in the public domain: essays in the morality of law and politics. OUP, Oxford
Raz J (1998) Postema on Law's autonomy and public practical reason. Leg Theory 4(1):2–19
Raz J (2002) Practical reason and norms. OUP, Oxford
Rousseau JJ (2004[1762]) The social contract. Penguin Books, New York
Saint Augustine (1992[400]) Confessions (trans: Chadwick H). OUP, Oxford
Shapiro SJ (2011) Legality. HUP, Cambridge
Simmonds NE (2011) The nature of law: three problems with one solution. German Law J 12 (1):601–624
Stone M (2010) Positivism opposed to what? Law and the moral concept of right (February 17, 2010). Cardozo Legal Studies Research Paper No. 290. Available at SSRN: https://ssrn.com/abstract=1554500
Waluchow WJ (1994) Inclusive legal positivism. Clarendon Press, Oxford

Part II
Legal Systems and Their Coercive Power

A Positivist Foundation of the Legal System: Popular Sovereignty as a Social Convention or Social Rule

Antonia M. Waltermann

Abstract A recurring question in legal theory regards the basis of the legal system. One possible answer is that it emanates from the people, as captured in the concept of popular sovereignty. This concept plays a role in many contexts ranging from political philosophy to constitutional law. However, it is not always clear what popular sovereignty means and how state power can be said to emanate from the people. This paper seeks to remedy this. In order to do so, it sketches a conception of popular sovereignty that explains how and in what way state power emanates from the people. This conception, following Hampton's account of political authority, bases state power on a social convention. However, an investigation into the nature of social conventions, drawing insights from legal theory and philosophy more generally, reveals that this conceptualisation is not accurate. Legal theory provides an alternative in the form of social rules, and this paper ultimately argues for a conception of popular sovereignty as the power of the people to constitute and maintain state power via the acceptance of and compliance with a social rule to this effect. This paper pursues two aims: firstly, it aims to develop a positivist and explanatory conception of popular sovereignty, which operationalises the concept for political scientists, constitutional (and European Union) lawyers, legal positivists and (legal) sociologists, linking political philosophy with legal theory. Secondly, it aims to investigate potential issues surrounding the use of social conventions in legal positivism, and to propose social rules as an alternative for some cases.

1 Introduction

The concept of popular sovereignty plays a role in many contexts ranging from political philosophy to constitutional law, it is invoked in many constitutions and some hold that it is a lack of popular sovereignty that leads to many of the European

---

A. M. Waltermann (✉)
Faculty of Law, Maastricht University, Maastricht, The Netherlands
e-mail: antonia.waltermann@maastrichtuniversity.nl

J. L. Fabra-Zamora, G. Villa Rosas (eds.), *Conceptual Jurisprudence*, Law and Philosophy Library 137, https://doi.org/10.1007/978-3-030-78803-2_5

Union's problems.[1] However, it is not always clear what popular sovereignty means and how state power can be said to emanate from the people. In this paper, I seek to remedy this while benefitting from and providing insight into legal theory.

The argument of this paper proceeds as follows: first, I sketch a conception of popular sovereignty that explains how and in what way state power emanates from the people. This conception of popular sovereignty is positivist[2] in nature and based on Hampton's account of political authority (Sect. 2). Hampton's account of political authority relies on a social convention and is comparable to HLA Hart's ultimate rule of recognition. In the following section, I investigate the nature of social conventions, drawing on insights from legal theory and from philosophy more general (Sect. 3). This investigation shows some difficulties with a characterisation of the positivist conception of popular sovereignty as conventional in nature (Sect. 4). I return to (legal) theory to find an alternative characterisation and argue that, departing from Hampton, a social rule rather than a social convention is the basis for popular sovereignty (Sect. 5). It bears mentioning that the positivist conception of popular sovereignty I sketch runs counter to a number of intuitions commonly held regarding popular sovereignty. I consider this justified because of the explanatory strength of this conception (Sect. 5).

This paper aims to do two kinds of things. On the one hand, it aims to offer a positivist conception of popular sovereignty. On the other hand, it aims to consider social conventions and social rules in legal theory more generally. More specifically, this paper aims to develop a positivist conception of popular sovereignty that explains the existence of the legal system and how "all state power emanates from the people." In doing so, it seeks to operationalise the concept of popular sovereignty for political scientists, constitutional (and European Union) lawyers, legal positivists and (legal) sociologists, and to link the concept of popular sovereignty to legal positivism,[3] thereby also linking political philosophy with legal theory. At the same time, this paper aims to investigate potential issues and problems surrounding social conventions for legal positivism, and to propose social rules as an alternative for some problematic cases.

Before I begin, it is useful to outline the assumption underlying this paper: I have argued elsewhere that sovereignty is a concept of which many conceptions are possible, and for which so many conceptions are used that it is not clear what "sovereignty" means at all.[4] Geenens makes a similar point when he writes that "[i]t is true that the element of 'supreme power' is somehow present in all meanings of the term sovereignty. But even with that element of commonality, the term

[1]Such as Della Sala (2012).

[2]I use the term 'positivist' to distinguish it from conceptions of popular sovereignty that justify a legal system, rather than explain its existence, but also—and perhaps predominantly—to indicate that this conception of popular sovereignty finds its basis in social fact. I would like to thank the anonymous reviewer who invited critical reflection on the label.

[3]For a more extensive exegesis of this conception, see Waltermann (2019).

[4]Waltermann (2019).

sovereignty still refers to such a variety of things that it is almost outlandish to always use the same term."[5] This makes it necessary to clearly define what one means when one uses the term "sovereignty" and to delineate one's use of the term from other definitions.

2 Positivist Popular Sovereignty

"Popular sovereignty" means that all state power emanates from the people. To say as much is not particularly controversial. Many constitutions contain provisions to this effect, such as section 3 of the Constitution of Thailand ("the sovereign power belongs to the Thai people"), article 3 of the Constitution of the Portuguese Republic ("sovereignty shall be single and indivisible and lie with the people"), article 3 of the Russian Constitution ("the bearer of sovereignty and the only source of power in the Russian Federation shall be its multinational people"), article 1(2) of the Constitution of the Hellenic Republic of Greece ("popular sovereignty is the foundation of government") or article 1 of the Brazilian Constitution ("all power emanates from the people"). Other constitutions contain similar references,[6] and the concept has received attention from both legal and political philosophical scholarship.[7] It is not sufficiently clear, however, what it means to say that state power emanates from the people. In this section, I would like to explore one conception of popular sovereignty that explains *how* state power emanates from the people and, in this way, allows for "popular sovereignty" to be used with precision and clarity in academic discourse. I call such a conception of popular sovereignty positivist because it fits well with the legal positivist school of thought that sought and seeks to describe and explain the existence and nature of law and the legal system.

The starting point for the positivist conception of popular sovereignty is a theory regarding political authority developed by the political philosopher Jean Hampton. In *Political Philosophy*, she considers the origin of political authority by investigating the origins of state power.[8] Before I discuss Hampton's theory in detail, I would like to point out that while Hampton focuses on political authority, she uses this phrase largely synonymously to the authority of the state. While there is a distinction between power and authority, I think that Hampton's understanding of authority and the "state power" that emanates from the people according to popular sovereignty coincide. Hampton holds that authority is "not the same as (sheer) power."[9] Raphael elaborates that power is the factual ability to force someone to do something, for example by holding them at gunpoint or by overpowering them in some other way,

[5]Geenens (2016), p. 35.

[6]Cf. German Basic Law, Article 20(2).

[7]Consider, by way of example: Kalyvas (2005), Sen (2011), Winterton (1998).

[8]Hampton (1997).

[9]Hampton (1997), p. 4.

while authority is recognized.[10] Given that no ruler can hold all their subjects at gunpoint at all times or otherwise overpower them, it is not possible for a ruler to rely on coercive power alone. Hence, coercive power is not sufficient for a claim to supreme authority.[11] I do not think that popular sovereignty means that coercive power emanates from the people, but that the state power in the phrase "all state power emanates from the people" is equivalent to what Hampton calls authority. Accordingly, Hampton's investigation into the origin and foundation of political authority coincides with the question of how and in what way state power (read: authority) can be said to emanate from the people.

Hampton argues that models such as the social contract which are based on the agency of the individual cannot sufficiently explain the existence of state authority. There are a number of reasons why this is the case: one of them is that such models lead to the paradox of being governed. If there is an agency relationship between ruler and people,

> how does it make sense to consider the people "ruled"? And if the people who are being "ruled" are themselves in charge of their rulers, how can their political society last? If babysitters are hired to supervise a bunch of unruly children and in reality the babysitters turn out to *be* the unruly children, the supervision is useless. And similarly, if the reason for creating a political institution is that people cannot govern themselves satisfactorily and the political regime that is created is one in which the people rule, the exercise appears useless.[12]

Another problem with agency-models like the social contract is the inconsistency of using a contract as the basis of government when it takes the government to enforce contracts.[13] The most serious challenge to the social contract model of political authority is the question if the people actually consented at all to political authority.[14] The argument that by continuing to live in a state means giving tacit consent is not convincing in a day and age in which it is not possible to live anywhere not subject to the authority of some state, and in which migration is highly regulated and often made difficult or even impossible.

Instead of relying on consent, Hampton develops a convention-based model of state authority: she argues that for state authority to exist, there must be a governing

---

[10]Raphael (1976), pp. 61–65.

[11]Raphael (1976), p. 61.

[12]Hampton (1997), p. 63.

[13]Hampton (1997), p. 64.

[14]Hampton (1997), pp. 64 f.

One might object that this question only touches those social contract theories that rely on actual consent, but not hypothetical contracts such as the social contract in Rawls' theory of *Justice as Fairness* (Rawls (1976)). Hampton anticipates this objection and points out that "if it turns out that throughout history states have been created in ways that have not involved subjects' consent and people have taken themselves to be subject to political authority *for reasons other than that they have consented to such authority*, then the consent that the contract argument requires in order to explain and legitimate that authority has simply not occurred [. . .]." Hampton (1997), p. 64 (emphasis added) and further "Hence whatever excellent use a hypothetical contract has in helping to illuminate the nature of justice [. . .], a contract that was never really made cannot explain real authority." Hampton (1997), pp. 65 f.

convention. Such a convention can be generated without agreement, but it requires that there is a salient equilibrium, meaning one choice that stands out above the rest. Such a salient equilibrium can be the outcome of a democratic process or of a warfare scenario. Hampton argues that the warfare scenario is often ignored by political philosophers because it does not suit their justificatory interests:

> Any theorist interested in showing what kind of state we *should* create and maintain does not want to use stories of state creation such as the warfare scenario in which the mightiest but not necessarily the most just leadership faction would prevail. It is natural to present a just government, which takes account of the rights of each individual subject, as the product of an agreement process in which those rights are respected. But even an unjust scenario is appropriate if that scenario is a way of understanding the structural forces that have actually precipitated the creation of states, and hence political authority, in human communities throughout history.[15]

In the warfare scenario, the governing convention is the result of a choice between accepting the leadership of the conqueror and receiving protection as a result or rejecting it and being harmed. It is the outcome of a democratic process when people in a given community vote on leadership candidates until a salient option emerges.[16] In either scenario, the governing convention is the source of authority for whatever governing institutions emerge. This authority "comes from the people; it is invented by them and bestowed upon rulers through the governing convention."[17] The political authority

> legislates so as to solve coordination and PD [prisoner's dilemma] problems in the community (via rules of property, contract, or marriage or rules of the criminal law); it adjudicates disputes, enforces the resolution of these disputes, and enforces law generally. To put it succinctly, political authority is understood by most philosophers to be an authority that demands obedience in order to *secure order*. All of the game-theoretic problems and the problems created by antisocial behavior are problems of order, requiring an institution that can enable people to achieve coordination, get the assurance necessary to make cooperation rational, and provide sanctions that encourage cooperative behavior in situations where it would otherwise be either irrational or at the very least unwelcome. While securing order in these various senses is surely not the only task of the state [...] this task is required in order for us to call any system of power and authority a genuine state.[18]

The governing convention creating this authority exists when two conditions are fulfilled, according to Hampton: firstly, that there exists a convention to regard the norms created by the governing institution(s) as pre-emptive and final (hereafter also: authoritative);[19] and secondly that there are means to enforce the norms created

---

[15]Hampton (1997), pp. 84 f.

[16]Hampton (1997), pp. 78–86.

[17]Hampton (1997), p. 90.

[18]Hampton (1997), pp. 74 f.

[19]The term "pre-emptive and final" is based on Joseph Raz's theory of reasons. He defines pre-emptive reasons as follows: "The fact that an authority requires performance of an action is a reason for its performance which is not to be added to all other relevant reasons when assessing what to do, but should exclude and take the place of some of them." Raz (1986), p. 46 This makes legal rules (norms generated by a political authority) into second-order reasons, meaning reasons

by the governing institution(s) and the willingness to use them. There is a third condition Hampton identifies that she does not consider necessary for the existence of the governing convention, namely that individuals consider the norms created the governing institution(s) as reasons to act accordingly.[20] I will return to this third condition in Sect. 5.

To summarize the argument so far: popular sovereignty means that all state authority emanates from the people. It does so because of a governing convention that exists when there is a convention to regard the norms of the state as authoritative, and when this convention is efficacious. Under this view, the legal system is an institutionalised part of social reality,[21] flowing forth from the governing convention. This situates this paper as following in the footsteps of a line of thought that moves from Austin to Hart and MacCormick and Weinberger.[22]

The positivist conception of popular sovereignty shows how the state and its legal system are based on and emanate from the actions of the people which create and maintain the governing convention. This positivist conception of popular sovereignty is explanatory in nature and as such does not have the legitimising function often ascribed to popular sovereignty.[23] Despite this loss in legitimising function that many regard as an important element of popular sovereignty, I would like to argue that a positivist conception of popular sovereignty can nevertheless fulfil an important function in academic discourse as a primarily explanatory tool.

Both philosophy and legal theory, and within that field legal positivists in particular, have considered conventions in some detail. In the next section, I will analyse insights from both. In doing so, it will become apparent that while Hampton's idea of a governing convention seems a plausible explanation for the creation of the legal system and the state, there are some issues regarding the reliance on a convention in this regard.

3 Conventions (in Legal Theory and Beyond)

HLA Hart is perhaps the most famous legal theorist of the last century to make use of a convention.[24] In *The Concept of Law*, Hart proposes the idea of rules of recognition. These rules, at least one of which—the ultimate rule of recognition—is a social

---

that impact first-order reasons, in this case by excluding them. This is why pre-emptive reasons are often called *exclusionary* as well.

[20] Hampton (1997), p. 97 f.

[21] Postema (2011), p. 343.

[22] For an elaboration of the fit between the positivist conception of popular sovereignty I put forward in this paper and the Austinian sovereign situated in an institutional system of law, accounting for Hart's criticism of Austin's work, see Waltermann (2018).

[23] See for example Kalyvas (2005) and Kumm (2016).

[24] Hart characterises the ultimate rule of recognition as a convention in the *Postscript*, calling it a social rule before. Given the parallels between Hampton's governing convention and the conditions

rather than a legal rule, determine how to identify (recognize) legal rules, thereby allowing the separation and distinction of law and the legal system from other norms, such as etiquette or morality.[25]

3.1 Rules of Recognition: Social Conventions According to Hart

A rule of recognition is a rule which identifies or determines how legal officials identify legal rules: a rule of recognition offers a test that allows a judge to tell a legal rule from a rule of morality, for example. A rule of recognition specifies what feature (s) a rule must possess in order to be a legal rule.[26] Rules of recognition furthermore fulfil the function of grouping together legal rules into a legal *system* by identifying membership criteria for the system.[27] Some rules of recognition might be found in legal rules themselves,[28] but at least the ultimate rule of recognition is a social rule. It is

> [...] constituted by a form of social practice comprising both patterns of conduct regularly followed by most members of the group and a distinctive normative attitude to such patterns of conduct which I have called 'acceptance'.[29]

The group in question that Hart has in mind is legal officials, and in particular judges. There has to be a pattern in which rules judges identify as legal rules and which they do not, and judges have to take a particular normative attitude toward this pattern, rather than considering it mere coincidence of happenstance.

It bears mentioning that while the ultimate rule of recognition must be efficacious and accepted, these are not requirements for individual legal rules. Hart specifies this with regard to efficacy:

> If by 'efficacy' is meant that the fact that a rule of law which requires certain behaviour is obeyed more often than not, it is plain there is no necessary connection between the validity of any particular rule and *its* efficacy, unless the rule of recognition of the system includes among its criteria, as some do, the provision (sometimes referred to as a rule of obsolescence) that no rule is to count as a rule of the system if it has long ceased to be efficacious.[30]

This quote also gives us an impression of how a rule of recognition can function in practice.

---

for it and the conditions for the ultimate rule of recognition in Hart's theory, however, I will begin by characterising both as conventional and test whether this is indeed the best characterisation.

[25]Hart (2012).

[26]Hart (2012), p. 94.

[27]Dickson emphasises this point, cf. Dickson (2007), p. 375.

[28]Hart (2012), p. 107.

[29]Hart (2012), p. 255.

[30]Hart (2012), p. 103.

According to Hart's postscript, the ultimate rule of recognition is a social convention, but it has a very different purpose and content to the governing convention that I, following Hampton, have proposed is created, maintained and deconstructed by popular sovereignty. The population of Hart's ultimate rule of recognition is not the people, but legal officials, and the rule of recognition functions as a test to tell law from non-law, rather than as the foundation of the state. Nevertheless, the two conventions raise many similar problems. Hart's theory has received a great deal of attention in legal scholarship, and many of these insights apply *mutatis mutandis* to the positivist conception of popular sovereignty. It is for this reason that I will continue in the following with Hart's rule of recognition, before returning to popular sovereignty in Sect. 4.

3.2 Beyond Hart: Lewis, Marmor and more

Marmor summarizes Hart's conditions for the existence of a social rule (such as the ultimate rule of recognition) *R* in a society *S* as follows:

1. There is a regularity of behaviour according to *R*, in *S*: namely that most members of *S* regularly conform to *R*.
2. Most members of *S* manifest a normative attitude toward *R*, which Hart called 'acceptance'.

The idea of 'acceptance' consists of basically two components:

(a) For most members of *S*, the existence of *R* constitutes reason for action in accordance with *R*.
(b) The existence of *R* is employed by members of *S* both as grounds for criticizing deviant behaviour and as a justification for exerting social pressure on other members of *S* to conform to *R*.[31]

Hart himself pointed out in the Postscript that social rules like the ultimate rule of recognition are social conventions. Comparing the two conditions for existence above with the requirements Hampton posits for the governing convention, the similarities are apparent. It seems that all that is required for a convention to exist is regularity in behaviour (which is efficacious and, if necessarily, enforced), and a particular normative attitude of the population in which this regularity exists toward said regularity. However, there is more to social conventions than this.

Lewis has analysed conventions, specifying and expanding on the work of Hume. According to him, conventions arise as the solution to recurring coordination problems: scenarios in which two or more individuals must coordinate their actions in order to achieve a preferred outcome. One example of such a situation is driving on the right (or the left) side of the road. Another is this: if a Skype call between my

[31]Marmor (2001), p. 195.

mother and me drops unexpectedly because my Wi-Fi cuts out, who should call back?[32] If we both wait for the other to call back, we will not get to continue our conversation. If we both call back, we will each get the busy signal and will not manage to continue our conversation, either. A convention might posit that whoever called first has to call back in such a case, thereby solving the coordination problem. Lewis defines conventions as follows:

> A regularity *R* in the behavior of members of a population *P* when they are agents in a recurrent situation *S* is a *convention* if and only if it is true that, and it is common knowledge in *P* that, in almost any instance of *S* among members of *P*,
>
> (1) almost everyone conforms to *R*;
> (2) almost everyone expects almost everyone else to conform to *R*;
> (3) almost everyone has approximately the same preferences regarding all possible combinations of actions;
> (4) almost everyone prefers that any one more conform to *R*, on condition that almost everyone conform to *R*;
> (5) almost everyone would prefer that any one more conform to *R'*, on condition that almost everyone conform to *R'*,
>
> where *R'* is some possible regularity in the behavior of members of *P* in *S*, such that almost no one in almost any instance of *S* among members of *P* could conform both to *R'* and to *R*.[33]

The population *P* could be the population of any country in the world, for example Sweden. The recurring situation *S* might be driving a car, in which case the regularity in the behaviour of the Swedish people with regard to driving a car is that they drive on the right side of the road. Almost everyone in Sweden in a situation to drive a car will drive it on the right side of the road, the occasional wrong-way driver notwithstanding. Swedish drivers certainly expect other drivers to drive on the right side of the road. Nevertheless, there is of course an alternative (*R'*): Swedes could drive on the left side of the road instead, and indeed have done so until 1967. This inclusion of an alternative in the definition of social conventions shows that conventions are essentially arbitrary: it matters little whether everyone drives on the right or the left side, so long as everyone drives on the same side—or at least, it matters more that everyone drive on the same side than it matters whether that is the left or the ride.

---

[32]This is an only somewhat updated version of an example not of my own making. Cf. Marmor (2001), p. 204; Rescorla (2015), para 3.2. This is not a perfect example of what Lewis had in mind when he wrote about coordination problems, in that someone might have a preference who calls back, especially in a variation of this scenario in which the caller pays. Such a preference makes this an 'imperfect' coordination problem.

[33]Lewis (2002), p. 78.

3.2.1 Coordination Problems and Arbitrariness

There are some issues with Hart's use of social conventions for legal theory in light of this, as Marmor points out, namely that rules of recognition hardly seem arbitrary, and that they do not seem to be the solution to recurring coordination problems.[34] If rules of recognition are not the answer to recurring coordination problems, are they social conventions at all?

Marmor thinks that this is the case because on his view, not all conventions need to solve recurring coordination problems. Before elaborating on his view, I would like to point out that Postema does not agree with Marmor that this problem exists at all:

> [A] coherent and unified legal system is possible only if conditions for the membership or validity of rules and norms in that system are established. This is accomplished by the practice of law-applying officials. In view of the high stakes involves, officials might disagree about what those conditions are or should be; still, they all recognize that, for the legal system to exist and maintain its unity, they must come to some agreement regarding those conditions. Thus, despite their disagreements (including disagreements of principle), they recognize the deeper need to coordinate their law-applying decisions around a common set of criteria.[35]

I do not find this argument convincing for the following reasons: while there may be a need to coordinate law-applying decisions in order to create or maintain a coherent and unified legal system, this does not show that the unified legal system is the answer to a coordination problem. In my view, this is precisely what must be shown, however: the legal system is not a goal in itself but must be the answer to a recurring coordination problem itself. Marmor compares law to chess in this regard, writing that

> [i]t seems rather awkward to claim that the rules constituting the game of chess are solutions to a recurrent coordination problem. Antecedent to the game of chess, there was simply no problem to solve. Of course, once the game is there to play, and it is played, it may give rise to certain coordination problems that might then get settled by additional conventions. But chess itself, as a game of a particular kind, is not a solution to a problem of coordination. 'Let's have a competitive intellectual game' or something like this is not a coordination problem along the lines suggested by Lewis. If it were, then 'Let's have a just Constitution' would also be a coordination problem, and, of course, it is not. Thus, the problem is this: either we stick to the idea of a coordination problem as a fairly structured set of conditions and preferences, in which case numerous conventions could not be described as solutions to such problems, or else we think of a coordination problem as something rather loose, applying to any set of circumstances where some form of collective action is pertinent [...].[36]

[34]Marmor (2001), pp. 201 f.

[35]Postema (2011), p. 494.

[36]Marmor (2001), pp. 205 f.

Earlier, I cited Hampton arguing that the state solves coordination problems.[37] It does so by legislating or adjudicating. That individual legal rules solve individual coordination problems does not mean, however, that the institutionalised legal system solves an individual coordination problem, unless we regard "how do we solve coordination problems?" as a coordination problem.

A possible explanation for this disagreement between Postema and Marmor might be found in Postema's argument that

> Following Hume, we can identify coordination elements in other kinds of games in which conflict is more pronounced, not only so-called Battle of the Sexes games, but also iterated prisoner's dilemma and hawk/dove games with uncertain termination points. We can refer to these as "cooperation problems" [...][38]

Here, Postema appears to take the idea of a coordination problem (or a cooperation problem) more loosely than Marmor does, choosing the second path proposed by Marmor. Despite this, it remains dubious to me whether either the rule of recognition or the creation of a legal system via a governing convention are really the response to a recurring coordination or cooperation problem. However, they are both certainly the response to a situation in which some form of collective action is pertinent.

Marmor's solution to the problem as he perceives it is not to broaden the idea of coordination problems, but to maintain that not all conventions must be the response and answer to recurring coordination problems. Marmor defines conventionality as follows:

> A rule, R, is conventional, if and only if all the following conditions obtain:
>
> 1. There is a group of people, a population, P, that normally follows R in circumstances C.
> 2. There is a reason, or a combination of reasons, call it A, for members of P to follow R in circumstances C.
> 3. There is at least one other potential rule, S, that if members of P had actually followed in circumstances C, then A would have been a sufficient reason for members of P to follow S instead of R in circumstances C, and at least partly because S is the rule generally followed instead of R. The rules R and S are such that it is impossible (or pointless) to comply with both of them concomitantly in circumstances C.[39]

Within this framework, he then makes a distinction between three types of conventions, namely coordination conventions, constitutive conventions and deep conventions. Coordination conventions are the type that has been discussed so far. Given that the positivist conception of popular sovereignty concerns the constitution (and maintenance) of the legal system, a closer look at constitutive conventions is in order. Marmor holds that constitutive conventions have two functions: they constitute a practice, and at the same time regulate conduct within the practice.[40] This is the

---

[37] Section 2. See again Hampton (1997), p. 74 f.

[38] Postema (2011), p. 489.

[39] Marmor (2009), p. 2.

[40] Marmor (2009), p. 36.

case both for chess and for law, according to Marmor. In both examples, the constitutive convention comes in a system of rules, which is a further distinction between constitutive and coordination conventions, which usually stand isolated.[41]

The introduction of constitutive conventions seems to solve the second of the problems Marmor identified, namely that the rule of recognition does not provide an answer to a coordination problem. According to Marmor, it does not need to do so in order to be a convention.[42]

This leaves one remaining problem, namely whether the rule of recognition fulfils the condition of arbitrariness. In this regard, Marmor holds that, for example, "the normative supremacy of the US Constitution is not just one arbitrarily chosen alternative among several other rules of recognition that are equally acceptable", and the same holds for the British rule of supremacy of Parliament.[43] However, whether or not this is truly so depends on what one understands under "arbitrariness". Marmor proposes the following definition:

> Given that *A* is the main reason[s] for members of a population, *P*, for following a rule, [*R*], in circumstances *C*, *R* is an arbitrary rule if and only if: there is at least one other rule, *R'*, so that if most members of *P* were complying with *R'* in circumstances *C*, then for all members of *P*, *A* would be sufficient reason to follow *R'* instead of *R*. The rules *R* and *R'* are such that it is normally impossible to comply with them concomitantly in circumstances *C*.[44]

Marmor argues, accordingly, that it is possible for a convention to be arbitrary even if the population in question has (strong) preferences concerning this convention, so long as these preferences do not outweigh the preference for coordination. In his later work, Marmor specifies that arbitrariness has two elements: first, the conventional rule must have an alternative. If there is no alternative rule that could be followed without a significant loss of function or purpose of the rule, it is not arbitrary.[45] Secondly, the conventional rule is followed *because* others follow it, too. Compliance is dependent, at least partially, on the compliance of others.[46]

Are rules of recognition arbitrary in this sense? Marmor bases his reasoning why this is the case on two observations:

> First, we know that different legal systems, even ones that are very similar in all other respects, have different rules or [sic] recognition. Second, there is very clear sense in which the reasons for following the rules of recognition are compliance-dependent in the relevant sense. This is one of the points that Hart has rightly emphasized in the postscript, namely, that the reasons judges and other officials have for following certain norms about the identification of the sources of law in their legal systems are closely tied to the fact that other officials follow those same norms.[47]

---

[41]Marmor (2009), p. 45.

[42]Marmor (2001).

[43]Marmor (2001), p. 201.

[44]Marmor (2001), p. 203.

[45]Marmor (2009), p. 9.

[46]Marmor (2009), p. 11.

[47]Marmor (2009), pp. 166 f.

Marmor regards these observations as uncontroversial. Dickson, meanwhile, argues that

> nothing in Hart's original account of the rule of recognition should lead us to conclude that he regards this rule as a conventional rule wherein common official practice constitutes part of the reasons which each judge has for treating it as binding.[48]

Equally, Postema criticises Marmor's account for failing to show that rules of recognition are compliance-dependent, and hence, for failing to show that the rule of recognition is a convention.[49] Nevertheless, Postema and Marmor agree that rules of recognition are conventions, if for different reasons, while Dickson disagrees. As I have already argued, I do not find Postema's reason to regard rules of recognition as solutions to coordination problems or cooperation problems particularly convincing. Equally, it is not entirely clear whether the reason legal officials have for following the rule of recognition of their system is dependent on the compliance of others in the way required for it to be conventional in nature.

However, I am in this paper not primarily concerned with finding out whether the rule of recognition is conventional or what which author thinks about that question. I am concerned with whether a positivist conception of popular sovereignty could be conventional in nature, as is suggested by Hampton's account of political authority.

4 Popular Sovereignty: A Convention?

In order to determine whether the positivist conception of popular sovereignty is conventional, as Hampton's account suggests, it makes sense to run through the conditions of a convention, broadly conceived. Such a broad view on conventions requires that at least the following conditions be fulfilled:[50]

(1) There is a regularity in the behaviour of a population.
(2) Almost all members of that population conform to the regularity.
(3) Almost all members expect almost all other members to conform to the regularity.
(4) The regularity is arbitrary. This means that
    a. There is an alternative regularity that could be followed instead for the same reason(s) or without loss of function or purpose.
    b. At least part of the reason why *this* regularity is followed instead of the alternative is because others follow this regularity.

---

[48] Dickson (2007), p. 382.

[49] Postema (2011), pp. 529 f.

[50] This is not meant to be a complete and exhaustive definition of conventions so much as a number of deliberately broadly conceived conditions that are necessary, but not necessarily jointly sufficient for the existence of a convention. This explains also the lack of condition or argument regarding the question if conventions must be the solution to a recurring coordination problem.

In the following, I will consider each of these elements individually.

4.1 Is There a Regularity in the Behaviour of a Population?

A first step toward answering this question is to identify the regularity in question.

I would argue that there is, in all or most states of the world, the regularity that (some) people regard the norms of the legal system as authoritative. Whether and to what degree this is in fact the case is a matter of sociological inquiry, but Hampton argues that it can and nearly always is a matter of degree, with some individuals regarding the norms of the system as authoritative, while others do not do so. Even in systems of widespread coercion, which Hampton calls mastery,[51] there will likely be some number of individuals regarding the norms of that system as authoritative:

> A pure form of mastery in a human community is very unlikely. Given human frailty and technological limitations (Superman and James Bond movies to the contrary), no ruler can hope to master people all by himself: He needs supporters to do so, and [. . .] this means there must be at least an agency relationship between him and his supporters.[52]

This suggests that there will likely always be at least some individuals which regard the norms of the legal system as authoritative.

An alternative regularity to consider in this regard is that individuals obey the law. While the consequence of regarding the norms of the legal system as authoritative will likely be compliance with the law, this second regularity leaves open the reason why individuals comply. Again, actual compliance with law is a matter of sociological inquiry, but a case can be made that in many legal systems, compliance exists to a large degree. If that is not the case, we do not regard the legal system to be efficacious and that often means that we regard it as non-existent or no longer in effect. (Consider, by way of example, the rules of Roman law.)

Given that one of the conditions for the existence of the convention is that a reason for compliance is the compliance of others, it may seem circular to include a reason for compliance in the regularity itself. Therefore, I will consider as the regularity in question not that the legal system is regarded as authoritative (which says something about reasons for compliance) but that they are treated as authoritative (by which I meant to make no statement about the attitudes of individuals, but merely about sociological facts of compliance and sanctions in cases of non-compliances).

---

[51] She defines mastery as follows: "to be *mastered* is *to be subject to the use of coercion in a way that disables one from participating in the process of creating or changing a governing convention*." Hampton (1997), p. 90.

[52] Hampton (1997), p. 92.

4.2 Do Almost All Members of that Population Treat the Legal System as Authoritative?

If treating the legal system as authoritative is understood, as I have suggested above, to mean that individuals generally comply and that sanctions are imposed in cases of non-compliance, I would like to argue that most legal systems in the world are sufficiently effective to answer this question affirmatively. Of course, "almost all" remains vague, and how many members of a population actually treat the legal system as authoritative is again a matter of sociological inquiry.

4.3 Do Almost All Members of That Population Expect Almost All Other Members to do the Same?

Without wanting to sound repetitive, I have to point out that an exact answer to this question is—again—a matter of sociological inquiry. I assume that on the whole, this is the case: people not only treat the legal system as authoritative themselves but have the expectation that they are not the only ones to do so. The legal system, in turn, supports this expectation by sanctioning non-compliance.

4.4 Is the Regularity Arbitrary?

There are two elements to arbitrariness, and I would like to argue that both of them are problematic when it comes to treating the legal system as authoritative. The first element of arbitrariness is that there is an alternative regularity that could be followed instead for the same reason(s) or without loss of function or purpose. While the reasons why individuals treat the legal system as authoritative may be varied (and I will consider reasons in more detail when it comes to the second element of arbitrariness) and while the same holds true for the functions and purposes of a legal system, a strong case can be made that the function of the legal system is to create order. As Hampton holds in an earlier-cited section, "[w]hile securing order in these various senses is surely not the only task of the state [...] this task is required in order for us to call any system of power and authority a genuine state."[53]

Is there an alternative regularity that could be followed instead without the loss of this function? One might think of place in which it is the church rather than the state that secures order. However, I wonder if we would not consider this a non-secular state creating laws, rather than an alternative regularity. One of the defining elements

[53]Hampton (1997), pp. 74 f, but see also Raphael (1976), p. 46 and of course Hobbes (2013).

of the legal system, it seems to me, is that it claims authority over other organisations.[54] In secular states, the church is included in those "other organisations", but that does not necessarily need to be the case. It may well be and in some states is part of the governing institutions of said state. Of course, if it is sufficient that not every legal system is identical, it is easy to state that there are alternatives. However, the level of abstraction at which to identify the alternative should be a higher one, it seems to me. The alternative to having some system of norms that is treated as authoritative and secures order (and I think it is likely that we would call any system that does so a legal one) is not having such a system of norms at all. This makes anarchy an alternative regularity, but anarchy would certainly mean a loss of function.[55] I doubt that treating the legal system as authoritative is arbitrary in the sense that there exists an alternative regularity that could be followed instead without loss of the function of securing order.

The second element of arbitrariness is that at least part of the reason why the legal system is treated as authoritative instead of the alternative is because others treat the legal system as authoritative. Even if we assume that there is an alternative (such as the church), I do not consider arbitrariness in this sense a given. There are many reasons why an individual may treat the legal system as authoritative. Some of them have been implicit in earlier sections of this paper.

Hobbes and game theory alike show that it is rational for individuals to treat the legal system as authoritative because the threat of sanctions allows for coordination where otherwise, it would be individually rational but collectively irrational to cooperate.[56] That it is rational for individuals to do so does not mean that this is the reason why individuals actually treat the legal system as authoritative. The same holds for the argument that the legal system is morally good or just or maximises utility. Nevertheless, all of these are possible candidates for reasons why individuals treat the legal system as authoritative, and none of them are immediately compliance-dependent, though it is true that the legal system can only fulfil its function of securing order if there is compliance. For this reason, there are in most, if not all legal systems, mechanisms to enforce compliance. I would argue that it is because of these mechanisms (sanctions in various forms) and because of the internalisation of norms that people treat the legal system as authoritative, not because others do the same. To me, it seems that the argument "if you do not obey the law, you will be punished" is a more likely reason for compliance than "others do it, too." Another likely reason for compliance is that people have internalised the idea that the legal system is authoritative in some way. On the whole, I do not think that the compliance of others is a sufficient reason for treating the legal system as authoritative.

---

[54]Raphael (1976), p. 55.

[55]Consider, again Hobbes (2013).

[56]Note that while specific legal rules (help) solve coordination problems, this does not mean that the legal system as a whole is necessarily the solution to a recurring coordination problem. I have argued this point in Sect. 3.2.1. above.

This means that the regularity that the legal system is treated as authoritative is not conventional because it lacks the arbitrary nature of conventions in at least one, of not both elements of arbitrariness. If this regularity is not conventional, the positivist conception of popular sovereignty put forward in Sect. 2 of this paper cannot be conventional. In the following, I would like to investigate if there is an alternative to conventions that might save the positivist conception of popular sovereignty from having to be abandoned.

5 Alternatives

In the first edition of *The Concept of Law*, Hart did not claim that his rule of recognition was conventional in nature, but that it was a social rule. Given Dickson's argument that Hart's original characterisation of the rule of recognition does not fit the definition of a convention, understanding the nature of social rules might provide an alternative to conventionality as the basis for a positivist understanding of popular sovereignty. I have covered Hart's conditions for the existence of social rules already under the heading of social conventions. He explains social rules by reference to (mere) habits, using the example of habitual obedience to law.[57]

> There is certainly one point of similarity between social rules and habits: in both cases the behaviour in question (e.g. baring the head in church) must be general though not necessarily invariable; this means that it is repeated when occasion arises by most members of the group: so much is, as we have said, implied in the phrases, 'They do it *as a rule*.' But though there is this similarity there are three salient differences.
>
> First, for the group to have a *habit* it is enough that their behaviour in fact converges. Deviation from the regular course need not be a matter for any form of criticism. But such general convergence or even identity of behaviour is not enough to constitute the existence of a rule requiring that behaviour: where there is such a rule deviations are generally regarded as lapses or faults open to criticism, and threatened deviations meet with pressure for conformity, though the forms of criticism and pressure differ with different types of rule.
>
> Secondly, where there are such rules, not only is such criticism in fact made but deviation from the standard is generally accepted as a *good reason* for making it. Criticism for deviation is regarded as legitimate in this sense, as are demands for compliance with the standard when deviation is threatened. Moreover, except by a minority of hardened offenders, such criticism and demands are generally regarded as legitimate, or made with good reasons, by both those who make them and those to whom they are made.[58]

Hart lists a third distinction which is implied in the prior two, namely that rules have a so-called *internal aspect*. This implies that there is a critical reflective attitude

---

[57]Hart here refers to Austin (1869). Nevertheless, habitual obedience is one element of how I have defined "treating the legal system as authoritative". Accordingly, Hart's view of this matter is acutely relevant to the current investigation into the nature of a positivist conception of popular sovereignty.

[58]Hart (2012), pp. 55 f.

by members of the group in which the social rule exists. If this is so, they regard the pattern of behaviour prescribed by the rule as a common standard, which is displayed in (self-)criticism, demands for conformity, regarding such demands as justified, and in normative terminology such as 'ought' or 'must'.[59]

In case of habitual obedience to a king, or in the case of popular sovereignty to the legal system, a social rule to regard the output of legal system (or the king) as authoritative transforms habitual obedience into recognition of authority and a system based on coercion and sanctions into a system based on authority.[60] In short, Hart's understanding of social rules, which he in the postscript of his second edition equated with social conventions, provides an accurate basis for the positivist conception of popular sovereignty.

Searle points out a further distinction, this one between conventions and rules, namely that conventions imply arbitrariness, but rules do not.[61] Searle also emphasises that (social) rules can be constitutive,[62] something Marmor has attempted to bring under the umbrella of conventions. This means that social rules can constitute practices and make that something counts as something else, often at the same time as regulating them. That certain pieces of paper count as (*are*) money is not a brute fact, that is, something to be found in the physical world, but a social fact based on the (social) rule that certain pieces of paper count as money.[63] Given that the arbitrary nature of conventions, in addition to the question of whether they must be the solution to recurring coordination problems, was the main issue with characterising the positivist conception of popular sovereignty as conventional, it seems there is no reason not to characterise it as a social rule instead.

Hage gives the example of a group of hikers to illustrate how social rules may come into being and what their effect is.

> Suppose that one member of the group, say Henriette, utters strong opinions about which path to take to the top of the mountain and that most of the group members tend to act on these opinions. After having several times chosen a particular path because Henriette proposed to take it, most group members recognize the leading role of Henriette. They believe that Henriette has become the group leader, that most other group members hold the same belief, and that Henriette is the leader of the group because she is recognized as such by most group members. In this example, the brute social fact concerns the possession by Henriette of the status of leader of the group.[64]

Henriette's leadership is a fact that depends on the recognition of the group; a social fact.

---

[59] Hart (2012), pp. 56–57.

[60] Hart (2012), p. 58.

[61] Searle (1995).

[62] Searle (2010), Searle (1995).

[63] For a thorough discussion of social facts and social rules as well as their relationship to each other and to other kinds of facts and rules, see Hage (2018a), sections III and IV in particular.

[64] Hage (2018b), pp. 116 f.

> If in our example about the mountain climbers the group members normally recognize the duties imposed by the leader of the group, whoever that may be, it may be said that the group has the rule that the group leader can impose duties. This rule exists through being recognized and therefore as a matter of social fact. The difference between having this rule and the recognition of the power of Henriette is the abstraction from the actual person having the power. When a power is not anymore ascribed to a particular person, but to a role – in this case the role of group leader – the acceptance of an ordinary social fact has become the acceptance of a social rule.[65]

The social rule in the example of the mountain climbers concerns the recognition of duties imposed by the leader of the group. However, it would not be a stretch to rephrase this social rule to say that the legislature can create rules, or to say that all rules created in accordance with other rules of an institutional system are authoritative. All three social rules describe the core of the positivist conception of popular sovereignty; all three explain how state power (equating the leader, the legislature or the institutional system with the state) can emanate from the people (that is, the members of the group).

Hage continues by pointing out that

> It is tempting to follow Hart in assuming that the existence of a social rule involves the existence of a critical reflective attitude with regard to behavior covered by the rule. This characterization of social rules is quite adequate for rules that prescribe behavior, but less so for other kinds of rules such as power-conferring rules. A broader, and therefore more adequate, characterization of a social rule is that *a social rule exists within a group if sufficiently many (sufficiently important) members of the group recognize the consequences of the rule when the rule is applicable.*[66]

While this may run counter to one's intuitions about the people as a whole having and exercising popular sovereignty, it corresponds to the point Hampton raises that the attitudes of individuals toward what she calls the governing convention and what should more accurately be named the governing social rule. In Sect. 2, I connected Hampton's conditions for the existence of political authority with the positivist conception of popular sovereignty. Incorporating the insight gained from the previous two sections that this conception (and hence also Hampton's political authority) is not conventional in nature, but rather based on a social rule leads to the following conditions for a positivist concept of popular sovereignty: there exists a social rule to the effect that the rules of the legal system count as (are) authoritative, that is, as pre-emptive and final, if two conditions are fulfilled. The first is that the social rule is efficacious, in that behaviour within the group conforms to the rule as a matter of fact. This can be for any reason, ranging from habit to the threat of sanction. The second is that the rule is recognised by sufficiently many sufficiently important

---

[65]Hage (2018b), p. 117. It is interesting to note that this transition from brute social fact to social rule corresponds to Hart's criticism of Austin, wherein Austin's habitually obeyed sovereign is sovereign as a matter of brute fact, while Hart's description of a possible transition of authority from Rex I to Rex II is on the basis of a social rule, much as Hage here describes. This shows that social rules concerning which or whose norms to treat as authoritative can play in groups as small as the mountain climbers or as large as a whole kingdom. Cf. Hart (2012), pp. 55 ff.

[66]Hage (2018b), p. 117.

members of the group. Recognition of the rule here means recognising the consequences of the rule.[67]

Hampton identified a third condition which she did not regard as necessary for the existence of political authority, namely that individuals consider the norms created by the governing institution(s) (or the legal system) as reasons to act accordingly. This condition is not necessary for the existence of a social rule, either. This leads to the—perhaps counter-intuitive—conclusion that popular sovereignty can be exercised by a group of sufficiently many sufficiently important individuals from within the people; it does not necessarily have to be exercised by the people as a whole. I consider this seemingly counter-intuitive conclusion justified because of the explanatory value of the positivist conception of popular sovereignty: it allows us to understand how and in what way state power actually emanates from (some of) the people. This understanding, in turn, makes it possible to evaluate which degree of popular sovereignty is present in any given state. Depending on one's evaluative framework and normative starting points, this may be a reason to consider certain states more or less justified and legitimate.

It seems that the positivist conception of popular sovereignty which explains how state power emanates from the people is based on a social rule, not a convention. Whether the conditions of existence of the social rule are fulfilled is a matter of sociological inquiry, just as it was for the conditions of a social convention. However, where even without such a sociological inquiry, there were serious doubts whether the conditions for the convention regarding arbitrariness would be fulfilled, I would like to argue that the same is not true for the conditions of a social rule to the effect that the rules of the legal system be treated as authoritative. I have already argued in Sect. 4.1 that it is likely that at least some members of the population (here, the people) regard the rules of the legal system as authoritative. Equally, for a legal system to exist, it must at least be somewhat efficacious. I would further posit that the members of the population regarding the rules of the legal system as authoritative are most likely at least legal officials of all three branches of government. Given the enforcement mechanisms of most, if not all, legal systems, these legal officials could be characterised as sufficiently important. It is likely, then, that a social rule to the effect that the rules of the legal system are authoritative exists. This indicates that popular sovereignty as I have defined it here is a matter of degree: because the number of members of the population who regard the rules of the legal system as authoritative can differ per legal system, not all people are equally sovereign in this sense. This runs counter to the idea that all people are equally sovereign but allows for the inquiry into how much popular sovereignty is actually (as a matter of fact) present with regard to a particular legal system and thus, in how far a particular legal system fulfils its claim to be based on popular sovereignty, if indeed it makes such a claim.

This positivist conception of popular sovereignty explains how state power emanates from the people and how states or legal systems come into and remain in

---

[67] Hage (2018b), p. 118.

existence: namely through initial and continued recognition of a social rule to the effect that the rules of the system are authoritative, combined with the efficacy of the system. A social rule provides a more accurate basis for the positivist conception of popular sovereignty than a social convention does, because social conventions are arbitrary in nature and (at least in some cases) the solution to a recurring coordination problem. It is not clear that the existence of the legal system provides the answer to a recurring coordination problem, though law can be and is used to solve coordination problems. More importantly, however, it is highly unlikely that the existence of the legal system and its recognition by (some of) the people are arbitrary in either of the senses of the word. Arbitrariness implies, on the one hand, that there is an alternative that might be followed instead without loss of function and for the same reasons. Authors such as Hobbes have made strong arguments as to why it is rational to have a coercive system of rules,[68] and while there may be variations in existing systems, I do not think that there is an alternative to having a coercive system of rules that does not come with a loss of function. Arbitrariness implies, on the other hand, that at least one, if not the main reason by people follow the convention is because others do so. While ultimately an empirical matter, I doubt that the reason or even one of the reasons why people obey the law is because others do so, too, and they want to coordinate their behaviour. Social rules are not arbitrary in the way conventions are, nor do the reasons why the rule is in place matter for its existence, making a social rule the more accurate basis for popular sovereignty.

6 Conclusion

The main aim of this paper was to explain how and in what way state power emanates from the people. As a first step toward this explanation, I have developed a positivist conception of popular sovereignty. This first conception, based on Hampton's theory of political authority, held that popular sovereignty is the power of the people to constitute and maintain a social convention to regard the norms of the governing institution as authoritative. However, a closer look at insights from legal theory and philosophy regarding social conventions shows that there are some issues in this regard. Explaining the existence of the legal system and how it emanates from the people by reference to a social convention fails because the existence of the legal system is not arbitrary (that is, there is no clear alternative that could exist without loss of function, and people to not treat the legal system as authoritative because others do the same) and because it is not clear that the legal system as a whole is the solution to a recurring coordination problem, though it does solve coordination problems. These issues also exist for HLA Hart's rule of recognition. The rule of recognition was first conceived as a social rule and later held to be a social convention. Investigating social rules shows them to be an alternative to

[68] Hobbes (2013).

social conventions. Social rules do not share the requirement of arbitrariness with social conventions and do not need to be the solution to a recurring coordination problem. This makes social rules a more accurate basis for the positivist conception of popular sovereignty.

Popular sovereignty, conceived in a way that coheres with positivism and explains how state power emanates from the people, does not justify state power or the legal system. The existence of a social rule that the legal system is authoritative says very little about the moral quality of that legal system. Furthermore, this conception makes popular sovereignty a matter of degree. It explains how legal systems (and state power) can exist even where large parts of the population are subject to coercion and what Hampton calls mastery, allowing for an assessment of how much (positivist) popular sovereignty is truly present in any legal system claiming to be justified on the basis of a non-positivist conception of popular sovereignty. Recognising the social rule that the legal system is authoritative is a collective enterprise, in that the recognition of one individual is not sufficient to create or maintain the rule. A collection of individuals—a bigger or smaller part of the people—exercises popular sovereignty by collectively recognising the social rule that the legal system is authoritative.

References

Austin J (1869) The province of Jurisprudence determined. John Murray

Della Sala V (2012) Europe's Autumn: popular sovereignty and economic crisis in the European Union beyond the Arab Spring: a new era of popular sovereignty and protest. Whitehead J Dipl Int Relat 13:35–44

Dickson J (2007) Is the rule of recognition really a conventional rule? Oxford J Legal Stud 27 (3):373–402

Geenens R (2016) E pluribus unum? The manifold meanings of sovereignty. Neth J Legal Philosphy 45(2):15–36

Hage J (2018a) Foundations and building blocks of law. Eleven International Publishing

Hage J (2018b) Of norms. In: Bongiovanni G, Postema GJ, Rotolo A, Sartor G, Valentini C, Walton D (eds) Handbook of legal reasoning and argumentation. Springer

Hampton J (1997) Political philosophy. Dimensions of philosophy series. Westview Press

Hart HLA (2012) The concept of law, 3rd edn. Clarendon Press

Hobbes T (2013) Leviathan. In: White E, Widger D (eds) Andrew Crooke, at the Green Dragon, St. Paul's Churchyard. https://www.gutenberg.org/files/3207/3207-h/3207-h.htm

Kalyvas A (2005) Popular sovereignty, democracy, and the constituent power. Constellations 12 (2):223–244

Kumm M (2016) Constituent power, cosmopolitan constitutionalism, and post-positivist law. Int J Const Law 14(3):697–711

Lewis D (2002) Convention: a philosophical study. Blackwell Publishers

Marmor A (2001) Legal conventionalism. In: Coleman J (ed) Hart's postscript. Oxford University Press

Marmor A (2009) Social conventions: from language to law. Princeton Monographs in Philosophy. Princeton University Press, Princeton

Postema GJ (2011) A treatise of legal philosophy and general Jurisprudence. Volume 11: legal philosophy in the twentieth century: the common law world. Springer

Raphael DD (1976) Problems of political philosophy. Revised Edition edn. Macmillan Press Ltd, London
Rawls J (1976) A theory of Justice. Oxford University Press
Raz J (1986) The morality of freedom. Clarendon Press
Rescorla M (2015) Convention. Stanford Encyclopedia of Philosophy, Summer 2015 edn. https://plato.stanford.edu/archives/sum2015/entries/convention
Searle JR (1995) The construction of social reality. The Free Press, New York
Searle JR (2010) Making the social world. Oxford University Press, Oxford
Sen S (2011) The constitution of India: popular sovereignty and democratic transformations. Oxford University Press, Delhi. https://doi.org/10.1093/acprof:oso/9780198071600.001.0001
Waltermann A (2018) Sovereignty and validity: on the relation between the concepts and the role of acceptance. In: Westerman P, Hage J, Kirste S, Mackor A-R (eds) Legal validity and soft law. Springer
Waltermann A (2019) Reconstructing sovereignty. Law and philosophy library. Springer
Winterton G (1998) Popular sovereignty and constitutional continuity. Fed Law Rev 26:1–14

On Law and Force

A Critical Account

Massimo La Torre

Abstract Legal positivism has been under attack, especially by doctrines contesting its proud claim of a conceptually necessary separation of law and morality. To such attack, the positivist reaction has been that of articulating on the one side a stricter, exclusivist version of the separationist thesis, and on the other side that of conceding to the possibility, though not to the necessity, of some (thus contingent) connection between law and moral requirements. An additional, traditional, third way of reasserting a positivist orthodoxy has been recently proposed, that of once again stressing the law as grounded in the use of force and sanction. This third way circumvents Herbert Hart's rejection of imperativism and the external point of view through the adoption of an eclectic, anti-essentialist epistemic strategy. However, such anti-essentialism is only apparent in so far as force and sanction are considered as basic conditions of the experience of law, and this is forcefully and indeed essentially reduced to some kind of violence. But such reduction, in spite of its proclaimed common-sense perspective, does not take account of the complexity and plurality of what law is assumed to be by those that practice it. The law as force doctrine also tries to justify itself as a methodology that would allow for an anti-ideological assessment of legal practice, while as, a matter of fact, making it impossible to articulate an antiauthoritarian account of legal operations.

A paper given at the 8th *Bonner Humboldt-Preisträger Forum*, "Zwischen Handwerk und Bekenntnis, Empirie und Normativität: Selbstbestimmung der Internationalen Rechtswissenschaft", Bonn, 17–21 November 2018. Many thanks to Professor Brian Bix for useful comments and suggestions.

M. La Torre (✉)
"Magna Græcia" University of Catanzaro, Catanzaro, Italy
e-mail: mlatorre@unicz.it

J. L. Fabra-Zamora, G. Villa Rosas (eds.), *Conceptual Jurisprudence*, Law and Philosophy Library 137, https://doi.org/10.1007/978-3-030-78803-2_6

1 The Law's Point

Law's function, if it has one, is that of allowing people to find a common standard of conduct. Now, this is easier said than in fact accomplished. People have different wishes, diverse interests, plural desires, multiple values, all of them actually or potentially conflicting the one against the other. How could one then have an intersubjectively agreed and secure guide for behaviour in such a conflictual existential situation? One traditional response is to make law be equivalent to force. An appeal to justice or morality would be yet too subjective and open to be challenged by competing values. Justice thus is uncertain, irremediably rooted in subjectivity, if not in idiosyncrasy. Force, on the contrary, seems to be evidence; everyone can see it, in so far as one's own will has to bend to it. Law as force could therefore be the solution to the perennial controversy, both conceptual and practical, about the nature and the identity of what law is, and of what is the law.

However, law as force is less evidently offering a clear of account of notion of the nature and content of law than it is sometimes assumed. It is nearly immediately exposed to perplexity. Indeed, in a discussion of law as force the first point to stress is that *force in the law* is quite a vague notion. It can mean various things. For instance: (i) That people are forced to follow an imperative directly, one could also say mechanically. (ii) That people are forced to follow an imperative indirectly, that is, through the threat of a sanction. (iii) That people are sanctioned, punished, because they did not follow an imperative. (iv) That people are not given the capacity to interpret the rules they are called to follow and have to apply them without deliberation or judgment. (v) Furthermore, that people will have to suffer some pain or evil or cost by following the imperatives or using the rules or claiming them.

Now, it is clear enough that a legal system's point is to avoid people being directly, that is personally, one by one, monitored and forced to obey rulings. It would be simply impossible to have an order that is able to prescribe in advance and detail, and directly guide, all possible conduct of individuals. This would require an officer accompanying any moment of a citizen's life and somehow pushing her in a mechanic way (by force, that is) to be law-abiding. Too expensive, and also absurd, since it would substitute the officer's judgment to the citizen's one, especially in situations where the following of the ruling is necessarily dependent on the ruling addressee's individual considerations. Citizens' life, that is their conduct, even under an authoritarian régime is their own; they decide if they want to go right or left, take a car or a bus, make a will or not, marry or remain single. The ruling application situation is manifesting only once the citizen's plan is manifest, and how this plan should be executed is again a matter of personal prudence. People evidently are not puppets. And this is just the reason why we have law and not mechanical force as a system of social coordination. We need rely on individual judgment, since we cannot anticipate the situational perspective of human conduct. The law as force doctrine however does not claim this extreme version of force guiding power, but nonetheless, it underplays the force of the notion of *force* and the implication of the phenomenology of rule-following in social intercourse. Such phenomenology already suggests that force, at least taken literally as a fully determinative compulsion, cannot meaningfully guide human conduct.

The law as force doctrine, however, tries to avoid absurd consequences and rather focusses on the *indirect* effect of law as force on behaviour. People will follow imperatives of law, because they are the law, without any consideration of personal interests, wishes, or values. This implies, in many cases, a fear of punishment or sanctions for ignoring the preemptive character of law. This might be a fact. But a fact is also that people are given instructions to follow, or rules to use, for having specific conducts and getting concrete aims. Law's point seems to coordinate people or to give them distinct perspectives of action, not primarily to bend their will. Seeing the law fundamentally as force, being force meant mainly as a power to push people in only one direction and not allowing room for self-determination, will thus miss a central point of having law.

The third meaning of law as force that people are sanctioned if legal rules are not followed may once again miss the "sense" of law, though sanctions are a usual appendix to laws. Imagine a society where people do not follow the rules but are implacably applied sanctions or punished for their not following rules. Could we think that this would be a well working, or a paradigmatic, system of law?

A system where only sanctions are applied, but no rule is followed would simply be absurd and somehow impossible, for the primary reason that legal sanctions are themselves applied by following rules. Of course, we could imagine a situation where one is punished even if one did follow the rules. In such a context then rules would not offer a common and secure standard of conduct; this would rather become the desperate attempt to so behave in order to avoid punishment, but since here punishment is not related to any rule, such an attempt would be perpetually and dramatically unsuccessful. Could this situation still be considered as subject to an order of law?

Suppose we could conceptually distinguish the two fields of conduct, *sanctioning* and *rule-following*, a society where only sanctions are applied, but no rules are followed, where only force is used, but no faculty of judgment is used. This would simply be a hell to live in, a more terrible form of anarchy, not law without force, Kant's definition of anarchy in his *Anthropologie*,[1] but rather *force without law*, sheer tyranny. Sanctions indeed are only a supplement to rules, not their central meaning and rationale. This could also be said of all kinds of directives, even of commands. "To command"—Herbert Hart reminds us—"is characteristically to exercise authority over men, not power to inflict harm."[2]

Law's point is not to punish citizens, but to coordinate their conduct and allowing for novel fields of action endowed with meaning. Providing for coercion is only a reaction to the possible failure of the directive force of norms, a *pis-aller*, that is, to

[1]See Kant (2000 [1798]), p. 269.

[2]Hart (1994), p. 20.

once again quoting Hart, a "secondary provision [...] for a breakdown in case the primary intended peremptory reasons are not accepted as such."[3]

Suppose now no people are given the capacity to interpret the rules they have to follow. How could they know that those rules are provided for the case they have to deal with? The situation will have to be subsumed in the rule, but this would presuppose an assessment of the fact and an understanding of the rule. We need not be Heideggerians to know that understanding needs some kind of interpretation. Rules in this way inevitably rely on the addressee's faculty of judgment. Judgment, however, needs not be decision from nothing, *ex nihilo*. There must be some ground for it, and some context to confront it with others. We can have discourses, and mutual recognition embedded in it. Force here is not central.

A further way of giving meaning to the law as force thesis is that law's addressees will have to suffer or be inflicted pain by following rules or by using or claiming them. This may again be sometimes the case. A trial, a process, is for any party a costly experience. It is painful both for the claimant and the defendant. The anxiety inherent in being involved in a trial is a prejudice that the law cannot avoid. On the contrary, there have been systems, such as for instance, the Court of Chancery equity jurisdiction so perceptively described by Charles Dickens in his novel *Bleak House*, there are systems like those, that indulge in increasing the parties' costs and anxiety.[4]

However, if a legal system to be implemented and effective should impose such extreme costs on his participants and subjects, the very effect pursued by the system would be put in danger and might be jeopardized. If a citizen, to follow or use a rule, should experience an intense experience of pain, she might prefer not to follow or use that rule, diminishing in this way the effectiveness of the rules in question. The coerciveness or, if you like, the "sadism" supporting or involved in being a law-abiding person should not go beyond a certain threshold. Otherwise, the motivation to follow the rules would strongly diminish, and the legal system might collapse. Coercion and force might thus be shown to be highly counterproductive for rule-following. One might then conclude that, if law is force, it should be such with much more than a pinch of moderation and self-restraint.

2 A Matter of Sanctions?

"The fact that the law is telling people what will happen to them if they do not obey it is a more salient feature of law than the fact that the law is expressing its unenforced preference how people ought to behave"—this statement summarizes the core of the law as force thesis.[5] According to this view, the sense of having law is not so much that citizens are given guidelines for living together in peace and coordinate their

[3]Hart (1984), p. 254. See also Gardner (2006), p. 209.

[4]La Torre (2018).

[5]Schauer (2015), p. 132.

conduct peacefully as rather that people are told that force will be used against them in specific cases. This view—we might remember—is objected by Herbert Hart's opposing a "puzzled man" to the "bad man," that is, to that sort of man that the realist tradition sees as the pivotal addressee of law.[6] A "bad man" will listen to the menace of force, and the arguments of costs and benefits. He does not have any sensibility for moral or normative reasons. He will act according to his prudential consideration, and can thus be convinced to follow a rule only if its violation is very expensive to his interests. The "bad man" is the kind of human being that the laws as force view need to render its central thesis plausible. Now, Hart objects to such view opposing it the figure of the "puzzled man."

Hart's assumption is that people look for the law not so much to avoid evils; they are not steering their lives through an obstacle course of rules. They, more often than not, ask the law for orientation in life. They do not know for sure what is the right course of action in many occasions, and to find it, to be oriented, they search what the law for the case at hand is; they could thus get a solution to their doubts, their "puzzle," and will then follow the law offering such solution. The "puzzled man" is not a sort of "noumenal" subject that is always doing what is told to be right. He's instead a perplexed citizen, that needs to have instruction about how to reduce the complexity of the situation in which he is involved. Or he needs some purpose for his conduct; he's in search of a field of sense, and this he can find in legal rules and principles. He seeks a way, a solution, a possible indication, which he may get in the law.

The "law as force" view can thus be challenged first of all by remembering that a law that just says *what will be done* without specifying *what ought to be done* will not meet the needs of the "puzzled" man, the man that asks for what he ought to do. Indeed, from the "puzzled man's perspective," a law that is just an announcement of future behaviour of state agencies (their use of force) will not be easily perceived as a law; a prediction or a declaration is not yet a prescription or an instruction. To be understood as such, it should be part of a more general normative context. Said differently, descriptive facts cannot themselves determine the content of law without some kind of additional rational determination.[7]

On the other side, what the law *will do* (here the infliction of a sanction) is only possible by law prescribing officials what they *ought to do*. Hans Kelsen, who fundamentally shares the law as force thesis, nevertheless was well aware that law, in order to announce what it will do to recalcitrant citizens, should formulate its announcement in a series of ought sentences concerning the enforcement of sanctions. Sanctions, therefore, are enforced through an understanding of *norms* having as their object those sanctions. There is, in any case, an existential priority of rules and understanding over force and strict causality.

Could we conceive, or imagine law that is just only coercion, that is only force? Don't we need to add something more? And is it not this something additional that

[6]The reference here is of course to O.W. Holmes, "The Path of Law" (1897).

[7]See Greenberg (2004).

would qualify law as such? The law as force view claims that "it is coercion in the most basic sense that enables us to understand law as it exists in bad societies as well as good."[8] In order to say that, one also needs to suggest that there is no law's claim to legitimacy, as it is shown —it is argued—by tyrannical or kleptocratic political régimes.

Force or violence are facts that are typically taking place from an external point of view; the observer's one. From the internal perspective, that is, the one of those that uses legal rules, some normative attitude is required to make it possible to judge a deviation from the rule as incorrect, *wrong*, and to claim that there is an obligation to take into account the rule and follow it. A legal rule, and even a legal system, just based on force, would not produce any critical attitude for the case of violation, no claim of being wrong in such a case. Force cannot either create an obligation, the sense of having an obligation, and not just the feeling of being obligated, of being subject to overwhelming factual power.

Force and brute power are empirically ascertainable, true. This is seen as a merit of the "law as force" thesis, that will thus claim to be neutral and objectively verifiable. But, as a matter of fact, we could have law without an observer's taking the external point of view, without legal theorists or philosophers of law, for instance. We couldn't have it on the contrary without participants, litigants or lawyers, or ordinary citizens, people using rules and approaching them as meaningful instructions for their conduct. Or at least we can have an observer's point of view only in so far as there is already operative the internal perspective, which is the one that is required for a normative practice to take place. A game like the law is the result of, and is given in reality, exists as, the use of its rules and principles. The external perspective is, in any case, parasitic with respect to the internal one.

This priority of the internal over the external perspective also implies that the looked-for notion of law should be capable of being somehow operative, that is, meaningful, from the internal point of view. It should offer an orientation, for instance, to the "puzzled man," the citizen looking for guidance, that is a content-based solution to a normative dilemma. As has been remarked, "the content of concepts affects what one is committed and entitled to by applying those concepts in judgment and argumentation."[9] The adopted concept of law thus should be able to provide the judge with some basis and argument for her decision. Now, "law as force" has no such capacity. One cannot justify any concrete decision in one sense rather than in another one by just referring to this notion. It would be hard for lawyers and citizens to accept as legally valid a judge's sentence that had as its only justification the fact that there is a rulemaking available the application of a sanction, something of the sort: "You are convicted because there is a sanction for the fact you are indicted of, and there is no more to say about it."[10]

[8] Schauer (2015), p. 96.

[9] See Brandom (2014), p. 19.

[10] Many thanks to Professor Luis Coutinho for suggesting this argumentative turn.

Or, said in a different way, and with an eye to a specific version of the law as coercion thesis claiming that law is coercion authorized,[11] suppose that a judge in front of a case would say and motivate her decision in the following way: "Since law is coercion authorized and I am authorized to coercion, I will apply coercion to citizen X, and this will be a piece of law, and there is no more to say".

As a matter of fact, we all know that force application could and might be the outcome of a judicial decision, but this decision could not be found nor justified on the ground of a "law as a force" thesis. We would need a notion of law that could be internally effective, which is possibly used as an argument or a justification for a decision. Probably, we would need an idea of law as force or coercion *rightly* applied, and thus authorized only *when it is right to do* so. But with this reference to the "right" or "rightness", we would go beyond the mere "law as force" thesis, and we will eventually render it uninformative, because incapable of direct or justify the *right* decision about the use of force. Such internal sterility of the "law as force" thesis is more generally—I believe—a flaw of all realist, purely external, definitions of law.

The law as force view of the nature of law, moreover, has the need to refer to a specific anthropology, that already mentioned of the "bad man." Law is not an angelic practice. It is there because people are bad and are ready to do wrong. This, however, is a somewhat double-face thesis.

The "bad man" is the one that uses law as force to pursue his egoistic and prudential purposes, both trying to minimize the force or violence that could be applied to him and to maximize the force or violence that he could direct to others for his own profit or benefit. Law as force in this way might have an ambiguous effect on the "bad man." It might tame him, but it could also make him "worse", instead of making him "better." Law as force, which mainly operates by the threatening of sanctions, could offer the "bad man," through the mechanism offered by those sanctions, a supplementary devise and motivation to be *bad*. It could even increase his "badness" by making him more powerful towards others. Law as force is not therefore guaranteed to play a civilizing role within a society. It might reduce private violence; but it might as well increase it. In any case, it is doubtful that it was apt to decrease public, state violence.

Be as it may, the law as force jurisprudent would insist that law as such does not grant a reason for action. In his view, there are only either moral, strong normative reasons, or just prudential reasons, purely cost/benefits considerations. A non-moral normativity of law is said to be "mysterious."[12] People either orient their conduct to strong moral universal arguments or most likely act following their egocentric interest. Law is abided by either because citizens believe that it is right or just, or else because they think that it is in their interest to do so, and this is mostly the result of a sanction appended to the legal prescription.

[11]See Himma (2016), pp. 593–626.

[12]See Schauer (2015), p. 148.

How could people otherwise think that there is a legal obligation? This is either referred and translated, fully made transparent to a moral duty, or else it would be reconsidered in terms of the costs or benefits that are triggered by the force applied to the law-breaker. This is also why Herbert Hart's puzzled man is criticized since he is seen as a principled law-abiding person. Such a principled legalist citizen would simply be, by anthropology and by the nature of practical reasons, impossible. This is a picture that claims to be realist, a plain fact, commonsensical view. But it is hardly so. If such a view were right, what the law is would no longer be an interesting question. The relevant issue here would be whether there is a moral requirement applying to the case or whether there is a predictable and unbearable cost as a consequence of one specific course of action.

One could furthermore object that there is not only law that claims to be binding as such, independently from sanctions and morality, but also social norms. But again from a law as force perspective these norms are reduced either to moral rules that are socially acknowledged and sanctioned or as rules that are backed by a strong social pressure, and this would be equivalent to "force" or sanction for such perspective. There would be no special normativity of social norms distinct from prudential calculus and morality. Indeed, all sorts of norms according to this approach are dissolved either in moral or in prudential requirements.

To such a picture one could object by pointing out the practice of language. Are language rules moral rules? Or are they just binding because of force? Is German or Italian a moral practice, or are they just binding and followed because of sanctions? If in a German sentence I do not put the verb in the second position, am I then infringing a moral rule? Or am I in this case acting in breach of a prudential calculation?

Now, the law as force jurisprudent might respond to the language case using his modelling of constitutive rules as rules once again backed by force. "Constitutive rules," we know, are those whose object is not possible or conceivable or perceivable without the rules themselves. Language as a meaningful practice is possible only through language rules. The chess rules constitute chess; they are a necessary condition for the practice of chess, which would not be possible nor understandable and practicable without these same rules. The rule "smoking is forbidden" on the contrary is a "regulative" rule, in so far as smoking is not logically possible or perceivable only by an understanding of such rule, or said differently in so far as smoking is possible independently from its prohibiting rule. In the regulative rule, its object is independent of the rule itself.

Constitutive rules, once followed, present or produce a special kind of normativity. We could hardly say that chess rules are moral rules, or transparent to moral rules; nor could we say that they are binding because they are backed by force. There is no real "force" as coercion behind them. If you violate the rules of chess, you simply are not playing chess. It would thus seem that these rules, constitutive rules, point out the possibility of a special normativity distinct from the moral one and also from that which is the outcome of the threat of a sanction.

The law as force jurisprudent will object to this conclusion. According to him, constitutive rules might as well be binding because of being sanctioned. The sanction would here consist of the nullity of the act performed in violation of the constitutive rule. Inefficacy following an incorrect use of constitutive rules, or their being ignored and not followed, could—it is argued—be considered as a form of sanction. In the same vein, however, one might then claim that a machine not working because it has not been properly turned on might also be a form of sanction for inappropriate instrumental behaviour.

Any form of failure in a means-end relationship might thus be reinterpreted as a form of coercion. In this way, however, we would end to widen so much this notion, I mean, coercion, to make it eventually useless and uninformative. But—it is then objected—constitutive rules from the internal point of view, "once one is inside the game,"[13] turn to be regulative or coercive or appear so. Their constitutive force would seem to be merely a property perceivable from an external point of view.

Indeed, inside the game, or within the practice opened by constitutive rules, these rules are binding. If being binding were to be equated with coerciveness, one would be right to affirm that they are coercive. Coercion in such view—we should remember—means being enforced through sanction. Now, from the point of view of the participant in the practice, as far as constitutive rules are concerned, such rules do not have a specific sanction. If I do not strike a goal, I just do not score in football. This is all and is a lot indeed for a player. But there is no distinct sanction in the game for not scoring. For sure, by doing so, because of my poor performance, I will more likely than not lose the match. But this could hardly be considered a "sanction" in a proper sense, that is a reaction to a violation of a rule, or a penalty for a wrong done. Unless we consider a "sanction" whatever failure or infelicity it is appended to our (ineffective or unlucky) conduct. But is a "fail" as a mark a true *sanction* for my more than modest performance at an exam? Am I by my ignorance of Chinese *sanctioned* for not having ever learnt that language?

3 A Hermeneutical Concept

Law is not a concept of a natural kind. It is not like a stone or water. A stone is there independently from its concept. This however is not the case of law. Law is a social practice that is shaped through its own definition. In a sense, law is its philosophy. Law is what we interpret and believe that it is.[14]

We could have law without an external perspective, without observers. But we cannot have law without participants.[15] This implies that the concept of law, its meaning, is given through its application, its use. In the law concept and practice are strongly interrelated and the primacy is given to the practice. The internal perspective of lawyers manifests itself fundamentally in legal reasoning, which is how they

[13] Schauer (2015), p. 30.

[14] See Dworkin (2006), Chapter 1.

[15] See Alexy (2002).

practice law. Legal reasoning could not thus be excluded from an investigation about the concept of law. This I think is sufficient to reject the idea that there is a "nature of law" that is opaque to the reasons required for a legal decision.

If the definition of law is a part of the practice of law, and is especially to be found in lawyers' reasoning, this renders law a controversial or contested concept. In fact, we know that legal reasoning is centered around the experience of a controversy, with parties claiming each other to be in their own right and modeling accordingly the notion of what is law for them. But if this is so, the activity of the philosopher or the theorist cannot be an enterprise developed form an ultra-external perspective, such as is suggested by the idea of the nature of law being an issue external to legal reasoning, which, however—one has to stress—is usually and commonsensically included in what law is.

If the nature of law were disconnected from legal reasoning and the ordinary practice of law, that is from the internal point of view, from the people using legal rules to shape their conducts and life style, the understanding of the nature of law could be a task only for philosophers, and not for lawyers or ordinary people. Lawyers and citizens being internally involved with law might be wrong about its "nature"; the philosopher, on the contrary, taking distance from practice and internal commitments would be in the appropriate position, a kind of eagle's perspective, to see the object of her study properly. Nonetheless, law in practice (which is all the law we have) is not what philosophers say it is but what lawyers and citizens agree that it should be. It has a plasticity, an "open texture," given to its symbolic and interpretive character. This eventually means that the discussion about the nature of law is conceptually related to its practice, and thus not neutral with regard to such practice and its core, legal and practical reasoning. What we say about law will precipitate in how law will be practiced.

Law is what we say it is from within its practice. If we thus say that law is force, law will more likely than not be force in the practice. We shall be inclined to consider as a paradigmatic, central case of law even that, or perhaps especially that where this, force, is used without limits or scruples.[16] If we define law as essentially coercive, this will be then translated in the practice of law as an endeavor basically coercive. Should we then understand rule of law as basically meaning *rule of coercion*, force's empire? If law is essentially coercion, why should lawyers not be mainly trained in the practice of coercive measures and force? Why all this stuff, and fuss, about legal reasoning, precedents, rights, procedures? Were a robust training in policing not much better and to the point?

The concept of law is not a neutral notion. It has not only a descriptive purport; it implicitly projects itself as a standard for conduct orientation. This point is stressed by Lon Fuller. "We must remember"—he writes—"that the word 'law' never serves purely as a term descriptive of actual events; there inheres in it a sense of prescription, of what ought to be".[17] This means that if we say that law *is* force or coercion,

[16]Cfr. Dyzenhaus (2016).

[17]Fuller (1968), p. 20.

we are somehow recommending that law *ought to be* force or coercion. Conceptualizing law as force thus, instead of having a critical, deconstructive effect about the possibility of using law as violence, reminding us that law is such, that is, violence or force, against any possible idle idealization, would more often than not be a reason, a construction for practicing or experiencing law as force without envisaging any possible alternative. One might object that the awareness of law being force could help in reducing the level of the coercion or force actually applied or used in the legal practice. This however is more than dubious.

If we paradigmatically define law as coercion, some social practices that being too coercive or radically opposed to the autonomy, wellbeing and dignity of subjects are usually and commonsensically excluded from what is considered to be law might now, on the contrary, be seen as included within law as indeed its most central items or instantiations. This might for instance be the case of slavery, or torture.

This conclusion will then imply a coda. If we want force and coercion to be reduced in the legal practice, if we intend for example slavery and torture to be expelled from the precinct of law, since we believe they are incompatible with the rule of law, if we want to defend a less authoritarian or even an openly antiauthoritarian approach to law, we should be very cautious about defining and defending law as at its core force and coercion.

References

Alexy R (2002) The argument from injustice: a reply to legal positivism (trans: Paulson BL, Paulson SL). Clarendon Press, Oxford

Brandom R (2014) Hegelian model of legal concept determination: the normative fine structure of the Judges' chain novel. In: Hubbs G, Lind D (eds) Pragmatism, law, and language. Routledge, New York, pp 19–39

Dworkin R (2006) Justice in Robes. HUP, Cambridge

Dyzenhaus D (2016) The ambiguity of force. Ratio Juris 29(3):323–347

Fuller L (1968) The anatomy of law. Penguin, Harmondsworth

Gardner J (2006) Law's aims in law's empire. In: Hershowitz S (ed) Exploring law's empire. The Jurisprudence of Ronald Dworkin. OUP, Oxford

Greenberg M (2004) How facts make law. Legal Theory 10:157–198

Hart HLA (1984) Commands and authoritative legal reasons. In: Id., Essays on Bentham: Jurisprudence and political philosophy. Clarendon, Oxford

Hart HLA (1994) The concept of law, 2nd edn. Clarendon, Oxford

Himma KE (2016) The authorization of coercive enforcement mechanisms as a conceptually necessary feature of law. Jurisprudence 7:593–626

Holmes OW (1897) The path of law. 10 Harv Law Rev 8:457–477

Kant I (2000) Anthropologie in pragmatischer Hinsicht. In: Brandt R (ed) Felix Meiner, Hamburg

La Torre M (2018) « La maison d'âpre vent » et le droit comme désespoir. Archiv für Rechts- und Sozialphilosophie 104(3):315–327

Schauer F (2015) The force of law. HUP, Cambridge

The Good, the Bad, and the Puzzled: Coercion and Compliance

Lucas Miotto

Abstract The assumption that coercion is largely responsible for our legal systems' efficacy is a common one. I argue that this assumption is false. But I do so indirectly, by objecting to a thesis I call "(Compliance)," which holds that most citizens comply with most legal mandates most of the time at least partly in virtue of being motivated by legal systems' threats of sanctions and other unwelcome consequences. The relationship between (Compliance) and the efficacy of legal systems is explained in Sect. 2. There I also show that (Compliance) must be rejected for it relies on unsubstantiated empirical assumptions. In Sect. 3, I claim that an alternative and more refined formulation of (Compliance) also lacks adequate support. I conclude with a few general remarks about the centrality of coercion in our thought and talk about legal systems.

1 Introduction

> When mores are sufficient, laws are unnecessary. When mores are insufficient, laws are unenforceable.[1]

The assumption that coercion is largely responsible for our legal systems' efficacy is a common one. Legal and political philosophers have claimed that 'law *needs* to be coercive,'[2] or that '[w]ithout coercion (. . .) law would be unable to succeed in being

For comments and suggestions that greatly improved this paper I'm thankful to Anthony Duff, Himani Bhakuni, James Edwards, Luís Duarte d'Almeida, Neil Walker, and the editors of this book.

[1]This quote is often attributed to Durkheim, though it is never found in one of his books.
[2]Finnis (2011), p. 266.

L. Miotto (✉)
University of Maastricht, Maastricht, The Netherlands
e-mail: lucas.miottolopes@maastrichtuniversity.nl

J. L. Fabra-Zamora, G. Villa Rosas (eds.), *Conceptual Jurisprudence*, Law and Philosophy Library 137, https://doi.org/10.1007/978-3-030-78803-2_7

practiced within a community,'[3] or even that '[n]o [human] society can subsist without government and coercion, and consequently without laws to control and restrain men's lusts and their unbridled urges.'[4]

I argue that this assumption is false. But I do so indirectly, by challenging the following thesis:

> (Compliance): in typical legal systems,[5] most citizens comply with most legal mandates most of the time at least partly in virtue of being motivated by legal systems' threats of sanctions and other unwelcome consequences.

The relationship between (Compliance) and the efficacy of legal systems is explained in Sect. 2. There I also argue that (Compliance) must be rejected for it relies on unsubstantiated empirical assumptions. In Sect. 3 I claim that an alternative, and more refined, formulation of (Compliance) also lacks adequate support. I conclude with a few general remarks about the place of coercion in our thought and talk about legal systems.

2 The Tale of the Bad Man

The claim that legal systems are efficacious can mean different things. Usually, however, legal philosophers hold that a legal system is efficacious only if a sufficient number of citizens—i.e., the addressees of legal mandates—*comply* with a sufficient number of legal mandates.[6] Under this description, the relationship between compliance and the efficacy of legal system is straightforward: compliance is a necessary condition of the efficacy of legal systems. For the purposes of the present discussion, I'll assume that this relationship holds and ignore a few complications about it.[7]

To say that citizens comply with a given legal mandate doesn't presuppose that citizens comply for any particular reason. Compliance is a thin notion; it can be achieved by any reason whatsoever; even by luck. But many—from Hobbes to public choice economists to contemporary legal and political philosophers—depict human beings as somewhat akin to Holmes's famous character, the *bad man*: someone who is primarily disposed to maximise self-interest and who is willing to

---

[3]Lamond (2001), p. 45.

[4]Spinoza (2007), secs 63–64.

[5]Throughout the paper I take "typical legal systems" to refer to those legal systems that currently exist in western democratic states and those that closely resemble them.

[6]See, Burazin (2019).

[7]I'll ignore complications associated with the relevant number of citizens that must comply with legal mandates and complications associated with the relevant number of legal mandates that must be complied with. I'll equally ignore the discussion about whether mandates of a certain type must be complied by a certain type of citizen for a legal system to be efficacious. As important as these discussions may be for a rigorous understanding of the efficacy of legal systems, there is no need to engage with them for the purposes of this paper.

flout the law whenever he can benefit from doing so.[8] They think that *in a world like ours*, a large and stable level of compliance can only be achieved by the coercive force of law. Without coercion—and by "coercion" it is meant nothing more than the threat of sanctions or other unwelcome consequences—compliance and cooperation would give in to anarchy and self-interest. Without coercion, therefore, our legal systems would cease to be efficacious.

Most actual legal systems are indeed efficacious. If it is true that a legal system in a world like ours wouldn't be efficacious but for coercion, then it must be true that coercion *does* motivate many, if not most, citizens to comply with most legal mandates in actual legal systems. So, for the claim that coercion is largely responsible for the efficacy of our legal systems to run, (Compliance) must also run.

(Compliance) seems to have some intuitive appeal. But its truth, as well as the accuracy of using the bad man as a description of the typical human character, hang on empirical considerations. One cannot assume these claims without checking the relevant empirical facts. That is what I'm going to do next.

2.1 *The Search for the Bad*

The empirical literature on deterrence provides a good starting point. Many studies have examined the extent to which the threat of legal sanctions deter breaches. The findings—especially those about the impact of criminal sanctions on citizens' behaviour—are interesting. Empirical studies show that deterrence is much less successful than often assumed.[9] Different factors contribute to that. For example, behavioural studies have found that deterrence sometimes fails in virtue of knowledge about criminal laws (i.e., knowledge of which conduct are criminalised, which actions are required, what excuses are available, what sanctions are applied, and of their magnitude) being weak among citizens; even among those who would benefit the most from knowing what the law requires.[10] The formulation of actual legal rules seems to have no impact on citizens' beliefs about what legal rules require.[11] Changes in the formulation of legal rules are often neither accompanied by a

[8]A number of legal philosophers have adopted a somewhat pessimistic view of human character and dispositions. For some recent examples of this presupposition in legal philosophy see, Plaxton (2012); Himma (2016). A similar presupposition is also widespread in political philosophy and economics. Elisabeth Anderson provides numerous examples in Anderson (2000). See also Brennan (2017).

[9]See, e.g., Tyler (2006a), p. 67. Robinson and Darley have reviewed the relevant literature and provided a number of helpful references on this point. See Robinson and Darley (2004).

[10]Robinson and Darley (2004), sec. 1A and passim.

[11]Sometimes this generates pernicious effects. For example, it has been shown that because of the lack of relevant legal knowledge, workers tend to enter employment contracts on the assumption that legal rules extend to them far greater protection against unfair employment contracts than they actually do. See Kim (1997).

corresponding change in citizens' beliefs about what the rules require nor by a change in behaviour.

These findings about citizens' knowledge, however, cannot by themselves explain why deterrence is weak. Certainly, they do show that the way legal rules are formulated doesn't directly impact citizens' behaviour and that sometimes citizens have no idea of what legal systems require. That may explain why some criminal rules (e.g., those largely unknown to citizens) don't deter or affect citizens' motivation in any way. But the point cannot be generalised. Requiring that, to be deterred, citizens must know the exact conduct which is criminalised or the sanctions that may be applied in case of a breach would be too demanding. Citizens need not know exactly which sanctions are applicable or the exact formulation of a legal rule in order to be deterred. Having a rough belief about what is criminalised and a belief that authorities are likely to do something unwelcome to those who engage in certain behaviours may suffice for deterrence. In fact, some studies corroborate this. They suggest that citizens believing both that authorities are likely to enforce sanctions and that unlawful behaviour is likely to be detected suffice to deter some breaches.[12]

There are, however, more factors which corroborate the view that deterrence is an overrated explanation for citizens' compliance with legal rules. Studies focused on criminal laws found that citizens 'commonly assume the law to be *as they think it should be*, so they assume the existence of criminal law rules that correspond to their own intuitions about justice' and act accordingly.[13] Reinforcing this last point, independent studies have found that moral beliefs (what social scientists often call 'personal morality') largely influence citizens' compliance with legal mandates.[14] Most citizens most of the time seem to comply with legal mandates simply because what legal mandates require corresponds to what citizens independently or collectively take to be the right thing to do. The fact that legal rules demand a particular behaviour and apply sanctions to deviations and the very fact that a legal rule requiring a given behaviour exists is usually irrelevant to citizens: legal mandates frequently don't number among the considerations citizens take into account when deciding what to do.[15]

Furthermore, empirical studies suggest that even when people do know what legal mandates require and the sanctions legal systems threaten, citizens still tend not to be motivated by them. This is because what legal mandates require clashes with what citizens think is fair,[16] or because the way legal regulation and enforcement are

[12]See, e.g., Paternoster (2010). For what is worth, even Robinson and Darley admit that. Robinson and Darley (2004), p. 173.

[13]Robinson and Darley (2004), pp. 176–177 my emphasis. See also, Darley et al. (2001); Darley et al. (1996).

[14]Tyler (2006a), pp. 67–68.

[15]See Darley et al. (2001); Nadler (2004); Tyler (2006a); Tyler (2006b); Schauer (2015), p. 59.

[16]Nadler (2004); Mullen and Nadler (2008); Robinson et al. (2010).

designed make non-compliance appealing,[17] or even, sometimes, because citizens are unable (e.g., in virtue of psychological problems) or unwilling (e.g., in virtue of the benefits of breaching the law, or in virtue of a strong desire to satisfy personal vendetta) to bring this knowledge to bear on their actions.[18]

Moreover, some studies show that sometimes intensifying the strength of sanctions or the ratio of enforcement may even increase non-compliance instead of decreasing it.[19] In certain contexts, sanctions can backfire: they end up promoting the behaviours they were supposed to deter. Instead of being taken as a disincentive and deterring behaviour, they are taken as a price worth paying to perform a particular action, or even lead to the development of harmful social norms.[20] The Prohibition in the 1920s United States is a telling example.

These findings aren't—and shouldn't be—surprising. Legal rules don't take place in a 'social vacuum';[21] they very often regulate behaviour which already possesses social significance, and which is heavily influenced by citizens' cultural, social, and moral norms and beliefs. And given the strength of these factors, often the best strategy for legal systems is, as far as possible, to work in tandem with them. That seems to be what typical legal systems attempt to do most of the time.

What is surprising, however, is the extent to which legal and political philosophers tend to ignore these points and continue to accord legal coercion a central place in both the explanation of citizens' motivation to cooperate with each other and in the explanation of their motivation to comply with legal mandates. This tendency has even been described as a bias.[22] Not only do many philosophers seem biased towards giving too much prominence to the role of legal sanctions in fostering compliance and cooperation, but also towards an overly pessimistic view about human character.

Contrary to this pessimistic view on human character, a large bulk of evidence from political science, social and cognitive psychology, and economics suggest that a more apt model for human character is that of the *good person*: someone who is disposed to do what she believes is fair and in agreement with her cultural, social, and moral norms and beliefs, and to cooperate when she believes that others are likely to do so.[23] Many studies have shown that, with some degree of variation across different cultures, humans have altruistic, prosocial, and cooperative

---

[17]Raymon Paternoster claims that even if we assume that agents are 'rational actors' (a la Holmes's *bad man*), there are reasons to think that the way actual criminal system is designed is insufficient to effectively change behaviour. See Paternoster (2010), sec. VI.

[18]Robinson and Darley provide a helpful review of the empirical literature on this point. See Robinson and Darley (2004), pp. 178–182 and references therein.

[19]Sherman (1993).

[20]Frey and Oberholzer-Gee (1997); Gneezy and Rustichini (2000); Fehr and Rockenbach (2003); Heyman and Ariely (2004); Abbink et al. (2017).

[21]Nadler (2017), p. 65.

[22]Brennan (2017).

[23]Notice that 'good person' here is not being used to suggest that people are generally morally good or virtuous. 'Good' is being used in the sense that people have a disposition to conditionally

dispositions and that cooperation tends to be favoured even when self-interest must be sacrificed.[24]

In addition, economists and social scientists have repeatedly emphasised that a large part of the social order we enjoy is not explained by the threat of legal sanctions or other unwelcome consequences. They have, time and again, pointed out how individuals and groups, by voluntarily cooperating and trusting each other, have collectively devised effective and ingenious solutions to a number of complex social and economic problems (ranging from the development of intricate systems of allocation and protection of property rights to systems of benefit-sharing and distribution of public goods) in the absence of the coercive sword of legal systems and the state.[25] To insist that the social order and stability that most current legal systems enjoy is largely a product of legal coercion is to disseminate a mistaken view.

All suggests that neither (Compliance), nor the overly pessimistic view of human character that many legal and political philosophers assume are accurate views. Granted: constructs such as the *bad man* might still be valuable to other theoretical purposes.[26] But in the face of current evidence, we have good reason to no longer tell the tale of the bad man when *describing* the usual human behaviour.

Of course, we cannot simply generalise and say that the threat of unwelcome consequences never motivates citizens to perform or to abstain from performing actions. There are many instances where the influence of the threat of unwelcome consequences on citizens' behaviour is well-documented.[27] Sometimes, legal systems do issue legal mandates that challenge citizens' cultural, social, and moral norms and beliefs. When that happens, the possibility of legal systems doing something unwelcome to citizens tends to figure in their motivation to comply with legal mandates. On some occasions, it is not an exaggeration to say that citizens' beliefs in the likelihood of being sanctioned is *the* reason why they comply with legal mandates. There is a garden-variety of examples. Examples ranging from the burkini ban to prohibitions on the use of recreational drugs, to laws requiring the use of helmets[28] and the imposition of curfews come to mind.

---

cooperate: to cooperate when they believe others will do the same. In that line, Samuel Bowles and Herbert Gintis, for example, calls humans the 'cooperative species'. Bowles and Gintis (2011).

[24]The literature is quite extensive. Some helpful examples are Dawes et al. (1990); Batson and Shaw (1991); Anderson (2000); Bicchieri (2006), chap. 4; Bowles and Gintis (2011); Embrey et al. (2018); Burton-Chellew et al. (2017).

[25]Ostrom (1990); Ellickson (1991); Stringham (2015); Ellickson (2017); Brennan (2017).

[26]Economists have extensively relied on a similar model of behaviour: the *homo economicus*. As some suggest, the *homo economicus* was a useful construct that allowed economists to build economic and mathematical models in a time where economic tools were more rudimentary than they are nowadays. Some contemporary economists, however, urge for the abandonment of the construct given that now we have better tools to build economic models based on a less simplified assumption of human character and rationality. See Thaler (2000). On the importance of the *homo economicus* construct to economic theory, see Ross (2012).

[27]Frederick Schauer provides many helpful references. See Schauer (2015), chaps 5–6.

[28]For a helpful analysis of how helmet laws clashed with the cultural values of some groups in the USA, see Jones and Bayer (2007).

Yet, as familiar and common as examples like these may seem to be, we should resist the temptation to take them as representative of what typical legal systems do to most citizens most of the time. Some legal mandates of typical legal systems are indeed complied primarily in virtue of the threat of legal sanctions (and for some citizens the bad man is certainly a more accurate model than the good person's). But, as far as our best empirical findings show, most legal mandates aren't. Even Frederick Schauer, a fierce advocate of the centrality of coercion to typical legal systems, has granted this point after examining the relevant empirical evidence. In his own words:

> [M]ost people make decisions about what to do and what not to do based on some complex mix of reasons of preference, prudence, and morality, but it is a mix that need not include the law. *For most people most of the time*, much that they do is consistent with the law, but is not done because of the law.[29]

This remark, however, may strike some as odd. How is it possible for someone, like Frederick Schauer, to admit that legal coercion doesn't influence most citizens' behaviour most of the time and still accord coercion a central place in explaining the efficacy of legal systems? Something must have gone wrong somewhere. That is what I try to find out in the next section.

3 Enter the Puzzled

There is a tension in simultaneously claiming that coercion has a central place in the explanation of the efficacy of legal systems and that coercion doesn't figure in most citizens' motivation to comply with most legal mandates most of the time. At times, this tension seems to be present in Frederick Schauer's recent work on the coerciveness of legal systems. It is possible, however, to construe Schauer's views in a more charitable way; a way that resolves this tension.

One of Schauer's main goals in his recent work is to find out how legal systems make a practical difference in citizens' lives, i.e., how they 'pla[y] a role in determining the actions and decisions of its subjects'.[30] One way to understand his broader project is to interpret it as an attempt to answer the following question: in virtue of what do legal systems influence citizens' behaviour? His general answer is that *when* legal systems make a practical difference in citizens' lives—i.e., when legal systems influence citizens' behaviour—they do so *mainly* in virtue of coercion.

We can interpret this answer in purely statistical terms.[31] Schauer seems to be defending the view that in the vast majority of circumstances where legal systems influence behaviour, the influence is due to the threat of unwelcome consequences. He sympathises with the view that law's non-coercive influence 'is so small as to be

[29]Schauer (2015), p. 50 my emphasis.

[30]Ibid., p. 54.

[31]Several passages in Schauer's recent book corroborate this view. See, for example, Ibid., p. 46.

hardly worth worrying about'.[32] All suggests that Schauer—and maybe others—has never really defended (Compliance). Instead he—and maybe others—has defended the following view:

> (Compliance*) Most of the time typical legal systems influence citizens' behaviour, they do so via the threat of unwelcome consequences.

Schauer—and maybe others—is, therefore, not strictly concerned with the relationship between coercion and the *efficacy* of typical legal systems. Instead, he is interested in the relationship between coercion and typical legal systems' actual influence on behaviour.

While believing that this is Schauer's view, I'm not too concerned with whether this is *really* his view or not. It is a view that is interesting and worth discussing regardless. More to the point, we can see that (Compliance*) is resistant to the objection that I raised in the previous section: even if true that most citizens most of the time don't comply with legal mandates because of coercion, it could still be true that in most occasions legal systems do succeed in influencing citizens' behaviour, the influence is due to the threat of unwelcome consequences.

Does (Compliance*) hold? Schauer thinks it does and accuses those who think otherwise of making an empirical mistake. According to Schauer, some philosophers and sociologists have assumed that most citizens are exclusively 'law-motivated', i.e. that most citizens 'comply with the law just because it is the law'.[33]

If most people are exclusively law-motivated—Schauer calls them '*puzzled people*'—then it must be false that legal systems influence most citizens' behaviour via the threat of unwelcome consequences.[34] Under the assumption that most citizens are puzzled people, it would follow that legal systems influence the behaviour of most citizens just by issuing legal mandates and letting citizens know the content of these mandates. Schauer, however, thinks that there are not as many puzzled people in the world as some philosophers and sociologists would have us believe.[35]

To some extent, Schauer's discussion of the puzzled person is itself puzzling. First, the way Schauer characterises the puzzled person makes us wonder what puzzles the puzzled person. If the puzzled person is generally motivated to comply with the law just because it is the law, it seems that she is not really puzzled about what to do. On the contrary, the puzzled person, as Schauer describes them, is more aptly described as a *law-maniac*; a devotee of the law who follows the law

[32]Ibid., p. 46. As I said, Schauer *sympathises* with this view. Schauer, however, never explicitly endorses it in such strong terms (though much of his book suggests that he does endorse this thesis in these terms). In the quoted passage, Schauer is talking about a view that someone may possibly hold (it is, by the way, a view explicitly endorsed by Michael Plaxton. See Plaxton (2012).

[33]Schauer (2015), p. 47.

[34]Ibid., pp. 47–48.

[35]See Ibid., chap. 5 and passim.

no-questions-asked.[36] More importantly, that description of people's motivation raises some questions. For one, it raises the question of whether any philosopher or sociologist has really defended the view that most people follow the law *just because* it is the law.

Before answering that, let me first deal with a preliminary worry: it is not entirely clear what it is for someone to comply with the law just because it is the law. The phrase seems to suggest that the simple fact that legal systems require an action is taken by someone as the sole reason or motive to perform or abstain from performing it. If that is how we should understand it, then the view faces a problem.

Suppose Puzzly tells us that she follows the law most of the time just because it is the law. In this case, it seems that we could still ask Puzzly for further explanation. In particular, we could ask her to present us the reasons why she thinks being the law makes something merit compliance in the first place. There can be multiple answers here. Puzzly, for instance, may think that if something is the law it is the right thing to do, or is what other people will likely do, or is what her country expects her to do, or is in her best interest, and so forth. A simple 'I follow the law just because it is the law' may hide many different motivations, including motivations based on prudence and morality that Schauer didn't expect to find in those who 'follow the law just because it is the law'. If this is true, then perhaps this explains why Schauer didn't find many instances of people who comply with the law *just* because it is the law.[37]

Coming back to a previous point: have philosophers and sociologists really assumed that most people comply with the law just because it is the law? No. Schauer's criticism is mainly directed towards H.L.A Hart,[38] from whom Schauer borrows the reference to the 'puzzled person'. Hart's characterisation of the puzzled person, however, is at odds with Schauer's in an important way. Here is the view Schauer attributes to Hart:

> Hart's puzzled person is thus someone who follows the law just because it is the law even when what the law requires seems not only not in her best interest but also contrary to her best judgment.[39]

For Hart, however, the puzzled person is not someone who is exclusively law-motivated. Instead, the puzzled—or 'ignorant'—person is just someone who is confused and looks at law for guidance. In Hart's own words, the 'puzzled man' or 'ignorant man' is someone 'who is willing to do what is required, if only he can be told what it is'.[40] This description is compatible with the puzzled person being someone who is willing to do what the law requires for a number of different

[36]Mark Greenberg has recently made a similar point. He thinks that Schauer's characterisation of the puzzled person is that of someone who has a fetish for the law. See Greenberg (2018), p. 376.

[37]I make a similar point in Miotto (2016), pp. 233–234. Mark Greenberg has also recently made a similar point and emphasises that the puzzled person can follow the law for moral reasons. See Greenberg (2018).

[38]Schauer (2015), pp. 46–48.

[39]Ibid., p. 62.

[40]Hart (2012), p. 40.

reasons. The puzzled person can be a patriot who wants to know what the law is in order to honour her country, or a lazy-conformant who follows the law because it spares her some effort, or someone who believes that the laws of her jurisdiction are generally fair and merit obedience.

The above is not just a charitable interpretation of what Hart has said about the puzzled person. It also aligns with Hart's broader view that actual people follow the law for a 'variety of motives'[41] and that legal systems still have a point in guiding and helping people's lives regardless of the reasons why they comply with the law.

The upshot is that, contrary to what Schauer suggests, Hart (but also others who Schauer criticises)[42] has never assumed that most people are exclusively law-motivated and thus cannot be blamed for making an empirical mistake about how legal systems influence behaviour.

Schauer's focus on the puzzled person is misguided for yet another reason. A reason that, even though obvious, is more fundamental to the present discussion. The reason is that, contrary to what Schauer seems to suggest, one need not defend the idea that most citizens fit Schauer's description of the puzzled person to refute (Compliance*). Requiring that—like Schauer does—is too demanding. Schauer may be right that most people in most legal systems don't comply with the law just because it is the law. But that just shows that most people aren't law-maniacs, which is hardly something anyone would dispute. To argue against (Compliance*), all one needs to establish is that most of the times legal systems influence citizens' behaviour they do so by ways other than the threat of sanctions or unwelcome consequences. In that regard, there are some empirical findings worth examining.

3.1 Covenants Without Swords

It is widely recognised—at least by sociologists and social psychologists—that legal systems influence behaviour independently from the threat of unwelcome consequences. Sociologists often highlight the relationship between the belief that a legal system is legitimate and the likelihood of citizens complying with legal mandates. The point is not new; it can even be traced back to Max Weber, to whom legitimacy was a key factor to make legal (and social) orders more stable.[43] A number of

[41]"[S]ome [people obey the law] from prudential calculation that the sacrifices are worth the gains, some from a disinterested interest in the welfare of others, and some because they look upon the rules as worthy of respect in themselves and find their ideals in devotion to them.". Ibid., p. 197.

[42]Tom Tyler is another example. Contrary to what Schauer suggests, Tyler doesn't assume that there is a vast number of puzzled people in our societies. Besides, in his empirical studies, Tyler distinguishes quite a few different motives for following the law (e.g., deterrence, legitimacy, peer disapproval, political factors, etc) and measures the influence of each of these distinct motives in isolation. Tyler also recognises that people often comply with the law for a mix of motives. See Tyler (2006a), p. 59.

[43]Weber (1978), pp. 31–33.

recent—or relatively recent—empirical studies have attempted to analyse the relationship between legitimacy and compliance in a more systematic way. For the purposes of empirical inquiry, sociologists and political scientists often presuppose a thin notion of legitimacy. They presuppose that a legal system is legitimate either when citizens believe they (morally) ought to obey the systems' mandates or when citizens express approval or allegiance to the system.[44]

Some studies found that legitimacy 'has a significant independent effect on compliance, even when other potential causal factors are controlled for'[45] and that the relationship between legitimacy and compliance is linear— i.e., 'as one increases so does the other'.[46] These studies on the influence of legitimacy on compliance, however, don't establish the exact proportion of citizens who are influenced by legal system's legitimacy (and not by the threat of unwelcome consequences). We cannot conclude, based on these studies alone, that *most* citizens are influenced by legal systems in virtue of legal mandates being legitimate. All we can say is that the number of citizens who are influenced by legal systems in this way is not insignificant.

There is, however, reason to believe that legal systems influence behaviour in ways other than legitimacy and coercion. In a number of occasions, people do what they think is morally right. But they don't do so just because that is what they would have done in the absence of legal systems' influence. Instead, people have—or take themselves to have—moral reasons to engage in some behaviours at least partly because these behaviours were required or permitted by a legal system. As the recent works of Robert Hughes and Mark Greenberg emphasise, legal systems influence behaviour—and, to what is worth, make a practical difference—by influencing citizens' 'moral profile', i.e., citizens' moral beliefs, reasons, and positions (their duties, permissions, powers, and so forth).[47]

There are at least two ways legal systems affect citizens' moral profile. The first, and milder, way is that issuing a given law at times influences citizens' perception of the rightfulness or wrongfulness of an action, which leads citizens to alter their behaviour.[48] Recent empirical studies corroborate this point. It has been found that legal systems influence people's moral beliefs and actions even when people are aware that sanctions won't be enforced. For example, Bert Huang's recent work has found that people tend to change their decisions in moral dilemmas when they believe that one of the options in the dilemma is favoured by the law (even when

[44]Tom Tyler provides a helpful overview of the concept of legitimacy presupposed in empirical studies. See, Tyler (2006a), pp. 27–30.

[45]Ibid., p. 58.

[46]Ibid., p. 57. See also Gibson et al. (2005); Tyler (2006a); Papachristos et al. (2012); Tyler and Jackson (2014).

[47]Greenberg (2018), p. 377; Hughes (2018).

[48]This way is not mentioned by Mark Greenberg or Robert Hughes. However, it is consistent with the point they make.

they know that there is no legal sanction for choosing the option proscribed by law).[49]

The second, and more robust, way legal systems affect citizens' moral landscape is by creating or altering citizens' moral reasons and positions.[50] Property rights are an example.[51] It is often said that most people refrain from theft for law-independent reasons; that people would not steal from one another in the absence of legal rules. But this is misleading. It is plausible to think that at least some property rights that we enjoy in current societies partly exist in virtue of legal rules. If this is so, then—at least in some cases—a 'moral motive for refraining from theft is not a law-independent motive';[52] its existence partly depends on the existence of a legal system and the property rules it creates.

The upshot is that some people who are taken, or who could be taken, and who I myself have taken in the first section of this paper to not be influenced by legal systems may in reality behave the way they behave partly in virtue of the (non-coercive) influence of legal systems. And that can be the case even when people are themselves not aware of the extent to which their actions and their moral beliefs, motives, and positions are influenced by legal systems.[53]

Determining which—if any—of the moral reasons are partly constituted by legal systems isn't an empirical issue. Whether, for example, some property rights are partly constituted by legal rules and, thus, whether citizens' moral reasons to respect property rights partly owe their existence to legal rules hang on a theory of property rights. It is not my job here to propose or defend such a theory. But it is not implausible—or at least not obviously implausible—to assume that examples where legal systems, as it were, shape citizens' moral reasons to comply with the law exist. (For instance, think of the moral reason to pay a specific amount of tax, or the reason to pay a specific amount of damages to a specific person, or the moral reason not to make noise of a particular magnitude at a particular hour, or the reason not to drive faster than a specific speed).

What is an empirical issue, however, is figuring out the precise proportion of citizens who comply with legal mandates for moral reasons that owe their existence (at least partly) to legal systems (assuming some moral reasons owe their existence at least partly to legal systems). As far as I'm aware, there is no empirical work on the topic, so it is not possible to say more than that this way legal systems influence behaviour *seems* to be common.

---

[49]Huang (2017).

[50]Greenberg (2018), p. 377 and passim; Hughes (2018), pp. 362–364. The general point being made here is an old one. It can be traced back to Aquinas and his idea of *determinatio*: that legal systems can create moral reasons by making precise what morality leaves imprecise. See, Aquinas (1947), p. Q.95.

[51]Hughes (2018).

[52]Ibid., p. 364.

[53]Ibid., p. 365.

Given what I've said so far about legal systems influencing behaviour by legitimacy and by influencing people's moral landscape, it is already possible to conclude that legal systems' non-coercive influence on behaviour appears to be more prominent than Schauer (and others) had suggested—it is at least not 'so small as to be hardly worth worrying about'.[54] That, of course, is still insufficient to establish that legal systems' non-coercive influence is pervasive and that legal systems' coercive influence is not (or that the coercive and non-coercive influence are on par, which would also be enough to refute (Compliance*)). There are, however, additional considerations that lend more plausibility to the view that legal systems' non-coercive influence is prominent.

3.2 *Expressive Powers and the Role of Expectations*

A considerable body of evidence has shown that people's compliance with rules—legal and otherwise—is strongly affected by both empirical and normative expectations.[55] Frequently, an agent is more inclined to comply with a given rule when and because she believes that others in her group or society are complying (i.e. when she has an empirical expectation). And an agent is also frequently more inclined to comply with a given rule when and because she believes that others in her group or society believe that she ought to comply with the rule (i.e. when she has a normative expectation). This influence of expectations in rule-compliance occurs both in the absence of the threat of unwelcome consequences and in the absence of people taking the rules as legitimate.[56]

There is evidence that legal systems can and, to a significant extent, do influence behaviour by creating expectations. A growing body of literature is dedicated to show that legal systems possess and utilise what is known as 'expressive powers'.[57] Two distinct expressive powers are taken to influence citizens' compliance with the law: the power to coordinate (i.e., the power to solve coordination problems) and the power to convey information. These powers are said to be 'expressive' because they are abilities to influence behaviour *by the mere expression* of rules, directives or guidelines.[58]

To see how legal systems' use of these powers are related to what I've said about expectations, consider simple (or 'pure', as it is often called) coordination problems;

---

[54] Schauer (2015), p. 46; Plaxton (2012).

[55] Cristina Bicchieri, for example, has carried out a number of empirical studies on the topic and provided an extensive and helpful discussion on it in a series of works on the topic. See, e.g., Bicchieri (2006); Bicchieri and Xiao (2008); Bicchieri and Chavez (2010).

[56] Gerald Gaus elaborates on some implications of this feature of Bicchieri's work to discussions in political philosophy. See Gaus (2016), p. 5.

[57] See McAdams (2000); McAdams and Nadler (2005); McAdams and Nadler (2008); McAdams (2015).

[58] McAdams (2015), p. 5.

problems where those involved have no preference for a particular solution but still prefer to adopt the solution favoured by most. Some traffic problems provide an example. Most people prefer to drive on the same side as other people and have no preference for a particular side.[59] Figuring out what side most people are likely to drive in the absence of certain rules or conventions may be difficult. Legal systems change that. By passing a law requiring citizens to drive on the right side, legal systems solve the coordination problem. And they solve the problem by creating a 'coordination focal point';[60] i.e., by making a given solution to the problem salient to the point that the advantages associated with adopting the solution create an expectation that most will adopt it.[61]

The point is that, in certain contexts—like in the traffic example—the mere expression of a law makes a given solution to a coordinative problem salient and leads people to believe that others are likely to adopt it. Because many don't want to be viewed as outliers and prefer to do what others will likely do in this type of situation, citizens comply with the behaviour required by legal systems without taking sanctions and unwelcome consequences into account, or without evaluating the legitimacy of what is required by law.[62]

There is reason to think that simple coordination problems are widespread and so are the cases where legal systems influence behaviour by simply making a solution to these coordination problems salient and by creating expectations.[63] Traffic laws are not the only examples. Many laws that provide (binding and non-binding) guidelines to traders, health providers, bankers, constructors, advertisers, manufacturers, and policy-makers; laws that set standards (e.g., laws that define what counts as legal tender, laws that set common communication protocols for international and domestic air-traffic control, laws that set standards for the operation of electrical grids, *etc.*); as well as a considerable bulk of administrative law and by-laws fall into this category.[64]

Even more widespread, however, is the presence of complex coordination problems; problems where everyone involved would be better-off by adopting the same solution but where different solutions are preferred—sometimes even strongly—by those involved.[65] An example is agreeing on how often a democracy should have elections. Citizens in a democracy may each have strong and conflicting preferences

[59] Of course, people who are accustomed to driving on a particular side of the road may have a strong preference for that side. My point presupposes a scenario where driving rules have been first introduced to a population new to driving. The central point being made in the passage, however, works for any kind of pure coordination problem. So, if the reader finds the driving example too unrealistic, I suggest them to adapt the example.

[60] McAdams (2015), p. 57 and passim.

[61] Ibid., pp. 42–43 and passim.

[62] Nadler (2017), pp. 64–65.

[63] A helpful and detailed case for this claim is made by Richard McAdams. See McAdams (2015), pp. 27–42.

[64] For examples in administrative law and by-laws see Nadler (2017), p. 66.

[65] McAdams (2015), chap. 2.

about the matter. But they will be better-off by agreeing on a common number than by insisting on their own preferences and failing to solve the problem.

Legal systems also influence behaviour independently from the threat of unwelcome consequences while providing solutions to complex coordination problems. The way legal systems influence behaviour in these scenarios is similar, but not identical, to the way they do while providing solutions to simple coordination problems. Examples are legion, they range from provisions in constitutional and in international law that are not backed by the threat of sanctions, to common contractual provisions in private law. To name a few: determining the minimum and maximum age for someone to occupy the presidential office, or the number of votes necessary for a constitutional amendment, or the terms and form of trade agreements, the margin of negotiation in employment contracts, *etc.*[66]

As interesting as these findings are and as numerous as the examples where legal systems influence behaviour independently from the threat of unwelcome consequences may seem to be, we should not be hasty and assume that law's non-coercive side is what mostly influences citizens' behaviour.

First, and as I have highlighted in the first section, knowledge of legal mandates is generally poor among citizens. And this impacts the non-coercive influence of the law just as equally as it impacts the law's coercive influence. As Richard MacAdams puts it:

> Not knowing a particular law exists, [citizens] will not fear legal sanctions for violating it, not defer to its legitimacy, not use it to solve a coordination problem, and (. . .) not update beliefs in light of the information the law reveals.[67]

Second, some of the studies are based on surveys and are not considered robust by some social scientists.[68] Third, there are certain studies that seem to favour the view that legal mandates only rarely influence behaviour by means other than the threat of unwelcome consequences. Schauer has cited a few in support of his thesis, though he has also acknowledged that they have serious limitations.[69] Finally, and more fundamentally, the empirical studies to date face significant methodological challenges. It is hard to effectively isolate the factors that influence citizens' behaviour. And, as it appears to be the case, the empirical studies to date—regardless of the conclusion they support—are yet to overcome these methodological challenges.[70]

To find out the extent to which the influence of legal mandates on behaviour is due to the threat of unwelcome consequences and the extent to which the influence is due to other factors we need to wait for more and better empirical evidence. While we wait for more and better evidence, the acceptable attitude is to suspend

---

[66]For more examples, see Ibid., pp. 67–92; Nadler (2017).

[67]McAdams (2015), p. 137.

[68]Nadler (2017), p. 63.

[69]Schauer (2015), pp. 64–65; Schauer (2017), p. 93.

[70]See Schauer (2015), p. 64; Schauer (2017), p. 92. See also McAdams (2015), p. 8.

judgement. As of now, we just cannot determine with enough confidence if (Compliance*) is true or not.

But what if new and more robust empirical studies emerge and show that (Compliance*) holds after all?

This would be an interesting conclusion, but its impact would be far less significant than one might think. Even if it turns out that coercion accounts for most cases where legal systems influence citizens' behaviour, we should not forget what we've concluded in the first section of this paper: that most people most of the time are not influenced by legal mandates. They comply with legal mandates for reasons which are independent from law's influence.

This doesn't happen by accident. Citizens often tend to favour prosocial behaviour and are influenced by their social, cultural, and moral norms and beliefs. Insofar as many social, cultural, and moral norms and beliefs are not harmful to society, the most obvious choice for legal authorities is to issue legal mandates that, as far as possible, match or strengthen citizens' pre-existing norms and beliefs. On top of that, legal authorities understand that coercion is extremely costly. Given the practical difficulties associated with coercing citizens, motivating citizens via the threat of unwelcome consequences is often intentionally left as a last resort. The increase of legal systems' reliance on alternative regulatory mechanisms—such as nudging—can attest to that.[71]

More fundamentally, on some occasions the threat of sanctions and unwelcome consequences can either backfire or have no effect in motivating citizens to comply with legal mandates. This makes us wonder why legal systems succeed in motivating citizens via the threat of unwelcome consequences in some circumstances and fail in others.

As recent empirical studies show, unless the threat of sanctions and unwelcome consequences are legitimated by underlying cultural, social and moral norms and beliefs, they are likely to fail in influencing behaviour. To put this in a different way: available evidence suggests that the influence of the threat of unwelcome consequences is parasitic on the fact that they are supported by underlying cultural, social, and moral norms and beliefs.[72]

[71]For a helpful, and somewhat historical, overview of the shift from regulation centred on negative incentives to alternative and more nuanced forms of motivating compliance with legal mandates, see Lessig (1998). The growth of alternative regulation such as nudging is not an unknown phenomenon; it has even made it to the news. For a news piece focused on the UK, see Rutter T (2015) The rise of nudge – the unit helping politicians to fathom human behaviour. In: The Guardian. https://www.theguardian.com/public-leaders-network/2015/jul/23/rise-nudge-unit-politicians-human-behaviour. Accessed 15 January 2021.

[72]Bicchieri et al. (2017). See also references therein. Gerald Gaus has made a similar point and explored these conclusions to political philosophy. See Gaus (2016). Gaus also mentioned this point in a recent interview. See Marshall R, Gaus G (2016) The Tyranny of the Ideal. In: 3:AM Magazine. http://www.3ammagazine.com/3am/the-tyranny-of-the-ideal/. Accessed 15 January 2021. In a similar vein, Richard McAdams argues for another sense in which the threat of unwelcome consequences is parasitic on legal system's non-coercive side. He defends that legal sanctions 'owe their

Schauer and others may end up being right about (Compliance*). But even if right, they have missed something important: that even if very often present, the influence of the threat of legal sanctions and other unwelcome consequences is still of secondary importance to our legal systems. Whatever role they play in affecting citizens' behaviour is conditioned upon the sanctions being supported by underlying social, cultural, and moral norms and beliefs.

4 Conclusion

H.L.A Hart once said that coercion has an ancillary role in legal systems. What he meant was that sanctions and unwelcome consequences were applied only when all else fails.[73] Given what we now know from empirical studies, we can go further than Hart and ascribe an even more exceptional and ancillary role to coercion. It is not just that coercive mechanisms motivate citizens in exceptional circumstances. When they do succeed in motivating citizens, their success tends to be due to the support of underlying social norms and the fact that citizens accept them as legitimate.

Hobbes' famous adage—'Covenants without swords are but words'—has played an enormous influence in legal and political philosophy as well as in our common understanding of our legal systems and the state. What we now know shows that it is time to reverse the adage and accord coercion a less prominent place in our thought and talk about typical legal systems: Swords without legitimate covenants are but cold blades.

References

Abbink K, Gangadharan L, Handfield T, Thrasher J (2017) Peer punishment promotes enforcement of bad social norms. Nat Commun 8:609. https://doi.org/10.1038/s41467-017-00731-0

Anderson E (2000) Beyond Homo Economicus: new developments in theories of social norms. Philos Public Aff 29:170–200. https://doi.org/10.1111/j.1088-4963.2000.00170.x

Aquinas T (1947) Summa Theologica (a treatise in theology). Benziger Bros, New York

Batson CD, Shaw LL (1991) Evidence for altruism: toward a pluralism of prosocial motives. Psychol Inq 2:107–122. https://doi.org/10.1207/s15327965pli0202_1

Bicchieri C (2006) The grammar of society: the nature and dynamics of social norms. Cambridge University Press, Cambridge

Bicchieri C, Chavez A (2010) Behaving as expected: public information and fairness norms. J Behav Decis Mak 23:161–178. https://doi.org/10.1002/bdm.648

Bicchieri C, Xiao E (2008) Do the right thing: but only if others do so. J Behav Decis Mak 22:191–208. https://doi.org/10.1002/bdm.621

---

power entirely to the law's ability to facilitate coordination expressively'. McAdams (2015), p. 7 and 57–67.

[73] Hart (2012), pp. 21, 39.

Bicchieri C, Dimant E, Xiao E (2017) Deviant or wrong? The effects of norm information on the efficacy of punishment. CeDex Discussion Paper Series

Bowles S, Gintis H (2011) A cooperative species: human reciprocity and its evolution. Princeton University Press, Princeton

Brennan J (2017) Private governance and the three biases of political philosophy. Rev Austrian Econ:1–9. https://doi.org/10.1007/s11138-017-0384-1

Burazin L (2019) The concept of law and efficacy. In: Sellers M, Kirste S (eds) Encyclopedia of philosophy of law and social philosophy. Springer

Burton-Chellew MN, Mouden CE, West SA (2017) Evidence for strategic cooperation in humans. Proc R Soc B 284:20170689. https://doi.org/10.1098/rspb.2017.0689

Darley JM, Sanderson C, LaMantia PS (1996) Community standards for defining attempt: inconsistencies with the model penal code. Am Behav Sci 39:405–420. https://doi.org/10.1177/0002764296039004005

Darley JM, Carlsmith KM, Robinson PH (2001) The ex ante function of the criminal law. Law Soc Rev 35:165–190. https://doi.org/10.2307/3185389

Dawes RM, Van de Kragt AJ, Orbell JM (1990) Cooperation for the benefit of us—not me, or my conscience. In: Mansbridge J (ed) Beyond self-interest. University of Chicago Press, Chicago, pp 97–110

Ellickson RC (1991) Order without law: how neighbors settle disputes. Harvard University Press

Ellickson RC (2017) Forceful self-help and private voice: how Schauer and McAdams exaggerate a State's ability to monopolize violence and expression. Law Soc Inq 42:49–59. https://doi.org/10.1111/lsi.12268

Embrey M, Fréchette GR, Yuksel S (2018) Cooperation in the finitely repeated Prisoner's dilemma. Q J Econ 133:509–551. https://doi.org/10.1093/qje/qjx033

Fehr E, Rockenbach B (2003) Detrimental effects of sanctions on human altruism. Nature 422:137–140. https://doi.org/10.1038/nature01474

Finnis J (2011) Natural law and natural rights, 2nd edn. Oxford University Press, Oxford

Frey BS, Oberholzer-Gee F (1997) The cost of price incentives: an empirical analysis of motivation crowding-out. Am Econ Rev 87:746–755

Gaus G (2016) The open society as a rule-based order. Erasmus J Philosophy Econ 9:1–13

Gibson JL, Caldeira GA, Spence LK (2005) Why do people accept public policies they oppose? Testing legitimacy theory with a survey-based experiment. Polit Res Q 58:187–201. https://doi.org/10.1177/106591290505800201

Gneezy U, Rustichini A (2000) A fine is a price. J Leg Stud 29:1–17. https://doi.org/10.1086/468061

Greenberg M (2018) How law affects behaviour. Jurisprudence 9:374–384. https://doi.org/10.1080/20403313.2017.1333256

Hart HLA (2012) The concept of law, 3rd edn. Oxford University Press, Oxford

Heyman J, Ariely D (2004) Effort for payment. A tale of two markets. Psychol Sci 15:787–793. https://doi.org/10.1111/j.0956-7976.2004.00757.x

Himma KE (2016) The authorisation of coercive enforcement mechanisms as a conceptually necessary feature of law. Jurisprudence 7:593–626

Huang BI (2017) Law and moral dilemmas (book review). Harv Law Rev 130:659–700

Hughes RC (2018) Would many people obey non-coercive law? Jurisprudence 9:361–367. https://doi.org/10.1080/20403313.2017.1333257

Jones MM, Bayer R (2007) Paternalism & its discontents: motorcycle helmet laws, libertarian values, and public health. Am J Public Health 97:208–217. https://doi.org/10.2105/AJPH.2005.083204

Kim PT (1997) Bargaining with imperfect information: a study of worker perceptions of legal protection in an at-will world. Cornell Law Rev 83:105–160

Lamond G (2001) Coercion and the nature of law. Legal Theory 7:35–57

Lessig L (1998) The new Chicago school. J Leg Stud 27:661–691. https://doi.org/10.1086/468039

McAdams RH (2000) A focal point theory of expressive law. Va Law Rev 86:1649–1729. https://doi.org/10.2307/1073827

McAdams RH (2015) The expressive powers of law: theories and limits. Harvard University Press, Cambridge

McAdams RH, Nadler J (2005) Testing the focal point theory of legal compliance: the effect of third-party expression in an experimental hawk/dove game. J Empir Leg Stud 2:87–123. https://doi.org/10.1111/j.1740-1461.2005.00032.x

McAdams RH, Nadler J (2008) Coordinating in the shadow of the law: two contextualized tests of the focal point theory of legal compliance. Law Soc Rev 42:865–898. https://doi.org/10.1111/j.1540-5893.2008.00361.x

Miotto L (2016) Evaluating the force of law's force. Aust J Legal Philosophy 40:229–236

Mullen E, Nadler J (2008) Moral spillovers: the effect of moral violations on deviant behavior. J Exp Soc Psychol 44:1239–1245. https://doi.org/10.1016/j.jesp.2008.04.001

Nadler J (2004) Flouting the law. Tex Law Rev 83:1399–1442

Nadler J (2017) Expressive law, social norms, and social groups. Law Soc Inq 42:60–75. https://doi.org/10.1111/lsi.12279

Ostrom E (1990) Governing the commons: the evolution of institutions for collective action. Cambridge University Press, New York

Papachristos AV, Meares TL, Fagan J (2012) Why do criminals obey the law? The influence of legitimacy and social networks on active gun offenders. J Crim Law Criminol (1973-) 102:397–440

Paternoster R (2010) How much do we really know about criminal deterrence? J Crim Law Criminol 100:765–823

Plaxton M (2012) The challenge of the bad man. McGill Law J 58:451–482

Robinson PH, Darley JM (2004) Does criminal law deter? A behavioural science investigation. Oxf J Leg Stud 24:173–205. https://doi.org/10.1093/ojls/24.2.173

Robinson PH, Goodwin GP, Reisig MD (2010) The disutility of injustice. N Y Univ Law Rev 85:1940–2033

Ross D (2012) The economic agent: not human, but important. In: Mäki U (ed) Philosophy of economics, 1st edn. Elsevier, North Holland, pp 627–671

Schauer F (2015) The force of law. Harvard University Press, Cambridge

Schauer F (2017) Preferences for law? Law Soc Inq 42:87–99. https://doi.org/10.1111/lsi.12281

Sherman L (1993) Defiance, deterrence, and irrelevance: a theory of the criminal sanction. J Res Crime Delinq 30:445–473. https://doi.org/10.1177/0022427893030004006

Spinoza B (2007) Theological-political treatise. Cambridge University Press

Stringham EP (2015) Private governance: creating order in economic and social life. Oxford University Press, New York

Thaler RH (2000) From homo economicus to homo sapiens. J Econ Perspect 14:133–141

Tyler TR (2006a) Why people obey the law. Princeton University Press, Princeton

Tyler TR (2006b) Psychological perspectives on legitimacy and legitimation. Annu Rev Psychol 57:375–400. https://doi.org/10.1146/annurev.psych.57.102904.190038

Tyler TR, Jackson J (2014) Popular legitimacy and the exercise of legal authority: motivating compliance, cooperation, and engagement. Psychol Public Policy Law 20:78

Weber M (1978) Economy and society: an outline of interpretive sociology. University of California Press, Berkeley

Part III
Law and Morality

Does Hart's *Postscript* Provide a Plausible Path to Inclusive Legal Positivism?

J. J. Moreso

Abstract In Hart's *Postscript* the following dilemma is introduced: either the thesis of moral objectivity is true and, then, determining what the law requires may depend on moral arguments, or else that thesis is false and, then, when the law refers to morality it only makes recommendations to the courts to make law in accordance with morality. This paper is intended to show that, on either horn of the dilemma—as Hart seems to understand it—his account remains in the sphere of exclusive legal positivism, and any room for *soft-positivism* is closed off.

1 Introduction

The importance of the posthumous publication of H. L. A. Hart's *Postscript* for legal theory —and for our reflections on the nature of law—can hardly be ignored.[1] Surely, not since the publication of Dworkin's *The Model of Rules*[2] has any work produced so much literature about the scope and limits of Hartian legal positivism, as presented in his masterpiece.[3] Since the publication of Hart's *Postscript*, legal positivism appears to be clearly divided between those who think that, for conceptual reasons, identifying the law never depends on moral arguments—i.e. defenders of *exclusive legal positivism*—and others who fundamentally argue that when

I am very grateful to the editors of the volume, Jorge Luis Fabra-Zamora and Gonzalo Villa Rosas, for valuable comments, corrections and suggestions. The work has benefited from two research grants: DER2016-80471-C2-1-R of the Spanish Government and 2017 SGR 00823 from the Generalitat of Catalonia.

[1]Hart (1994).
[2]Dworkin (1967).
[3]Hart (1961).

J. J. Moreso (✉)
Pompeu Fabra University, Department of Law, Barcelona, Spain
e-mail: josejuan.moreso@upf.edu

J. L. Fabra-Zamora, G. Villa Rosas (eds.), *Conceptual Jurisprudence*, Law and Philosophy Library 137, https://doi.org/10.1007/978-3-030-78803-2_8

sources of law appeal to morality, determining what the law requires depends on moral arguments—i.e. defenders of *inclusive legal positivism*. Accordingly, the former theorists hold that when legal sources appeal to morality, they refer to judicial discretion, while the latter theorists reject this extreme.[4] Inclusive legal positivism is apparently how Hart himself understood positivism, and indeed he says so in the *Postscript*, where he terms this view *soft positivism*.[5]

In this brief commentary, I want to show that, in the *Postscript*, Hart also poses a dilemma that, it seems to me, leaves no conceptual room for inclusive positivism. And this is what I shall try to argue next.

2 The Dilemma

When Hart argues in his posthumous text about the possibility that law refers to morality, he refers to the question of whether it is acceptable to think that moral judgements have an 'objective standing.'[6] According to Hart, that question should be left open by legal theory. He adds:

> If the question of the objective standing of moral judgements is left open by legal theory, as I claim it should be, then soft positivism cannot be simply characterized as the theory that moral principles or values may be among the criteria of legal validity, since if it is an open question whether moral principles and values have objective standing, it must also be an open question whether 'soft positivist' provisions purporting to include conformity with them among the tests for existing law can have that effect or instead, can only constitute directions to courts to *make* law in accordance with morality.[7]

Therefore, and this is the dilemma, either the thesis of moral objectivity is true and, then, determining what the law requires may depend on moral arguments, or else that thesis is false and, then, when the law appeals to morality it only makes recommendations to courts to make law in accordance with morality.[8] Then, Hart accepts that the truth of the thesis of moral objectivity is a necessary condition for the adequation of *Inclusive Legal Positivism.* I shall next try to show that, on either horn

[4]The same year the *Postscript* was published, the first systematic presentation of inclusive legal positivism was published by Waluchow (1994); see also Kramer (1999), Coleman (2001), and presentations of its main ideas in Moreso (2001) and Himma (2002). For exclusive legal positivism, see the defence formulated by Raz (1979, 1994, 2004); see also Gardner (2001), Shapiro (2011), Marmor (2011), and a good general presentation in Marmor (2002).

[5]Hart (1994), p. 250.

[6]Hart (1994), pp. 253–254.

[7]Hart (1994), p. 254.

[8]This passage has attracted attention and sparked discussion; see e.g. Himma (1999); Kramer (1999), pp. 152–161; Orrego (2004); Finnis (2007), pp. 48–53; Green (2012), pp. xlii–xlv. See also Moreso (2001): if I then thought I had a way to defend Hart's position, I have since changed my mind, as will become clear shortly. The expression 'objective standing', as Hart himself admits (200), p. 253, comes from Dworkin (1984), p. 250.

of the dilemma—as Hart seems to understand it—his account remains in the sphere of exclusive legal positivism, without leaving any room for *soft positivism*.

3 Objective Standing and Reasons for Action

In one of his last writings, Hart's position about legal norms and their capacity to become reasons for action,[9] seems to approach Raz conception of legal norms as protected reasons for action: first-order reasons to do what legal rules require, and exclusionary second-order reasons not to act in accordance with any first-order reasons that are contrary to legal rules.[10] A conception that leads Raz, via his conception of authority, to the idea that legal norms as protected reasons always pre-empt other considerations in practical reasoning, and so, in order to identify their content we should not appeal to moral reasons or arguments, because that would amount to losing their capacity to pre-empt: appealing to moral reasons consists precisely in deliberating about first-order reasons for action and about their force or scope.[11] Also, Hart (1982, ch. 10), acknowledging his debt to Raz (1975, 1979) in this respect, and reflecting on the idea of command in Thomas Hobbes and Jeremy Bentham, argues that legal norms, like promises, provide us with reasons for action that are *peremptory and content-independent*: reasons that exclude deliberation about the merits of carrying out such action. And, in this way, this conception of legal norms precludes the possibility that law can be identified through moral considerations. If this were so, Hart's conception could end up like Raz's: recognizing that legal duties are a kind of moral duty, albeit excluding deliberation. Hart (1982, pp. 262–263) considers this possibility but rejects it:[12]

> Of course, if it were the case, as a cognitive account of duty would hold it to be, that the statement that the subject has a legal duty to act in a way contrary to his interests and inclinations entails the statement that there exist reasons which are 'external' or objective, in the sense that they exist independently of his subjective motivation, it would be difficult to deny that legal duty is a form of moral duty. At least this would be so if it is assumed that ordinary non-legal moral judgments of duty are also statements of such objective reasons for action. For in that case, to hold that legal and moral duties were conceptually independent

[9] Hart (1982) ch. 10.

[10] Raz's (1975).

[11] See e.g. Raz (1994).

[12] This way of rejecting it, however, leads Caracciolo (2009) essay 14 to argue that, for Hart, the rejection of moral objectivism is a conceptual feature of legal positivism—as it was for Ross (1998), for von Wright (1985), and at some point for Bulygin (i.e. his position in Caracciolo (1993) later amended in Bulygin (2006))—because if morality were objective, then legal duties would be a kind of moral duty. Perhaps Hart's thesis is not so strong: he holds that if legal duties were to imply objective reasons for action, then legal duties would be a kind of moral duty; but he rejects the antecedent of that conditional, and perhaps could remain neutral about the thesis of moral objectivity (i.e. allowing that moral reasons can provide objective reasons to act). See Moreso (2016).

would involve the extravagant hypothesis that there were two independent 'worlds' or sets of objective reasons, one legal and the other moral.

So, if Hart were to accept a cognitive account of duty, it would lead him to a position like Raz's: legal propositions are a kind of practical proposition that are not committed but rather detached and adopted from a determinate point of view.[13] This would likely lead him to a doctrine of authority like Raz's that implies exclusive legal positivism: not incorporating morality when identifying what the law requires. But Hart rejects this path. He does so because he doesn't believe that legal authorities' claim to authority can be compared with the claim of theoretical authorities, which, in its two versions, is founded either in the recognition of those authorities' wisdom or in (some people's) belief in such wisdom. For Hart, this is not accurate in the case of legal authorities: the habit of doing so is enough, a kind of 'technically confined way' of speaking.[14]

Moreover, Hart seems to reject the existence of objective or external reasons for action. As Finnis points out in his commentary,[15] near the end of his life, while reviewing Bernard Williams's influential *Ethics and the Limits of Philosophy*, Hart (1986) seems to accept the Humean version of Williams, according to which all reasons for action are internal, i.e. somehow linked with our motivational structure, and hence there are no external reasons for our motives and desires.[16]

Hart's metaethical position is not always clear. And this is not the place to enter into the debate that was opened by Williams's position on reasons for action.[17] It is worthwhile, perhaps, to caution that there are ways to argue that all reasons are internal, but not subjective or merely motivational—compatible with moral objectivism—for instance, by arguing that the reasons one has for action are those that one would have, if one were completely rational and had a coherent and ordered set of desires.[18]

Be that as it may, Finnis is right that in this text Hart shows the more Humean and subjectivist side of his metaethics.[19] Inclining it, then, not towards a neutral position about the objectivity of morality, but rather towards a skeptical position about the objectivity of morality. In that case, he would again fall into something like exclusive positivism, now not *Razianally* as a consequence of the doctrine of authority, but simply because morality has no *objective standing*.[20]

---

[13]Raz (1979).

[14]Hart (1982), p. 266.

[15]Finnis (2007).

[16]Hart (1986) reviewing Williams (1985).

[17]Williams (1979).

[18]See Smith (1994).

[19]A position that, as Finnis himself notes, is confirmed by a Hart *connoisseur* as fine as Raz (2001), pp. 4–6.

[20]This is precisely Bulygin's position (2006).

That doesn't mean that Hart would take the rejection of moral objectivism to be a defining feature of legal positivism,[21] but without a doubt, if he considered moral objectivism to be a false doctrine, his acceptance of *soft positivism* becomes somewhat more unstable.

4 Conclusion

If we accept that Hart failed to ground his defence of inclusive legal positivism,[22] then perhaps we must conclude that he should take two distinct routes to support it: on the one hand by allowing room for the objectivity of morality—which doesn't necessarily mean embracing *moral realism* as a metaphysical thesis—and on the other hand, by adopting a theory of authority in law that doesn't entail rejecting moral argumentation as part of our reasoning towards identifying what the law requires.

The first could perhaps be achieved through some constructivist perspective,[23] or through some form of objectivism that is not metaphysically committed, in the sense that there is a place for moral reasons without causal relations to other facts and, therefore, compatible with naturalism for empirical sciences. In an analogous way, there I a place for mathematical, abstract, entities without causal relations to other facts, but clear candidates to the objectivity.[24]

The second entails a way to allow moral reasoning into law without giving up on explaining its institutional nature.[25] Referring to the Raz's doctrine for authority, which excludes moral considerations for the identification of law, Dworkin notes: 'Raz thinks law cannot be authoritative unless those who accept it *never* use their own conviction to decide what it requires, even in this partial way. But why must law be blind authority rather than authoritative in the more relaxed way other conceptions assume?'[26] Perhaps a conception able to reject the so-called *Standard Picture*, which presupposes that 'a norm is legally valid simply in virtue of its being

[21]In fact, already in his important (1958) Hart had rejected, upon consideration, the synonymy between legal positivism and moral non-cognitivism.

[22]As is well known, the preface of *The Concept of Law* (1961) starts by declaring that the objective of the book is an adequate understanding of law, coercion and morality, as distinct yet interrelated social phenomena. Perhaps this tension in Hart's work shows his difficulties in showing precisely what room he leaves for law between coercion and morality. But this issue would take too far afield.

[23]A good overview can be found in Bagnoli (2015).

[24]As Parfit (2011) has recently argued, along the lines of Nagel (1986), Dworkin (1996) or Scanlon (2014).

[25]For the institutional dimension, see Atienza and Ruiz Manero (2001).

[26]Dworkin (1986), pp. 429–430 note 3.

authoritatively pronounced,'[27] would explain how moral considerations contribute to identifying what the law requires.[28]

Both suggestions, sadly, must wait for another occasion.

References

Atienza M, Ruiz Manero J (2001) La dimensión institucional del derecho y la justificación jurídica. Doxa 24:115–130

Bagnoli C (2015) Constructivism in Metaethics, *The Stanford Encyclopedia of Philosophy* (Spring 2015 Edition), Edward N. Zalta (ed.), URL = http://plato.stanford.edu/archives/spr2015/entries/constructivism-metaethics/

Bulygin E (2006) El positivismo jurídico. Mexico, Fontamara

Caracciolo R (1993) Entrevista al Prof. Eugenio Bulygin. *Doxa* 14:499–515

Caracciolo R (2009) Realismo moral vs. positivismo jurídico. In: Caracciolo R (ed) *El Derecho desde la filosofía. Ensayos*. Centro de Estudios Constitucionales, Madrid, essay 14

Coleman J (2001) The practice of principle: in defense of a pragmatist approach to legal theory. Oxford University Press, Oxford

Darwall S (2006) The second-person standpoint: morality, respect, and accountability. Harvard University Press, Cambridge

Darwall S (2013) Morality, authority, and law: essays in second-personal ethics. Oxford University Press, Oxford

Dworkin R (1967) The model of rules. Univ Chicago Law Rev 34:14–46

Dworkin R (1984) A reply to critics. In: Cohen M (ed) Ronald Dworkin and the contemporary jurisprudence. Rowman & Allanheld, Totowa

Dworkin R (1986) Law's Empire. Harvard University Press, Cambridge

Dworkin R (1996) Objectivity and truth: you'd better believe it. Philos Public Aff 25:97–139

Finnis J (2007) On hart's ways: law as reason and fact. Am J Jurisprud 52:25–53

Gardner J (2001) Legal positivism: 5 ½ myths. Am J Jurisprud 46:199–226

Green L (2012) Introduction. In: Hart HLA (ed) The concept of law, 3rd edn. Oxford University Press, Oxford, pp xv–lv

Greenberg M (2011) The standard picture and its discontents. Oxf Stud Philos Law 1:39–106

Greenberg M (2014) The moral impact theory of law. Yale Law J 123:1288–1342

Hart HLA (1958) Positivism and the separation of law and morals. Harv Law Rev 71:593–629, now in Hart HLA *Essays in Jurisprudence and Philosophy*. Oxford, OUP, 1983, pp. 21–48

Hart HLA (1961) The concept of law. Oxford University Press, Oxford

Hart HLA (1982) Commands and authoritative legal reasons. In: Hart HLA (ed) Essays on Bentham. Oxford University Press, Oxford, ch. 10

Hart HLA (1986) Who can tell right from wrong review of ethics and the limits of philosophy by Bernard Williams'. *New York Review of Books,* July 17:49-52

Hart HLA (1994) Postscript. In: Hart, HLA The concept of law, 2nd edn, P. Bulloch and Joseph Raz (eds), Oxford, Oxford University Press.

Himma KE (1999) Incorporationism and the objectivity of moral norms. Legal Theory 5:415–434

27 Greenberg (2011), p.102.

28 See, for instance, Greenberg (2011, 2014). Perhaps complemented by some recent applications of Darwall's conception (e.g. 2006, 2013) from a second-person moral perspective, but see also Karr (2007) and Monti (2018).

Himma KE (2002) Inclusive legal positivism. In: Coleman JL, Shapiro SJ (eds) The Oxford handbook of jurisprudence and philosophy of law. Oxford University Press, Oxford, pp 125–165
Kar RB (2007) Hart's Response To Exclusive Legal Positivism. Georgetown Law J 95:393–461
Kramer M (1999) In defense of legal positivism. Law without trimmings. Oxford University Press, Oxford
Marmor A (2002) Exclusive legal positivism. In: Coleman JL, Shapiro SJ (eds) The Oxford handbook of jurisprudence and philosophy of law. Oxford University Press, Oxford, pp 104–112
Marmor A (2011) Philosophy of law. Princeton University Press, Princeton
Monti E (2018) On Darwall's case against the normal justification thesis. Ethics 128:432–445
Moreso JJ (2001) In defense of inclusive legal positivism. In: Chiasoni P (ed) The legal Ought. Torino, Giappichelli, pp 37–64
Moreso JJ (2016) Ethica more iuridico incorporata: Caracciolo. In: Navarro PE, Redondo MC (eds) La filosofía desde el derecho. Homenaje a Ricardo Caracciolo. Fontamara, Mexico, pp 73–84
Nagel T (1986) The view from nowhere. Oxford University Press, Oxford
Orrego C (2004) Hart's last legal positivism. In: Himma KE (ed) Law, morality, and legal positivism: proceedings of the 21st World Congress for Philosophy of Law and Social Philosophy (IVR); Lund, Sweden, 12-18 August 2003. Franz Steiner, Wiesbaden, pp 73–79
Parfit D (2011) On what matters: volume two. Oxford University Press, Oxford
Raz J (1975) Practical reason and norms. Hutchinson, London
Raz J (1979) The authority of law. Oxford University Press, Oxford
Raz J (1994) Ethics in the public domain. Oxford University Press, Oxford
Raz J (2001) Two views of the nature of the theory of law: a partial comparison. In: Coleman JL (ed) Hart's postscript: essays on the postscript to the concept of law. Oxford University Press, Oxford, ch. 1
Raz J (2004) Incorporation by law. Legal Theory 10:1–17
Ross A (1998) Validity and the conflict between positivism and natural law [1961]. In: Paulson SL, Paulson BL (eds) Normativity and norms. Critical perspectives on Kelsenian themes. Oxford University Press, Oxford, pp 148–163
Scanlon TM (2014) Being realistic about reasons. Oxford University Press, Oxford
Shapiro SJ (2011) Legality. Harvard University Press, Cambridge
Smith M (1994) The moral problem. Basil Blackwell, Oxford
Von Wright GH (1985) Is and ought. In: Bulygin E, Gardies JL, Niiniluoto I (eds) Man, law and modern forms of life. Reidel, Dordrecht, pp 263–281
Waluchow WJ (1994) Inclusive legal positivism. Oxford University Press, Oxford
Williams B (1979) Internal and external reasons. In: Harrison R (ed) Rational action. Cambridge University Press, Cambridge, pp 1001–1113
Williams B (1985) Ethics and the limits of philosophy. Fontana Press, London

Law as an Expression of Adopted Justice

Matti Ilmari Niemi

Abstract In this chapter, Matti Ilmari Niemi sets the stage for a novel approach to legal theory that captures the fundamental intuitions of natural law and positivist theories of law while fending off the core objections against them. Concerning natural law jurisprudence, Niemi argues that this approach properly captures that legal systems share many common values and protect human goods. However, mainstream natural law theorists are problematic because their principles either have a religious foundation or might appear as arbitrary. In turn, while legal positivism captures the factual dimensions of law, it fails to adequately capture the role that principles of morality and justice have in the interpretation of legal materials and the application of laws to specific cases. To overcome these issues, Niemi outlines the foundation of a view of law as an "expression of adopted justice." In his view, this theory captures both the factual dimension of legal materials emphasized by positivists, while also describing the role of principles and substantive reasons in legal interpretation and the application of these materials.

1 Introduction

Different theories of law have different views on the relationship between law and morals. The crucial question is about the role of justice in legal knowledge and interpretation. Traditionally, natural law jurisprudence and legal positivism have maintained two opposite views on the role of justice.

According to the *natural law jurisprudence*, valid law is an actualization of a certain kind of justice. As far as legal validity is concerned, given principles of natural law, protecting human goods, have the ruling position. Therefore, and in this sense, there is a necessary relationship between law and morals.

On the contrary, a supporter of *legal positivism* treats law as a factual phenomenon. Per this view, law appears as rules, decisions and outcomes of human will, and

M. I. Niemi (✉)
University of Eastern Finland, Joensuu, Finland
e-mail: matti.niemi@uef.fi

J. L. Fabra-Zamora, G. Villa Rosas (eds.), *Conceptual Jurisprudence*, Law and Philosophy Library 137, https://doi.org/10.1007/978-3-030-78803-2_9

law is not dependent on justice or morals. Often, morals are understood as personal feelings or opinions and as such powerless in relation to law.

The author of this article treats law as an expression of justice. On the other hand, certain and given principles of justice or morals are not adopted as the starting point. This approach is introduced as the *legal point of view*, in the form of *legal knowledge* understood as *interpretation* and *understanding*, employed by judges and legal scholars.

In legal interpretation, sections of *statutes* and/or *precedents* are treated as the given *starting points*. On the other hand, they are understood as an *expression of justice* as well as other *substantial reasons*. There are certain principles of justice and other substantial reasons adopted and confirmed in a society in the forms of statutes and precedents. The adopted and confirmed justice can be shown and known with the help of statutes and precedents. In this way, the pointed principles of justice as well as other substantial reasons are exploited as effective reasons in legal interpretation.

Legal knowledge appearing as legal interpretation and understanding is a combined operation of and the *interplay* between formal and substantial reasons.

2 On Natural Law Jurisprudence

Natural law jurisprudence had the predominant position in Europe from the Middle Ages until the nineteenth century. That is, until the adoption of modern societies and states as well as the rise of positivistic legal thinking. *Necessary relation between law and morality* is the most fundamental feature of traditional natural law jurisprudence and its most distinctive feature separating it from a positivistic understanding of law. According to the natural *law* tradition law is treated as a *special case of morality*.

Thomas Aquinas is the father and paragon of traditional natural law school in Europe. Besides him, here, the focus has been laid on *John Finnis* who has continued Aquinas' project.[1]

According to traditional natural law, jurisprudence demands of morality appear as the *orders of practical reason*. In Aquinas's words, law is nothing else but a dictate of practical reason, and as such, it is eternal and a manifestation of divine reason.[2] The natural law is promulgated by the very fact that God instilled it into man's mind so as to be known by him naturally.[3] Therefore, the natural law is nothing else than

[1]See Bix (1996), p. 228.

[2]Aquinas (1943), first part of the second part, question 91, article 1.

[3]Aquinas (1943), first part of the second part, question 90, article 4. Accordingly, here, the will of God is treated as the foundation of morals and law. This is the foundation of voluntaristic natural law theories. See Bix (2002), p. 68.

the rational creature's participation of the eternal law.[4] No doubt, according to Aquinas, all laws have a certain given foundation and provenance: God's order. In addition, following the principles of *Aristotelian philosophy*, Aquinas regards law first and foremost as the order to the common good.[5]

According to Finnis, however, natural law can be understood without adverting to the questions of the existence of God and certain faith. In addition, his own approach to natural law offers such an interpretation.[6] The possibility for a secular approach is a significant feature of European modern natural law thinking after the seventeenth century.[7]

The principles of natural law constitute a crucial point of natural law doctrine. They are certain, given principles protecting human goods. They are eternal and immutable.[8] According to John Finnis, they have no history.[9] They are certain and given things because human beings as creatures are certain and given things. Therefore, there is *no history* of human beings or human goods either. Accordingly, it is presumed that human beings and their goods are self-evident, eternal and immutable.[10] The basic features of human societies are eternal and immutable as well. The doctrine of natural law appears *static*, which has been one of the traditional objects of critique provided by the leading legal positivists.[11]

According to the basic principles of natural law theory, *positive* (human) *law*, that is, law created and enacted by human societies, *derives its validity from natural law*, that is, from the certain and given principles in two different ways. First, as conclusions from premises, that is, from the principles of natural law, and second, by way of determination of certain generalities.[12]

Because of the second way, there are variable *determinations* in the frames of the principles of natural law. Positive laws are different in different places and times; they are variable determinations.

---

[4] Aquinas (1943), first part of the second part, question 91, article 2. See Finnis (1980), p. 398.

[5] Aquinas (1943), first part of the second part, question 90, article 3.

[6] Finnis (1980), pp. 49, 402 and 403.

[7] Bix (2002), p. 67. See also Finnis (2002), p. 6.

[8] See Finnis (2002), p. 1.

[9] Finnis (1980), p. 24. In addition to natural and human (positive) law Thomas Aquinas defines and mentions two other laws: eternal and divine (divided into old and new). On the other hand, Aquinas seems to deny law in the fomes of sin. See Aquinas (1943), first part of the second part, question 91 and 93. According to Aquinas, the principles (precepts) of the natural law are many in themselves but are based on one common foundation and principle (the first principle). The first principle is "good is to be done and pursued, and evil is to be avoided". Aquinas (1943), first part of the second part, question 94. Finnis mentions the fulfilment of all basic human goods as the master principle. Finnis (2002), p. 28.

[10] See, for instance, in the case of knowledge ("knowledge is good") as a basic value and a practical principle. Finnis (1980), p. 64.

[11] See, for instance, Kelsen (1961), p. 399; Hart (1994), p. 92.

[12] Aquinas (1943), first part of the second part, question 91, article 3 and question 95, article 2. Determination means here "making specific or concrete". See Bix (1996), p. 225.

Principles of natural law are general, and therefore, adjustments, qualifications and choices are needed. On the other hand, it is presumed that all the *positive laws*, in order to be correct and valid, are *enacted on the condition of the principles of natural law*. That is, in terms of Finnis, "natural law 'already somehow in existence' does not itself provide all or even most of the solutions to the co-ordination problems of communal life."[13]

Natural law is in the dominant position in relation to positive law, but natural law proves to be insufficient in this respect. In addition, because of human weaknesses and in order to maintain peace and virtues, it is necessary for positive laws to be framed.[14] For practical reasons, legal procedures and forms are necessary. Ultimately, they are exercised for the protection of human goods.[15]

Determination in the form of legislation and precedents is needed because of the general nature of principles of natural law. However, sections of statutes, as well as precedents, prove to be vague and imprecise as well. Therefore, determination in the form of conventional legal *interpretation* is needed as well.[16]

Conflicts between natural law and positive laws are possible. According to Aquinas, every human law has just so much of the nature of law, as it is derived from the law of nature. But if at any point a human law deflects from the law of nature, it is no longer a law but a perversion of law.[17] Despite its formal correctness and enforcement, such a law is unjustified and *lacks legitimation*, moral authority as well as the "true" legal authority.[18] From the viewpoint of natural law jurisprudence, such laws are valid in the formal sense but *defective*.

---

[13]Finnis (1980), p. 28.

[14]Aquinas (1943), first part of the second part, question 95, article 1. On the other hand, positive law also is deficient in relation to natural law. Positive law does not forbid all vicious acts, by the obligation of a precept, as neither does it prescribe all acts of virtue. Aquinas, first part of the second part, question 96, article 2 and 3.

According to Aquinas (1943), the natural law is a participation of the eternal law and therefore endures without change, owing to the unchangeableness and perfection of the Divine Reason, the Author of nature. But the reason of man is changeable and imperfect: wherefore his law is subject to change. The natural law contains certain universal precepts, which are everlasting: whereas human law contains certain particular precepts, according to various emergencies. Moreover, human law is rightly changed, in so far as such change is conducive to the common weal. Aquinas (1943), first part of the second part, question 97, articles 1 and 2.

[15]See Finnis (2002), pp. 30 and 34.

[16]Finnis (2002), p. 38.

[17]Aquinas (1943), first part of the second part, question 95, article 2. Here, Aquinas appeals to Saint Augustine.

[18]See Finnis (1980), p. 354; Bix (1996), p. 226; Finnis (2002), pp. 12 and 22.

The eternal and given principles of natural law appearing as practical reasoning and moral (good) reasons and as part of law and legal reasoning demonstrates the necessary relation between law and morals. As far as acceptable positive law and jurisdiction is concerned, the necessary relation is granted. On the other hand, sections of statutes, precedents or other judgements, that is, positive law or its applications can be immoral and unacceptable, that is, contrary to the principles. In this sense, paradoxically, there is no necessary relation between law and morals even according to natural law thinking. The first approach bears internal approach to law, the essential approach, obeying the

The adopted relationship between natural law and positive law is applied even to *rights* of citizens. According to Aquinas, a right is a matter of relations between persons, and the natural basis is equality. As a natural dimension of rights (a natural right), for instance, there is the principle of the proper price (as an application of Aristotelian *iustitia commutativa*). On the other hand, there are dimensions of rights founded on positive law, that is, human determinations (positive rights). Positive law means here both private agreements and their terms and public agreements as statutes or precedents.[19]

Accordingly, all acts of virtue, considered as virtuous, belong to the natural law. This is the area of *speculative reason*. Speculative reason is busied chiefly with the necessary things, which cannot be otherwise than they are, its proper conclusions, like the universal principles, contain the truth without fail. Therefore, by human nature, we may mean which is proper to man, and in this sense, all sins, as being against reason are also against nature. As a rule, the natural law is altogether unchangeable. But virtuous acts, considered in themselves in their proper species, are not necessarily prescribed by the natural law. Many things are done virtuously, to which nature does not incline at first, but which, through the inquiry of reason, have been found by men to be conducive to well-living. This is the area of *practical reason*. The truth or rectitude of the proper conclusions of practical reasoning are not the same for all and neither, where they are the same, are they equally known by all.[20]

According to natural law theory, on a large scale, *law is a universal order*. The differences between legal systems are secondary. As far as the most important elements of law are concerned, law is treated as a universal issue and affair common to all societies and people. According to Aquinas, it is evident that, as regards the general principles whether of speculative or of practical reason, truth or rectitude is the same for all, and is equally known by all.[21] These principles are self-evident but, on the other hand, understanding and mature reasoning is needed in order to see them.[22]

The first principles of natural law are treated as given things, as self-evident and indemonstrable. According to Aquinas, their *foundation* is the *given* and immutable eternal and divine *orders*. Ultimately, the existence of legal order has a religious explanation.[23] The defence of natural law thinking has often been allied with the authority of the Catholic Church.

---

principle 'no ought from mere is' and the second one the external approach to law describing certain decisions as "legal facts". The latter one is not treated as a sufficient or intrinsic approach. See Finnis (2002), pp. 11, 14 and 16.

[19]Aquinas (1943), second part of the second part, question 57, article 1 and 2.

[20]Aquinas (1943), first part of the second part, question 94, articles 3, 4 and 5.

[21]Aquinas (1943), first part of the second part, question 94, article 4.

[22]Finnis (1980), p. 31.

[23]Bix (1996), p. 225.

According to Finnis, however, the *first principles* are *not inferred from anything*. Principles of right and wrong are derived from the first principles.[24] The derivation is made with the help of intermediate principles, which indicate basic requirements of practical reasonableness.[25]

The natural law *method* appears as working out the (moral) 'natural law' from the first (pre-moral) 'principles of natural law'. The aspiration of the method is to show reasons why (and thus the ways in which) there are things that morally ought or ought not to be done.[26]

Both Aquinas and Finnis treat positive law, like statutes and precedents, as norms of proper law when enacted on the condition of the principles of natural law. *Knowledge of law*, legal interpretation and jurisdiction appear as *practical reasoning* made on the condition and in the frames of the given principles of natural law.[27] On a large scale, positive law is treated as derived from natural law.[28]

The sphere of law proves to be large and open to *substantial reasons*. As a matter of fact, all speak of normativity is legal.[29] Accordingly, all moral arguments founded on practical wisdom bearing the given principles are essential parts of legal reasoning, and their objectivity is granted. Arguments from and for justice, protecting human goods and promoting them are natural legal reasons.[30] Natural law principles are treated as necessary conditions of a flourishing community, and they indicate the standards of proper and natural life of human beings. Even *contra-legem* interpretations and judgement, that is, deviations from the wordings of statutes or precedents, founded on the objective moral reasons, are conventional solutions.

3 Critical Notes on Natural Law Jurisprudence

Traditional natural law jurisprudence is often founded on the assumption of *divine order* as the given foundation of human beings and human societies. This is the approach adopted by Thomas Aquinas. It seems to be, however, that the presumed universal order appearing as the principles of natural law is a dimension of the *Christian world*, and more precisely, in the frames of the Catholic Church. The "universe" of the adopted universalism seems to, after all, restricted.

---

[24] Finnis (1980), p. 33.

[25] Finnis (1980), p. 33; Bix (1996), p. 229.

[26] Finnis (1980), p. 103.

[27] Bix (1996), p. 223.

[28] Aquinas (1943), first part of the second part, question 95, article 2 and Finnis (1980), p. 281.

[29] Finnis (2002), p. 1. Because of the large and open sphere of law jurisprudence expand to the field of ethics as well as political philosophy and vice versa. There are no strict borderlines. Finnis (2002), p. 18.

[30] See Finnis (2002), p. 28.

The *religious foundation* appears irrelevant, redundant and even misleading from the legal point of view. Association with beliefs of a particular religious tradition, doctrine and faith appears either unnecessary or harmful. The approaches adopted by many supporters of rationalist natural law during the seventeenth century and that after, for instance, made by John Finnis, are good examples. They bypass or abandon the presumption of the existence of God and the certain divine order as the foundations of natural law and legal systems.

Accordingly, I take as granted that legal knowledge is not founded on religious or theological arguments. They are irrelevant from the legal point of view. In addition, they might turn out to be even harmful from the viewpoints of equality and freedom of religion.

Secular versions of natural law thinking prove to be insufficient and misleading as well. I put forward *two critical notes* on these approaches. The aspiration of the first one is to show the missing foundation of the natural law approach. The aspiration of the second one is to show the irrelevancy of the natural law approach from the point of legal knowledge.

The presumed divine order provides, as such, a solid foundation for both natural and positive law according to a natural law theory. It is a consistent explanation for the given starting points, that is, the certain axioms of a theory and the basic inferences from them.

Abandonment of the presumed divine order means the *abandonment of the* given *foundation* of natural law theory. Despite the abandonment of the divine foundation, the very same axioms and starting points are, nevertheless, preserved, maintained and treated as the given starting points of inferences in a theory of natural law. In other words, despite the abandonment of the given foundation of the axioms the *same axioms* are, nevertheless, adopted and treated as given things but without any explanatory or justifying foundation.

The theory of Finnis is a good example. According to Finnis, principles of natural law, protecting basic human goods, have no history. They are self-evident. They cannot be demonstrated, and they need no demonstration. Accordingly, the axioms of Finnis' theory are given things, but there is *no explanation* or foundation *for the givenness*.

It is true that the basic forms of good, enumerated by Finnis are relevant for human beings. They are, no doubt, objects of legal protection. On the other hand, understanding of these objects does not tell us about their protection. It is not possible to derive norms protecting human goods from the goods themselves. The *protection* can be *arranged in many ways*. The adopted protection and its details bear the crucial legal issues.

It is true, as well, that *practical reasoning*, in the way Finnis has described it, bear an important dimension of legal reasoning. On the other hand, mastering practical reasoning *is not sufficient* in order to gain legal knowledge. Practical reasoning, presented by Finnis, refers to substantial reasons exploited both in legal interpretation and jurisdiction. Substantial reasons are important legal reasons but, nevertheless, they are in the secondary position in legal reasoning. References to *statutes* and/or *precedents*, that is, conventional legal sources are *primary legal reasons*. That is, references to the chosen ways of legal protection of human goods indicate the primary legal reasons. In addition, mastering practical reasoning designates merely mastering a method of legal reasoning. The content and, in the sense of interpretation, objects of legal reasoning are, here again, statutes and/or precedents.

The question framing introduced by the supports or natural law jurisprudence proves to be misleading from the viewpoint of conventional legal knowledge. Legal questions are not questions about given human goods and, after that, about the best possible protection of them. Instead, legal questions are about the *adopted ways of protecting human goods*. There are various ways with various emphases in protecting human goods.

Basically, certain given human goods bear not the given starting point of legal knowledge or reasoning. Instead, the adopted and decided ways of protection of the goods bear the starting point. Therefore, the starting point of reasoning is valid and applicable sections of statutes and precedents. With their help, it is possible to make conclusions about protected human goods and about the ways they are protected as they are adopted in a legal system.

In short, in legal reasoning, legal protection is not inferred from given human goods. On the contrary, protected *human goods are inferred from adopted legal protection*. With the help of knowledge and understanding of adopted legal protection, that is, statutes and/or precedents, it is possible to know and understand human goods protected in a society at certain time.

In words of natural law concepts, in conventional legal knowledge and interpretation, human, that is, *positive law* is in the *primary position*. The principles of "natural law", that is, *substantial reasoning*, referring to the content and justification of positive law, is in the *secondary position*.

This is not, however, an order of importance but a *logical order*. It is the way how knowledge on adopted values and other substantial reasons as parts of legal order is reached in legal interpretation, which is here treated as the form of legal knowledge, as we can see in detail later.

Basically, the assumed universal legal order, on the level of the given principles of natural law and determining different positive legal orders on a large scale, is not a relevant assumption. That kind of assumption is not made by legal scholars or judges when they interpret law. Instead, they start with applicable statutes and precedents of a legal system, and with the help of them, as well as with the help of legal interpretation, they can understand the protected human goods and the ways the goods are protected here and now, that is, as a part of a certain legal system.

Accordingly, natural law theory seems to be rather an ethical theory than a theory of law relevant from the viewpoints of legal doctrine or jurisdiction.[31]

---

[31] According to Bix, "Natural law theory often has little if anything to do with 'law' as that term is conventionally used". Bix (2002), p. 70. Bix's sentence can be interpreted in the following way. Natural law theory is remote and irrelevant from the viewpoint of conventional legal knowledge, legal reasoning and legal doctrine. Instead, it can be treated as an ethical theory, and as such it is, nevertheless, relevant on the level of jurisprudence. This is why we are here discussing about natural law theory.

4 On Positivistic Jurisprudence

The birth and rise of positivistic legal theories at the end of nineteenth century and the beginning of twentieth century is easy to connect, for instance, to the birth of European national states, to the adoption of the Enlightenment and other new European ideologies, to codifications of new state laws, to the rise of philosophical positivism and secularization. In the era of the *new modern Europe*, the traditional doctrine of natural law seemed outdated and unfit. It did not appear anymore as a relevant or realistic study on law.

Here, attention is paid to two important representatives of legal positivism, *Hans Kelsen* as an exclusive positivist and *H.L.A Hart* as an inclusive positivist.

The two most important characteristics of positivistic thinking are the social and separability theses.[32] According to them, law is a matter of fact as decisions or as other social facts, and there is no necessary connection between law and morals. These theses are closely connected.

The *social thesis* is one of the cornerstones of the approaches of both Kelsen and Hart. Kelsen saw legal rules in the form of sections of statutes as legal facts and as the content of the lawgiver's will.[33] For Hart, law appears as existing and valid rules of a legal system identified by the rule of recognition. For him, the existence of a legal system is a social phenomenon.[34]

For Kelsen, legal rules as sections of statutes (basically, the legal ought in the form of imputation) are the defined and existing objects of the statements of legal doctrine. These statements are true or false, and hence, true statements are value-free and objective descriptions of their objects. Moreover, Kelsen employs correspondence as the definition of truth. Accordingly, valid legal rules are social facts, and there is a *special branch of reality* as the object area of legal doctrine.[35]

On the other hand, the existence of legal norms differs from the perceivable reality. Here, existence means *validity*. The special kind of legal reality embodies the will of the lawgiver (in a non-psychological sense).[36] The existence of laws depends on the decisions of the lawgiver. With the help of these philosophical points of departure, Kelsen defended legal doctrine as an acceptable branch of *science* but, at the same time, as an independent branch. The criteria of acceptability were,

From this viewpoint, the description of natural law approach, introduced by Finnis, is understandable. According to him, natural law approach manifests an internal viewpoint. The dominant concern is judging for oneself what reasons are good reasons for adopting or rejecting specific kinds of option. Standards and norms of conduct are never constituted by the facts of convention, custom or consensus. Finnis (2002), p. 4.

[32]Coleman and Leiter (1996), p. 241.

[33]Kelsen (1970), pp. 73 and 79.

[34]Hart (1994), p. 201.

[35]Kelsen (1970), p. 4; Kelsen (2013), p. 196.

[36]Kelsen (1961), pp. 30, 46 and 153; Kelsen (1970), pp. 4, 72 and 76. I interpret the term "a norm" employed by Kelsen as a rule.

nevertheless, provided by philosophical positivism.[37] In addition, there seems to be no room for evaluations in the Kelsenian statements of legal doctrine. For instance, interpretative sentences containing principles of justice are doomed to be subjective.

For Hart, the existence of legal rules or, rather, the *existence of a* certain *legal system* bears, on the one hand, social facts but, on the other hand, validity without any ontological commitments in relation to individual recognized rules. The existence of rules is explained by the membership of a legal system. Validity for Hart is a certain way to *understand language*, which is basically a factual (and contingent) practice.[38] The criteria of validity, in turn, refer to certain *rules of recognition* adopted by a certain society at a certain time. These criteria are reduced in the same way to a certain established *practice* of people and a society.[39] Basically, the existence of the rules of recognition means the existence of a certain practice of judges and other officials and, hence, Hart closes the gap between is and ought, too.[40]

Both main theses of legal positivism, that is, social and separability theses together, entail the *difference* in quality between *law* and *morals*: descriptions of valid law (or expressions of valid law) differ radically from moral evaluations. The existence of legal rules is a social fact, but moral reasons appear as different personal opinions, attitudes, feelings or personal interests, that is, subjective expressions of persons but not descriptions of a certain society.

This presupposition appears in the major texts of positivists. Relativity of moral values in these texts means, in fact, different and contrary personal moral evaluations or values or interests of different groups of persons but not values of societies, that is, shared values of the members of a society as the subjects of a legal system.[41]

---

[37]Humanities and social sciences were under a great pressure assessed by the prevailing positivistic philosophy at the end of nineteenth and at the beginning of twentieth century. Kelsen, like many other theorists, felt obligated to defend legal doctrine as an acceptable branch of science. In addition, Kelsen found it necessary to transform legal doctrine into a branch of science acceptable from the viewpoint of positivistic philosophy. On the other hand, supporters of legal realism went ahead much further in this way.

[38]See e.g. Hart (1960), p. 145; Hart (1984a), p. 23; Hart (1994), p. 94. The influence of the mature Wittgenstein on Hart is obvious here. That is why the phrase 'use in the language' (*Gebraucht in der Sprache*) is important in this respect. An existing practice can be seen as the core of Wittgenstein's idea. See Wittgenstein (1958), I, p. 43. At the level of legal issues, Hart interprets this approach as the thesis according to which a concept's meaning (content) is determined by its use (as a social practice). For the dynamic character of positive law, see also Kelsen (1961), p. 399.

[39]Hart (1994), pp. 101 and 109. About the crucial role of officials as the foundation of existence of a legal system, see Lamond (2013), p. 110.

[40]Both Kelsen and Hart define a crucial crossing point which belong to the world of ought (*sollen*) and to the world of is (*sein*). Kelsen defines legal rules as existing facts with the content of ought. Hart defines the rule of recognition as a norm and, at the same time, an existing fact of a society. See Kelsen (1970), p. 4.

[41]I interpret the texts of Kelsen and Hart as expressing the emotivistic or subjectivistic view on morals. See Kelsen (1970), p. 63; Kelsen (1948); Hart (1994), p. 200; Hart (1984b), p. 82.

According to the positivistic understanding of law, the *sphere of law* is treated *narrowly*. The sphere of law is restricted to *positive law*, that is, in practice, to official sources of law. There are no other kinds of law. Legal reasons are formal reasons referring to statutes or precedents. Instead, moral reasoning appealing to justice or other substantial reasons are doomed to be subjective evaluations, that is, non-legal reasons.

On the other hand, a judge can use substantial reasons in the form of *judicial discretion*. According to positivists, a judge exercising judicial discretion is *acting as a lawgiver*; that is, she or he is creating new law. In controversial cases (hard cases) law proves to be incomplete. In such cases, incomplete law does not provide answers to legal questions. Controversial cases are unregulated cases and, therefore, judges must exercise restricted law-making function. This is a crucial part of the legal doctrine of Kelsen. In such cases, the new rules given by a judge are called individual legal rules.[42] Hart adopts a similar doctrine of judicial discretion.[43]

Finnis criticizes the legal positivists' descriptive approach. According to Finnis and founded on Aristoteles, jurisprudence is part of practical philosophy, and practical philosophy is a disciplined and critical reflection on the goods that can be realized in human action and the requirements of practical reasonableness. It is necessary to assess the importance or significance of similarities and differences within defined subject-matters.[44]

Even descriptive theorists, like legal positivists, should make these choices according to Finnis. They have to define crucial concepts, and they have to decide central cases (typical cases) of the subject matter. On the other hand, they refuse to show the necessary reasons and foundation of their choices and definitions. So, the crucial question is where the concepts and central cases come from. They are excluded from the sphere of law to the pre- or post-legal sphere, for instance, to the sphere of morals as something independent from law by the positivists. Instead, they insist on variable considerations and evaluations of people.[45] Therefore, the positivistic theory is short of its necessary foundation and it proves to be insufficient and misleading.

According to Finnis, practical philosophy, like jurisprudence, must have a practical foundation, that is, reflections on human goods. Legal concepts and central cases as the tools of jurisprudence have to be founded on certain choices embodying the adopted normative goals and justifications of law as the supporters of human flourishing. Central cases have to be identified with the help of requirements of practical reasonableness. Therefore, there is a necessary relation between law and morality, that is, human practical reasonableness.[46]

---

[42] Kelsen (1970), pp. 234 and 237.

[43] Hart (1994), p. 252.

[44] Finnis (1980), pp. 11, 12 and 19.

[45] Finnis (1980), pp. 13–15 and 18.

[46] Here Finnis appeals to Max Weber. See Finnis (1980), p. 16.

5 Critical Notes on Positivistic Jurisprudence

Legal positivism can be blamed for the *misunderstanding about* the role and significance of *statutes* and *precedents* as crucial features of modern societies.

Historical reasons for that, especially in Continental Europe, are obvious. Supporters of modern societies considered the new European societies different from the previous pre-modern societies founded on static and traditionalist worldview. New European societies were detached from the pre-modern traditions and from the influence of religion. A new enlightened society was founded on reasons, and its laws were expressions of the will of the people written in the form of state statutes and enacted by parliaments or heads of the states. In addition, the crucial position of state law, rather, exactly written statutes, was seen as a guarantee of legal certainty and equality of citizens. State laws were not any more expressions of a certain immutable tradition, but expressions of a variable legislative will.

Even the positivistic jurisprudence is *nonhistorical* but in a different sense and way compared with natural law jurisprudence.

Even in the frames of English common law tradition, the nature of law and precedents were seen in a new way, in a positivistic way. Accordingly, it was not convincing or plausible any more to provide certain principles of natural law expressing given, immutable and determinative factors of law.

Legal positivism bears a *narrow conception of law*. It is too narrow, which has been pointed out by the famous criticism of *Ronald Dworkin*.[47] Adoption of the principles of modern society does not compel one to adopt a narrow conception of law. There are, however, even more severe deficiencies included in positivism. Both the main theses of positivism, that is, social and separability theses can be disputed.

According to positivism, law as an object of knowledge appears as social facts. These facts appear as sections of statutes or precedents, and they are described by a judge or a legal scholar. According to Kelsen, as decisions, they are manifestations of the will of the lawgiver.[48] According to Hart, they are known and shown with the help of the rule of recognition, basically founded on practices of judges and other officials.

As social facts law differs from moral evaluations in a crucial way, there is either a deep categorical difference between them (exclusive positivism), or the relationship between is contingent (inclusive positivism).

The idea of knowledge of law as descriptions of social facts can be contested. As far as the narrow conception of law is abandoned, the knowledge of law understood as fact descriptions is not sustainable anymore. The *employment of principles* referring to justice and values is an essential feature of legal knowledge in addition to references to sections of statutes and precedents.

Why are the *principles* important in Dworkin's critique? According to my understanding, principles unite law and morals in a necessary way. Principles appear

---

[47]Dworkin (1977), p. 22.

[48]Kelsen (1970), p. 4.

as *embodiments of justice* and values, and they are independent of the existence or wordings of certain statutes and precedents. Appealing to the justice of a society as well as other moral values is a necessary and significant feature of legal knowledge and reasoning in Western Societies.

In addition, there are *other substantial reasons* employed as legal reasons, like policies, administrative and economic goals and consequences of different options of interpretations or decisions. Advanced legal interpretation and decision making contain many kinds of relevant and applicable reasons independent of wordings of certain sections of statutes or precedents.

Often, principles of justice, policies and goals are seen as the necessary background of sections of statutes and precedents. They are treated as *justifications* and *explanations* of statutes and precedents. Therefore, it is natural and justified to employ them as legal reasons and as a means of interpretation of these sections of statutes or precedents.

In addition, principles of justice, policies and goals are employed in broader ways. *Analogical interpretation*, that is, leaning on sections of statutes or precedents not straight applicable in a situation or case can be justified with the help of principles of justice, policies and goals. The same holds true with the so-called *gaps* in law and *contra-legem* decisions. Many of them can be seen as the Dworkinian hard cases.

Considering the consequences of different interpretations or decision options is similar substantial reasoning independent of wordings of statutes and precedents. It is an essential feature of legal interpretation and decision making.

Appealing to principles of justice, policies, goals and consequences of interpretations and decisions is *substantial reasoning supplementing appealing to applicable sections of statutes or precedents*. It is not a matter of describing law as facts but *understanding law* as a normative and meaningful whole in a justified way. There is a crucial difference between describing facts and understanding something.

Understanding law contains references to applicable sections of authoritative materials, that is, statutes and/or precedents as well as appealing to principles of justice, policies, goals and consequences of interpretations or decisions. This is the real content of advanced knowledge of law. It appears as conventional and advanced legal interpretation. Understood in this way, it is clear that legal knowledge as legal interpretation contains a necessary connection between law and morality, and it does not bear fact descriptions.

6 A Fresh Start: On the Relationship Between Law and Morals in the Frames of Legal Knowledge

In connection with critique against legal positivism, I *assumed* the *necessary relationship between law and morality*. On the other hand, in connection with the critique against natural law thinking, I *abandoned the certain and given system of principles* as the necessary foundation of legal systems and as the given starting point of inferences. Therefore, no doubt, the assumed relationship between law and morality needs clarification.

Here, the adopted viewpoint is a *legal approach*. More precisely, the subject matter is legal knowledge as a topic of jurisprudence. What kind of knowledge is at the stage? What is the role of values in legal knowledge and interpretation? The object of this study is the knowledge of law judges, and legal scholars possess and exercise in their job.

In the field of ethics, it is possible to presume certain human values as the starting point. A common or universal system of human values is often presumed. It is possible to see human norms as applications of these values. This seems to be the viewpoint of natural law theory as well. In the frames of legal viewpoint, the layout is different. The *differences between legal systems* have to be taken seriously. In this respect, the supporters of legal positivism are right. There are different legal systems containing different norms in the contemporary world.

No doubt, there are many *common norms* shared by all legal systems, at least most of them, and there are many *common values* as the groundwork of many, perhaps, all legal systems. In this respect, supporters of natural law jurisprudence are right.

Nevertheless, a legal system bears an *independent system* and, as a whole, an independent object of knowledge. This is the undisputed starting point and presumption in all legal systems. Competent legal knowledge is knowledge in the frames of a certain legal system. Basically, all legal knowledge is knowledge about a legal system. The conventional legal point of view is not a universal viewpoint.

Differences between legal systems or different norms of the systems do not exclude the necessary relationship between law and morals. In the frames of a legal system, *moral values* can be treated as the *foundation of the system*. It is even possible that several systems or all systems share the same values. On the other hand, it is possible that the same values are *interpreted*, that is, applied, emphasized and weighted in *different ways*. Human goods can be protected in many different ways and with the help of many different procedures. Values as such are on the general level. From the legal viewpoint, the crucial issue is the varying ways they are implemented and adapted. As a matter of fact, these differences bear the main source of different norms of different legal systems despite common and shared values.

For instance, in a certain legal system, the adopted balance between contrary principles, expressing adopted values and their adopted weights in the society, is specified and expressed with the help of legal rules. The differences between legal systems are embodied as different legal rules. Moreover, often, the adopted values as the groundwork of the legal system are not an interesting topic as such on the level of legal reasoning. Instead, the adopted balance between values and between conflicting principles is the interesting topic. In addition, in unregulated situations or cases, the proper balance between conflicting principles has to be decided without the straight help of legal rules.[49]

The same holds true with relationships between values and other substantial reasons as the justifying groundwork of legal regulation.[50] Policies or goals of a society are often treated as self-evident and undisputed matters. The interesting matter is the influence and weight of a policy or a goal in relation to certain principles and values, especially in certain situations or cases. An adopted policy or a goal often conflicts with an adopted principle or a value. Protected rights of citizens are often in tension with the policies of their societies.[51]

Therefore, it is not helpful to indicate certain values or goals as such. Normally, there is no disagreement about them. Instead, the crucial and interesting question is whether those values or goals are treated as operative and effective legal reasons and what are the exact weights of those substantial reasons as parts of legal reasoning or decision-making.

Does this mean that there are certain given values expressed with the help of given principles and certain given policies and goals bearing the given starting point of legal interpretation and reasoning? No doubt, my answer is negative. I have already stated that certain given human goods bear not the given starting point of legal knowledge. Instead, the adopted and decided ways of protection of the goods bear the starting point. Therefore, the *starting point* of legal reasoning is valid and applicable sections of *statutes* and/or *precedents*. They are norms about rights and duties as well as procedures. *With their help, it is possible to make conclusions about protected human goods* and especially about the ways they are protected as adopted in a legal system at a certain time.

In a concrete interpretation situation, like a court case or a subject of discussion in legal doctrine, an *established practice of legal reasoning* has been adopted. The first step is to *show applicable* sections of *statutes* or *precedents*. They are applicable if they match the facts of the case or situation in a sufficient way. They are considered effective because of their form. In other words, they are employed as formal reasons in legal interpretation. Even in unregulated situations or cases, this is the first step. Possible rules as the foundation of legal analogy or the lack of applicable rules are the outcome of this step.

---

[49]See Dworkin (1977), pp. 24 and 35.

[50]See Dworkin (1977), p. 82.

[51]Here appears an additional difference compared with traditional and conventional natural law thinking. Following Aristotelian philosophy, it is presumed in natural law tradition that personal goods can be reduced to common good, that is, the goals of the societies of people. Therefore, there cannot be any genuine difference or tension between justified goods of individual people and the goals of their societies. However, the tension between rights belonging to people and common good, that is, policies of their societies is one of the main theses of contemporary legal thinking, emphasized, for instance, by Ronald Dworkin. See Aristotle (2002), book I, chapter 2, 1094b, Aquinas (1943), first part of the second part, question 91, article 2, Finnis (1980), p. 214 and Dworkin (1977), pp. 22, 82, 90.

However, finding applicable sections and/or precedents and considering the applicability or suitability of a section or a precedent contains already legal interpretation. The situation or case has to be described in legal terms, that is, the situation or case has to be perceived in and with the help of proper and suitable legal terms. The crucial question is: *What is this all about in the legal sense?* The relevant question is how the situation or case shall be described and understood from the legal viewpoint and in the frames of the legal system. Here, systematics and relevant concepts of the system are applied. This is a crucial step and form of legal understanding, that is, legal interpretation. Even so-called easy or routine cases always contain this kind of interpretation.

Often, however, different rival sections of statutes or precedents are proposed by the parties of a case or by different legal scholars. The *choice* between proposed sections or precedents will be made with the help of interpretation. It is presumed that the alternative equipped with the *best legal support* will be chosen. Even the applicability and suitability of the only proposed section of a statute or a precedent has to be justified in the same way. There are always many alternative ways to understand a statute or a precedent and many alternative applications of them.

This is the stage of interpretation in which references to *principles* (values), *policies*, *goals* and *consequences* of different options of interpretation start to take place. They are understood as the *justifying factors behind the formal reasons*, that is, statutes and precedents, as their background. Application of a certain section of a statute or a precedent is justified with these substantial reasons. In other words, the application of certain official sources of law (sections of statutes or precedents), that is, formal reasons of interpretation, is justified by substantial reasons.

The order of the stages of legal interpretation is the important issue here. First, the attention is pointed out to the possibly applicable sections of statutes and/or precedents, that is, formal reason of interpretation. Second, the attention is pointed out to the substantial reasons. Substantial reasons are treated as the justifying factors of the applied sections or precedents, that is, something behind the applied sections or precedents and their wordings as their justifications.

The aspiration of legal interpretation is to *understand* the applicable sections of statutes or precedents. It is the core of legal knowledge. The crucial question is: what the purpose or target is, that is, the true normative meaning of this regulation. Understanding wordings is the starting point, but it is not enough. Advanced interpretation requires an understanding of substantial reasons as the justifying reasons for the applied sections or precedents. I take it as granted that all legal decisions and interpretations must be justified in a substantial sense.[52]

[52]In practice, nevertheless, expressions of substantial justifications of decisions or interpretations are limited. Often, references to sections of statutes are enough. Easy or routine decisions, for instance, made by a policeman or another officer, are normally made without any references to principles, values or other substantial reasons. For practical reasons, it is not necessary. Lack of substantial justifications means here that the decision-maker considers the case easy and unproblematic. Even in these cases, however, the decision or interpretation has to be justified and, for instance, in a case of appeal or contest, one must be able to show the substantial

In the cases of legal *analogy* and in *unregulated situations* or cases, principles and other substantial reasons are employed as justifications of analogy and the adopted interpretation in the gap situation. In other words, in these hard cases, because of the lack of applicable rules interpretation and/or decision has to be made directly on the ground of substantial reasons.

Advanced legal interpretation requires an understanding of the applicable *systematics* and *concepts* adopted in the legal system too. In addition to the need for legal perception of situations and cases, specific systematic principles are employed. Systematic reasons function in interpretation in the same way as substantial reasons. Basically, systematic reasons are founded on material justice. Similar cases collected together and being subordinated to a certain concept are treated equally.

Accordingly, values are treated as parts of the justifying framework of statutes and precedents. Statutes and precedents are expressions of adopted justice in a society, and they are understood with the help of adopted values as their background. As a rule, statutes and precedents are applied, but the applications are influenced by values as justifying reasons. Therefore, legal interpretation contains the *necessary relationship between law and* values, that is, *morals*.

The significance of the justifying reasons does not restrict merely to applications of certain sections of statutes or precedents in a certain adopted way. Often, they are treated as the justifying groundwork of a larger part of the legal order. In this way, they can act as justifying reasons in analogical interpretations, and even *contra-legem* decisions are possible and rational. An important and heavy substantial reason can overrule a section of a statute or a precedent, most often, however, in a certain situation or a case.

Examination and analysis of adopted principles of justice and other substantial reasons behind and as the foundation of the wordings of statutes and precedents provide means of *critical discussion and interpretation* as well. A certain section of a statute or an interpretation adopted in a precedent might turn out to be problematic in relation to the values and other substantial reasons behind the statute, other statutes, systematics or the whole legal system. The adopted section, precedent or interpretation under the criticism might prove to be poorly justified. Restrictive interpretation or application or, here again, even *contra-legem* decisions are possible. Often, convincing, heavy and overruling substantial reasons are provided by a constitution. In the end, legal interpretation is always made in the frames of a whole legal system.

In this arrangement and according to the established logic of legal interpretation, values, often enunciated in the forms of principles, appear as the justifying framework of statutes and precedents. From the legal point of view, certain statutes and precedents are adopted in a legal system and, at the same time and together with the statutes and precedents; certain values with certain weights are adopted in the

justifications in the needful extent. In other words, they shall not prove to be problematic in the substantial inspection. Eventually, in the profound analysis, it must be possible to show the material justice of all decisions and interpretations.

society. These *values and their significance* are *confirmed* by the adoption of the statutes and precedents.

In other words, a society has adopted certain values with certain weights. This adoption and the weights of the adopted values can be proved with the help of the wordings of the adopted statutes and precedents, that is, by decisions as to the formal reasons of legal interpretation. On the other hand, their form as decisions and social facts is not the determinative issue. It is merely the necessary formal aspect of decision making. The important issue is the normative meaning of the statutes and precedents as well as the values and other substantial reasons as justifying factors of legal interpretation confirmed by the adoption of the statutes and precedents.

7 Conclusions

The basic principles of traditional *natural law jurisprudence* prove to be *problematic*. The traditional religious framework is alien to the legal viewpoint. Even the secular interpretations of the theory prove to be problematic. From the viewpoint of a legal system and legal knowledge, the certain given principles of natural law appear arbitrary.

No doubt, legal systems share many common values and protect human goods. On the other hand, the adopted different ways of protection in the frames of different legal systems is the crucial point. Legal knowledge is about a legal system and competent in the frames of the system.

The starting point of legal knowledge consists of sections of statutes and/or precedents. They are manifestations of the adopted principles of justice and other substantial in a legal system. The adopted values and the ways they are protected in a society can be shown and known with the help of statutes and precedents.

Because of the important role of values, principles of justice and other substantial reasons, the *positivistic approach* to law and legal knowledge proves to be *problematic* as well. Legal knowledge as legal interpretation does not consist of descriptions of law as facts. Rather, sections of statutes and precedents appear as objects of understanding. Moreover, there is a necessary connection between law and morals.

Sections of *statutes* and/or *precedents*, that is, formal reasons function as the *first stage* of interpretation. With the help of them, it is possible to *show* and *know* values, principles of justice and other *substantial reasons as the justifications* of the sections and precedents adopted in a legal system and society. As justifications, values, principles of justice and other substantial reasons function as efficient legal reasons as well. Legal knowledge as legal interpretation and understanding is interplay and collaboration of formal and substantial legal reasons. Both of these reasons are employed as premises of the conclusions of legal interpretation.

References

Aquinas T (1943) Summa Theologiae Translated by Fathers of the English Dominican Province. http://www.documentacatholicaomnia.eu/03d/1225-1274,_Thomas_Aquinas,_Summa_Theologiae_%5B1%5D,_EN.pdf
Aristotle (2002) Nicomachean ethics. Translation by Christopher Rowe and Introduction and Commentary by Sarah Broadie. Oxford University Press, Padstow
Bix B (1996) Natural law theory. In: Patterson D (ed) A companion to philosophy of law and legal theory. Blackwell Publishers, Padstow, pp 223–240
Bix B (2002) Natural law: the modern tradition. In: Coleman J, Shapiro S (eds) The Oxford handbook of jurisprudence & philosophy of law. Oxford University Press, Oxford, pp 61–103
Coleman JL, Leiter B (1996) Legal positivism. In: Patterson D (ed) A companion to philosophy of law and legal theory. Blackwell Publishers, Padstow, pp 241–260
Dworkin R (1977) Taking rights seriously. Harvard University Press, Cambridge
Finnis J (1980) Natural law and natural rights. Oxford University Press, Hong Kong
Finnis J (2002) Natural law: the classical tradition. In: Coleman J, Shapiro S (eds) The Oxford handbook of jurisprudence & philosophy of law. Oxford University Press, Oxford, pp 1–60
Hart HLA (1960) The ascription of responsibility and rights. In: Flew A (ed) Logic and language, first series. Blackwell Publishers, Oxford, pp 145–166
Hart HLA (1984a) Definition and theory in jurisprudence. In: Hart HLA (ed) Essays in jurisprudence and philosophy. Oxford University Press, Oxford, pp 21–48
Hart HLA (1984b) Positivism and the separation of law and morals. In: Hart HLA (ed) Essays in jurisprudence and philosophy. Oxford University Press, Oxford, pp 49–87
Hart HLA (1994) The concept of law, 2nd edn. Oxford University Press, Oxford
Kelsen H (1948) Law, state and justice in the pure theory of law. Yale Law J 3(57):377–390
Kelsen H (1961) General theory of law and state (trans: Wedberg A). Russell & Russell, New York
Kelsen H (1970) Pure theory of law. University of California Press, Berkeley
Kelsen H (2013) A 'realistic' theory of law and the pure theory of law: remarks on Alf Ross' on law and justice. In: d'Almeida LD, Gardner J, Green L (eds) Kelsen revisited. New essays on the pure theory of law. Hart Publishing, Oxford and Portland, Oregon, pp 195–221
Lamond G (2013) The rule of recognition and the foundations of a legal system. In: Duarte L, Dolcetti A (eds) Reading HLA Hart's the concept of law. Hart Publishing, Oxford and Portland, Oregon, pp 97–122
Wittgenstein L (1958) Philosophical investigations. Blackwell Publishers, Oxford

Milgram and Hart on Resisting Oppressive Regimes

Andrés Molina-Ochoa

Abstract This paper examines "the Resistance argument," one of HLA Hart's arguments for legal positivism. For Hart, a positivist concept of law that separates law from morality compares favourably to non-positivist ones for it facilitates resistance against oppressive regimes. Since law is separable from morality, the argument goes, law loses part of its "aura of majesty" and thereby, the legality of a norm is not a conclusive reason for citizen obedience. Molina-Ochoa argues that the evidence provided from the Milgram Experiments about obedience to authority figures provides empirical support for Hart's hypothesis. The author also suggests that these experiments provide elements to doubt of non-positivist concepts of law, particularly those in which law displays some form of moral correctness, such as the one advanced by Robert Alexy.

1 Introduction

In *The Concept of Law*, Hart writes:

> What surely is most needed in order to make men clear-sighted in confronting the official abuse of power, is that they should preserve the sense that the certification of something as legally valid is not conclusive of the question of obedience, and that, however great the aura of majesty or authority which the official system may have, its demands must in the end be submitted to a moral scrutiny.[1]

At first glance, this appears to be uncontroversial: that legal systems are fallible is, at face value, a legitimate argument, as such systems do not always stand up to the normative conditions that we use to evaluate them. As Leslie Green states, "[t]he

[1]Hart (1994), p. 210. In Hart (1958, p. 620) claims that, "If with Utilitarians we speak plainly, we say that laws may be law but too evil to be obeyed. This is a moral condemnation which everyone can understand, and it makes an immediate and obvious claim to moral attention."

A. Molina-Ochoa (✉)
South Texas College, McAllen, TX, USA
e-mail: amolinao@southtexascollege.edu

J. L. Fabra-Zamora, G. Villa Rosas (eds.), *Conceptual Jurisprudence*, Law and Philosophy Library 137, https://doi.org/10.1007/978-3-030-78803-2_10

thesis is correct, but it is not the exclusive property of positivism. Aquinas accepts it, Fuller accepts it, Finnis accepts it, and Dworkin accepts it [. . .] Law may have an essentially moral character and yet be morally deficient."[2] The claim that a recognition of the law's fallibility is required to resist oppressive regimes is also uncontroversial. If the law were infallible, there would be no moral reason to disobey it, nor could a system be oppressive.

The controversy arises when we understand—as it seems Hart intended to do—the resistance argument (RA) as an argument in favor of legal positivism. If it is clear that legal systems are fallible, then that we need to separate laws from morals to "preserve the sense that the certification of something as legally valid is not conclusive of the question of obedience" is a controversial notion. For instance, it is possible to claim that although some laws are morally flawed, they must only satisfy the minimum requirements of morality. In this sense, an extremely immoral law is not valid, but a moderately immoral law is. Supporters of this argument may use it as effectively as legal positivists to justify the violation of extremely immoral laws and resistance of oppressive regimes.

The objective of this article is to evaluate RA as an argument in favor of legal positivism, in light of the lessons offered by the obedience experiments carried out and inspired by Stanley Milgram. Milgram's experiments on obedience were a series of social psychology experiments that evaluated the inclination of participants to obey an authority commanding them to act against their own morals. Here, I am particularly interested in asking whether it is true that we need to separate morals and the law to resist oppressive regimes, and if so, when and under which circumstances? Despite the ethical concerns and legal restrictions concerning obedience experiments, more than 3000 people have participated in experiments like Milgram's.[3] The initial experiment has been repeated in different countries, societies, and with different methods.[4] According to Muzafer Sherif, the influential social psychologist who conducted the famous experiments at a summer camp, "Milgram's obedience experiment is the single greatest contribution to human knowledge ever made by the field of social psychology, perhaps psychology in general."[5] Such evidence must be considered in discussing whether it is true that the separation of law and morals is required, or at least contributes to violations of orders and rules of oppressive regimes.

This paper falls within the current experimental philosophy approach: the main idea is to use the evidence collected by experimental psychologists to evaluate Hart's claims about the separation of law and morals and the resistance to oppressive

[2]Green (2003b).

[3]Blass (2009).

[4]The Milgram experiment is usually ranked in surveys as the most famous psychological experiment. See: Banyard, P., and Grayson, A., *Introducing psychological research: seventy studies that shape psychology*. London: Palgrave.

[5]Takooshian, cited in Blass (2000, p. 10).

regimes.[6] I agree with Nadelhoffer and Nahmias that experimental philosophers assume that "the degree to which philosophers' own intuitions and their reports of ordinary intuitions correlate with layperson's actual intuitions is an empirical question and that it is amenable to controlled and systematic examination."[7] However, in this paper, the empirical question I analyze is not a correlation between a philosopher's intuition and layperson's intentions, but instead, a correlation between a philosopher's intuition and the way we react to the laws of oppressive regimes. Because this is a well-established field with plenty of data, I do not need to collect new data; instead, I will rely on existing data from the experiments on obedience.

In Sect. 2 of this paper, I revisit Hart's argument for RA and use what is, in my opinion, the strongest version as an argument in favor of legal positivism. I contrast this refined version of Hart's argument for RA with Milgram's experiments on obedience in Sect. 3, and I discuss some possible objections in Sect. 4. In the concluding portion, Sect. 5, I suggest various consequences for legal philosophy and new avenues of research related to this topic.

2 Hart's Resistance Argument Revisited

2.1 Hart's Formulation

RA is Hart's reworking of several ideas that first appeared in *Positivism and the Separation of Law and Morals*,[8] a paper he wrote in the aftermath of the Second World War in response to a series of papers by Gustav Radbruch,[9] in which Radbruch blamed legal positivism for the participation of distinguished judges in the Nazi Holocaust. As he does in *The Concept of Law,* Hart suggests in *Positivism and the Separation of Law and Morals* that claiming a rule is legally valid is not "conclusive of the final moral question: Ought this rule of law to be obeyed?"[10] In this article, Hart also claims that if we reject the idea that laws may be legitimate even when they are immoral, "we confuse one of the most powerful, because it is the simplest, forms of moral criticism."[11] Without this analytical tool, resistance is not possible.

[6]According to Ernst Sosa (2007, p. 99), Experimental Philosophy "puts in question what is or is not believed *intuitively* by people generally. And it challenges the *truth* of beliefs that *are* generally held, ones traditionally important in philosophy."

[7]Nadelhoffer and Nahmias (2007, p. 125).

[8]Hart (1958, pp. 593–629).

[9]Radbruch (2006, p. 6) claims that, "Positivism, with its principle that 'a law is a law', has in fact rendered the German legal profession defenceless against statutes that are arbitrary and criminal."

[10]Ibid, p. 618.

[11]Ibid, p. 620.

The Hart-Radbruch debate framed, to some extent, the beginning of contemporary analytical jurisprudence. Hart's defense of the separation between laws and morals is precisely what provoked Fuller to write a rebuttal that sparked the famous Hart-Fuller debate. In this debate, Hart defended the idea that law and morals are separate, while Fuller claimed that legal systems have an "internal morality" guaranteed by the procedural standards of legal systems.[12] Despite this—and the numerous papers in which Hart's arguments in favor of the separation of law and morals are presented—RA has largely been ignored, perhaps because the *zeitgeist* has changed, and philosophers are now more interested in explaining why we must obey the law, rather than in exploring the best strategies to resist oppressive regimes.[13]

It can also be argued that some empirical evidence might prove RA wrong. For example, legal systems and institutions have been used to resist injustice. In the past, Americans have used the judicial review process to resist oppressive laws. It was through judicial review that Americans were able to overcome racial segregation in schools and challenge the ban on inter-racial marriage, among other cases. The strategy used in these cases is rooted in the idea that the law is not valid when it violates the moral principles enshrined in the US Constitution. Social activists were able to achieve important political reforms by appealing to the idea that there is a connection between law and morality, at least in the American legal system.[14] Of course, this fact is not necessarily an objection to legal positivism,[15] but it does show that, in some cases, a separation of law and morality is not needed to overcome oppressive institutions.

2.2 The Moderate Version

Nevertheless, RA may still be valid if moderated. Perhaps the separation of law and morals is not always required to resist oppressive regimes, but a person may be more successful resisting oppressive regimes if they adhere to this thesis. Given that it is difficult to resist the official abuse of power, it is reasonable to adhere to the moderate version of RA (MRA), even if there are other possible strategies.

---

[12]For an analysis of the debate, see Lacey (2008, pp. 1059–1087).

[13]The proliferation of books and articles about the authority of law are examples of this change in the zeitgeist of contemporary legal philosophy.

[14]According to Jerome Bickenbach (1985, p. 81), "If the legal institutions and those involved with them are merely fallible and not corrupt, the citizen aware of the constitutional framework of her legal system would surely not be justified in saying [. . .] 'This is law; but it is too iniquitous to be applied or obeyed.' Rather, she should say, 'This is a mistake; being iniquitous this putative law violates the constitution and is thus invalid."

[15]In the *Postscript,* Hart (1997, p. 250) claims "The rule of recognition may incorporate as criteria of legal validity conformity with moral principles or substantive values."

However, even if this is true, there is still a second question: In what sense does MRA support legal positivism, and why, if MRA is true, is legal positivism a better theory? In other words, what kind of separation between law and morality supports the resistance of oppressive regimes and, more importantly, why is this separation characteristic of legal positivism?

This is a complex question for at least two reasons. First, the concept of legal positivism is contentious. As Dan Priel claims, "Many legal positivists [. . .] have come to see the 'no necessary connection' slogan as 'absurd' and its association with legal positivism a 'myth.'"[16] Second, it has never been clear what kind of separation between law and morality positivists support. For instance, Leslie Green lists four possible connections between law and morals, concluding that a positivist thesis that defends any of these possible connections is false.[17]

Despite the complexity of the topic, it is clear that, for Hart, a central tenant of legal positivism is "the simple contention that it is in no sense a necessary truth that laws reproduce or satisfy certain demands of morality, though, in fact, they have often done so."[18] In other words, it is possible for extremely immoral laws to exist that are also valid. For this reason, MRA can be analyzed as an argument in favor of Hart's version of legal positivism, though this is still a controversial and vague concept.[19]

In summary, the objective of this paper is to discuss whether there is empirical evidence to support a moderate version of Hart's Resistance Argument in favor of the thesis that laws do not necessarily satisfy moral standards. Whether this thesis defines or does not define legal positivism is a topic for a different article.

3 Milgram's Studies on Obedience

3.1 The Experiment

In July 1961, the same year *The Concept of Law* was published, Stanley Milgram began what are considered by many to be the most influential psychological experiments in history.

---

[16]Priel (2019, p. 268).

[17]Green (2003b).

[18]Hart (1994, pp. 185–186).

[19]Hart's version of legal positivism is probably the most influential on analytical jurisprudence. Dworkin (1977, p. 17), for instance, wrote that, "I want to examine the soundness of legal positivism, particularly in the powerful form that Professor H. L. A. Hart has given to it. I choose to focus on his position, not only because of its clarity and elegance, but because here, as almost everywhere else in legal philosophy, constructive thought must start with a consideration of his views." In the same sense, Kent Greenwalt (1996, pp. 3–4) claims that, "H. L. A. Hart [is] the most influential modern positivist in the English-speaking world."

Milgram's experiments began when a series of advertisements asking for male volunteers to take part in a learning study at Yale University were published in local newspapers. Participants would receive $4.50—approximately 40 dollars in 2021—for simply agreeing to take part in the experiment.

At the beginning, volunteers were introduced to another participant named Mr Wallace, who was actually a confederate. Both the participant and the confederate drew straws to determine their roles, but the game was fixed so that Wallace was always the learner. Wallace was then sent to another room while the teacher stayed with the experimenter and an electric shock generator. The learner was told to remember a list of word pairs, and the teacher was asked to administer an electric shock every time the learner made a mistake, increasing the charge by 15 volts per error, to a maximum of 450 volts. Although the shock generator was not connected to the learner, the teacher believed that he was actually inflicting increasing electric shocks to Wallace and that Wallace was suffering excruciating pain after the 150 volts mark.

If the teacher did not want to continue with the electric shocks, the experimenter encouraged him to continue with the following prods:

Prod 1: Please Continue. Prod 2: The experiment requires you to continue. Prod 3: It is absolutely essential that you continue. Prod 4: You have no other choice but to continue.

In the first set of experiments, more than two-thirds of the participants (65%) continued inflicting electric shocks up to the highest level of volts; all volunteers continued to at least 300 volts.

3.2 Relevance for Jurisprudence

Most participants were willing to obey the experimenter's commands, even when these actions were against their own moral beliefs. Commenting on the lessons from Milgram's experiments, Thomas Blass rightly claims, "Humans have a powerful propensity to obey authority. Did we need Milgram to tell us this? Of course not. What he *did* teach us is just how strong this tendency is—so strong, in fact, that it can make us act in ways contrary to our moral principles."[20] Milgram thought that the findings of his experiment, which revealed the human tendency to obey orders from an authority without question, could help to explain why Germans were prone to obey Nazi orders during the Second World War.[21] If in RA, Hart suggests the separation thesis is a necessary strategy to resist oppressive regimes, Milgram thought that his experiments could help to explain the participation of thousands in the atrocities committed by the Nazis: "Gas chambers were built, death camps

[20] Blass (2009).

[21] According to ibid (p. 5), one fact that "led Milgram to his obedience research was his attempt to fathom the Holocaust."

were guarded, daily quotas of corpses were produced with the same efficiency as the manufacture of appliances. These inhumane policies may have originated in the mind of a single person, but they could only have been carried out on a massive scale if a very large number of people obeyed orders."[22]

The question is, then, why did participants do it? Why were they compelled to inflict pain upon a stranger and to act in contradiction with their own morals? Milgram advances an interpretation of his experiment known as the *agentic state* interpretation, according to which "a man feels responsible *to* the authority directing him but feels no responsibility *for* the content of the actions that the authority prescribes."[23] For Milgram, the participant sees himself as an instrument of authority, depriving him of any possible moral agency. Milgram notes that the participants believed that it was the experimenter, and not them, who bore the responsibility for the pain inflicted upon Mr Wallace that caused them to continue with the experiment.[24]

However, some authors suggest that this is not a valid interpretation, neither of the experiment nor the Holocaust. Haslam and Reicher, for instance, point to the fact that Nazis were not simply obedient automats but enthusiastic adherents. They "had a very good understanding of what they were doing and took pride in the energy and application that they brought to their work."[25] They were not simply fulfilling responsibilities but carrying out orders with pride. This seems to suggest that Nazis both thought that their actions were contributing to a valuable endeavor and did not consider themselves as simple instruments of authority, as Milgram suggests. Similarly, most participants in Milgram's experiment resisted the orders given by the experimenters: they contradicted their instructions and showed physical signs of aversion to what they were doing. These signs of distress have also been demonstrated in recent experiments conducted in virtual environments, which revealed an "aversive state of personal distress and not one of emphatic concern,"[26] in the participants. How could participants show pain for their actions if they thought they were only instruments of the experimenters, as Milgram suggests? Moreover, the prod "the experiment requires that you continue" was, in most cases, all that was required to change the participant's mind. The idea that they were part of a good endeavor—the scientific experiment—was, in the end, all that was necessary to ease the participants' feelings of distress and make them obey the experimenter's orders. By contrast, Burger's replication of Milgram's experiments in 2009 found that every time the prod "You have no other choice, you must go on" was used, participants

[22]Milgram (1974, p. 1).

[23]Ibid, pp. 145–146.

[24]According to ibid, "The most far-reaching consequence of the agentic shift is that a man feels responsible *to* the authority directing him but feels no responsibility *for* the content of the actions that the authority prescribes."

[25]Haslam and Reicher (2012, p. 2). See also: Reicher et al. (2014, pp. 393–408).

[26]These feelings of distress were replicated in a recent experiment similar to Milgram's that used an avatar instead of a human being, and which measured the brain activity of the participants. See: Cheetham et al. (2009).

decided not to continue with the experiment.[27] This suggests that participants did not understand themselves to be mere tools of authority, but rather deliberative agents seeking to contribute to science through the experiment. Haslam and Reicher also point to the fact that Milgram reduced the participants' discomfort by praising their contribution to science, which led them to support similar experiments in the future.[28] Even after the experiment, participants were engaged in the study, and not in a state of passive fulfillment, as Milgram suggests.

3.3 Milgram's Experiments Support for a Moderate Resistant Argument (MRA)

Legal systems also claim to be part of a good endeavor: they claim to have the authority to rule society to advance important goals, such as the protection of human rights.[29] This claim is what Robert Alexy calls the claim to correctness; namely, the idea that "Individual legal norms and individual legal decisions, as well as legal systems as a whole, necessarily lay claim to correctness."[30] The claim of correctness is evident in the human rights charters and preambles of almost every modern constitution. Legal systems not only claim authority; they claim that their authority is founded in morality. If Haslam and Reicher's interpretation of Milgram's experiment is accurate, there is an important similarity between the experimenter and the law: both are considered to be legitimate authorities in the sense that following their orders is necessary for the achievement of valuable goals. More importantly, history is rife with cases in which people commit horrible atrocities by obeying the law, thinking they were doing the right thing. Legal moral claims, as well as the scientific justification of Milgram's study, absolve human beings of the responsibility of moral deliberation that is required to resist unjust orders.

If the power to make people obey the law, even when it contradicts their own morals, is grounded in the principle of moral correction, it seems that the best way to weaken this power is by denying that there is a necessary connection between law and morals. It is precisely this intuition that Hart expresses in *The Concept of Law*. Regardless of the many chapters of modern constitutions dedicated to human rights, it is important to keep in mind that laws are not necessarily morally desirable; this idea is necessary (or at least useful) in confronting our natural tendency to obey the authority of both people and institutions that pretend, as legal systems do, to be

27 Burger (2009b).

28 Milgram (1974, p. 3, pp. 145–146).

29 As Leslie Green (2003a) suggests: "Many philosophers and social scientists agree that a social order is a legal system only if it has effective authority. An effective (or de facto) authority may not be justified, but it does stand in special relation to justified (de jure) authority. Justified authority is what effective authorities claim, or what they are generally recognized to have."

30 Alexy (2004, pp. 35–36).

created to achieve desirable goals. When obeying legal systems, we must certainly keep one eye on the moral justification of the legal system, but just as importantly, both ears turned to the crimes that have been committed in its name.

4 Possible Objections

In the previous section, I claimed that the authority of both legal systems and the experimenter is grounded in the principle of correctness. The idea of a just end is precisely what forces people to break with their moral beliefs to obey immoral orders. Accordingly, the separability thesis—the idea that laws do not necessarily satisfy moral criteria—is at least useful for resisting the tendency to obey legitimate authorities.

4.1 Interpreting Milgram's Result

However, this conclusion depends on the validity of Milgram's experiments. Some scholars, Gina Perry, for instance, have questioned both Milgram's procedures and the veracity of his findings.[31] Defending Milgram is beyond the scope of this paper; however, even if it is true that Milgram's findings are not reliable, his experiments have been replicated in different countries and by other scholars with similar outcomes. Jerry M. Burger, a professor at Santa Clara University, replicated Milgram's study in 2009 and found similar compliance rates to those found in the original experiment.[32] In 2015, a group of social psychologists at SWPS University of Social Sciences and Humanities in Poland replicated Milgram's experiment and obtained similar results; they even concluded, "The original explanations proposed by Milgram are difficult to refute."[33] While more evidence in support of Milgram's claims must be found, sufficient evidence exists for our philosophical inquires on the problem of obedience. Though we may suspend a final verdict, there is no reason to reject the findings of several studies on this topic.

Some may not argue against the use of Milgram's experiment, but instead against the interpretation I have chosen. For example, Don Mixon—contradicting Milgram's own interpretation of the experiment—claims that it is the scientific context of the experiment that explains the obedience of the participants. For him, volunteers obeyed not because they trusted the experimenter's legitimacy in advancing a good cause—science, in this case—but rather because experts informed them that nothing bad would happen to Mr Wallace. For Mixon, the experimenter was not

[31] Perry (2013).

[32] Burger (2009a, pp. 1–11).

[33] Doliński et al. (2017, p. 932).

perceived as a legitimate authority, but instead, as an expert authority—a doctor whose expertise is sufficient to assure participants their actions will not produce harm to the learner.[34]

Mixon's interpretation may demand a different analysis of MRA; however, it is not likely to be an insurmountable objection. If Mixon is right, the only kind of expertise a legal agent may have is what may be called moral expertise. If this is the case, the separation thesis is still a valid tool to use against oppressive regimes.

Consider the different areas of expertise of experimenters and judges. According to Mixon, participants were willing to continue with the experiment because they were reassured that nothing was going to happen to Mr Wallace, and they believed the experimenter because he was an expert. Why should we believe a lawyer or a legislator? They can indeed inform us that our actions will not have adverse legal consequences (i.e., that we will not be arrested or fined). However, this kind of expertise does not explain the commitment that, for instance, Nazis had during the Second World War, nor does it explain why people obey the law even when they know they will not suffer negative consequences if they violate it.[35]

If we understand that the law reflects moral values and principles, then it can be said that legal agents are also experts on morals. When a person justifies their actions using the famous Latin phrase *Sed lex dura lex* (the law is hard, but it is the law), they are not only pointing to the legality of an action; they are also claiming that there are moral reasons to follow a specific course of action precisely because it is legal. As with prod 2 in Milgram's experiment (the experiment requires you to continue), the sentence *It is the law* eliminates the need for moral deliberation on the course of action that is demanded. Practitioners know that their actions will not harm Mr Wallace because the experimenters have told them he would not suffer any harm; people obey the law because they believe the law informs them of the course of action they must follow.

Some may not be convinced by Haslam and Reicher's interpretations and may instead suggest that Milgram's *agent state* theory is the right one. However, as with Mixon, this is not an insurmountable objection, as both accounts are not necessarily contradictory. According to Doliński et al., the studies conducted by Haslam, Reicher, and Miller provide "only a more precise labeling of the reason why participants carry out the commands of the experimenter-scientist."[36] It is possible that the agentic shift described by Milgram occurred because participants thought it necessary to contribute to the scientific goals of the experiment. A soldier who kills a person with a drone will likely believe that the real person responsible for their actions is their superior, as they (the soldier) were only following orders; however, the soldier submitted to the authority of the superiors because the soldier adhered to the principles defended by that army.

---

[34]See Mixon (1976, pp. 89–104) and Mixon (1989).

[35]For a similar argument, see Chapter Two of Hart (1994).

[36]Doliński et al. (2017, p. 932).

It is also possible to be skeptical about the use of obedience experiments to explain legal obedience. After all, legal rules are constantly disobeyed, and legal systems require a system of law enforcement. However, the authority pull is only one out of many an agent may experience. If participants were asked to apply electric shocks to themselves, it is likely that they would never have engaged in the experiment. Similarly, we have more reason to disobey a law that requires personal sacrifice, either by ourselves or our loved ones. This could explain why oppressive regimes are so effective in violating the rights of minorities.

4.2 Does Milgram's Experiments Support the Separability Thesis?

Finally, it is also possible to argue that to resist oppressive regimes, we should not use the Separability Thesis, but must instead use the Fallibility Thesis, which argues that laws are not always moral. However, the problem with the Fallibility Thesis is that it shares the same assumptions regarding legal systems as participants regarding the authority of the experimenter. The Fallibility Thesis assumes that the law is a valuable endeavor, the orders of which we must almost always obey. The Separability Thesis, by contrast, accepts that legal systems are sometimes morally valuable but suggests that there is nothing in their structures that guarantees this is the case.[37]

The previous point can be explained with an example. Patrols working along the US border are sometimes ordered by authorities to dump out water that humanitarian organizations have left for immigrants. A report by *No More Deaths* and *La Coalición de Derechos Humanos* notes that 3586 gallons of water were vandalized at the border, mostly by patrols.[38] This is one cause of the thousands of deaths that occur at the border. According to a report by the New York Times, "More people have died illegally crossing the southwestern border of the United States in the last 16 years than were killed in the Sept. 11, 2001, terrorist attacks and Hurricane Katrina combined."[39]

Assume that a border patrol is ordered to dump water left at the border. They know that their actions will likely cause the death of immigrants—even children.

[37]In *Col* and in other writings, Hart denies Fuller's thesis that the structure of legal systems had an inherent moral value. Hart suggests that systems of rules, such as the one imposed during Apartheid, had all the features of a modern legal system but were oppressive and immoral. See Fuller (1958, pp. 630–672); Hart (1965, pp. 1281–1296).

[38]La Coalición de Derechos Humanos, No More Deaths, and The Abuse Documentation Working Group, *Disappeared: How the US border enforcement agencies are fueling a missing persons crisis*. http://www.thedisappearedreport.org/uploads/8/3/5/1/83515082/disappeared%2D%2Dintroduction.pdf, accessed January 8, 2021.

[39]Fernandez, Manny, "A Path to America marked by more and more bodies," *New York Times*, May 4, 2017, https://www.nytimes.com/interactive/2017/05/04/us/texas-border-migrants-dead-bodies.html, accessed January 8, 2021.

They may also think that their actions are immoral and may even feel even the same repulsion that participants felt during Milgram's experiments. However, if they think that the legal system of their country is a morally desirable endeavor, even if it is fallible, they might believe that their action is justified by the moral goals expressed in the US Constitution. If the border patrol follows the Separability Thesis, there are no moral goals to protect, enabling them to pay attention to the suffering of children and elderly who may die at the border, suffocating under the scorching sun. More importantly, the border patrol will not judge the minority crossing the border as a criminal who is challenging the moral values of the legal system they are defending, but instead view the migrant as a human escaping from misery or certain death. Perhaps, this new perception will expand the border patrol's empathy and give them the tools required to disobey the orders.

5 Conclusion

Howard Zinn once wrote that "historically, the most terrible things—war, genocide, and slavery—have resulted not from disobedience, but from obedience."[40] Generals obeying Hitler's orders massacred millions of people and devastated Europe, while slaves saw their lives destroyed amid strict adherence to the American Constitution. In the aftermath of the Second World War, philosophers such as Gustav Radbruch and H.L.A. Hart debated the validity of their theories, arguing about the possible contributions they could offer to avoid the repetition of the atrocities of the Second World War.

Five decades later, legal philosophers are now more interested in finding reasons to obey the law or, in Dworkin's case, to justify their punitive powers. Meanwhile, legal systems continue to sanction and contribute to the perpetuation of atrocities around the world. Millions die at the borders of industrialized countries because of actions committed by legal agents obeying the law. Bombs are dropped in cities, while the proportion of civilian casualties in contemporary wars increases.

Perhaps, it is time to change perspectives in the discipline of legal philosophy. Instead of assuming that the moral claims of legal systems are argumentative tools that enable judges to achieve morally reasonable sentences, we may begin to apply again a more critical perspective—one that sees a role for legal philosophy in supporting the rejection of unjust laws, the struggle against oppressive regimes, and the protection of minorities. As I express in this paper, elements of experimental psychology may contribute to the development of this perspective, though more studies are necessary. This paper is my contribution to this project.

[40] Zinn (2009, p. 420).

References

Alexy R (2004) The argument from injustice. Clarendon Press, Oxford
Bickenbach JE (1985) Law, morals, and the fallibility thesis. Univ Tor Law J 35(1):67–85
Blass T (2009) From New Haven to Santa Clara: a historical perspective on the Milgram obedience experiments. Am Psychol 64(1):37–45
Burger J (2009a) Replicating Milgram: would people still obey today? Am Psychol 64(1):1–11
Burger J (2009b) In their own words: explaining obedience through an examination of participants' comments. Paper presented at the Meeting of the Society of Experimental Social Psychology, October 15–17, Portland, ME
Cheetham M et al (2009) Virtual Milgram: emphatic concern or personal distress? Evidence from functional MRI and dispositional measures. Front Hum Neurosci 3(29). https://doi.org/10.3389/neuro.09.029.2009
Doliński D et al (2017) Would you deliver an electric shock in 2015? Obedience in the experimental paradigm developed by Stanley Milgram in the 50 years following the original studies. Soc Psychol Personal Sci 8(8):927–933
Dworkin R (1977) The model of rules. In: Taking rights seriously. Harvard University Press, Massachusetts
Fernandez M, A path to America marked by more and more bodies. New York Times, May 4, 2017. https://www.nytimes.com/interactive/2017/05/04/us/texas-border-migrants-dead-bodies.html. Accessed 8 Jan 2021
Fuller L (1958) Positivism and fidelity to law—a reply to Professor Hart. Harv Law Rev 71 (4):630–672
Green L (2003a) Legal obligation and authority. Stanford Encyclopedia of Philosophy. https://plato.stanford.edu/entries/legal-obligation/
Green L (2003b) Legal positivism. Stanford Encyclopedia of Philosophy. https://plato.stanford.edu/entries/legal-positivism/, retrieved October 2, 2018
Greenwalt K (1996) Too thin and too rich. In: The autonomy of law. Clarendon Press, Oxford
Hart HLA (1958) Positivism and the separation of law and morals. Harv Law Rev 71(4):593–629
Hart HLA (1965) The morality of law by Lon L. Fuller. Harv Law Rev 78(6):1281–1296
Hart HLA (1994) The concept of law, 2nd edn. Oxford University Press, Oxford
Hart HLA (1997) Postscript. Clarendon Press, Oxford
Haslam A, Reicher S (2012) Contesting the nature of conformity: what Milgram and Zimbardo's studies really show. PLoS Biol 10(11)
La Coalici6n de Derechos Humanos, No More Deaths, The Abuse Documentation Working Group. Disappeared: how the US border enforcement agencies are fueling a missing persons crisis. Accessed 8 Jan 2021
Lacey N (2008) Philosophy, political morality, and history: explaining the enduring resonance of the Hart-Fuller Debate. N Y Univ Law Rev 83:1059–1087
Milgram S (1974) Obedience to authority: an experimental view. Harper & Row, New York
Mixon D (1976) Studying feignable behavior. Represent Res Soc Psychol 7(2):89–104
Mixon D (1989) Obedience and civilization: authorized crime and the normality of evil. Pluto Press, London
Nadelhoffer T, Nahmias E (2007) The past and future of experimental philosophy. Philos Explor 10 (2):123–149
Perry G (2013) Behind the shock machine: the untold story of the notorious Milgram psychology experiments. The New Press
Priel D (2019) Law as a social construction and conceptual legal theory. Law Philos 38(3):267–287
Radbruch G (2006) Statutory lawlessness and supra-statutory law (1946). Oxf J Leg Stud 26 (1):1–11

Reicher S, Haslam A, Miller A (2014) What makes a person a perpetrator? The intellectual, moral, and methodological arguments for revisiting Milgram's research on the influence of authority. J Soc Sci 70(3):393–408
Sosa E (2007) Experimental philosophy and philosophical intuition. Philos Stud 132(1):99–107
Takooshian H (2000) How Stanley Milgram taught about obedience and social influence. In: Blass T (ed) Obedience to authority. Taylor & Francis, New York, pp 9–21
Zinn H (2009) The Zinn reader: writings on disobedience and democracy. Seven Stories Press, New York

The Concept of Law in Legal Ethics: Towards a New Perspective

Andrea Romeo

Abstract This chapter explores the emerging jurisprudential theories in lawyering, with the intention to point out how the conceptualization of the lawyers' role and the nature of their professional commitments are both a function of the concept of law we endorse, with special regard to what is called "positivist turn" in legal ethics. Positivist legal ethicists fashion their legal ethics account in a jurisprudence broadly influenced by H.L.A. Hart and Joseph Raz and the concept of legal positivism, also basing the lawyers' role and professional commitments in the normative structure of legality. The paper critically focuses on such emerging authoritarian theory in legal ethics trying to suggest a new workable alternative, which conceives lawyers as "*legal abuse filters*." Given that rules do not provide about their own application, such consideration could provide room for a general practical discourse that regards the scope of advocacy and recognizes a proper role for legal ethics that would be independent from the respect of the settled law.

1 Introduction: A Brief Inquiry into the Legal Ethics Jurisprudence

Legal ethics—i.e. the study of the standards of the legal profession—is beginning to bloom as a jurisprudential field, whose theoretical roots lie in the province of contemporary legal debate and many legal conceptual issues.[1] Such jurisprudential developments in approaching the lawyering issues are also a result of the increasing relevance of the internal point of view in analyzing the concept of law. Per this view, we should address the question of the meaning and nature of law from the participants' perspective in the legal practice, since they use and interpret the legal

[1]See Kruse (2011), p. 501. For a deep analysis see also Schneyer (1984), pp. 1529–1572. See also Markovits (2008).

A. Romeo (✉)
"Magna Græcia" University of Catanzaro, Catanzaro, Italy
e-mail: a.romeo@unicz.it

J. L. Fabra-Zamora, G. Villa Rosas (eds.), *Conceptual Jurisprudence*, Law and Philosophy Library 137, https://doi.org/10.1007/978-3-030-78803-2_11

materials. Although some neo-essentialist scholars still hold that it possible to study the nature of law without considering the interpretation of legal practice, it is a mainstream view that we cannot properly analyze the sense, the "wits"—to boast Wittgensteinian term—of law if we do not seriously look at it within practices, inside its practical dimension.

Nevertheless, the European legal tradition has devoted scant attention to the figure of the lawyer for, at least until recently, it has focalized its attention on the leading figures of the lawmaker, the legal scholar and, above all, the judge.[2] Lawyers, as it is well known, do not perform any (official) paradigmatic activities: they do not play a direct role in lawmaking processes (different from the one they play as ordinary citizens), they do not authoritatively apply legal rules or settle legal cases, nor provide a systematization of legal materials. Although lawyers represent in some ways the symbol of the forensic discourse, since advocacy is properly grounded in the argumentative rationality which would characterize the trial dimension, there has not been serious reflections on the relationship between advocacy and the concept of law, as legal ethics was not perceived as a scientific issue to address.[3] Conversely, in the North-American legal tradition, legal ethics and the theoretical issues raised by advocacy seem to have enjoyed a greater "academic fortune," and the recent emergence of jurisprudential theories seems the result of the relevance of such theoretical focus in the legal conceptual domain.[4]

The chapter explores and critically evaluates the schools of thought within jurisprudential legal ethics, mapping the jurisprudential issues implicated in the activity of lawyering. The main question raised regards how lawyers should interpret and represent the law to their client, and how they should move within the scope of the bounds of law. This is a very crucial point in addressing the law-interpreting role of lawyers since legal consultations often "determines the shape of law as it exists in society."[5] Analyzing jurisprudential theories in legal ethics emerge how the conceptualization of the function of the lawyer in the law system, as well as the content and structure of the professional commitments, are both a function of the general concept of law adopted.

The argument proceeds as follows. The chapter begins with a reconstruction of the "standard" or "dominant" view—inspired in the views of legal realists and some

---

[2]La Torre (2012), pp. 1ff:

> If one had to pick three characters who figure prominently in the string of legal positivist theories that have come to pass since the epoch, indeed the epic, of codification, especially in Europe, they would have to be the judge, the legislator, and the law professor (the last of them being, in the modern age, a self-styled "scientist" of law). Scarcely a word is devoted to the lawyer: neither Savigny nor Jhering, nor Jellinek, nor Kelsen, nor Hart – just to mention a few of the great luminaries of the legal positivist tradition – have had much to say about the lawyer, except by way a few passing remarks.

[3]For some prominent exceptions in the Italian context, see, among others, La Torre (2002b, 2010); Cosi (1998), pp. 13ff; Olgiati (1990).

[4]See generally Crystal (2012).

[5]Kruse (2011), p. 494. see also Kruse (2005).

positivists—according to which law is a neutral "hired gun" in defence of their clients. In response, some natural lawyers and non-positivists have argued that, given certain connections between law and morality, lawyers are to act as moral counsellors for the clients or should attempt to reconstruct the moral foundations of settled law. We will devote special attention to what is sometimes called "positivist turn" in legal ethics. Positivist legal ethicists fashion their legal ethics account in a jurisprudence broadly influenced by H.L.A. Hart and Joseph Raz and the concept of legal positivism, also basing the lawyers' role and professional commitments in the normative structure of legality. In the final section, I develop a new workable alternative to such emerging authoritarian theory in legal ethics. Per this view, lawyers are *filters against legal abuse.* Given that rules do not provide about their own application, such consideration could provide room for a general practical discourse that regards the scope of advocacy and recognizes a proper role for legal ethics that would be independent of the respect of the settled law.

2 The Rise of the Dominant Jurisprudential View: Lawyers as Maximizers of Their Client's Interests

From the perspective of jurisprudential analysis, the most important paradigm of lawyering is influenced by the morally and normatively skeptical perspective of the (American) legal realism.[6] This view advocates for the *hyper-zealous* lawyering paradigm,[7] where the good lawyer is conceived as a cold and neutral "hired gun" of her client[8] and is committed to exploiting all effective legal actions in the effort to provide the best legal service to her client.

On the basis of such a jurisprudential approach, also labelled *Standard view,*[9] or *Dominant view,*[10] lawyers are committed to maximizing the client's interest, even if it would mean bringing up to the indefinite bounds of law, through creative and manipulative interpretations of the letter of the norms.[11] So, attorneys must pursue everything that sounds *not technically* illegal or too much inconsistent with the expressed *ratio* of the law. It claims, in other words, that every possible gap in the law system, cavil or loopholes, is to be exploited with no care or remorse for the possible prejudice or wound to other parties. Such legal ethics' account is also endorsed by the Italian legal philosopher Giovanni Tarello.[12] For Tarello, advocacy is to be performed in the most effective way possible and must keep account only the

---

[6]See Wilkins (1990), pp. 468–524. See also Pepper (1995).

[7]See Dare (2009), p. 7ff; Pepper (1986).

[8]Schneyer (1999), p. 11.

[9]Kruse (2011), p. 502; Postema (1980), p. 73; Schneyer (1984), pp. 1529–1572.

[10]Simon (1998), pp. 217–253.

[11]Dare (2009), pp. 5ff. See also Dare (2004), pp. 24–38.

[12]Tarello (1982), pp. 215–216.

bounds of settled law (whose words on this matter, as La Torre ruminates,[13] is to be interpreted in the most restrictive way), and this with a view to fully effecting a client's basic rights and freedoms.

In substance, the standard conception "commits [lawyers] to the aggressive and single-minded pursuit of the client's objectives not only *within* the law, but all the way *up to* [. . .] the limit of the law".[14] As many scholars stress, the professionalism principle is nothing more but a declination of the pivotal *duty of partisanship*, according to which lawyers must pursue everything their clients require them to do by means of exploiting professional techniques or legal interpretations that sound technically consistent with the letter of the law, but might actually wound the law's *spirit* or purpose, and to do it up to "the bounds of law,"[15] thus providing legal services "without fear [. . .] and without regard to any unpleasant consequences to themselves or to any other person."[16] In accordance with this Archimedean principle of legal ethics, the sole loyalty of the lawyer should be to the client's will.[17] Such principle, as Tim Dare notes, requires to the attorneys "to do all they possibly can, within the rules of the game, to see that their client's interests prevail,"[18] and to pursue and secure those goals with a high degree of zealous advocacy,[19] also labelled *hyper-zeal*[20] or "*zeal at the margin.*"[21]

The duty of professionalism, as it is traditionally conceived in the dominant view, implies two other fundamental standard view's tenets: (i) the *neutrality principle* (sometimes also labelled *professional principle* or *partisanship principle* by some legal ethicists)—according to which advocacy should be "neutral" with respect to the legal merit of the client's claim.[22] It requires lawyers representing their clients regardless of their own view on the justice of the client's goal and, consequentially, it argues for the impossibility to exercise personal moral judgments on the specific legal case. After all, according to the division of labour thesis, lawyers should not enroach the judge role. (ii) The *non-accountability* principle—i.e. lawyers are not susceptible to the ordinary moral blame, whereas they act zealously to secure the client's goal.[23] Furtherance of advocacy commits attorney to special moral-role-obligations when they act on behalf of the client's interests, which considerably

---

[13]La Torre (2007), p. 110.

[14]Postema (1980), p. 73, italics in the original.

[15]Dare (2009), p. 7.

[16]Dare (2009), p. 7; See also Freedman (1992), pp. 470ff.

[17]Dare (2009), p. 7.

[18]Dare (2009), p. 7.

[19]Ayers (2013), p. 6.

[20]See Dare (2009), pp. 7, 76.

[21]The expression is used by Luban (2007), pp. 19 and 26.

[22]See, among others, Wasserstrom (1975), p. 6.

[23]Dare (2009), p. 10; Wendel (2010), p. 6.

depart from the ordinary morality that commonly bounds and guides man's conduct.[24] These professional commitments arguably stem from, or are an implication of, the partisanship principle.

Now, within this package of professional principles, which notably are the standard position pillars, it is noteworthy stressing that *non-accountability principle* provides with the core-idea of such conception—i.e. role-commitments are to be distinguished from those imposed by ordinary morality. To summarize such a legal ethicist account, we might say that a lawyer could never be judged on the moral status of his own client's intentions, albeit without the assistance of the attorney the client cannot translate her plans into something that could sound like a legal argument or claim.

3 Challenging the Standard View's Account of Legal Ethics: The Moralistic Approach and the Dworkinian Legal Ethics

From the dominant legal ethics standpoint, law ultimately is nothing more than the interest of the (politically) *stronger*, as Thrasymachus says in Plato's dialogue. In turn, the lawyer's role is conceived as a sort of instrument for the fulfillment of the client's needs and desires, even if the latter may be worthy of moral blame. In other words, we might say that the standard account of legal ethics supports a "mercenary" portrait of lawyering and that because attorneys are to be professionally deaf to truth and justice.[25] What definitively counts, one might claim, is just the client's purpose, that must be pursued by means of any arguable interpretation of law. Such an idea resonates with the famous aphorism of King Louis XII: "[l]awyers use the law as shoemakers use leather; rubbing it, pressing it, stretching it with their teeth, all to the end of making it fit their purposes."[26] On such a thesis, therefore, "we will occasionally be reminded that the lawyer's point of view is that of the 'bad man,' or the immoral man, and that this is part of the systemic practice of law."[27]

Many legal ethicists rejected such legal realist-influenced standard view by reason of its ethically problematic implications. In turn, as the majority of them were moral philosophers by training, as Kruse notes,[28] they attempted to fashion a sort of "counter-reform" to the dominant-view turning to the moral theory discourse and arguing that lawyers might have additional professional constraints grounded in

[24]See, among others, Andre (1991), p. 73. Focusing on this particular point, Katherine Kruse had noted that legal realist conception of law could be meant as the core component of the implicit operating jurisprudence of everyday lawyers. Kruse (2011), p. 498.

[25]See La Torre (2002b), p. 121.

[26]Quoted by Wendel (2010), p. 69.

[27]La Torre (2012), p. 3.

[28]See, for a deep analysis of such counter-shift in legal ethics, Kruse (2011), pp. 501ff.

ordinary moral judgments.[29] From such a perspective, which is diametrically opposed to the standard-view bare neutrality, lawyers would have the burden of assessing the moral merit of their clients' claims and, consequently, might refuse legal service to those whose claims are inconsistent with ordinary morality.[30] To make up for the moral gaps raised by the operating jurisprudence of legal ethics, the early opponents to the standard view's account conceived a model of lawyering as a moral activist. In this view, attorneys have to carry out strategies of moral counselling, taking "upon themselves to judge and shape client project" in order to "steer [their] clients in the direction of the public good,"[31] and to exercise moral judgments in providing legal services.[32] It follows that lawyers will have to step beyond the law, and beyond the client's legal claims, drawing on their own personal judgments and beliefs concerning what ought morally to be done. Advocacy—they might hold—will be based on something other than the existing requirements of settled valid law, on the one hand, and will depart from blind compliance to clients' requirements, on the other hand.

Such a moralistic approach is shared, to some extent, by the Italian jurisprudent Lombardi Vallauri.[33] Moving from the idea that trial situation represents a sort of "pathological process of law," the Italian jurisprudent provides a different account of advocacy, according to which—as La Torre notes—a lawyer could be understood as "preventer at law," acting as a "family doctor" in legal counselling.[34] In analyzing Lombardi Vallauri's model of lawyering, La Torre highlights how the attorney, on such a thesis, seems to become a sort of judge, or even better, a "pre-judge" or, in the Lombardi Vallauri's terms, an "expert in structures," a "goodwill promoter," a "good father and family man."[35]

However, such moral accounts of the lawyer's role are open to criticism and raise several serious concerns. First of all, as many scholars observed, we might run the risk of a dramatic failure in the rule of law, which might be replaced with a sort of "oligarchy of lawyers."[36] Moving from the standpoint of the moral disagreement that characterizes the modern pluralistic society, many legal ethicists, taking seriously such jurisprudential issues, point out the problems with deploying personal moral judgments in lawyering. Now, such a possibility, as Dare fears, may sound like a sort of legal warrant for lawyers to morally drive their clients' life choices by exercising

---

[29]See Kruse (2011), p. 501.

[30]Luban (1986), p. 644.

[31]Luban (1988), p. 721.

[32]See Kruse (2011), p. 498. Such moral-advocacy—as Luban notes—implies the activity of "discussing with the client the rightness and wrongness of her projects, and the possible impact of those projects [on the people] in same matter-of-fact and (one hopes) un-moralistic manner that one discusses the financial aspects of a representation." Luban (1990), p. 1026.

[33]Lombardi Vallauri (1981), p. 625ff.

[34]La Torre (2007), pp. 111–113.

[35]La Torre (2007), p. 113. Quotations of Lombardi Vallauri are from Lombardi Vallauri (1981), pp. 625–627.

[36]See generally Wasserstrom (1975), p. 6.

personal moral judgments on their business dealings. Some scholars, across the spectrum, object the lawyers' lacking moral expertise in addressing moral issues and, consequentially, fear the possibility to run the risk of a serious moral-overreaching in providing legal services.[37] In addition, the acceptance of such a possibility might signal a serious threat to the rule of law values, since law could be characterized and applied differently to the citizens—i.e. depending on the lawyers' different moral horizons; a situation, this last, that would clash with the principles of legal certainty and equality supporting the rule of law idea.

To make up for the problematic consequences of moral activism, some legal ethicists—the most prominent is undoubtedly William Simon—tried to ground their counter-reform to the standards view and their advocacy commitments, in the idea of justice permeating the legal order as a whole.[38] The central core of Simon's proposal is to replace the principles and duties of the standard view, which borrow too much from the realist school of thought, with a single imperative that commits lawyers to take such actions that, considering the relevant circumstances of the particular case, seem likely to promote justice, or what he labels "legal merit."[39] This advocacy model clearly draws inspiration from Dworkinian thesis about the *full law*, which necessarily includes principles of political morality that positive law embodies or expresses, and such principles provide the settled law with its best interpretation and moral justification (the *best constructive interpretation*).[40] Based on Dworkin, Simon argues that addressing legal issues is a business requiring a style of legal reasoning closer to that adopted by judges, taking into account not only the "letter of the law," but also (and above all) the fundamental values and general principles providing the legal order basis, and are necessary embodied and expressed in law application.[41] Therefore, lawyers must pursue and promote concrete legal justice, and have done it not by means of the exercise of own moral judgments on client's goals, as the moralistic approach explains, but on the grounds of the guidance provided by principles crystallized into law, which "are part of the law in the sense that they affect the decisions of cases."[42]

As Kruse stresses, we might take Simon's account as a jurisprudential advance over the moralistic approach and the lawyers conceived as a moral counsellor because it is grounded in legal principles routinely employed in settling legal cases. It also compares favorably to the hired-gun model, as it appeals to the inner justice in law. However, as many legal ethicists have stressed, such is open to several objections.[43] It is perhaps worth highlighting that this assessment of "legal merit" in the client's case is a hard task, and Simon has to recognize that "not all lawyers [*will*]

---

[37]See Kruse (2011), p. 498.

[38]Kruse (2011), p. 508ff.

[39]Simon (1998), p. 138. See also Simon (2006), p. 1453ff.

[40]Dworkin (1986). See also Strassberg (1995).

[41]See Simon (1998), p. 139.

[42]Simon (1998), p. 138.

[43]See Kruse (2011), pp. 510–511.

agree in any given situation on how the applicable principles apply."[44] As a result, the research for the "one right answer" when hard cases are involved, and the requirement for "the best interpretation" could be problematic since lawyers do not settle legal cases as judges do in the furtherance of their professional duty to decide cases. Some ethicists, mainly those sympathetic to the positivist project, have found fault with Simon's thesis, as "[w]ithout the premise that Dworkinian interpretation yields a 'one right answer' the 'best interpretation' of law most of the time, the implications of Simon's jurisprudence are troubling."[45] Ultimately, his legal ethics account raises questionable issues not too far departed from those raised by moral activism.[46] In the end, what claims to be the main workable alternative to the standard view's cynical realism makes a different argument, trying to stem hired gun professionalism by making no appeal to justice, external to law or internal to it, but grounding advocacy in respect of law's authority. It is to that legal ethics account that we now turn.

4 Grounding Legal Ethics in Law's Authority

The standard view's alternatives we have briefly explored are far from a broad consensus. As noted in the preceding section, the main criticism, both to the moral-counselling solution and to Simon's Dworkinian lawyering style, comes from the (self-proclaimed) positivist side of the debate. These scholars postulate a more or less radical non-cognitivism or relativism regarding moral facts and hold that can be room for competing moral viewpoints claiming equal worth and respect due to the deep and irreconcilable moral pluralism of modern liberal society. Such an idea lies at the basis of what has been labelled as the "*positivistic turn*" in legal ethics contemporary debate, although the label *positivistic* must be understood in a broad sense.[47] Legal ethicists as Bradley Wendel and Tim Dare (undoubtedly two leading pioneers of such jurisprudential shift in legal ethics) both root their legal ethics account in a jurisprudence broadly influenced by H.L.A. Hart and Joseph Raz. Per

---

[44]Simon (1998), pp. 51–52.

[45]Kruse (2011), p. 498, p. 515. "Legal scholar Brad Wendel and philosopher Tim Dare"—Kruse explains—"have each advanced a positivist jurisprudence of lawyering derived from a professional duty to respect the authority of law as a framework for enabling coordinated social activity in the face of deep and persistent normative disagreement in a morally pluralistic society."

[46]For a criticism of Simon's view see, among others, Wilkins (1996), p. 269ff.

[47]See Simon (2012), pp. 709–725. *See* also Salyzyn (2014), p. 1063. "While in legal theory scholarship the label "positivism" carries various nuances and controversies, its use in the legal ethics context is, as a general matter, more straightforward and uniform. Broadly speaking, positivist accounts of legal ethics share a general view that the law owes its normative content to its ability to solve coordination problems and settle moral controversies. This view of the *law*, in turn, informs a particular view of *the lawyer* as governed in her actions by the legal entitlements at issue, as opposed to, for example, considerations of morality or justice writ at large."

this view, positivism is not only a theory of law, but it also provides ground to the lawyers' role and professional commitments in the settled law. Lawyers, in the furtherance of advocacy, have to respect the authority of law since the law provides the resolution of contested moral and political disagreement of a given society: this is synthetically the clarion call of the positivist account of legal ethics. From such a legalistic perspective, it seems noteworthy stressing here, "law owes its normative content to its ability to solve coordination problems and settle moral controversies."[48] Legal certainty and respect for the authority of the law are, now, the supporting pillars of such legal ethics jurisprudence, even if the compliance with these tenets would mean to steer legal service even against the client's purpose when it could sound inconsistent with law.[49]

The theoretical purpose of such a thesis is to provide a concept of lawyering that would make up for the (legally and morally) problems that the hired-gun lawyer's paradigm raises, both rejecting any conception requiring to sacrifice the client's interest in the name of the fulfillment of professional duty to exercise moral judgment (as the moral activists argue), or to exercise discretionary and contextualized judgments to promote only those legal cases with a "legal merit" (as Simon ruminates on his contextual hermeneutic approach).

However, if the core scope of the positivist account of legal ethics is to guarantee the respect of law's authority, it follows that this theory conceives a new function for lawyering and assigns to attorneys a closer-to-officials' role in the processes of settled law enforcement. Such a crucial point is concerned with a novel perspective on the idea of professional loyalty: *fidelity to law*—Wendel's famous expression—whose reasons lie in the fact of pluralism. "Law exists"—Wendel puts it—in order to provide a framework for coordinated social action in the face of persistent moral disagreement."[50]

Tim Dare has long stressed the theoretical perils and operative problems hidden in the idea of assigning to lawyers the responsibility for pursuing substantial justice in addressing legal cases: "[l]awyers who calibrate their professional efforts according to their own view of the good-or indeed according to any particular view of the good"—as Wendel warns us—"not only 'privilege' the view they favor and disenfranchise the view of the client, they undercut the strategy by which we secure community between people profoundly divided by reasonable but incompatible views of the good."[51] Nevertheless, Bradley Wendel, the other upholder of the authority view, not only claims the axiological pre-eminence of "effectiveness" and "validity," but also attempts to identify the justifying reasons for law obedience, which would yield in the law's capability to achieve social coordination and to settle

[48]Salyzyn (2014), p. 1063.

[49]See Wendel (2012), p. 741: "Without the constitutive obligation of fidelity to law, lawyers are just sophists – offering nothing beyond the kind of half-baked moral advice that any decent client could supply for herself."

[50]Wendel (2004), p. 368.

[51]Dare (2009), p. 74.

the normative controversy due to the pluralistic dimension of contemporary liberal and democratic society. The plurality of incommensurable and not fully hierarchizable values (on the basis of axiological importance or moral weight) land people in a situation of moral conflict, which makes society "unable to establish a stable basis for cooperative activity with reference to comprehensive doctrines of the good, or substantive theories of rights."[52] But, here, law takes place and settles the problem of such pluralism, of our "plurality of conceptions of the good" (thus echoing a Rawlsian famous expression).[53]

In summing up, law provides a "provisional settlement" of moral disagreements and offers a solution for settling practical disputes about what is required to do in specific situations.[54] So, what stems out from such concept of law is the following further point: "[t]he authority of law"—so Wendel holds—"depends on its capacity to enable collective social action in the face of persistent disagreement,"[55] as well as, consequentially, on the "capacity of law to transform brute demands into claims of legal entitlement."[56]

Thus, the resulting account is a positivist-sounding one, invoking the Archimedean idea of the "separation thesis," according to which, conceptually, a law's existence is independent of its moral merit—i.e. what law ought to be. Then, from that perspective, we should conclude that law (validity claim) and morality (justice claim) are to be considered as distinct phenomena. Wendel, however, tries to fashion a strong justification for the authority of law that would lie beyond the merely pragmatic idea of "social settlement," and do so by appealing to the normative attractiveness of democratic decision-making processes. In fact, we could argue that the social coordination-settlement could be achieved even by installing a dictatorial regime, arguing for the idea that democracy is not necessary to coordination.

Nevertheless, Wendel anticipates such criticism and tries to overcome it by invoking the substantial justice that democratic procedures could (or should) actually provide. The key point is that democratic lawmaking processes "treat equals, entitled to an equal measure of respect no matter what their substantive views about justice and morality,"[57] and guarantee "an equal voice to participants in a political debate, so that the resulting legal settlement reflects the view[s] of everyone, as much as possible."[58] By means of fair democratic procedures—which claim and require equality of all participants—we may cut off the "Gordian knot" of moral disagreement, on the grounds that all potential actors are involved in the political decision-making process.

---

[52]Wendel (2004), p. 368.

[53]Rawls (1993).

[54]Wendel (2005a), p. 88.

[55]Wendel (2004), p. 368.

[56]Wendel (2010), p. 89.

[57]Wendel (2010), p. 91.

[58]Wendel (2010), p. 98. See also Wendel (2009).

Dare makes a similar point and claims that the legitimacy of law is independent of its content, and it results from the overlapping consensus converging on procedures for enacting positive norms. Dare tries to make clear the point by referring to the famous "coin-toss example."[59] When two contenders dispute over a crucial issue, splitting on different reasons, but, at the same time, they desire to find a way to set aside the controversy, the only route to set up the disagreement is by turning to a procedural solution, which would transcend underlying justice conceptions. The paradigm of such procedural shift is given by the coin-toss model: the contenders decide to settle the dispute rely on a coin-toss, because it would provide a way of going on, despite the disagreement.[60] Nevertheless, Dare cannot counterfactually argue that modern societies seriously rely on coin-toss processes for enacting legal binding decisions. But what is worth emphasizing, here, is the core concept of "exclusionary reasons" that the coin-toss model, as well as neutral democratic procedures, provides for achieving the settlement of the moral controversy among partecipants, offering second-order reasons for complying with the result.

If we try to look to lawyers' partisanship from such a broadly positivist standpoint, advocacy's goals will radically change. Now, on such a thesis, attorneys must pursue "what the law, properly interpreted, actually provides"[61]—rather than the zealous pursuit of a client's interests. The idea that lawyering is to be ruled only by legal rules (ruling out any other not-legal or moral-sounding consideration) is shared, to some extent, also by Dare, who, in attempt to defend a neo-positivist re-shaping of the standard view, replaces the "hyper-zeal advocacy"—that the realist conception supports—concerned "to pursue any advantage obtainable for the clients through the law,"[62] with a "merely-zealous" advocacy, that is directed to the pursuit of client's rights or legal entitlements.[63] The crucial distinction would be drawn on the goal which such zeal refers to, thus distinguishing between *right-zeal* and *advantage-zeal.*[64] Then, attorneys should approach the law in good faith, justifying any given assertion about the law "in light of the interpretive understanding of professional

---

[59]See Dare (2009), p. 62.

[60]See Dare (2009), p. 62: "After the toss, however, you can give me a new reason namely the fact that the decision procedure we accepted has selected your preference. The normative force of this reason, however, does not depend upon me thinking that you were right about the substantive matters – and concludes by adding that: "I can accept it as a reason for action while continuing to hold on to my own view of what, from substantive perspective ought to have been done."

[61]Wendel (2010), p. 59.

[62]Dare (2009), pp. 7, 76. See also Dare (2004), pp. 24–28.

[63]Dare (2009), p. 7: "Merely zealous lawyers"—Dare writes—"are concerned solely with their clients' legal rights. They pursue those rights 'without fear [...] and without regard to any unpleasant consequences to [themselves] or to any other person'. According to an alternative understanding, the principle requires lawyers to exercise what we can call 'hyper-zeal'. Hyperzealous lawyers are concerned not merely to secure their clients' legal rights, but instead to pursue any advantage obtainable for the clients through the law. Indeed, they are not really attempting to defend legal rights at all: they are attempting to win."

[64]Dare (2004), p. 27.

community."[65] Nevertheless, many scholars found fault with the jurisprudential implications of authoritarian legal ethics, stressing how such theory could lead legal ethics to be largely insignificant or to overlap the legal commitments completely. The following section is going to explore such criticism.

5 Some Critics to the Positivist Approach of Lawyering

The *authority view's* account of legal ethics, as Dare and Wendel conceive it, raises many interpretative issues, both concerning the concept of law and the lawyers' role in the legal system, as well as the idea of law governing lawyers.

Simon, for example, holds that such an authority view could be seen as a clear signal of the more recent trend toward authoritarianism that is at odds with the libertarian flavour of classic writings in legal ethics.[66] Simon steers his criticisms against Wendel's fear of anarchy, stressing how that fear would lend him to overestimate the law's function to solve coordination problems and settle moral controversies, grounding on it the same legitimacy of the legal system. It is noteworthy to stress here—as Simon does—that many laws or legal rules are not about coordination.[67] Rules about driving on the right or the left side, Simon argues, are probably enacted to settle coordination problems, but laws prohibiting human killing or sexual rape seem hard to be considered legal tools to achieve only coordination goals.[68]

Simon criticizes Wendel's point about the exclusionary legal judgment: if rules provide exclusionary reasons for action, then rules would need an "exclusionary judgment" in the application process—i.e. without any regard for the unpleasant consequences of the rule application. Nevertheless, Simon holds that, sometimes, relying on an exclusionary judgment (i.e. strict enforcement of the rules) might not be the best way for achieving social coordination, and many situations could require a "particular contextual judgment." "If rules about which side to drive on lend themselves to exclusionary reasoning"—Simon explains the point through a (perhaps too) easy example—"rules about highway driving speeds lend themselves to inclusionary reasoning."[69] One of the primary targets of Simon's criticism is the centrality of rules in the positivist account of law (and consequently in legal ethics

---

[65]See Wendel (2005b), p. 1170.

[66]Simon (2012), pp. 709–726.

[67]Simon (2012), p. 722.

[68]Simon (2012), p. 722.

[69]Simon (2012), pp. 722–723. "More importantly, even in the realm of specific coordination, exclusionary legal judgment is often not the most appropriate way to achieve our goals. Sometimes it is better to let people make contextual judgments about how the policy behind the rules—coordination—can best be achieved. If rules about which side to drive on lend themselves to exclusionary reasoning, rules about highway driving speeds lend themselves to inclusionary reasoning. Traffic flows better when people drive at what they consider a reasonable speed given

account). As it is well-known, legal scholars split over the key issue whether "lawyers' ethics is structured by rules on the one hand or by principles and policies on the other;"[70] a jurisprudential issue that echoes the Hart-Dworkin famous debate. On the Dworkinian account of law, as it is well known, rules are "explicit and categorical," thus are "all or nothing" standards.[71] Insofar rules are conceived as "conclusive reasons for action," legal rules cannot conflict. Or, to be more accurate, when two rules clash, then one of them cannot be a valid rule. Conversely, principles do not provide for the cases to which they are to be applied.[72] So, legal principles may clash, and they have a "weight" that means that they provide reasons to various courses of action.[73] Now, in the authoritarian account of legal ethics, bounds of advocacy are specified by rules. By contrast, many legal ethicists argue that such constraints are conceived in terms of principles. The critical argument is that an authoritarian view cannot properly account for the existence of principles in legal ethics issues.

Wendel does not deny that law includes principles as well as rules, but, on Simon's critical analysis, "he worries that too much preoccupation with principles and policies jeopardizes the separation of law and morality."[74] Nevertheless, the contrast between rule-based and principles-based perspectives raises many other issues. If we conceive confidentiality as a close-to-absolute norm, with no other rules providing accommodations or exceptional clause, a lawyer would never infringe such mandatory commitment even if it was necessary for saving an innocent in a defective convict-case. There is no room for reasonable or justifiable infringement. Or still, the dominant view mandates a lawyer to impeach a truthful witness (for example, by claiming that the witness got a prior perjury conviction, even if she knows he is now truthful). Turning the situation under the authoritarian light, as Simon points out, no legal ethics rule prohibits the truthful-witness impeachment, then attorneys should adopt a default rule that the client's decision prevails. However, Simon holds that a principled-based view might support the idea stakeholders should not mislead facts.[75] Obviously, given the weight-dimension of principles, the reason for impeachment might ride on the ground of the pre-eminence of the principle according to which "even a guilty defendant is entitled to put the prosecution to proof."[76] Thus, if we accept the existence of competing principles, we have to settle the issue by means of the principle that results, in the case, with a more specific

the conditions they observe around them. Strict enforcement of the rules would impede this coordination."

[70] Simon (2012), p. 722.

[71] See Dworkin (1978), p. 24.

[72] Dworkin (1978), pp. 25–27.

[73] Dworkin (1978), p. 32.

[74] Simon (2012), p. 712.

[75] Simon (2012), p. 713.

[76] Simon (2012), p. 713.

weight.[77] By contrast, a ruled-based legal ethics would lead to a different conclusion: without a clear rule prescribing certain conduct, what counts is only the loyalty to the client's willingness.[78]

Nevertheless, the (so labelled) positivist account of legal ethics worries about the application of legal ethics principles. Because of the vagueness end open-texture of principles, people (and officials) will disagree about their specific content or application. The argument rides on the pluralistic dimension of society which represents the authoritarian legal ethics Archimedean point. However, Wendel and Dare both hold that interpreting the law respectfully with due regard for its *ratio* implies compliance with intersubjective criteria of validity, and that in order to prevent any lawyers' manipulatives or creatives interpretations (to which the hired-gun standard paradigm bounds lawyers to do). These criteria are grounded in social practices, providing a sort of "rule of recognition" for all valid or plausible interpretations.[79] What is relevant to points out, here, is that such *rule of recognition* stems from the same practice of operating jurisprudence of everyday lawyering. Thus, when lawyers face a range of plausible interpretations, they need to be driven by the fixed star's light of the coordination function. Wendel, on the specific point, argues that "there is enough objectivity and determinacy in the law that the set of inadequately supported legal positions is not empty."[80] It follows that lawyers "should understand their role in the process of legal interpretation as coordination-enhancing."[81]

Nevertheless, this argument raises severe criticism, even within the same positivist account of legal ethics. Without the fulfilment of the premise that law provides a settlement of social disagreement, the whole fidelity-to law-architecture seems to collapse ruinously.[82] However, in addition, rethinking the standard conception in narrow positivist terms leaves many questions still open. Positivist account of legal ethics lacks justifications for the lawyers-role in the legal system, and yet it seems to be grounded on *weak* reasons meanwhile lawyering and role-morality sometimes seem calling for strong justifications that would lie beyond the mere appeal to acting within a legal practice.

Such a legalistic approach, which grounds a theory of legal ethics in respect for the law, seems to be open to a further critique. If the lawyers' fidelity must be to the authority of law, as Dare and Wendel hold, it could mean that legal ethics and legality could overlap in the end, because lawyers would be only bounded not to infringe the law.[83] Under such a conception of legal ethics, as Wendel clarify,

---

[77]Simon (2012), p. 713.

[78]Simon (2012), p. 713.

[79]Wendel (2010), pp. 196–97.

[80]Wendel (2010), pp. 196–97.

[81]Wendel (2010), p. 393.

[82]Kruse (2011), p. 517.

[83]Salyzyn (2014): "Those advancing positivist accounts of legal ethics take a different view, rejecting a vision of the lawyering role that revolves around considerations of substantive justice

attorneys are duty-bound not to spoil the achievement of law "by reintroducing contested moral values into the domain of law, either in the guise of principles of interpretation or as the basis for an ethically motivated decision to act or not to act on behalf of a client."[84]

But say it means acknowledging that there is no room for ethics in providing legal service, because all that lawyers must do is to comply with the letter of the law. It means nothing more, and it means nothing less. In other words, if a lawyer's response, or act, sounds morally defective but consistent with law, the defectiveness must be referred to the law on the ground that the lawyer acted legally. Legal ethicists will only question how, or if, changing the defective legal rule, not about the lawyer's conduct when it falls within the scope of the legal warrant. But if we accept this account, what would be the meaning of legal ethics? How can we distinguish legal ethics and ordinary settled laws?

If the skeptical dominant view provides a hired-gun attorney ready to break the law for pleasing her client, and while the moralistic approach could jeopardize legal certainty by deploying in personal moral judgments, the positivist account, on its part, undermines jurisprudential legal ethics at all, making it a non-sense argument. In the conclusive section, we will try to address these issues and provide a workable alternative.

6 Beyond the Bare Fidelity to the Law: A Different Advocacy Model

The framework of the legalistic approach strips legal ethics rules of their normative content and therefore devalues the normative meaning of law governing lawyers. If we accept the positivist account (or, to say it better, such particular version of legal positivism) as a set feature of legal ethics, all professional commitments of lawyering fall within the scope of legality—i.e. ethical duties stem out from the respect of the settled law's authority. What an attorney must do is to pursue the legal entitlements of her client, ensuring what law properly (and properly interpreted) assigns him. Therefore, lawyers should not treat legal rules instrumentally, and never stretch legal interpretation, or legal enforcement, to meet their own conceptions of substantive justice.

Such a solution, according to Dare, Wendel and many other legal ethicists, provides a workable way out of those problematic issues that the standard view commonly raises—i.e. the shoemaker-lawyer model which is duty-bound to characterize and manipulate law in an instrumental way, trying to pursue the clients'

or morality. Instead, they offer a distinct alternative (or modification) to the Standard Conception by arguing that the normative content of the law mandates that the duties of lawyers must be oriented toward respect for the law itself, not ordinary moral considerations."

[84]Wendel (2004), p. 366.

interests at all costs by driving legal interpretation to be consistent (*only in appearance*) with client's goals. After all, as Dare argues, lawyers are to be "concerned solely with their clients' legal rights" (according to the positivist *merely-zeal* paradigm), so they have not to pursue any advantage obtainable for the clients through the law (as the *hyper-zeal* model would require them).[85] Such claim echoes what David Luban—who is notably an opponent of the legalistic approach—stressed in addressing the distinction between legal rights and advantages which are obtainable through legal rules: "My legal rights are everything I am in fact legally entitled to do, not everything the law can be made to give."[86] On the legalistic approach, lawyers and clients are indistinguishable because their loyalty is to the same object: the authority of law. However, if on this account of legal ethics, there is no gap between legality and legal ethics, and so the latter, as a jurisprudence, would sound completely pleonastic. My point here is concerned with the idea that it is not at all like that.

Conversely, legal ethics and legality are not the same things, do not play the same game, and legal ethics jurisprudence might be necessary to guide attorneys in the furtherance of advocacy, also and above all when they act within the bounds of law. In order to see why this is so, we need to bring to light the circumstance that legal rules—as Wittgenstein teaches us, and the same great legal positivist Herbert H.L Hart has long recognized[87]—*do not provide about their own application*. Such consideration could provide room for a general practical discourse that regards the scope of advocacy. Legal rules, according to many jurisprudents, do not determine their own meaning and, consequently, do not rule their applications in specific cases. Sometimes in the interpretation of legal rules there is room for a range of all-reasonable competing applications. So, to choose among these workable possibilities seems to invoke a practical discourse situation and implies investigating reasons that go beyond the "letter of the law" and the mere coordination purpose. Now, the rule-application situation figures out for the case that lawyers must pursue their client's legal rights. The rule that recognizes what the right-holder is entitled to do, to get or to claim, most of the cases do not provide for the ways of pursuing it. So, in pursuing her client's legal right, an attorney could face many competing possibilities—due to the open texture of the norms or the vagueness of some legal terms—, that seem all workable and all consistent with legality (not a mere "appearance of compliance," as the dominant view would request to grasp). Nevertheless, if the guidance of the law runs out in case of specific enforcement, what could drive the lawyer's professional choices when she is concerned with the pursuing of a client's legal entitlement?

My point here is that for such practical guidance, we have necessarily to rely on legal ethics, that might provide a morally permeable membrane in law's enforcement. Let us turn, here, to the example of a lawyer committed to pursuing a due and

[85]Dare (2009), p. 7.

[86]Luban (2007), p. 75.

[87]Hart (1988), p. 106.

payable debt on the ground of a single debt instrument. There are two workable possibilities consistent with legal provisions that the attorney could face: (i) enforcing the debt instrument in a way that the debtor could pay only once, discharging himself; or (ii) splitting the instrument itself, giving rise to some multiple execution, in order to maximize the creditor interest providing many property executions on debtor's assets. Let suppose, now, that law governing payment obligations does not state anything about such different possibilities, leaving many alternatives workable, each able to comply with the legal commitments. Since the relevant law does not mandate which solution is to be applied, the way of enforcing legal entitlements is up to the client's or the lawyer's will. Now, if we endorse the standard hired-gun standpoint, the choice will always lie on the client's side, and she will steer the enforcement in the specific case. In such a situation, the lawyer is just a neutral instrument. The positivist account, on the other hand, cannot provide us with any solution in this regard, since any application that seems to be consistent with law fulfills the authority view's commitments when law, properly interpreted, allows such range.

In my view, the practical guidance in such cases should stem out from legal ethics, without reliance on lawyers' moral judgments to supplement and limit the harmful law-consistent application. In cases where the law falls short in governing interpretation or, to say it properly, when legal rules do not provide about enforcement of legal rights (do not properly rule their application), there is room for competing way of acting, lawyers must pursue that action which, in the range of legal ones, causes the least possible sacrifice to the others. Turning to the example above mentioned, a lawyer has to opt for the less damaging way-of-enforcement, which could wound the debtor as little as possible, therefore by suiting for a single settlement of the debt. In other words, lawyers are (ethically, not legally) committed to preventing possible legal abuses, or abuses of legal entitlements, when they act to purse client's legal entitlements. And in performing that, the sole compliance with the authority of law is not enough.

A legal entitlement, as it is well known, states what I am entitled to do, allowing me the possibility to decide *if* do it, *when* do it, and sometimes *how to* enforce it, maybe through a legal suit. Thus, it does not mandate to take care of the harmful consequences of such enforcement (after all, we could say: *qui suo iure utitur neminem laedit*).

Such an idea is today challenged by many jurisprudents and legal philosophers. La Torre, among these, conceives a standard governing the enforcement of subjective rights, that he labels *tolerance principle,* on the ground that the actual enforcement of subjective legal entitlements, or their pursuance, must be accomplished in the least harmful way possible. On the practicing level, the exercise or the enforcement of a legal entitlement cannot spread the "legal damage" beyond those limits that are strictly necessary for the effective pursuance of the interest protected.[88] So we need an "applicative practical discourse" beyond the justificatory one, and

[88] La Torre (2002b), pp. 161–162.

lawyers are those legal professionals who may be required to engage such discourse, acting as *a filter* against possible abuses of legal entitlements.

Instead of saying simply that some actions would lack merit and should, therefore, be criticized and abandoned (because lawyers have to engage moral discourse with their client in order to drive their will)—as the moralistic approach suggests—, my thesis, here, is that lawyers as filters against legal abuse. Per this view, lawyers must act autonomously in the space left open by the interpretation of legal commitments regarding their own application, pursuing client's legal rights in the least harmful way possible to the other people. After all, we should not forget that many codes of professional conduct—recognizing the *amphibious* nature of attorneys and the ambiguity of the lawyer's discourse[89]—commits professionals to sometimes *difficult-to-reconcile* duties. The Preamble of the ABA Model Rules states that "a lawyer, as a member of the legal profession, is a representative of clients, an officer of the legal system and a public citizen having special responsibility for the quality of justice," adding soon "a lawyer may serve as a third-party neutral, a nonrepresentational role helping the parties to resolve a dispute or other matter." The workable way to comply with such conflicting commitments is by pursuing client's legal rights without exercising personal moral judgments, on the one hand, but also by driving pursuance of client's rights independently, thus providing legal service that could filter out possible legal abuses and the harmful consequences of legal enforcement. So, by claiming that lawyers should pursue their clients 'legal entitlement and not their legal interests, and only what law properly interpreted provide, lacks practical guidance when the law warrants for a range of all-legally compliant enforcements, some of which *legally* harmful. Thus, the application-discourse, addressing rule-application issues, requires a style of legal reasoning that could not stop at the threshold of the mere authority of law.

Obviously, the *lawyer-as abuse-filter* thesis could properly work only for non-criminal contexts. The justifications of role-morality in criminal-context are different, ethically stronger, and deeply rooted in the trial-exceptional-situation, where the greater emphasis should be placed on the protection of individuals from possible abuse of the over-reaching power of settled institutions; and this aim should be considered prevailing over justice itself. In such a context, facing an over-reaching power, even the worst man prosecuted seems defenceless with respect to the outstanding institution's strength; then lawyers would seem to wear the sparkling armour of the upholder of human dignity, as Luban notably claims, in the effort "to keep the State honest."[90]

---

[89]La Torre (2002b), p. 162.

[90]Luban (2007), p. 30.

References

Andre J (1991) Role morality as a complex instance of ordinary morality. Am Philos Q 28:73–80
Ayers A (2013) What if legal ethics can't be reduced to a maxim? Geo J Leg Ethics 26:1–48
Cosi G (1998) La responsabilità del giurista. Etica e professione legale. Giappichelli, Torino
Crystal NM (2012) Developing a philosophy of lawyering. Notre Dame J Law Ethics Pub Policy 14:75–101
Dare T (2004) Mere-zeal, hyper-zeal, and the ethical obligation of lawyers. Leg Ethics 7:24–38
Dare T (2009) The Counsel of Rogues?: A defence of the standard conception of the lawyer's role. Ashgate, Farnham, Surrey
Dworkin R (1978) Taking rights seriously, 2nd edn. Duckworth, London
Dworkin R (1986) Law's empire. HUP, Cambridge
Freedman MH (1992) Professionalism in the American Adversary System. Emory Law J 41:467–472
Hart HLA (1988) Essay in jurisprudence and philosophy. OUP, Oxford
Kruse KR (2005) Lawyers, justice, and the challenge of moral pluralism. Minn Law Rev 90:389–458
Kruse KR (2011) The jurisprudential turn in legal ethics. Ariz Law Rev 53:593–531
La Torre M (2002a) *Tolleranza*. In: La Torre M, Zanetti G (eds) Seminari di filosofia del diritto. Categorie del dibattito contemporaneo. Rubbettino, Soveria Mannelli (Catanzaro)
La Torre M (2002b) Il giudice, l'avvocato e il concetto di diritto. Rubbettino, Soveria Mannelli (Catanzaro)
La Torre M (2007) Constitutionalism and legal reasoning. A new paradigm for the concept of law. Springer, Dordrecht
La Torre M (2010) Avvocatura e retorica. Tra teoria del diritto e deontologia forense. In: Manzin P, Moro P (eds) Retorica e Deontologia Forense. Giuffrè, Milano
La Torre M (2012) Lawyers, advocacy and the concept of law. Rechtstheorie 43:1–25
Lombardi Vallauri L (1981) Corso di filosofia del diritto. Cedam, Padova
Luban D (1986) The Lysistratian Prerogative: a response to Stephen Pepper. Am Bar Found Res J:637–649. https://doi.org/10.1111/j.1747-4469.1986.tb00259.x
Luban D (1988) Lawyers and justice. An ethical study. Princeton University Press, Princeton
Luban D (1990) Partisanship, betrayal and autonomy in the lawyer–client relationship:a reply to Stephen Ellmann. Colum Law Rev 90:1004–1043. https://doi.org/10.2307/1122923
Luban D (2007) Legal ethics and human dignity. Cambridge University Press, New York
Markovits D (2008) A modern legal ethics: adversary advocacy in a democratic age. Princeton University Press, Princeton
Olgiati V (1990) Saggi sull'avvocatura. L'avvocato italiano tra diritto, potere e società. Giuffrè, Milano
Pepper SL (1986) The lawyer's amoral ethical role: a defense, a problem and some possibilities. Am Bar Found Res J 4:613–634. https://doi.org/10.1111/j.1747-4469.1986.tb00258.x
Pepper SL (1995) Counseling at the limits of the law: an exercise in the jurisprudence and ethics of lawyering. Yale Law J 104:1545–1610
Postema GJ (1980) Moral responsibility in legal ethics. N Y Univ Law Rev 55:63–89
Rawls J (1993) Political liberalism. Columbia University Press, New York
Salyzyn A (2014) Positivist legal ethics theory and the law governing lawyers: a few puzzles worth solving. Hofstra Law Rev 42:1063–1076
Schneyer T (1984) Moral philosophy's standard misconception of legal ethics. Wisconsin Law Rev:1529–1572
Schneyer T (1999) Some sympathy for the hired gun. J Leg Educ 41:11–27
Simon WH (1998) The practice of justice: a theory of lawyers' ethics. Cambridge University Press, Cambridge (Mass)
Simon WH (2006) After confidentiality: rethinking the professional responsibilities of the business lawyer. Fordham Law Rev 75:1453–1471

Simon WH (2012) Authoritarian legal ethics: Bradley Wendel and the positivist turn. Tex Law Rev 90:673–690
Strassberg M (1995) Taking ethics seriously, beyond positivist jurisprudence in legal ethics. Iowa Law Rev 80:926–953
Tarello G (1982) Due interventi in tema di deontologia. Materiali per una storia della cultura giuridica 12:207–218
Wasserstrom R (1975) Lawyers as professionals: some moral issues. Hum Rights 5:1–24
Wendel WB (2004) Civil obedience. Colum Law Rev 104:363–465
Wendel WB (2005a) Legal ethics and the separation of law and morals. Cornell Law Rev 91:67–128
Wendel WB (2005b) Professionalism as interpretation. Northwest Univ Law Rev 99:1167
Wendel WB (2009) The lawyer's role in a contemporary democracy, promoting the rule of law, government lawyers, democracy, and the rule of law. Fordham Law Rev 77:1333–1362
Wendel WB (2010) Lawyers and fidelity to law. Princeton University Press, Princeton
Wendel WB (2012) Legal ethics is about the law, not morality or justice. Tex Law Rev 90:727–741
Wilkins DB (1990) Legal realism for lawyers. Harv Law Rev 104:468–524
Wilkins DB (1996) In defense of law and morality: why lawyers should have a prima facie duty to obey the law. WM Mary Law Rev 38:269–295

Part IV
Law, Normativity and Practical Reason

Hard Cases and Legal Validity: The Internal Moral Significance of Law

Sari Kisilevsky

Abstract One of Hart's central insights about law, and his major advance over Austin, is to argue for law's internal normative structure, and to place this at the centre of his theory of law. Hart not only showed that law consists of an ordered system of rules rather than a collection of commands backed by threats, but he also argued that this internal normative framework is essential for a theory of law. This paper argues for the moral significance of law so conceived. As against instrumentalist accounts of law, I argue that it is the internal normative structure of law that gives it its distinctive moral force. Here, I argue that the moral significance of such an internally structured system of rules is lost or distorted when one focuses on law's external ends. With this understanding of law in mind, I argue, positivists can solve the difficulty of hard cases raised by *Riggs v. Palmer*, which is often understood to raise a problem of *external* moral considerations in law. I argue that the internal normative structure that Hart places at the centre of his account of law is sufficient for positivists to meet this challenge raised by Dworkin and his followers.

1 Introduction

The question of the role of morality in law has dominated analytic jurisprudence for the past half a century. Positivists ask how, if the existence of a legal system, and which legal system exists are matters of social fact, one can explain the prevalence of morality in law. Non-positivists wonder, if law is necessarily moral, then what role do social facts play? They thus dispute their moral and legal significance.

One central focus of this debate is the argument from *hard cases*.[1] Hard cases are cases where the posited law points to a clear outcome, but the question of what the

[1]Dworkin (1978), esp. ch. 2, "The Model of Rules."

S. Kisilevsky (✉)
Department of Philosophy, Queens College CUNY, New York, NY, USA
e-mail: sari.kisilevsky@qc.cuny.edu

J. L. Fabra-Zamora, G. Villa Rosas (eds.), *Conceptual Jurisprudence*, Law and Philosophy Library 137, https://doi.org/10.1007/978-3-030-78803-2_12

law requires remains open. Consider *Riggs v. Palmer*, the pivotal case at issue.[2] *Riggs* is a case in which a grandson, Elmer Palmer, murdered his grandfather in order to expedite his inheritance. Elmer was clearly named as a beneficiary in the will, the will was validly enacted, and there was no posited law overriding the Statute of Wills, the governing statute at the time, or prohibiting murderers from inheriting. Nonetheless, the majority held it is the "universal law administered in all civilized countries"[3] that no one should profit from his own wrong, and for this reason, denied Elmer the inheritance.

This case poses a challenge for positivists because it appears that the Court relied on a rule that had no posited source in rendering its decision. Even so, the judges argued that they were deciding what the law *is*, rather than what it ought to be. This calls the two fundamental positivist tenets regarding the social nature of law into question. It challenges the sources theses, the principle that social sources are necessary for legal validity, because it appears that the principle that no one should profit from his own wrong is an unposited legally valid rule. This also challenges the separation thesis, since the mere fact that the posited law pointed to a given outcome did not settle the question of what the law required; the majority still looked to morality in order to decide the issue. The intuitive plausibility of *Riggs* suggests that a complete theory of law must be capable of explaining the legal validity of these further considerations as well.

The parties to this debate take *Riggs* to illustrate the possibility of legally binding moral considerations that are not anticipated by posited ones. They thus take the challenge posed by *Riggs* to lie in the possibility of explaining the legal force of these considerations, given that the existence of a legal system is a matter of social fact. This throws the debate about the nature of law into sharp relief. Legal positivists respond by acknowledging the role of morality in law, though insisting that its presence is in turn a matter of social fact. Dworkin and his followers argue that law is an aspect of morality, one that is dependent on contingent facts about the system.

I take a different tack. Lost in this dispute is one of Hart's central contributions to legal philosophy, namely the centrality of law's internal normative structure to a theory of law. Beyond remedying the structural deficiencies with Austin's view, Hart sought to explain the fundamental effect of law on the normative landscape of a community. In arguing for the importance of secondary and power-conferring rules in a theory of law, Hart remarks,

> if such rules of this distinctive kind did not exist we should lack some of the most familiar concepts of social life, since these logically presuppose the existence of such rules. Just as there could be no crimes or offences and so no murders or thefts if there were no criminal

[2]115 NY 506, 22 NE 188 (1889). [Hereinafter *Riggs*.] Dworkin raised a number of cases in this discussion to illustrate his point, but *Riggs* is the one that has most gripped theorists' imagination and dominated subsequent discussions of the problem. This is probably because it is most plausibly characterized as a judgment of what the law *is* rather than an alteration of the law based on what it ought to be. See ch. 2 Dworkin (1978) generally for Dworkin's famous attack on legal positivism from the problem of hard cases.

[3]*id.* at 511f; 190.

> laws of the mandatory kind which do resemble orders backed by threats, so there could be no buying, selling, gifts, wills, or marriages if there were no power conferring rules; for these latter things, like the orders of courts and the enactments of law-making bodies, just consist in the valid exercise of legal powers.[4]

Hart is here alluding to a central aspect of law. Among the various non-legal advantages or disadvantages that might result from the establishment of a legal system, law also introduces new, distinctively *legal* ways that people might relate to one another. These might be related to underlying moral considerations that bear on people's relations, but they are not reduced to them, and they are not wholly explained in terms of underlying, non-legal concepts. So, e.g., just as the rules of a game make possible new ways to move, score, win, lose, take a turn, etc. according to its rules, so too does the introduction of a system of legal rules to a community make it possible for people to buy property, sell it, own, steal from, get married, commit a crime, and bear other relations towards one another. These are distinctive in that they expand ways that people can relate to each other, enriching the normative possibilities of a community, and they are capable of authorizing the state to uphold them. Unlike games, however, and clubs, universities, and other social institutions, the establishment of law is fundamental to the normative structure of a community. Hart underscores its importance:

> the introduction into a society of rules enabling legislators to change and add to the rules of duty, and judges to determine when the rules of duty have been broken, is a step forward as important to society as the invention of the wheel. Not only was it an important step; but it is one which, as we shall argue in Chapter IV, may fairly be considered as the step from the pre-legal into the legal world.[5]

The introduction of secondary power-conferring rules and the legal powers and institutions that they establish is one of the central organizing factors of modern society. The establishment of a system of law is a fundamental a societal shift, as important and innovative, Hart contends, as the invention of the wheel.

I will elaborate on this idea and argue for its moral significance. I will argue that law, so understood, coordinates the actions of people conceived as independent rational actors, capable of setting and pursuing their ends for themselves. In essence, it takes its subjects to be "choosing beings," as Hart remarks in his discussion of the role of excuses in law, or as a community of "choosing beings," capable of exercising their power of choice independently, but whose ends and actions can conflict with one another.[6] This is morally valuable because, as I shall argue, it both makes possible a range of normative relations that people can bear towards one

[4]Hart (2012), p. 32.

[5]Hart (2012), pp. 41f.

[6]As will become clear, this isn't the exact picture of law that I defend, but like Hart, I think it is part of the idea of law as the union of primary and secondary rules that it takes its subjects to be rational actors capable of setting their own ends. See Hart (1968), p. 44 defending a "mercantile view" of law, on which people should consider "law not as a system of stimuli but as what might be termed a choosing system, in which individuals can find out, in general terms at least, the costs they have to pay if they act in certain ways."

another and secures these with the power of the state, while at the same time guaranteeing that the state will secure just these relations, leaving all other interactions free from the threat of state interference. This does not mean that law is necessarily just, or that the posited law must satisfy some moral criteria in order to be valid; positivists wholeheartedly deny both theses. But, I suggest, when the law is just, the enriched normative relations that law makes possible are *morally* valuable, because, among other things, they allow people to interact as independent actors.

I will argue that this important aspect of law follows from Hart's conception of law as the union of primary and secondary rules, united by an ultimate rule of recognition. Together, these explain the idea of law as a system of rules, and, resultingly, the notion of a rule as a valid standard of the system. Specifically, Hart's conception of law can explain law as a binding system of rules, issued by an authorized source and backed by a public sword. As Hart painstakingly argues against Austin, a theory of law that ignores these crucial notions fails to explain law. Discussions of the normative significance of legal positivism thus ought to attend to this crucial distinction between Hart and Austin.

The idea that law governs people capable of setting and pursuing ends for themselves makes law specially vulnerable to hard cases like *Riggs*, or so I shall argue. This is because it is always possible for rational actors to act so as to subvert law's aims, as Elmer did in *Riggs*. Dworkin is thus right to hold that the problem of hard cases is inescapable for positivists. However, I argue, those very features of law that make it vulnerable to hard cases also provide the resources to resolve them. When the law confers a system of rights, it also reserves the authority to uphold them, and the decision in *Riggs* is just an attempt by the law to reassert its authority over one who usurped its power for illegitimate ends. Nothing more than appeal to law's systematic nature, as an authoritative system of rules coordinating the activities of independent actors, is needed to resolve this case. Most importantly, no further appeal to morality is necessary. My solution thus remains a positivist one.

2 Riggs v. Palmer

Riggs is a civil case brought by Francis Palmer's two daughters, Mrs. Riggs and Mrs. Preston, against his grandson, Elmer Palmer, after Elmer was charged and found guilty of murdering his grandfather in order to expedite his inheritance. The plaintiffs argued that notwithstanding the validity of the will, and the clear language, clearly bequeathing Elmer the remainder of the estate, it is an affront to law and to common sense that it should allow the property to devolve to the murderer in such a circumstance. Elmer was clearly set to inherit under the Statute of Wills that governed the case at the time, and there were no contravening posited laws overriding the Statute. Nonetheless, the Court split in its judgment, with the majority siding against Elmer. It is true, the majority argued, that under the posited law, Elmer stood to receive his grandfather's inheritance. The judges also conceded that this was the law governing the matter and that there were no further posited considerations that bore on the issue. However, this alone did not settle the question. Instead, they argued, it was a "fundamental maxim of the common law"[7] that is grounded in the "universal law administered in all civilized countries"[8] that no one should be permitted to profit from his own wrong, and that this principle superseded Elmer's entitlement to inherit under the governing statute. In other words, they argued, despite its lack of recognized pedigree, and despite the fact that the posited law points to the opposite conclusion, the principle governing the issue in this case is that no man should profit from his own wrong, and that it is legally binding because of its appropriateness to the circumstances.

The controversy that the Court encountered in rendering a judgment in *Riggs* did not arise from gaps in the law, or because the law on the matter was unclear. There were no omissions or mistakes in the language in the governing statute. Nor was *Riggs* a borderline case where the court had to decide where to draw the line on an issue. The facts in *Riggs* clearly fell under the statute, and the wording of the statute was clear on the matter: the will was a valid one, and Elmer was designated as the beneficiary. The judges also all agreed about what happened; the facts of the case were not in dispute. In all these respects, *Riggs* was an easy case. Rather, the difficulty that the Court encountered in *Riggs* was that the posited law did not, on its own, settle the question of what the law on the matter was. Even though they agreed on the facts of the case and what the posited law dictated, the presiding judges continued to dispute what the law required. And, in rendering its decision, the majority in *Riggs* relied on a further, unposited consideration, namely, the principle that no man should profit from his own wrong. Most importantly, the majority insisted that even though this principle was binding in virtue of its merits, not its sources, the decision remained a judgment about what the law *was*, and not what it ought to be. The challenge posed by *Riggs* is to explain the possibility of legally valid considerations that are binding in virtue of their merits, not their sources.

As mentioned in the introduction, this problem is interpreted in terms of explaining the role of morality in law. The moral repugnance of awarding Elmer the inheritance is thought to be just too appalling for the Court to countenance. Positivists have responded by arguing that the legal validity of considerations binding by virtue of their merits is itself a matter of social fact.[9] Anti-positivists deny that the ultimate test for legal validity can be a social one.[10]

My claim then is that *Riggs* does not pose a problem of unposited legally valid moral considerations at all. It is decided on the basis of the inner workings of law conceived as an authorized system of inter-related rules, as Hart insisted in his rejection of Austin's approach. In short, I believe, it is an instance of the law

---

[7]*Riggs* at 511; 190, as per Earl, J.

[8]*id.* at 511f; 190.

[9]Inclusive and exclusive positivist responses to this problem laid out the terrain of scholarship for decades to come. Some key responses include Hart's Postscript in Hart (2012), p. 238; Joseph Raz (1972); Lyons (1977), Coleman (1982); Waluchow (1994); Shapiro (2011).

[10]Dworkin (1986), Greenberg (2006).

speaking in one voice, as Dworkin might say. This idea lies in the difference Austin drew between a society governed by law and one held together by "mutual intercourse" alone, or in Hart's sharper distinction between law and a "gunman scenario writ large," a distinction I argue that Hart makes the centre of his account. These latter notions lack the internal normative structure of law and, I shall argue, the moral significance of being governed by such an authorized system of rules.

3 The Distinctive Features of Law

The idea that a theory of law must explain law's distinctive binding force can be traced back to John Austin.[11] Austin took the first task for a theory of law to be to identify the law of a society and distinguish it from all other rules and standards to which people are subject.[12] Laws are rules "properly so-called" for Austin; they are obligation-conferring or categorically imperative. They tell people what they must do, and not just what they should do or what would be good for them to do given their ends and inclinations. They are thus different from social habits or patterns of behaviour and positive morality like rules of fashion or honour which typically bind hypothetically. They are also different from laws of nature and rules governing instinctive behaviour of plants and animals, which are inviolable or categorical in a sense, but don't act on the will. In short, Austin notes rules "properly so-called" are set "set by intelligent and rational beings to intelligent and rational beings;"[13] they operate through the will and reason rather than by instinct or nature.

This raises a puzzle for Austin because law is socially contingent. Its content and existence amount to nothing more than things people say and do and their inclinations to comply or not comply with existing practices. How then can law bind people categorically regardless of their ends and desires? Austin solved this problem by positing an uncommanded commander and designating its commands as the source of all law. The threat of sanction gives them imperative force, binding people categorically regardless of their desires. The uncommanded commander, or the highest person or office in a chain of command, is the sovereign of a community and the presence of such an office is the mark of an independent political society. Austin thus identified the distinctive features of law, and distinguished a society governed by law from one in a state of nature, or a society held together by "mutual intercourse" alone.

Despite Austin's failures, Hart inherited from him the problem of legal validity as the defining problem for a theory of law. Like Austin, Hart placed legal validity, or law's distinctive binding force, at the centre of a theory of law, and took the problem of reconciling it with law's social nature to be the core puzzle to be solved. The

[11] Austin (2000).

[12] See Austin's discussion in Austin (2000), Lecture I.

[13] Austin (2000), Lecture I, p. 4.

structural failures of Austin's theory of law are well-known, leading Hart to describe Austin's view as a "gunman scenario writ large."[14] Law as commands backed by threats[15] issued by one who is habitually obeyed cannot explain power-conferring rules, the distinction between acting in a public or private capacity, the persistence of laws and succession of legislative authority, the existence of constitutional democracies, and so on.

Hart crucially rejected Austin's attempt to explain the *normative* features of law as well. Hart detailed at length Austin's inability to explain why legal rules impose obligations or confer rights; the legal authority to issue law; how this authority can be created or extinguished, how it can be transferred from one official to another without interruption or how it can persist even when the occupants of these offices change; Austin also can't explain the normative relations among rules, particularly their ability to serve as reasons for decisions and actions people take under the law and their ability to justify conclusions that officials and people subject to the law might draw under its rules. Together these features constitute what I call the *internal normative structure* of law, and Hart shows, these are also central to a theory of law.

Hart explains the notion of rules in terms of the problematic concept of an internal point of view. This idea is fraught with difficulty and the source of much confusion, in large part due to Hart's explanation of it in terms of the adoption of a critical attitude towards or endorsement of a rule or a system of rules, which, as many writers have pointed out, need not be present for the existence of a rule. Thankfully though, the key insight can be reformulated in terms of the reason-giving force of rules and the rational relationship between them in a system of rules and their ability to ground inferences and serve as reasons for conclusions and actions people might take under the rules.[16] The problem of explaining the distinctive nature of legal validity and law's internal normative structure thus amounts to the problem of explaining the reason-giving force of legal rules (where they have it), and the rational relations they bear to one another.

The "root cause," Hart argues, of Austin's failure in the basic components of his theory – commands threats, and habits of obedience—these "do not include, and cannot by their combination yield, the idea of a rule, without which we cannot hope to elucidate even the most elementary forms of law."[17] This is a key claim but it is somewhat obscure. Why not? What does the notion of a rule add to Hart's account that is missing from Austin's approach to law as habits, obedience, and threats? In short, rules, unlike the threat of sanctions or mere incentives, can provide the appropriate kind of reason and operate on the will in the way described by Hart and Austin as distinctive of legal validity. They issue in obligations "properly so-called," as Austin required, or can serve as legal reasons in the manner required

---

[14]See Hart's discussion in Hart (2012) ch. IV and *passim*.

[15]Note that Hart rejected Austin's use of the term "command," and replaced it with the notion of "orders," since even commands imply an element of authority to issue them. Hart (2012), p. 19.

[16]For a classic discussion of these issues, see Raz (1999).

[17]Hart (1968), p. 80.

by Hart. By so doing, they presume those subject to them to be "choosing beings," providing them with reasons to comply, rather than well-placed stimuli, "goading the individual by its threats into conformity."[18] Law conceived as a system of rules thus presumes the rationality of those subject to it and their ability to act for reasons and choose for themselves, rather than conceiving of people behaviouristically, responding to stimuli placed in their path.

Hart's solution to the difficulties that Austin encountered was to introduce the distinction between primary and secondary rules and to conceive of law as the union of these two types of rules united by an ultimate rule of recognition. These are necessary for explaining the distinctive features of law. They explain power-conferring legal rules allowing people to get married, make wills, contracts, legislate, etc. They are also necessary for explaining the notion of legal obligation, the subjection of officials to legal rules, the distinction between acting in a public or private capacity, the persistence of laws and succession of legislative authority, the existence of constitutional democracies, etc.

Most importantly, Hart's conception of law as the union of primary and secondary rules ordered by an ultimate rule of recognition explains how these various authorities and duties fit together as a system, structured by the posited rules, and organized as a coherent whole. Hart's conception of law explains how legal rules can serve as reasons for legal conclusions, and how they can authorize the decisions and actions that people take under them. As such, they give effect the important normative relations that people can bear under law, like owning and exchanging property, punishing a crime, being under a legal obligation (or having a legal right) and the other examples that Hart listed in the quotation in the introduction. As Hart makes clear, a theory of law that cannot explain these has failed to fully explain law.

It is thus in the idea of law as the union of primary and secondary rules ordered by an ultimate rule of recognition, and not in commands backed by threats issued by one who is habitually obeyed that one can find the "key to the science of jurisprudence." The existence of an ordered system of these types of rules is the identifying mark of law and distinguishes societies governed by law from mere natural societies or ones held together by "mutual intercourse" alone.

Law thus occupies an awkward position for Hart of being in a sense more normative than unconnected commands or social rules, but not giving rise to full-blown moral rights and obligations, and not necessarily having moral content or serving moral ends.[19] It is like sports or a game for Hart: consisting of a systematic and internally ordered set of rules, but furthering no particular external purpose. The challenge for positivists since Hart has been to explain this position without running afoul of Austin's mistake of stripping law of all normativity or conceiving of law as

---

[18]Hart (1968), p. 44, discussing his "mercantile" view of law on which people can choose for themselves whether to comply or violate the law by weighing the costs and benefits for themselves.

[19]Hart remarks of the rule of recognition, "by providing an authoritative mark it introduces, although in embryonic form, the idea of a legal system: for the rules are now not just a discrete unconnected set but are, in a simple way, unified." Hart (2012), p. 95.

necessarily moral as natural law theorists do, while anti-positivists maintain the untenability of this middle ground. My aim is to draw out some of the moral implications of these features of law for a positivist theory of law and for the purposes of the problem posed by *Riggs*.

Positivists often insist on a strict separation between law's internal and external normativity, and limit law's external morality to formal ends like stability, predictability, security, etc. and its ability to coordinate people's activities.[20] This cannot be all that law does however. This is because it leaves the distinctive features of law that distinguish it from Austin's set of commands backed by threats unexplained. Coordination, stability, predictability, etc. require that people have *some* common set of rules or considerations, of which they are all aware, and to which they can all appeal when planning their affairs requires them to take into consideration the activities of others. But this is not all that law provides. As Hart takes pains to show, law not only gives people an indication of how those around them will behave; it gives people a legal *right* to have others behave this way, and imposes a legal *obligation* on others to so behave. Second, in order to confer these rights and obligations on people, law must also be issued from an *authorized source*; otherwise, it consists of the arbitrary exercise of power. Finally, not all harms count as legal sanctions. Instead, law backs these rights and obligations with a *public* sword; it entitles each person to call upon the power of the state in order to protect her rights against others and to enforce people's obligations against one another. As we know from Hart, these are distinctive marks of law. An account of the moral significance of law that leaves out these key aspects ignores those fundamental features that makes law *law*, beyond the fact that it constitutes just some set of standards and incentives for coordinating people's behaviour. As I shall argue, this is key to explaining law's moral significance *as law* compared to just any system of social rules.

My emphasis on law's moral significance is closely related to Lon Fuller's account of law's "inner morality,"[21] in that the moral values I emphasize follow from the conceptual nature of law or law's internal normative structure, and not from any external aims or purposes to which law is put. In this respect, our views are quite similar. Hart's main objection to Fuller is that if the formal values he attributed to law (publicity, generality, prospectivity, clarity, etc.) hold for any purposive activity and are at best conditions of efficacy, consistent with good or wicked ends; they are hardly moral at all.[22] To the extent that law's morality is merely formal in this sense, it poses no threat to positivism. This is consistent with my view, which aims to

---

[20]Hayek (1944, 1960) are good examples of this view.

[21]Fuller (1964).

[22]In response to Fuller, Hart notes that "Poisoning is no doubt a purposive activity, and reflections on its purpose may show that it has its internal principles. ("Avoid poisons however lethal if they cause the victim to vomit," or "Avoid poisons however lethal if their shape, color, or size is likely to attract notice.") But to call these principles of the poisoner's art "the morality of poisoning" would simply blur the distinction between the notion of efficiency for a purpose and those final judgments about activities and purposes with which morality in its various forms is concerned." Hart (1965), p. 1286.

identify the distinctive moral significance of law, where the law of a community is good. More importantly, however, my view does not posit any aims or purposes for law. Positivists often take law's moral value to lie in its instrumental value or the external aims or purposes it serves.[23] No doubt these are important. My point is that an account of these aims that ignores the distinctive features of law is missing an important aspect of law's moral significance. I aim to elucidate this internal moral aspect of law.

4 Law as the Union of Primary and Secondary Rules

My claim is that the distinctive normative structure of law conceived as a system of authorized primary and secondary rules united by an ultimate rule of recognition makes possible a certain kind of rational behaviour for people and that this is morally valuable.

Specifically, it makes it possible for people to coordinate their actions as independent actors, or people capable of setting and pursuing ends for themselves and entitled to do so, separate from the ends and pursuits of all others. In short, it allows people to interact with one another as strangers; they can interact without knowing or taking into account the ends and pursuits of everyone else. This makes possible many of the interactions that are familiar aspects of modern social life. It does so by introducing a range of normative relations that people can bear to one another. These interactions are possible without law, but they are not as secure as when they are enshrined in law and backed by the power of the state. This added security, along with the authorization to engage in these legally-sanctioned interactions, backed by a public sword, facilitates these interactions and enhances the normative landscape of the community. This does not mean that law is necessarily good or that the posited law always lives up to this ideal. It is always possible that the posited law is wicked or that it fails to enact these important normative notions. But, where there is good law, it gives effect to this important aspect of morality. This, I suggest, is distinctively morally important about law. And it results from the advances Hart makes over Austin's theory or law, namely conceiving of law as an authorized system of primary and secondary rules that are all united by an ultimate rule of recognition.

I shall argue that this results in a system of rules that is *fixed, public,* and *coordinated.* When people are governed by a legal system, they are subject to a set of rules conferring a coordinated set of rights and duties on them. Specifically, when people are governed by a legal system, they are subject to a set of rules securing for each person a range of action over which she is entitled to be free from

[23] See especially John Gardner (2012) ch. 8, "On the Supposed Formality of the Rule of Law," emphasizing this idea in connection with legal positivism. Indeed, Andrei Marmor takes the idea that law is fundamentally a means to be a "core commitment" (and the least controversial one) that all positivists share (Marmor 2006).

interference by those around her, but limiting this range of action to that which is consistent with others' entitlement to the same; people thus also incur a set of obligations to respect the rights of all other subjects of the system.

The law secures these rights and obligations with the threat of force. When someone has a right at law, she is entitled to call upon the power of the state to protect it from encroachment by others, and when she is under an obligation, she is subject to the threat of state coercion for its violation.

This does not mean that the state will protect people's interests from all sources of interference, nor is it a promise to provide people with the conditions for achieving their aims come what may. It is always possible that, say, despite their best efforts, people fail to achieve the ends they set for themselves: I might do all that I can do but my efforts might be thwarted by natural forces, or, say, someone else gets there first, and so on. These are all unhappy results, but they are not violations of my legal rights. The entitlement to be free from interference is also not a promise that people will in fact refrain from interfering with one another's rights. Rights and duties are rational constraints; it is up to the actor to decide whether or not to comply. By backing legal rights and obligations with the power of the state, however, law gives public warning that violations of these rights and duties are taken at the risk of state coercion, and that the state might force the wrongdoer to redress her wrong.

At the same time, the state is limited to protecting *just* those interests secured by legal rights and duties; people can engage in all other activities free from the threat of state coercion. People are of course subject many other obligations to one another, the violation of which can result in many other sanctions. People, e.g., make promises to one another, are members of families, form friendships, and so on, all of which subject people to obligations and threaten people with various forms of sanction for their violation. But, the law limits the exercise of *state* coercion to upholding just those that are prescribed by law; there are no further types of behaviour that the state is justified in coercing.

I suggest that law can provide the security it does because, as Hart shows, it consists of the union of primary duty-imposing rules and secondary power-conferring rules, and it is founded in an ultimate rule of recognition.[24] This is because such a system of rules enables law to issue rules conferring a set of legal rights and duties on the people living under it. This set of rules is fixed, public and coordinated. We can see this if we consider the various elements of Hart's theory, and the distinctive features of law that I am emphasizing.

Primary rules are action-guiding rules. They tell people what, according to the law, they can and cannot do. Power-conferring rules are rules setting out the conditions under which people can create, amend, or extinguish primary rules. Intuitively speaking, power-conferring rules are rules establishing legal institutions, like legislatures, courts, judges, police, etc. Legal systems must include such rules in order to render intelligible the idea that, under some circumstances, members of a

[24] Hart (2012) ch. V.

community act and speak in an official law-creating, applying, and enforcing capacity, separate from acting on their personal desires and judgments.

Power-conferring rules also include rules setting out the conditions for making a valid will or contract, and other ways that private parties can alter their legal status with respect to each other. These rules are a kind of power-conferring rules because people are acting like private legislators when they change their legal status in accordance with these rules. But, there remains a significant difference between the actions that private parties take pursuant to these rules and the actions of officials; private parties do not act in an official capacity when they, say, make a will, get married, incorporate, and so on. Moreover, the powers they have to change their legal status consist in just those that the law confers on them; the law prevents people from unilaterally changing their legal status with respect to each other. Indeed, as we shall see, this is the central idea that the notion of a secondary rule explains.

Finally, law is founded in an ultimate rule of recognition setting out the authoritative criteria for validity for all the subordinate rules of the system. This rule imposes a hierarchical order on all the subordinate rules of the system, thereby establishing a means of resolving conflicts between them, should they arise. The rule of recognition thus unites all the various rules of the system into a systemic and coherent whole, and the various judgments and actions of the officials of the system into that of a single public authority capable of speaking in a unified voice.

Such a system of rules enables law to issue rules conferring a set of legal rights and duties on the people living under it. This set of rules is fixed, public and coordinated.

First, to say that these rules are fixed is not to say that these rules are unchanging or unchangeable. On the contrary, as Hart points out in his criticism of John Austin, one of the distinctive features of a legal system is that it provides the procedures for creating, amending, and extinguishing its own rules.[25] The rules conferring rights and duties are fixed in the sense that they are determined by facts that are independent of the whims and activities of private actors. This is because these rules are those that are enacted pursuant to the recognized procedures of the system, and it is just to the extent that a rule is enacted in accordance with these procedures that it confers a legal right or duty; no other rights or duties, no matter how weighty, morally good, or widely practiced, are enforced by law. To say that law provides people with a fixed set of rules then is to say that it provides them with a set of rules that are fixed at any given time by facts that are independent of people's private behaviour and attitudes in this respect.

Secondly, by making legal validity depend on conformity with specified procedures, the existence of power-conferring rules makes people's legal rights and duties public. This is because on this conception of law, whether or not a given rule is a rule of the system depends the actions and judgments of public officials; they are issued by public officials, acting in their public capacities, in accordance with public procedures. In this respect, people's legal rights and duties depend on facts that are

[25] Hart (2012) ch. III.

available to all subjects of the system, and the continued existence of these rights and duties, or their extinction, remains a matter of public fact; they may not be changed or be extinguished in secret.[26] These rules are not always easily discernable, nor is there always a clear answer to what the law requires in any given case. As we well know, legal systems can be indefinitely complex and people often need significant expertise in order to determine what the law requires in a given case. But, legal rights and duties are public in that the facts that make it true that a given person is under a legal right or duty are available to the public at large, and, that these are the relevant facts for determining people's rights and duties under the system is also a publicly available fact.

Finally, power-conferring rules also make it possible for law to issue a coordinated set of rules conferring a coherent set of rights and duties. Law confers a coordinated set of rules insofar as its rules work together to promote, rather than impede action. So, for example, where the law grants a right, it also imposes corresponding obligations to respect it; the law does not permit and prohibit the same action; it does not require people to engage in conflicting actions, or do and refrain from engaging in the same action, or otherwise require practical impossibilities. This does not mean that conflicts are impossible, or that they do not arise between the various rights and duties conferred by the system. In a system that is sufficiently complex, and that is created and maintained by many individuals, conflicts between rules are not unlikely. But, power-conferring rules allow law to resolve conflicts when they do arise by including rules for ordering the subordinate rules of the system and deciding conflicts. Where there is no such explicit rule for settling a conflict, the law will direct people to an authoritative official whose judgment on the matter settles the question. The important point here is that where conflicts between rules do arise, their resolution is also a question for the legal system; the system does not leave conflicts to be resolved by the subjects themselves. This is so just by virtue of the fact that the power-conferring rules return questions arising from the issuing, application, and enforcement of its rules to the system.

5 Independence

This makes possible the complex kinds of interactions between people that people typically associate with life under a legal system, and think are absent in pre-legal societies.

Where there is no law, whether or not people's interactions go well or badly for them depends on the particular characteristics of those around them. People might be

[26]This is a slight overstatement, but the basic idea is correct. Rules might sometimes be created or changed in secret, because e.g. they are classified or for the sake of national security, etc. Ordinarily though when this happens, the criteria for secrecy are public, so at the very least there is public oversight over the procedure. This is an impoverished notion of publicity to be sure, but I believe the principle remains the same.

kind and generous towards one another, and they might respect the interests of those around them, but they might not, and whether or not they do depends on the particular attitudes and inclinations people have on the matter. This is not to say that people are subject to the *mere* whims and inclinations of those around them where they have no law. Absent a system of fixed legal rules, people may well develop practices of, say, respecting one another's holdings and engage in trades or exchanges of them; they might refrain from injuring one another, and inflict harm on those who do injure people, and so on. These practices can help to force some people to treat those around them well, even when they are not so inclined. But, whether or not such practices are in place, and which practices people adopt remains a function of the particular characteristics of the members of the community, as does their continued existence. It is thus just to the extent that the members of a community are inclined to adopt and enforce such practices that they are in place. As a result, where there is no fixed set of rules for settling such conflicts, there is *nothing further* than people's whims and choices to which people can appeal. That is, there is no further standard to which they can hold one another, other than that which is set by the particular choices of particular people in order to settle such conflicts and redress wrongs when they occur.

This makes people's relations with one another doubly insecure. On the one hand, people are independent actors, capable of choosing their ends and pursuits for themselves, independently of ends and pursuits of others. Although they might take their ends and pursuits of those around them into consideration when deciding what to do, they need not. As a result, when people interact with one another, they are vulnerable to the risk that others might act against their interests and injure them. On the other hand, where there is no fixed, public, and coordinated set of rules for governing people's activities with respect to one another, people are vulnerable to the possibility of suffering *any* injury at the hands of another; there is no limit to the ways in which people might harm one another. As a result, people are wholly vulnerable to the whims and inclinations of those around them.

One way of mitigating against these risks is to physically insulate oneself from the activities of others, making the risk of harm by one's neighbours physically impossible, or unlikely. People might thus, e.g., build fortresses around their homes, or impose other physical barriers between themselves and those around them. This is a useful strategy, and it is especially important for protecting things that are not fungible, like one's person. So, for example, people, have reason to drive defensively even when they have the right of way because the available remedies for accidents are poor compensation for the potential injuries that one might suffer.

Another way to mitigate the risk of injury at the hands of another is to provide people with an avenue of recovery should an injury occur. The availability of recourse for recovery does not necessarily make the possibility of injury less likely (though it may help, since it increases the cost of engaging in risky activities). But it can reduce the harm that people suffer when an injury does occur by displacing some of the resulting costs of the injury. The availability of recourse can thus relieve people of the responsibility for bearing the full burden of the loss. It is thus another way of making people's interactions with one another more secure, even though it does not (necessarily) reduce the risk of injury directly.

Where there is no law, people are vulnerable to both kinds of risk. They are vulnerable to the possibility people take no heed of the needs and interests of those around them into account, and they are vulnerable to the risk that any of their aims or pursuits might be thwarted by the activities of another. To be sure, people might adopt alternative means for relieving each other of these risks and making their interactions with each other more secure. As we saw above, people might, say, physically insulate themselves from the activities of others, or institute practices of, say, respecting one another's interests, and, say, forcing people to compensate one another for what is owed. As we have seen, however, whether or not they do engage in such practices depends on the whims and inclinations of the members of a given community, making people once again vulnerable to the particular characteristics of those around them.

Law, of course, does not relieve people from the physical risk of suffering a harm at the hands of another. Law does not consist in a set of physical constraints, that physically prevent people from harming one another, and this is what would be needed in order to protect people from the possibility of harm in this way. Rather, as we have seen, it gives people *reason* to act or refrain from acting in certain ways. It does so by consisting in a system of rules prescribing the legal rights and duties that its subjects can invoke the power of the state to claim against one another, coupled with the assurance that these are the only claims that the state will enforce against its subjects; there are no further complaints that subjects can call upon the state to enforce against one another beyond those prescribed by law. It thus remains possible for people to harm one another in violations of the rights and obligations that the law imposes on them, even when they are subject to a legal system.

But the distinctive features of law described above—namely, that it is fixed by facts that are independent of any person or group's personal characteristics, that these facts are publicly available to all the subjects of the system, and that they form a unified system, directing questions of conflict or indeterminacy back to the system to be resolved—relieve people of the risk that people might refuse or fail to take the needs and interests of those around them into account, and that there is no limit to harms to which they are vulnerable. It does so by being a fixed, public, and coordinated system of rules in the manners described. This provides people with a further set of standards that, first, do not depend on the whims and inclinations of any particular person or group, and whose continued existence is independent of what anyone thinks of these rules, or whether or not people comply with them. Second, people can determine according to these standards, for any given action, whether or not it is subject to the threat of state coercion, and they are entitled to hold those around them to this standard as well. And, third, these standards set out the conditions of state coercion conclusively, so that where questions as to the rules' requirements do arise, as in cases of conflict or indeterminacy, they are not left to be settled by the subjects themselves. Although, as mentioned above, the existence of such a set of rules does not make violation impossible, it assures people that they can seek recourse when they do occur, and that these are the only claims that people can call upon the power of the state to enforce against one another, thereby relieving people of some of the risks they face when interacting with other actors.

The availability of such a set of rules makes it possible for people to interact with strangers or with one another as strangers without facing the insecurity described above. It does so because it guarantees to all subject a legal system that they can seek recovery from if they are injured by another party to an interaction, but that they are responsible for no more than the cost of the harm in the case of an injury; they cannot be made to shoulder *all* of others' misfortunes. This makes possible many of the complex and limited interactions among strangers that are familiar aspects of social life.

So, for example, it is of course possible that, even without a legal system in place, people can designate routes for travel, that they develop conventions coordinating their travel, and that these conventions are steady and well-established, so that people can safely get from one place to another. But, it is the existence of a fixed system of rules securing people's right of way on the green light but not the red; at the crosswalk but not in the middle of the road; designating the roads for drivers but not, say, lawns or sidewalks, and so on, and rules denying people the authority to unilaterally change these rules, that makes possible the complex systems of traffic that we currently have. Similarly, even without a legal system, people may, say, trade goods with one another, establish a marketplace, institute mechanisms for holding one another to the bargains they strike, and so on. But, it is only with such a set of rules in place that people can, e.g., book a flight on the internet, or make a trade on the stock market. These are all risky activities, in the sense that they involve non-trivial stakes, and people stand to lose a lot in the case of injury. They are also risky in that they require the coordination of many people who often know nothing about one another, and who frequently bear no other relation to one another beyond their mutual involvement in these interactions. There are of course many rules telling people to treat each other well—rules of morality, religion, honour, social conventions, and so on. All of these make it possible for people to get along, and interact with one another as strangers, or without knowing very much about each other. But law reduces the risks of such interactions—of encountering a bad actor, e.g.—in a way that makes social interaction much easier. It is only with a system of publicly available rules publicly establishing people's rights and duties towards one another and guaranteeing that they can be held to just those rights and duties, absent further public notice, that people can engage in the all the complex, coordinated, and risky activity involved in modern-day social life.

The problem is not merely people's wickedness or uncertainty (or disagreement) about the rules of morality, though it is certainly made worse by these. Even if people are perfectly good and scrupulous in their dealings with one another, though, they still need an authoritative system of rules for fixing the boundaries of people's rights in order to pursue their ends as independent persons in the manner described above.

Morality can, for example, tell people that it is wrong to help themselves to the belongings of others, that they ought to return objects lent to them, that they ought to compensate people when they destroy their belongings, and so on. Morality can tell people that they ought to return the actual book lent, not a copy or a different book that is equally good (assuming the original hasn't been destroyed), but that, e.g., they can return a different cup of flour after the initial one they borrowed was baked into a cake. But it cannot always identify the object of a right.

Morality does not tell us, e.g., when one person writes another's page, that it is the paper that persists, even when the text is a piece of poetry, and even when it is written in gold, obliging the borrower to return the paper to its original owner, but when a borrower paints on a canvas, the canvas is destroyed and a new object—the painting—is created, obliging her to compensate the owner for the destruction of his property.[27] There is nothing morally necessary about these outcomes; either is permissible and the law could easily have reached the opposite outcomes and been equally morally sound. The value of the resulting objects; their separability from the initial object; the relative interests of the parties' in one or the other outcomes are insufficient for determining the legal result.[28] Morality dictates the return of the actual object of the right or compensation for its destruction, but it often cannot resolve precisely what that object is or which situation the parties are in. It thus cannot direct the parties in these cases to, say, return the paper with the text on it to its owner, but to compensate the owner of the canvas for the destruction of her property. And this is what it is needed in order for people to satisfy their moral obligations.

The same holds for the other rules that law provides for reconciling people's independent activities. In order for people to, e.g., drive safely in the presence of other drivers trying to do the same, they need authoritative rules specifying what counts as a road and who has right of way, no matter how careful or considerate they are; in order for people to limit their liability in their dealings with others, they need

---

[27] See Nicholas (1962), p. 134 for a discussion of the Roman law of accession in connection to these cases.

[28] Importantly, rights in objects do not necessarily follow the underlying natural object itself. Naturally separate or separable objects can be considered a single thing at law and hence the subject of a single right, as in the wheels on a truck (*Purnell v. Fooks* (1923)), sails on a ship (*Southworth v. Isham* 5 N.Y. Super. Ct. (3 Sandf.) 448), or an animal and her offspring (Justinian, *Institutes* II, i, 37, holding that "in the fruits of animals are included their young, as well as their milk, hair and wool; and, therefore, lambs, kids, calves, colts, and young pigs immediately on their birth become, by the law of nature, the property of the *usufructory*."), imposing on the borrower an obligation to return the entire expanded objects, even if she supplied the wheels, sails, care and nourishment for the animals, or if the offspring were born on her property. (She might, perhaps, be able to seek compensation for her lost materials and efforts though.) On the other hand, a single natural object can be the object of multiple rights, as when a person bequeaths an estate to his wife for life, and then to his son. (This example comes from Nicholas (1962), p. 145 (comparing the English doctrine of estates to Roman law).) Here the wife and son hold simultaneous rights in the estate, where neither right is diminished by the existence of the other as it would be if they each owned half of the estate or if they owned the estate jointly, each having half a share in the ownership of the whole, even though the son's right does not vest immediately. Another example of multiple rights existing in a single natural object would be acquisition by prescription, where one person's right in a thing is extinguished and another's is created, even though there is no corresponding change in the underlying natural object.

rules specifying the conditions under which they can incorporate, no matter how scrupulous they are. Morality might dictate that people should honour their agreements, that each citizen deserves a vote, that the guilty deserve a fair punishment, etc. But it cannot determine when a contract has been concluded or what are its terms; it cannot determine who counts as a citizen, fix the procedures for submitting a vote or the procedures governing a fair trial and authorizing the state to impose a sanction, and so on. This is so even when people are perfectly good and in perfect agreement on morality's dictates. Satisfaction of moral obligations when engaged in these practices (citizenship, voting, etc.) likewise requires the existence of a fixed and public answer to these questions.

This problem is a deep one. Rendering people's disparate aims and the actions they take in their pursuit consistent with one another does not require reconciling every action that a person can take with the pursuits of every other actor in the world. So holding would make action virtually impossible. This is because virtually every time someone acts, she limits the range of action of all other actors. If people had to take every action that every person might choose into account every time she acted, they could almost never act. Law releases people from this general obligation, on the condition that they respect others' power to act as well. But, it provides people with only a limited range of actions over which their choices are sovereign, and puts them under a corresponding obligation towards only a limited range of people, and morality cannot supply the boundaries for fixing this range of actions, or of persons towards whom people are under reciprocal obligations. As a result, although interacting in terms of independence is morally permissible, and although morality can provide people with general guidelines for governing such interactions, it cannot specify the determinate particulars for fixing the boundaries in which they can occur. It thus cannot supply people with determinate rules for rendering their independent actions consistent with one another.

The point is not that these distinctive relations can only have a bearing in the context of a legal system giving them effect. Murder and theft are wrong whether or not they are recognized as crimes under law, though the idea of them as public wrongs and the state's authority to punish them are legal notions. People could also still exchange their belongings, uphold their agreements, become families, make collective decisions, etc. without law. Legal norms are not like the rules of a game in this respect. Castling, trumping, hitting a home run, and so on have no sense beyond their specification by the rules of the game. Law is not like this. Although some important legal concepts are perhaps wholly a matter of legal artifice (perhaps, e.g. corporations), many can be grasped independently of law. Criminal wrongs (so-called *mala in se* crimes), casting a vote, making a sale, becoming a family, and many other familiar legal notions can have bearing in a community even without being fully specified by law. Law can give effect to these important notions, however, and authorize some of the decisions and actions that people take pursuant to the normative bearing that these have in ordinary social life. And, when the system in place is a just one, law can help to realize the important role that these normative relations play in a well-ordered community.

The moral significance of these internal legal concepts is intrinsic to their place within a legal system. It cannot be wholly explained in terms independent non-legal moral considerations or the beneficial results that they tend to produce. Advantages like stability and security, etc. that law produces are important, and communities can have many reasons for establishing the rule of law. But taking these to be the main, or the only moral advantage of law distorts the internal normative structure that is central to a complete understanding of law, and drains Hart's advances over Austin of their important insight. Whether a wrongdoer owes compensation, whether a contract should be upheld, whether a ruling quashed, etc. are determined through the operation of law and the normative concepts in play here are products of the system. The decision to establish or not establish a legal system, and which rules it contains can be made with reference to the non-legal ends that law serves. But, as Hart emphatically argues, law has a distinctive internal normative structure making possible a range of important normative relations that people might bear towards one another. My point is that these can also have moral significance in their own right, and this arises by virtue of their place in the system.

When a legal system is a just one, the law thus gives effect to this important aspect of morality. But law can coordinate the actions of people as independent actors even when the rules are unjust. The mere fact that they are fixed, public, and coordinated that makes such interactions possible; all that is needed for securing people's interactions with one another is a fixed, public warning about the state's use of force, and the assurance that these conditions will persist until further public notice. Of course, where the rules of the system are not good ones—where, say, they do not accord their subjects equal status, where they deny people rights that are morally valuable, etc.—subjects will likewise be incapable of lawfully engaging in free or just interactions with one another, or, at least, their ability to do so will be significantly curtailed. But, their mere ability to interact with one another as independent actors—i.e., their mere ability to set and pursue their ends for themselves and to refrain from interfering with the attempts of others – will remain intact, even where the system fails to set out moral or good conditions for interaction.

Law thus makes it possible for people to interact with one another even though they are vulnerable to one another's power of choice by establishing authoritative rules fixing the boundaries of people's rights with respect to each other, and by establishing fixed procedures for determining the creation, amendment and extinction of these rules. This makes it impossible for any particular person or group unilaterally to change these rules governing the state's use of its power on a private desire or whim. Instead, it is only under certain circumstances—namely, when officials, acting in their official capacity, change these rules in accordance with set procedures—that one can effect a change in these rules. This makes the kind of complex interactions that we typically associate with life under law possible because it allows people to interact with one another—e.g., to drive on a highway, to make a trade on the stock market, etc.—on terms of independence, or without any concern for the particular ends and pursuits of those around them. My final claim is that the fact that law can authoritatively coordinate the actions of free actors makes law vulnerable to hard cases like *Riggs*. However, law's ability to so coordinate people's actions also explains how it can decide such cases. Consider again the difficulty posed by *Riggs*.

6 *Riggs* Revisited

The Court in *Riggs* held that even though Elmer was clearly set to inherit under the will, and even though there was no countervailing posited law prohibiting murderers from inheriting, it is fundamental principle of law that no one should profit from his own wrong. For this reason, it denied Elmer the inheritance. Moreover, the Court held that this principle governed the case even though it had no posited source.

Riggs is not a hard case in the sense that it requires judges to apply a wicked or unsavoury law, nor is it hard in the sense that it arises from defects, moral or otherwise, in the formulation or application of legal rules; the Court in *Riggs* was not charged with applying unjust or wicked laws. Nor further is it hard in the sense that the relevant rules are hard to apply, or that it is unclear whether it falls under the rules in question. In all these respects, *Riggs* is an easy or clear case: the rules governing the disposition of property are just ones; the will clearly named Elmer as a beneficiary; it was clearly valid; it clearly fell under the Statue of Wills; and there was no posited law prohibiting murderers from inheriting, or otherwise vitiating the Statue. The difficulty that *Riggs* raises, then, does not lie in the application of the particular rules themselves.

Dworkin suggests that the difficulty with *Riggs* arises from the immorality of permitting Elmer to benefit from his wicked act, and the possibility that the law is implicated in such a wrong. Further commentators have adopted this analysis as well. All have supposed that the law's appeal to the principle that no man should profit from his own wrong constitutes an appeal to a moral principle in an attempt to prevent the law from furthering Elmer's immoral ends. The law on the matter is not so straightforward, however.

First, the principle upon which the Court in *Riggs* relied—that no man should profit from his own wrong—is too broad as stated. The law certainly sometimes permits people to profit from the fact that they have committed a wrong, even if they are not profiting from the wrong directly. So, for example, although many states have laws prohibiting criminals from profiting from the publication of the details of their crimes (so-called "Son of Sam" laws), not all states do, and whether or not so profiting is legally prohibited depends upon whether such a law has been enacted, rather than on a conceptual feature of law. Adverse possession and breach of contract are two other obvious examples of instances in which the law permits people to profit from their wrongs. The law thus need not prohibit all attempts to profit from one's wrong.

More importantly, however, modern legal systems typically prohibit the imposition of a penalty beyond that provided by the criminal law for the commission of a crime.[29] In general, they do not divest a person of her civil rights or her property because of a lack of desert, or dirty hands. This is so even when allowing a person the benefit of her property or civil rights is morally repugnant. So, for example, the administrators of a retirement fund cannot deny a retired police officer his pension on the grounds that he has been convicted of drug trafficking.[30] The mere fact that the officer is morally undeserving of this benefit cannot serve as the reason for denying it to him. In general, considerations of moral desert or lack of desert do not form the basis of a decision about who benefits at law. This is certainly true of the American legal system at the time that *Riggs* was decided. The Court's denial of Elmer's claim thus cannot be explained by mere appeal to his lack of *moral* entitlement to the inheritance.

Instead, the problem in *Riggs* is that the defendant committed a legal wrong *so as to gain from someone else's legal power.* Elmer's act did not just consist of the prohibited act of murder, though it was also murder. Instead, he killed his grandfather *in order to* prevent him from changing his will and disinheriting him. In other words, Elmer sought to benefit from a power that the law confers on his grandfather, namely, his power to dispose of his property as he sees fit, and he did so through legally prohibited means.

By so doing, Elmer tried to usurp his grandfather's legal right for his own gain; he tried to help himself to his grandfather's right to name the beneficiaries of his estate in order to secure his claim on the estate. But, when the law confers a power on people to dispose of their property as they see fit upon their death, it confers this power *just* on those people. No one else has the legal power to decide how they will divest their property. Of course, people might ask for advice from their family or, say, their lawyers on how to best dispose of their estate. But, the ultimate decision, at law, remains theirs; no one else's decision can have the legal effect of naming a beneficiary under a person's will. By murdering his grandfather so as to benefit under the will, Elmer attempted to subvert this power.

It is thus true that the will named Elmer as the beneficiary, that it was validly enacted, and that there was no countervailing posited law preventing murderers from inheriting in New York State at that time. But, the Court asked, "what law, human or

[29]Article III of the U.S. Constitution states that "no Attainder of Treason shall work Corruption of Blood, or Forfeiture except during the Life of the Person attainted," U.S. Const. art. III, § 3, cl. 2. This clause has been liberally construed and has been read to prevent all official attempts to impose further punishment for crimes committed. See *United States* v. *Brown*, 381 U.S. 437 (1965), 442. See also *Cummings* v. *Missouri*, 71 US 4 Wall. 277 277 (1867), holding that the deprivation of any right can count as a punishment if it is imposed as such. Similarly, article I of the U.S. Constitution prohibits federal and state Congresses from passing *ex post facto* laws and bills of attainder. Art. I, §§ 4, 9 and 10, respectively.

[30]*Board of Trustees of Police Pension and Retirement System of Oklahoma Board of Trustees of Police Pension and Retirement System of Oklahoma City v. Weed* 719 P.2d 1276, holding that the Police Pension and Retirement Board's attempt to divest an otherwise meritorious officer of his earned pension on the grounds of his criminal conviction violates the prohibition on corruption of blood and forfeitures of estates.

divine, will allow him [Elmer] to take the estate and enjoy the fruits of his crime?" It continued,

> If he had met the testator and taken his property by force, he would have no title to it. Shall he acquire title by murdering him? If he had gone to the testator's house and by force compelled him, or by fraud or undue influence had induced him to will him his property, the law would not allow him to hold it. But can he give effect and operation to a will by murder, and yet take the property? To answer these questions in the affirmative, it seems to me, would be a reproach to the jurisprudence of the state, and an offense against public policy.[31]

In other words, by murdering his grandfather in order to prevent him from changing his will, Elmer negated his claim to inherit under it just as he would have lost his claim to the title had he taken the property by force, or had he fraudulently induced his grandfather to will it to him.

The posited law's vulnerability to the possibility that its subjects unilaterally act so as to subvert the power it confers is an unavoidable feature of its structure. As a system of rules that imposes a coordinated scheme of rights and duties on people backed by the threat of state force, the law takes its subjects to be rational actors, capable of exercising their reason independently so as to result in action, but whose actions can come into conflict. By imposing such a scheme of rights and duties, the law seeks to give people reason to render their actions consistent with each other. But, by so doing, the law merely gives people reason to so act; it leaves the ultimate choice of action with the actor. It is thus always open to people to act in violation of the law.

This coordinated set of rules thus *legally* prohibits acting so as to subvert this scheme; it provides its subjects with legal reason to comply with its dictates and uphold rather than undermine this scheme. However, as rational actors, it is always open to legal subjects to attempt to subvert the law; there is no conceptual impossibility in their doing so. It is thus always possible for actors under this scheme to help themselves to its guarantees in order to seek a legally prohibited advantage; i.e., it is always open to the subjects of this scheme, as free actors, to seek to benefit from the law's protection of, for example, someone else's right to dispose of his property as he chooses, through legally prohibited means.

No combination of posited rules can prevent actors from choosing to act in this way, no matter how complete or carefully crafted. This is because no system of rules can make it impossible for subjects to abuse or subvert its guarantees. In addition to the possibility that they violate its rules, people can also abuse the law's guarantees by attempting to usurp its authority and attempting to claim for themselves powers that it reserves for other subjects, or for its officials.

Such a system of rules is vulnerable to the possibility that its subjects act this way regardless of who it designates as a subject, and which actions it permits or prohibits. This is because it is the mere fact that it seeks to govern the actions of free actors through the imposition of a fixed set of permissions and prohibitions that it leaves open the possibility that a legal actor, whoever it is, will commit a prohibited act,

---

[31] As per Earl, J., writing for the majority in *Riggs*, 512f, 190.

whatever it is, so as to gain from a legal permission. This is so even if the law denies status to, say, women or African-Americans, or, say, confers it to households or ships,[32] and even when it prohibits good acts and permits wicked ones. The law's appeal to the prohibition against profiting from one's own wrong only appears to be an appeal to a moral principle in *Riggs* because the law in this case was just.

Dworkin is thus correct to say that the positive law's inherent structure renders it vulnerable to cases like *Riggs*. But its inherent structure also provides it with the resources to resolve such cases. The law secures for the testator the exclusive right to name the beneficiaries of his estate by reserving to itself the power to determine its rules. As we know, legal rules can only be changed in accordance with fixed legal procedures since only such actions can have legal effect. It is not open to a private party unilaterally to change the rules of the system. This includes the rules conferring the power on a testator to decide who is to inherit his property when he dies. Elmer's actions constitute such a unilateral attempt. Recall the facts of *Riggs*. In this case, Elmer had warning that his grandfather might attempt to change his will and disinherit him. Elmer murdered his grandfather in order to pre-empt this possibility and guarantee his inheritance. Elmer's murder of his grandfather thus constitutes an attempt to usurp the power that the law reserves to itself to set the rules for deciding who gets to dispose of someone's property when he dies. The law can prevent such attempts just by virtue of the fact that, in setting out the conditions under which its rules are created, amended or extinguished, it makes these conditions exhaustive. Private, unilateral attempts to change the rules of the system are legally void. It is for this reason that it must hold Elmer's attempts to be void as well and deny his claim to the estate.[33]

Cases like *Riggs* are easily multiplied. Consider another example. The law can also prohibit keeping the profits from the sale of timber that was wrongfully taken from another's land and then improved.[34] This is so even if the defendants have a greater *moral* claim to the timber than do its owners. In *Wooden-Ware*, timber was taken by Indigenous peoples off land owned by the federal government but reserved

---

[32]The household is taken to be the primary legal actor under Roman law, and under U.S. Admiralty law, ships can be taken to be legal actors for the sake of proceedings *in rem*. See, Nicholas (1962), for a discussion of the Roman law of persons, and e.g., *The Ville de St. Nazaire*,124 F. 1008 (D. Or. 1903), for the discussion of the U.S. doctrine of proceedings in *rem*.

[33]One might object that by conceiving of the murder of a person in order to stop him from changing his will as a prohibited means of benefiting under the will, but, say, not the tempting or seducing of another in order to achieve this result, I am implicitly relying on a moral judgment about what does or does not count as a prohibited means of effecting a legal outcome, thereby illegitimately reintroducing a moral element to law. This misunderstands the point, however. The reason why the law does not award the estate to those who murder their benefactors in order to inherit, but does allow seducers and temptresses to inherit is not because it is wrong to murder someone in order to prevent him from changing his will (though it is wrong). Rather, it is because the murderer is adopting legally prohibited means in order to benefit from someone else's legal power, just as if he had taken the property by force or fraud. I thank Mark Greenberg and A. J. Julius for pressing me on this point.

[34]*Wooden-Ware Co.* v. *U.S.* 106 US 432, 1 S. Ct. 398 (1882).

for them. Arguably, the defendants in this case are morally entitled to the benefits of the land, even if they do not have title at law. The law, however, upheld the rights of the lawful owner as against the defendants. It did so because it prohibits such unilateral attempts to subvert its rules, even if they are morally justified.

Similarly, the law can also prohibit keeping the profits from the sale of a book in which the author intentionally commits libel for the sake of selling more books[35] or from improvements made on coal that is taken from another's mine,[36] and so on. As above, in such cases the law is preventing itself from being used as an instrument to subvert its own aims. It is true that the benefits sought by the defendants in these cases are ones that the system in question protected: in these cases, the system in question protected the profits gained from otherwise lawful sales, and those accrued through improvements one makes to one's property. But, in these cases, the defendants committed a legal wrong *so as to* benefit from these protections: Cassell & Co. helped themselves to Captain Broome's reputation *in order to sell more books*; the defendants in the coal cases helped themselves to others' coal *in order to gain from its resale*, and so on. As in *Riggs*, their acts constitute unilateral attempts to usurp powers that the law confers on others, namely, the power to control one's reputation and to seek profit from the sale of one's property. And, as above, the defendants in these cases committed these wrongs so as to benefit from the law's protections. The denial of their claims, however, is not an *ad hoc* attempt to ignore the posited law when it points to an outcome too unsavoury to uphold, or to insert morality to curtail unwanted consequences of the posited law. Nor are these cases examples of the seamless connection between law and morality. They are not an open door for the inclusion of all moral considerations in legal reasoning, as Dworkin suggests. Instead, they are instances of the law's attempt to reassert itself as an institution that delimits the range within which people are authorized to act in the face of the legally authorized powers of other agents to act. These limitations on the exercise of legal rights do not need to be posited in order to be law. Instead, they follow just from the systematic nature of law, and the fact that this precludes the unilateral attempt to change its rules.

Indeed, we can even generate another principle like the one applied in *Riggs* using this same line reasoning. In addition to preventing people from committing a prohibited act so as to benefit from another's exercise of his right, a legal system can also prevent people from exercising their legal rights so as to benefit from another's commission of a legal wrong.[37] So, for example, I cannot refuse to contract with one person unless he breaks his contract with another.[38] This is so even though

[35]*Cassell &Co. Ltd.* v. *Broome* [1972] AC 1027; [1972] 1 All E. 801.

[36]*Martin* v. *Porter*, 5 Mee. & W. 351; *Morgan* v. *Powell*, 3 Ad. & ENS. 278; *Wood* v. *Morewood*, 3 id. 440; *Hilton v. Woods*, Law Rep. 4 Eq. 432; *Jegon* v. *Vivian*, Law Rep. 6 Ch. App. 742, all cited in *Wooden-Ware*.

[37]See Holmes (1894) for raising this point in this connection.

[38]Holmes (1894), p. 12, fn. 1. Holmes cites *Temperton* v. *Russell* (1893) 1 Q.B.D. 715 in support of this point.

the system gives me the freedom to contract, including the freedom to refuse to contract, and even though, typically, legal systems relieve people of responsibility for the wrongs of others. These prohibitions do not require explicit enactment in order to be legally binding. Nor do they indicate the existence of unposited moral considerations in law. Instead, they follow just from the fact that a legal system systematically coordinates the rights of each with the rights of others, but it protects nothing more than people's entitlement to one another's rightful actions.[39]

My suggestion, then, is that the unposited moral considerations that Dworkin thinks are missing from the positivist account but that remain legally binding are just those that arise from the fact that law consists in a system of rules that confers a coordinated scheme of rights and duties on people capable of setting and pursuing ends for themselves. Doing so requires that it denies legal effect to unilateral attempts to change its rules. Hard cases arise under such a system because law governs free actors, who are capable of attempting to subvert law's structure, whatever it is. The law has the resources to resolve them because it maintains ultimate authority to determine its rules: unilateral action only has legal effect when the law confers a power. No further appeal to morality is necessary.

Dworkin is thus correct to suggest that the law is inescapably vulnerable to the possibility of the type of hard cases described above, and that, when confronted with them, the law has the resources to resolve them even when their solution cannot be traced to a posited source. A complete theory of legal validity must therefore explain law's ability to handle these cases. But, Dworkin is wrong to think that law's vulnerability to such cases poses a threat to positivism. Explaining law's ability to issue a coordinated set of rules is precisely what Hart set out to do in conceiving of law as the union of primary and secondary rules unified by an ultimate rule of recognition. And, I suggest, we need to appeal to nothing further in order to explain law's ability to resolve hard cases. In particular, no further explanation of the legal validity of moral considerations is needed.

7 Conclusion

My solution to the problem of hard cases like *Riggs* and my account of legal positivism thus emphasizes the central role that the internal normative structure of law plays in an account of law, and its independent moral significance. This might seem like a far cry from the received view of legal positivism, which takes the central

---

[39]Note that my claim is just that law *can* license these decisions by appeal to the posited law alone, not that it *must*. Legislatures can enact rules expressly prohibiting such judgments, and courts can decide otherwise. My claim, however, is sufficient to defend positivism against Dworkin's attack, since all that is needed for this is to show that the posited law is capable of deciding hard cases like *Riggs*; not that they must be decided this way. I thank Seana Shiffrin for raising this point in this connection.

task for a theory of law to provide a descriptive of what the law is, and to leave questions of its moral value to moral theory.

Notwithstanding the importance I place on law's moral significance, the account of law I propose remains a positivist one. I take law to consist only in a system of primary and secondary posited rules united by an ultimate rule of recognition, and I rely only on the advances that Hart makes over Austin's theory in explaining law's moral significance. This perhaps makes my position a normative positivist one,[40] though perhaps not,[41] and in any event, it is not a defence of positivism based on the non-legal moral benefits of law to a community.[42]

Crucially, the posited rules retain normative priority on my account. The heart of the anti-positivist challenge lies in questioning the priority of the posited law over moral considerations in determining questions of law. Dworkin and his followers take the posited law to have force just to the extent that it is backed by the relevant moral considerations.[43] Like all positivists, I deny this, and, following Hart, I take the independent legal force of the posited law to be central to a theory of law. My point is that this important aspect of law, that Hart made clear and that Austin mischaracterized, is morally significant, and that this is sufficient to resolve the problem of hard cases.

I have thus proposed a resolution to the problem of hard cases by examining the nature of legal validity. I have argued that the very features of Hart's account that resolve the puzzle raised by legal validity, namely, the difficulty of reconciling law's social nature with the fact that it binds people independently of their inclinations, and whether or not they want to be bound, solves the problem of hard cases as well. It does so because the existence of secondary rules establishes the public institutions and voice from which law is issued and enforced, but it also limits all law-creating and enforcing acts to just those that are issued by such public officials; as we have seen, no further private acts can be legally efficacious in this way. It is for this reason that Elmer's unilateral attempt to usurp his grandfather's power to divest of his property as he sees fit is void at law.

This solution differs from other positivists' resolutions by denying that hard cases raise a problem of how morality enters law. It also avoids the difficulties Dworkin encounters by arguing that all of morality is already in law. It resolves the problem of hard cases by appealing to nothing more than systematic features of law, and, as I have argued, the problem of hard cases, and *Riggs* in particular is best understood as raising questions about these features. As a result, no appeal to unposited moral considerations is necessary. Instead, I argue that the distinctive features of law that distinguish it from all other rules and considerations that people are subject to and that explain its internal normative structure and systematicity at the same time

[40]See Waldron (2001); Perry (1988); Campbell (1996); MacCormick (1985).

[41]Marmor (2006).

[42]Gardner (2001).

[43]Greenberg (2006) similarly takes moral considerations to have priority over posited ones in determining the content of law, but for different reasons.

explain its moral significance, and this is all that is needed in order to explain, and resolve, *Riggs*.

References

Austin J (2000) The providence of Jurisprudence determined. Prometheus Books
Campbell T (1996) The legal theory of ethical positivism. Dartmouth, MA, Aldershot
Coleman J (1982) Negative and positive positivism. J Legal Stud 11:139
Dworkin R (1978) Taking rights seriously. Harvard University Press, Cambridge
Dworkin R (1986) Law's Empire. Harvard University Press, Cambridge
Fuller L (1964), The morality of law, 2nd edn. Yale University Press, New Haven
Gardner J (2001) Legal positivism, 5 ½ myths. Am J Jurisprud 46:199
Gardner J (2012) Law as a leap of faith: essays on law in general. Oxford University Press, Oxford
Greenberg M (2006) "How Facts Make Law I" and "How Facts Make Law II,". In: Hershovitz S (ed) Exploring law's empire: the Jurisprudence of Ronald Dworkin. Oxford University Press
Hart HLA (1965) Book review of the morality of law. Harv Law Rev 78:1281
Hart HLA (1968) Legal responsibility and excuses, punishment and responsibility: essays in the philosophy of law. Oxford University Press, Oxford
Hart HLA (2012) The concept of law, 3rd edn. Clarendon Law Series, Oxford
Hayek FA (1960) The constitution of liberty. University of Chicago Press, Chicago
Hayek FA (1972) [1944] The road to serfdom. University of Chicago Press, Chicago
Holmes OW (1894) Privilege, malice, and intent. Harv Law Rev 8:1–14
Lyons D (1977) principles, positivism, and legal theory. Yale Law J 87(415):423–424
MacCormick N (1985) A moralistic case for a-moralistic law. Valparaiso Law Rev 20:1
Marmor A (2006) Legal positivism: still descriptive and morally neutral. OJLS 26(4):683–704
Nicholas B (1962) An introduction to Roman law. Clarendon Press, Oxford
Perry SR (1988) Hart's methodological positivism. Legal Theory 4:427–467
Raz J (1972) Legal principles and the limits of law. Yale Law Rev 81:823
Raz J (1999) Practical reason and norms. Oxford University Press, Oxford
Shapiro SJ (2011) Legality. Harvard University Press, Cambridge
Waldron J (2001) Normative (or ethical) positivism. In: Coleman JL (ed) Hart's postscript, Oxford University Press, Oxford
Waluchow WJ (1994) Inclusive legal positivism. Clarendon Press, Oxford

Between Authority and Interpretation: The Scope of Morality in Raz's Account of Law

Paula Gaido

Abstract Joseph Raz calls our attention to the conceptual link between legal norms and reasons for action. We cannot understand what legal norms are without understanding their role in our practical reasoning as protected reasons for action. In this paper, I want to challenge some of Raz's theses on legal reasoning, with his theory of law as background. Raz argues that legal interpretation and judicial adjudication are both fundamentally open to moral argument, where the voice of the legitimate legal authority is just a first voice. I think this idea clashes with the main theses that frame his theory of law. My argument is that Raz argues that even when law is effectively authoritative and settled (it is not indeterminate), judges have the power to change it based on certain reasons (excluded for the citizen, such as justice) and that, sometimes, they must change it (if the balance of reasons to change the law defeats the reasons to leave it as it is). My thesis is that this power of judges to review the law based on reasons that are excluded for citizens is incompatible with accepting the moral authority law claims to have. Raz's conception of law states a dilemma: either law is authoritative for judges and they cannot change it, or judges can change it but then it is not authoritative for them.

1 Introduction

> The crucial point is that our interest in legal authority lies in how it establishes the moral authority of the law, or parts of it. We are interested in the authority of law, if any, in order to

---

For very helpful comments to previous versions of this writing and friendly conversations, I would like to thank Ricardo Caracciolo, Cristina Redondo, Gerald Postema, Margaret Martin, Dimitrios Kyritsis, Kenneth Himma, Ezequiel Monti, Lewis Kornhauser, Juan Carlos Bayón, Larry Alexander, Horacio Spector, George Letsas, Fernando Tesón, Thomas Bustamante, Alexander Green, Simon Palmer, Rodrigo Sánchez Brigido, Alejandro Chehtman and Fabio Ortiz Pulido. I also want to especially thank Jorge Luis Fabra-Zamora and Gonzalo Villa Rosas for their suggestions and invitation to be part of this book.

P. Gaido (✉)
National Research Council of Argentina (CONICET)-National University of Córdoba (UNC), Córdoba, Argentina
e-mail: paula.gaido@conicet.gov.ar

J. L. Fabra-Zamora, G. Villa Rosas (eds.), *Conceptual Jurisprudence*, Law and Philosophy Library 137, https://doi.org/10.1007/978-3-030-78803-2_13

establish whether we have an obligation to respect and obey it. Moreover, the grounds for the authority of the law help to determine how it ought to be interpreted.[1]

Joseph Raz calls our attention to the conceptual link between legal norms and reasons for action.[2] We cannot understand what legal norms are without understanding their role in our practical reasoning as protected reasons for action. In this paper, I want to challenge some of Raz's theses on legal reasoning, with his theory of law as background. Raz argues that legal interpretation and judicial adjudication are both fundamentally open to moral argument, where the voice of the legitimate legal authority is just a first voice. I think this idea clashes with the main theses that frame his theory of law. My argument is that Raz argues that even when law is effectively authoritative and settled (it is not indeterminate), judges have the power to change it based on certain reasons (excluded for the citizen, such as justice) and that, sometimes, they must change it (if the balance of reasons to change the law defeats the reasons to leave it as it is). My thesis is that this power of judges to review the law based on reasons that are excluded for citizens is incompatible with accepting the moral authority law claims to have. Raz's conception of law states a dilemma: either law is authoritative for judges and they cannot change it, or judges can change it but then it is not authoritative for them.

In what follows I will closely analyze the main theses that frame Raz's theory of law and then explore how they relate to legal interpretation and judicial adjudication. In Sect. 2, I will articulate Raz's core thesis of law. In Sect. 3, I will critically analyze his theses on legal reasoning. Finally, I will share my conclusion.

2 Raz's Core Theses of Law

2.1 Legal Norms as Exclusionary Reasons

Raz maintains that the existence of law requires, on the one hand, institutional sources that claim legitimate authority and intentionally formulate directives with the purpose of regulating and being a guide to the behavior of their subjects.[3] On the other hand, it requires agents (typically, though not only, judges) who accept the legitimate authority of those institutional sources.[4] There is no law without this authoritative relationship between sources, norm-applying institutions and subjects. Arguably this is why Raz concludes that to understand law we need to articulate the conceptual commitments of those involved in it.[5] From the participant's

[1]Raz (2011a), p. 332.

[2]Raz (1990).

[3]Raz (1979a), pp. 37 ff.; Raz (1994a), pp. 194 ff.; Raz (1996a), pp. 249–286.

[4]Raz (1984), p. 130.

[5]Raz (1986), p. 28.

perspective,[6] Raz tells us, for conceptual reasons, legal norms should be understood as protected reasons for action.[7] That is, as complex reasons that include a first-order reason to act as they prescribe and a negative, second-order reason, which excludes the practical relevance of further considerations against the action required.[8] For Raz, what must be excluded, barring an explicit warning, are those considerations against the action required by the norm, and which would lead to rejecting the required action if they prevailed.[9] Of course, it is taken for granted here that the authority has decided within its competence or jurisdiction.[10] It is only within the scope of its jurisdiction that it has the power to prescribe certain actions and exclude the practical relevance of further considerations against the action required.

True, it is consistent for Raz to recognize that legislators or second-order norms of a legal system (e.g., constitutional norms) might set limits on exclusion, that is, set some reasons beyond the scope of exclusion. However, the more he allows for such constraints on exclusion, the less room there is for issues to be settled in advance by the legal authority.[11] Much of Raz's theoretical effort has been devoted to showing that agents who reason on the basis of protected reasons—that is, based on a partial judgment and not all things considered–retain rationality.[12]

Decisively, for Raz, the understanding of legal norms as protected reasons conceptually depends on the understanding of the legal authority as a legitimate moral authority.[13] In other words, to take legal norms as protected reasons would only be intelligible if it is assumed that its source, a legal authority, has the legitimate moral authority that it aspires to have. The central idea that is implied is that one better conforms to reasons if one follows the authoritative directives than if one acts on the basis of one's own criteria.[14] This idea includes the fact that it is possible for the authority to continue to be legitimate even though it sometimes makes moral errors.[15] This is so because, for the authority to be legitimate, it suffices with making it more likely for people to act in conformity with reason, but that conformity does not necessarily have to be ensured on every occasion. Thus, from the participant's

---

[6]That is, from the point of view of those who accept law's authority.

[7]Raz (1990), pp. 184–185.

[8]Raz (1990), pp. 49–84; Raz (1979b), pp. 22–23. In fact, only certain legal norms have for Raz this complex character. He has in mind specifically legal norms of obligation. I will refer in this paper only to these types of norms.

[9]Raz (1998), footnote 39, p. 17.

[10]Raz (1979b), p. 22; Raz (2006), pp. 1019–1020.

[11]I would like to thank Gerald Postema for underlying this point.

[12]Raz (1990), pp. 144 ff.

[13]For a critical analysis of Raz's account regarding this relationship, see Martin (2014), esp. chapters 4 and 5.

[14]Raz (2006), pp. 1012 ff.; Raz (1986), pp. 23–69; Raz (1996b), p. 11.

[15]Raz (2006); Raz (1986); Raz (2011a), esp. footnote 14, p. 343.

perspective, legitimate (legal) authorities are understood to have an instrumental character and are conceived as potentially imperfect agents.[16]

A related but different issue is the important restriction Raz places on the idea of authority that is conceptually presupposed from the participant's perspective. For Raz, from the participant's perspective there is no timeless authority.[17] The idea here seems to be that the practical force of their directives is constrained by time.[18] It seems that, for Raz, the passage of time gradually deprives the lawmaker of its moral standing. The assumed notion of authority implies that the lawmakers' chances of identifying the right reasons decline over time. Then, the authoritative relationship that structures law presupposes not only the belief in the fallible moral capacity of the legal authority, but also the belief that this capacity cannot last very long.[19] This time constraint on lawmakers deprives legal provisions of practical force—as long as no further argument is offered to replace the authority as the ground of their validity.

We can conclude that Raz's idea of legitimate legal authority is clearly delimited: it is not an almighty authority.[20] Simultaneously, there is still an important idea Raz wants us to consider: the idea of legal authority that underlies our conceptual practice implies the notion of having a matter resolved in advance by someone else.[21] Moreover, to accept the authority of legal sources means committing to take its directives as protected reasons for action. Legal systems are composed of legal norms that put an end to the practical relevance of any further deliberation, inasmuch as they are rules formulated by the legitimate authority that settle the issues at stake. Thus, from the participant's perspective—that is, from the point of view of those who accept law's authority—the authority of law seems to have two sides: it is related to the identification and force of law. From that perspective, legal authority is understood as a service for identifying the right thing to do.

Of course, as Raz argues, it is possible for people not to follow certain law because they do not care for it or find it unjust. I have in mind here those reasons of justice excluded by law. But such attitudes imply, for conceptual reasons, denying its authority.[22] Notice that although possible, such denials of authority could not be pervasive. Otherwise, the authoritative relationship Raz identifies as a necessary feature of law would disappear, and with it so would law.

---

[16]Raz (2003), p. 12; Raz (2004), p. 9.

[17]Raz (1996a), pp. 278 ff.

[18]Raz (2011a), p. 341.

[19]Raz (2011a), p. 341.

[20]This is compatible with Raz's idea of legal systems claiming the right to regulate whatever they want. Notice that what is at stake here is a restriction of time, not substance.

[21]Take this general formulation ("someone else") to involve different kind of legal sources—customs included.

[22]Raz (1996b), p. 15.

2.2 Legal Systems as Exclusionary Systems

Raz does not believe legal norms to be conclusive reasons, but *pro tanto* reasons to act.[23] Now, what kind of reasons can defeat valid legal norms as protected reasons for action in the legal field? Or, putting it differently, what are the reasons that compete in the arena of law (given that, from the participant's perspective, the idea of law implies the notion of reasoning on the basis of a partial and potentially imperfect judgment and not reasoning all things considered)? At first sight, it seems that, from the participant's perspective, *if there is settled law to the case which does not refer to extralegal considerations*, nothing further can matter. Remember that, barring an explicit warning, legal norms as protected reasons imply the idea that considerations against the action required by the legal norm are excluded. This is because of the concept of authority that is presupposed from its perspective. The idea is that "... while it is in force, the law resolves the argument and the struggle about how things should be in society."[24]

Often law does refer to extralegal considerations, and Raz admits different scenarios where legal norms, as protected reasons, do not determine what is required. On the one hand, Raz conceives of the possibility of valid laws in genuine conflict with each other.[25] On the other hand, extralegal considerations remain that are not excluded by legal norms, and which can conflict with them.[26] In both cases, a new balance of reasons would be required, where non-excluded extralegal considerations play a crucial role. Balancing valid laws in genuine conflict with each other and valid laws with those considerations that are not excluded seem to match the authoritative relationship in which participants are involved. I have no problem in admitting with Raz that law does not settle every issue. My concern is that I do not think Raz can sustain that extralegal considerations always have a role to play in legal interpretation and judicial adjudication when there is settled law that does not refer to extralegal considerations.[27]

We can explore Raz's understanding of legal norms as having just a *pro tanto* force by analyzing his theses regarding legal interpretation and judicial adjudication. According to his reconstruction of law, the room for further normative considerations in legal reasoning is rather constrained. However, Raz argues not only that judges have discretion to fill in gaps where existing law is indeterminate, but also that moral argument reigns in legal interpretation and judicial adjudication of concrete cases. Let me show you the tensions I see here.

---

[23]Raz (2006), p. 1023.

[24]Raz (1996b), p. 14.

[25]Raz (1994b), p. 59; Raz (1979c), p. 33; Raz (1994c), p. 257; Raz (2006), pp. 1019–1020.

[26]Raz (1990), p. 77.

[27]I will come back to the role Raz assigns to extralegal considerations in legal interpretation and judicial adjudication in the following paragraphs.

3 Raz On Legal Reasoning

3.1 Raz On Legal Interpretation

The conceptual link Raz identifies between legal norms, protected reasons for action and legitimate legal authority extends, in principle, to his theses on legal interpretation. That makes sense otherwise his theory of legal norms would remain void. The idea is that as long as law is the product of deliberate creation, and the moral legitimacy of the lawmakers is assumed, interpretation should reflect the intentions of its creators.[28] Clearly, I am focusing here on that settled law that assume that all further consideration against the required action are excluded.[29] The minimal intention Raz ascribes to lawmakers is that the passed laws are to be understood as one would normally understand them according to the circumstances and legal culture in which they were promulgated (Authoritative Intention Thesis). Raz wants to differentiate this minimal intention with the "real" intentions of the lawmakers.[30]

Participants of legal practices are conceptually committed to establishing the existence and meaning of laws according to this minimal intention. This is so, because from the participant's perspective, it is assumed that this is the best way to conform to reason. The authoritative relationship that frames law is the reason why legal interpretation has to be conducted in that way.[31] The type of interpretation at stake is a 'conserving' one.[32] In Raz's terms, a conserving interpretation sets out the meaning of a legal provision according to a specific reference group (author, original audience, etc.), which may or may not coincide with the common understanding at the moment of interpretation.[33]

Raz maintains that we have to identify the settled law using the interpretive conventions prevailing at the time it was promulgated.[34] And this has to be so unless

[28]Raz is articulating here his "Authoritative Intention Thesis." Raz gives reasons why this thesis could be applied not only to legislation but also to norms originated in common law. That depends, he clarifies, "... whether the common law is more like enacted law, with decisions becoming precedent if deliberately laid down as such by a court with an authority to bind itself or other courts. Or whether the common law is really customary law, consisting of the practices of the courts." In the end, he says, it rests "on the way the judge-made law of the country concerned is to be understood." Raz (1996c), pp. 359–360. See also Raz (1996a), pp. 259 ff. It must be added he thinks that—unlike legislative law-making—judicial law-making need not be intentional. A judge may make a new rule while thinking she only applies existing law. Raz (1979d), p. 207.

[29]See reference footnote 9.

[30]Raz (1996a), pp. 267–268, 271 ff.

[31]For an analysis of Raz's theses on legal interpretation, but apparently reaching different conclusions, see Dickson (2014).

[32]Raz (1996a), p. 272.

[33]Raz calls this latter kind of interpretation 'conventional interpretation.' See Raz (1996a), p. 253.

[34]Raz (1996a), pp. 267-8-5, 271 ff. It is possible to argue Raz is thinking these interpretive conventions are part of the rule of recognition of the legal system. However, as far as I know, Raz does not articulate the issue in those terms.

the authority explicitly said otherwise.[35] Raz disagrees that there are any conceptual commitments with specific interpretive conventions.[36] Different legal practices or the same legal practice across time could refer to different interpretive conventions; which one would be those interpretive conventions is an empirical issue, not a conceptual one.[37] However, I think his thesis certainly rules out some interpretative methods. His thesis implies that not every method of interpretation is compatible with it.[38] At least not without changing our concept of law. The thesis implied by the doctrine of authority conceptually excludes methods of interpretation that maintain that we have to interpret law according to what law should be or any other method of interpretation that gives practical relevance to further deliberation. Such methods of interpretation have to be excluded because of the very idea of legitimate authority as a service in the identification of the right thing to do. Raz's theory of law seems to rule out, for example, moral reading as an available method of interpreting settled law.

On the same ground, it seems that the relevant methods of interpretation at stake could only be those that refer to considerations of facts related to the moment the law was passed.[39] Moreover, it seems that the prevailing methods of interpretations on which the authorities should rely, should be consistent or at least provide in advance mechanisms for solving the possible contradictions that may arise while using them in the process of interpreting law.[40] Otherwise, the lawmaker would neither be able to know the meanings of her decisions in advance nor be a service in the identification of the right thing to do. In cases of contradictory results according to the prevailing methods of interpretation, the right thing to do would not be identified. Thus, the Authoritative Intention Thesis says something about which interpretive conventions are conceptually plausible: they have to refer to facts and provide in advance criteria for resolving potential inconsistencies if something such as settled law is to be identified.

Surprisingly, conserving interpretation seems to retain a modest role in Raz's account of interpretation, while innovative interpretation seems to have a significant role to play. It is not at all clear to me how this crucial role he assigns to innovative interpretation does not end up swallowing the exclusionary role he ascribes to law. I will develop this issue in the following paragraphs.

---

[35]Raz (1996a), pp. 268 ff.

[36]Raz (1996a), pp. 269 ff.

[37]Raz (1996a), p. 250.

[38]Raz (1996c), pp. 251, 255–256.

[39]For example: semantic conventions, technical and judicial stipulations, historical background, etc.

[40]Raz (1979d), pp. 182, 193.

3.1.1 The Room for Changing the Law

As we noted, the regulating idea of legitimate authority at stake is not an almighty one. It has limits. The central idea is that we better conform to reason if we follow authoritative directives as opposed to when we act on our own criteria. This includes the fact that it is possible for the authority to continue to be legitimate even though it incurs in error. Its errors do not undermine its legitimacy. However, for Raz, there are cases in which we are required to overcome the authoritative constraints, and change the law.[41] For Raz, there are two situations where the change of law is conceptually required: on the one hand, when the doctrine of authority supports the deviation from the Authoritative Intention Thesis; on the other hand, when the doctrine of authority itself loses its force.[42] Let's briefly explore them.

Raz argues that there are two cases where the doctrine of authority supports deviation from the Authoritative Intention Thesis: one is the case of coordination laws; the other is the case of the lawmaker's further intentions.[43] In the case of coordination laws, Raz asserts that all that matters is securing one coordinating convention. Thus it is irrelevant whether or not it was the one intended by the lawmaker. The lawmaker's intent would be secured as long as one coordinating convention is guaranteed.[44] Raz also conceives that lawmakers can incorporate further intentions for the interpretation of their provisions that can override their minimal intention. Conserving interpretation yields when the authority explicitly states, for example, that she wants her provisions to be interpreted in order to satisfy certain social goals.[45] In those cases, what the prevailed interpretive conventions say is only a first step in the practical deliberation that has to assess the concrete achievement of those further intentions.

Raz also conceives cases where the doctrine of authority directly loses its force.[46] Raz mentions two examples: on the one hand, the ostensive failure of the lawmaker's competence; on the other hand, old laws.[47] In the first case, as a result of the lawmaker's gross errors, the belief in their competence, by those to whom the norms are addressed, can no longer be maintained.[48] In the second case, instead, as mentioned, what happened is that, for Raz, the passage of time gradually deprives the lawmaker of its moral standing.[49] The case of gross errors opens the door for changing the law. The case of old laws, on the other hand, seems to imply that

[41]For an articulation of his ideas of "applying" and "creating" law, see Raz (1979c), esp. pp. 206–209.

[42]Raz (1996a), pp. 272 ff.

[43]Raz (1996a), pp. 272 ff.

[44]Raz (1996a), p. 273.

[45]Raz (1996a), pp. 274 ff; esp. footnote 27.

[46]Raz (1996a), pp. 274 ff.

[47]Raz (1996a), pp. 272 ff.

[48]Raz (1996a), pp. 276 ff.

[49]Raz (1996a), pp. 277 ff.

changing the law is only one possibility. In those cases, moral reasoning could assign special value to continuity and justify a conserving interpretation as well.[50]

However, the absence of articulated criteria to test the presence of gross errors or the moment in which the lawmaker loses its moral standing or when reasons for continuity overcome reasons for change seems to demand inescapable assessments of the moral content of all settled legal provisions, tacitly putting their practical relevance in suspense, and with it their nature as protected reasons for action. Of course, Raz clearly embraced the view from the outset that law's claim to authority is only good as far as there are sound reasons for taking the law's directives as authoritative. No doubt. Then, someone might argue that, if that is the condition under which law has authority, subjects to law must be entitled to some kind of monitoring of law's authority. There must be room for some engagement in practical reasoning by those addressed by law's directives, assessing whether, in effect, the promised benefit of acting in accordance with reasons that apply to them is realized. However, the monitoring of those results does not come alone. It tacitly implies putting in suspense the practical relevance of the balance made by the legal authority. That implies, for conceptual reasons, denying its service in identifying the right thing to do.[51]

3.1.2 Innovative Interpretation Everywhere

I want to focus now on the openly pervasive role Raz assigns to innovative interpretation in constitutional law. An innovative interpretation is, to him, one that shows a new meaning of the original. It is understood by Raz as a specific way to create law constrained by the existing meanings and conventions of interpretations.[52] Raz argues for two main theses here. Firstly, he holds constitutional interpretation must always look backward and forward. Secondly, he maintains that there are no given criteria to balance backward and forward-looking considerations.[53] It is not only where constitutional law is unsettled that a balance of backward and forward considerations should take place, but when constitutional law is settled as well. Conserving and innovative interpretation, therefore, are always present in constitutional interpretation. Which one will prevail will depend on a moral argument, and there are no criteria available beforehand to guide it.[54] I think the pervasiveness of moral argument in constitutional interpretation undermines Raz's crucial idea of law as having at least certain matters resolved in advance by someone else. Let me delve into Raz's ideas at stake.

---

[50] Raz (1996a), p. 297.

[51] I thank Gerald Postema for stressing the necessity to articulate this point.

[52] Raz (2011b), pp. 319, 321.

[53] Raz (2011a), p. 355 ff.

[54] Raz (2011a), pp. 357 ff.

Here, for Raz, the question of how to interpret constitutional law is once again closely connected to a conceptual question: the question of what a Constitution is; that is, what the concept of having a constitution from the participant's perspective implies.[55] Constitutions are conceived to stand the test of time, and are consequently destined to become old law.[56] Remember that Raz assumes that lawmakers lose their authority (probability of identifying the right reasons) over time. Thus, Raz maintains that the authority of the lawmaker cannot be the justification for a long-standing Constitution.[57] The drafters of the Constitution play a secondary role in Raz's approach to the authority of the Constitution: they launch the constitutional tradition.[58] It is the constitutional practice and tradition (as long as it remains within the boundaries set by morality) that justifies the Constitution itself.[59]

Raz takes this notion of Constitution to argue that conserving interpretation plays a primary role in constitutional interpretation.[60] Conserving interpretation is understood here as the articulation of the current meaning of the constitutional provisions, set by the constitutional practice and tradition (what is presupposed is that this was the intention of its authors). He wants to stress that while the meaning assigned by the prevailing conventions of interpretation when the Constitution was promulgated plays a role in the early days of the Constitution,[61] it is the layers of interpretive decisions that constitute the relevant meaning to be identified in the years to come; and that is so for conceptual reasons.[62] It is the concept of "Constitution" that binds anyone who adopts the participant's perspective with this version of conserving (backward-looking) interpretation.

Raz also claims that given the moral relevance of constitutional issues, the question about the need for changing the current constitutional law always has to be raised. The current constitutional law could clearly determine the issue. However, Raz tells us, it cannot have the last word. Constitutional interpretation also and always has a forward-looking part.[63] Raz maintains not only that to address the question of the need for changing the law is inescapable and that moral reasoning is required to respond to it, but also that there are no general criteria for reaching an answer about whether or not to change it.[64] Now Raz seems to be openly advocating

[55]Raz (2011a), p. 329.

[56]The notion of 'constitution' he is explicitly assuming comprises the idea of a norm that: is superior within a legal system, establishes the structure of power and basic rights with a judicial review to guarantee its superiority; is meant to be of long duration, canonical written and entrenched; reflects the common ideology that governs public life; see Raz (2011a), p. 325.

[57]Raz (2011a), pp. 343 ff.

[58]Raz (2011a), p. 352.

[59]Raz (2011a), p. 348. Remember that, for Raz, participants of legal practices are conceptually committed to understanding that law (constitutional law, too), rests on a moral value.

[60]Raz (2011a), p. 348.

[61]Raz (2011a), p. 365.

[62]Raz (2011a), p. 365.

[63]Raz (2011a), p. 368.

[64]Raz (2011a), p. 360.

for a moral reading of the Constitution. And the thesis of the moral reading of the Constitution seems to clash with Raz's own primary idea of how participant's of legal practices are conceptually committed to seeing law as "put[ting] an end to the argument and the struggle about what is to be done." According to his account of law, participants of legal practices (judges included) have no conceptual space for such pervasive innovative interpretation. As we noticed, of course it is possible for people (judges included) not to follow the law because they do not care for it or find it unjust. Certainly, we can also have anarchist judges. But such kinds of attitudes towards law imply, for conceptual reasons, denying its authority. And such denials of authority could not be pervasive, without swallowing the authoritative relationship without which law, for Raz, cannot exist.

3.2 Raz On Judicial Adjudication

Regarding legal adjudication, Raz argues that our legal practices have incorporated clauses of justice to ensure that (settled) law in its application is not unfair.[65] Raz seems to be thinking that in our contemporary legal practices it is *always* the case that the relevant valid laws compete with considerations of justice in determining the correct solution to the case. However, the authoritative relationship that frames law does not seem to leave room for giving practical relevance to further normative considerations *in each case*.[66] At least, if we take his idea of legal authority seriously as a service in the identification of the right thing to do. The idea of accepting an authority as legitimate implies not only its instrumental character, but also its potential fallibility. And that implies the idea of being committed to taking its directives as protected reasons for action, even if some of them are morally wrong.[67]

The idea of judges regarding their judgment as based on a partial assessment of the valid reasons as rational, which includes an understanding of law as having preemptive force, makes it conceptually difficult to fit Raz's thesis of the clauses of justice within his account of law. To the extent that considerations of justice should be taken into account in all cases (settled cases included), legal norms would lose the place in practical reasoning that according to Raz is essential to its very nature.

[65]Raz (1998), p. 114.

[66]For a similar view, see Postema (1996), Martin (2014). As is well known, Raz distinguishes between two kinds of legal reasoning: 'reasoning about law' and 'reasoning according to law'. Reasoning about law is reasoning directed at identifying the content of law and is characterized by its autonomy. Reasoning according to law is reasoning from that content to the decision that has to be reached in the particular case. Raz argues that this latter reasoning is characterized by its lack of autonomy, since it inevitably implies that other types of normative considerations—different from the legal ones—are relevant by law in the determination of the correct legal solution. To be clear, it is only in the case where the law does not settle the issue that moral reasoning can come, conceptually, into play; Raz (1994d), pp. 311 ff.

[67]Raz (1990), p. 144.

Along with the clauses of justice, Raz would be expanding his theory of judicial discretion, depriving law from its authoritative role in courts' hands.

Raz's strategy to reaffirm the authoritative character of law is to differentiate settled law that applies to the courts from settled law that applies to the litigants before them.[68] Clearly, law plays a different role for citizens and courts.[69] Citizens have protected reasons to act guided by law. Courts have protected reasons to evaluate the citizens' behavior according to the legal norms excluding other considerations.[70] But this distinction, Raz assumes, does not prevent law in both cases from having authoritative character. However, I think this distinction plus the 'clauses of justice thesis' does not help Raz to save the core of his account of law, which includes the idea of law as having a guiding function.

Of course, what courts should or should not do depends on secondary rules, and not on the primary rules that are part of legal systems. These secondary rules indicate that the courts have a reason to apply settled law, unless it is relevant to give greater weight to considerations of justice. Now, what would remain of Raz's legal authority after the requirement to the courts to apply the law by taking into account considerations of justice in each case? Along the incorporation of such secondary rules in our legal systems, the idea of law as a service in the identification of the right thing to do, definitely becomes an idea difficult to grasp, when it reaches the hands of courts.

I think that following Raz's argument would imply citizens and judges being committed to different concepts of law (conceptually bound to different concepts of legal authority and legal norms). One where settled law implies the idea of not giving practical relevance to further deliberation, and another where settled law implies just the opposite action. This option does not seem to match Raz's methodological assumptions. He is assuming that in our conceptual practices there is one concept of law, our concept of law, and that elucidating this concept implies articulating the conceptual commitments of those that adopt the participant's perspective.[71] Raz takes officials (judges included) to be the paradigmatic participants in legal practices. Consequently, there is no theoretical support within Raz's account to sustain that law binds citizens and courts differently.

Law's function to guide citizen's behavior would be put into question as well. Just as Raz himself put it:

> it is obvious that it is futile to guide one's action on the basis of the law if when the matters come to adjudication the courts will not apply the law and will act for some other reasons.[72]

My point is not that considerations of justice should not play any role in defining how we should act. It is that law to conserve some guiding function should give

---

[68] Raz (1998), p. 18.

[69] I would like to thank Lewis Kornhauser, Dimitrios Kyritsis, Margaret Martin and Ezequiel Monti for advancing this line of objection.

[70] Raz (1998), p. 18.

[71] Raz (1996c), p. 358. For a development of the methodological implications that the priority of the participant's perspective has in Raz's theory of law, see Gaido (2012).

[72] Raz (1979e), p. 217.

similar directives to judges and citizens in concrete cases. If law wants to retain some guiding function, considerations of justice need to be available to determine how to justify decisions not only for courts, but for all citizens in concrete cases as well. Law could conserve some guiding function only if clauses of justice have for courts and citizens in concrete cases the power to constrain law's force.[73] Making considerations of justice available not only for judges but for citizens to justify their decision will be not enough. It seems that while it is in force, the law would not resolve the argument and the struggle about how things should be in society anymore. Then, under this picture Raz would need to reframe the idea of legal authority (and the type of reasons that it provides) that is necessary to understand law.[74] Legal authority -from the participant's perspective- would be not one that identifies the right thing to do anymore, but one that just provides reasons that are required to be balanced with considerations of justice.

4 Conclusion

The main purpose of this paper was to assess the reach of Raz's theses regarding the exclusionary role of law. The thesis, in a nutshell, states that the very idea of law implies the idea of legal authorities as a service in identifying the right thing to do. The legal authoritative directives conceptually need to be identified independently of any value consideration and treated as being pre-emptive, at least in some cases. Raz strives to reintroduce an idea of rationality in the hands of courts making for them available further normative arguments in the resolution of each case. I think this last option is excluded by the concept of legitimate legal authority that is assumed from the participant's perspective, according to his account. I tried to show how with this move the distinctive role legal norms were supposed to play in practical reasoning gets blurred.

References

Bayón JC (2002) Derecho, convencionalismo y controversia. In: Navarro PE, Redondo C (eds) La relevancia del derecho. Ensayos de filosofía jurídica, moral y política, Barcelona, Gedisa
Dickson J (2014) Interpretation and coherence in legal reasoning. The Stanford Encyclopedia of Philosophy (Summer 2014 Edition), Zalta EN (ed) forthcoming URL=http://plato.stanford.edu/archives/sum2014/entries/legal-reas-interpret/
Gaido P (2012) The scope of the participant's perspective in Joseph Raz's theory of law. Canadian J Law Jurisprud 25(2):347–357
Martin M (2014) Judging positivism. Hart, Oxford

[73]For a sophisticated argument in this direction see Waluchow (2000).

[74]A leading and pioneer argument articulating a similar criticism can be found in Bayón (2002).

Postema G (1996) Law's autonomy and public practical reason. In: George RP (ed) The autonomy of law. Essays on legal positivism. Clarendon Press, Oxford, pp 79–118
Raz J (1979a) Legal positivism and the sources of law. In: The authority of law. Essays on law and morality. Clarendon Press, Oxford, pp 37–52
Raz J (1979b) Legitimate authority. In: The authority of law. Essays on law and morality. Clarendon Press, Oxford, pp 3–27
Raz J (1979c) The claims of law. In: The authority of law. Essays on law and morality. Clarendon Press, Oxford, pp 28–36
Raz J (1979d) Law and value in adjudication. In: The authority of law. Essays on law and morality. Clarendon Press, Oxford, pp 180–209
Raz J (1979e) The rule of law and its virtue. In: The authority of law. Essays on law and morality. Clarendon Press, Oxford, pp 210–229
Raz J (1984) Hart on moral rights and legal duties. Oxf J Leg Stud 1(4):123–131
Raz J (1986) The morality of freedom. Oxford University Press, Oxford, p 1986
Raz J (1990) Practical reasons and norms. Princeton, Princeton University Press
Raz J (1994a) Authority, law and morality. In: Ethics in the public domain. Clarendon Press, Oxford, pp 210–237.
Raz J (1994b) Legal reasons, sources, and gaps. In: Ethics in the public domain. Clarendon Press, Oxford, pp 53–77
Raz J (1994c) Legal rights. In: Ethics in the public domain. Clarendon Press, Oxford, pp 254–276.
Raz J (1994d) On the autonomy of legal reasoning. In: Ethics in the public domain. Clarendon Press, Oxford, pp 326–340.
Raz J (1996a) Intention in interpretation. In: George RP (ed) The autonomy of law. Essays on legal positivism. Clarendon Press, Oxford, pp 249–286
Raz J (1996b) On the nature of law. Archiv für Recht und Sozial Philosophie 82:1–29
Raz J (1996c) Why interpret. Ratio Juris 9(4):349–363
Raz J (1998) Postema on law's autonomy and public practical reasons: a critical comment. Legal Theory 4:1–20
Raz J (2003) About morality and the nature of law. Am J Jurisprud 48:1–15
Raz J (2004) Incorporation by law. Legal Theory 10:1–17
Raz J (2006) The problem of authority: revisiting the service conception. Minn Law Rev 90:1003–1044
Raz J (2011a) On the authority and interpretation of constitutions: some preliminaries. In: Between authority and interpretation. Oxford University Press, Oxford, pp 323–372
Raz J (2011b) Interpretation: pluralism and innovation. In: Between authority and interpretation. Oxford University Press, Oxford, pp 299–323.
Waluchow WJ (2000) Authority and the practical difference thesis: a defense of inclusive legal positivism. Legal Theory 6:45–81

Not Everything Is Normativity: A Critique to Plunkett and Shapiro's Account of General Jurisprudence

Pau Luque and Ismael Martínez Torres

Abstract This chapter offers a critical analysis of David Plunkett and Scott Shapiro's novel account of general jurisprudence, which parallels this field to metaethics. We hold that this conception requires legal discourse to be exclusively normative, which is problematic on two counts. On the one hand, many important jurisprudes deny that, strictly speaking, legal discourse is normative in any relevant sense. On the other hand, even if we concede that part of legal discourse is normative, Plunkett and Shapiro's conception of what general jurisprudence is about would not illuminate an important part of legal thought and talk that is descriptive. If our observations are correct, it is hard to appreciate the programmatic appeal of Plunkett and Shapiro's proposal. Contrary to what they think, their account does not illuminate existing positions in general jurisprudence and cannot be used by legal scholars to advance the philosophical discussion in some important respects about legal thought, talk, and what, if any, such thought and talk are about.

1 Introduction

David Plunkett and Scott Shapiro have recently proposed a novel account of general jurisprudence.[1] Roughly, according to their proposal, general jurisprudence is parallel to metaethics. This move would allow illuminating many general jurisprudence positions. In this sense, the spirit—so to speak—of their proposal is rather ecumenical.

In this article, we offer a critical analysis of their account. Their conception of general jurisprudence needs the legal discourse to be exclusively normative. But this is controversial. On the one hand, there are many important jurisprudes that deny

[1] Plunkett and Shapiro (2017).

P. Luque (✉)
Universidad Nacional Autonoma de México, México City, Mexico

I. Martínez Torres
University of Edinburgh, Edinburgh, UK

J. L. Fabra-Zamora, G. Villa Rosas (eds.), *Conceptual Jurisprudence*, Law and Philosophy Library 137, https://doi.org/10.1007/978-3-030-78803-2_14

that, strictly speaking, legal discourse is normative in any relevant sense. On the other hand, even if we concede that part of legal discourse is normative, Plunkett and Shapiro's conception of what general jurisprudence is about would not illuminate an important part of legal thought and talk that is descriptive.

Our discussion is divided into three sections. In Sect. 2, we aim to do two things; first, we aim to reconstruct the part of Plunkett and Shapiro's account with which we take issue; second, we make explicit some theoretical commitments entailed by their account. In Sect. 3, we introduce a first objection against Plunkett and Shapiro's account. We argue that some well-known jurisprudes would not be jurisprudes under their account, and show why this is implausible. In Sect. 4, we introduce a second objection against Plunkett and Shapiro's account. To do so, we draw attention to legal statements of a particular kind and claim that, even if not normative in a relevant sense, such statements are part of legal thought and talk. In Sect. 5, we conclude by highlighting some of the main claims we argued for in the paper.

2 Plunkett and Shapiro's Account

In this section we reconstruct Plunkett and Shapiro's account of general jurisprudence and point out some theoretical commitments they undertake. It is worth pointing out that our reconstruction below is not (and doesn't pretend to be) exhaustive.

2.1 *General Jurisprudence as a Branch of Metanormative Inquiry*

One of the core moves Plunkett and Shapiro make in advancing their account of general jurisprudence is to claim that general jurisprudence is a branch of another overarching explanatory project they call "metanormative inquiry." According to them, metanormative inquiry "aims to explain how normative and evaluative thought and talk—and what (if anything) such thought and talk are distinctively about—fit into reality overall."[2]

To support the claim that general jurisprudence is a branch of metanormative inquiry, they introduce an argument that runs roughly as follows. At first, they introduce a distinction between "two different kinds of normativity."[3] Formal normativity, on the one hand, is characterized by reference to the notion of "formal norm." For Plunkett and Shapiro, formal norms are "standards that can be used to

[2] Ibid., p. 47.

[3] Ibid., p. 48.

assess whether something (e.g., an action, a style of dress) accords with it."[4] This type of normativity is characteristic, for instance, of the rules of chess or the standards of fashion. On the other hand, "robust normativity" pertains to what agents should ethically really do, all things considered. Robust normativity, Plunkett and Shapiro tell us, goes beyond the mere relation between an agent and some formal norms.

By appealing to the distinction between formal and robust normativity, Plunkett and Shapiro identify two ways to understand the metanormative project. The "wide understanding" aims at explaining "...how thought, talk, and reality that involve formal normativity fit into reality...",[5] while the "narrow understanding" aims at explaining "...how thought, talk, and reality that involve robust normativity fit into reality."[6] Depending on whether we conceive of normative claims as *formally normative* or *robustly normative*, we would engage with one version of the metanormative project or the other.

The following move in Plunkett and Shapiro's argument is to show that there are different (at least two) cases that can be made as to why metalegal inquiry is part of the metanormative project. What case we make depends on two things: what understanding of the metanormative project we are working on and our substantive views about legal thought, talk, and reality. The first case can be made by arguing that the law involves formal norms. According to Plunkett and Shapiro, when one argues that law involves formal norms, one uses the notion of formal normativity and, as a consequence, general jurisprudence results a part of metanormative inquiry.

The second case is, in some sense, more complicated. According to a well-known argument in legal philosophy[7] (to which Plunkett and Shapiro do not necessarily commit themselves), the law claims robust normativity. That is, it is claimed that the kind of demands that the law makes on its subjects purport to be authoritative "with respect to all-things-considered facts about what to do."[8] From accepting that the law claims robust normativity, it follows that general jurisprudence is a branch of the narrow understanding of the metanormative project. However, as acknowledged by Plunkett and Shapiro, to say that the law claims robust normativity is a contested thesis. A philosopher may still deny it. However, for Plunkett and Shapiro, even if skepticism about the robust normativity of the law were true, it wouldn't follow that general jurisprudence is not a branch of metanormative inquiry. What follows, they argue, is that general jurisprudence is part of the wide understanding of the metanormative project. Denying that there is a relation between law and robust normativity is fully compatible with accepting that there is a relation between law and formal normativity, or so Plunkett and Shapiro claim.

---

[4]Ibid., p. 48.

[5]Ibid., p. 49.

[6]Ibid., p. 49.

[7]Plunkett and Shapiro cite See Raz (2002), Marmor (2011) and Shapiro (2011).

[8]Plunkett and Shapiro (2017), p. 50.

2.2 Theoretical Commitments

Before advancing any objection against Plunkett and Shapiro's account, it is worth casting some light on two theoretical commitments entailed by conceiving of general jurisprudence as a branch of the metanormative project. We can start by asking about the scope of such a conception. As stated, according to Plunkett and Shapiro's view, if we accept that general jurisprudence is a branch of the wide understanding of metanormative inquiry, we are committed to accepting that the law *involves* formal norms. On the other hand, if we accept that general jurisprudence is a part of the narrow understanding, we are committed to accepting that the law *involves* robust norms.[9] Since we claim that our observations will apply without distinction whether we work on the wide or the narrow understanding, there is no harm in using the term "norms" to refer to both formal and robust norms. In what follows, we will stick to this stipulation unless stated otherwise and would claim that, according to Plunkett and Shapiro, the law involves norms.

To accept that general jurisprudence is a part of the metanormative project is to accept that the law *involves* norms. It is not clear to us what particular relation between the law and norms Plunkett and Shapiro have in mind when they use the term "to involve."[10] However, for our purposes, a clear understanding on this matter is not necessary. Whatever "to involve" means, there seems to be two ways in which the law might involve norms. One the one hand, norms might be *exhaustive* with respect to the things that the law involves. In other words, one might claim that the law involves *exclusively* norms. On the other, one might claim that the law involves (at least) *some* norms. There is certainly no explicit evidence through the text that we could find to attribute Plunkett and Shapiro any of these readings of their theory. Nonetheless, we argue that it follows from accepting that general jurisprudence is a part of the wide or the narrow understandings of the metanormative project that the law involves *exclusively* norms. In other words, we argue that by accepting that general jurisprudence is a part of the metanormative project, one is committed to the view that law involves exclusively norms. Let us elaborate.

Suppose that, as a matter of fact, it is not the case that the law involves exclusively norms. Suppose it also contains, for example, descriptions that carry no normative import.[11] It seems to us that, under this depiction of things, there would be no reason not to consider those (non-normative) descriptions part of *legal reality*. If they are

[9]Although Plunkett and Shapiro are not explicit about it, we see no reason to reject a third possibility: general jurisprudence would still be a branch of the metanormative project if the law were to involve formal and robust norms. We maintain that our conclusions would also apply to this scenario.

[10]We take it that by "to involve," Plunkett and Shapiro mean something close to what other philosophers refer to by the more intuitively graspable term "to contain", for instance, Hart. See Hart (1961). We will proceed on the assumption then that to say that the law involves norms is to say that it *contains* norms. However, in order to keep our presentation of Plunkett and Shapiro's ideas as unaltered as possible, we won't make any terminological changes in this respect.

[11]For instance, descriptions of legislative debates.

part of legal reality, there would most likely be as well (legal) talk and thought about them. We could ask then: Would general jurisprudence, as conceived by Plunkett and Shapiro, aim to explain as well that non-normative part of legal thought, talk and reality? Suppose our answer is yes. The part of general jurisprudence that would aim to explain non-normative legal thought, talk and reality, could not be part of the metanormative project. We should then attribute Plunkett and Shapiro something like the following claim: general jurisprudence is a part of the metanormative project, but it also aims to explain non-normative legal thought talk and reality (i.e., legal thought, talk and reality that bear no connection to normativity). Plunkett and Shapiro, it seems clear to us, wouldn't welcome such an interpretation of their view.

There are at least three reasons to support that Plunkett and Shapiro would reject such an interpretation. First, nowhere in the paper they suggest, neither explicitly nor implicitly, anything like it. Second, to claim that there is a part of general jurisprudence that is not a part of the metanormative project seems to be in sharp contrast with the emphasis they put in arguing that general jurisprudence is a part of the metanormative project. Third, the most natural way to understand the phrase "being (a) part of" is as suggesting inclusion, not intersection. When we say that "A is part of B," we usually say that A as a whole (every part of A) is contained in B, instead of saying that A and B intersect with respect to some of their parts. If general jurisprudence is a part of the metanormative project, this reading would suggest, none of its parts could be not a part of the metanormative inquiry.

If our observations are on the right track, it seems correct to attribute Plunkett and Shapiro the view that the law involves exclusively norms. In other words, it seems to follow from accepting that general jurisprudence is a part of the metanormative project that norms are exhaustive with respect to legal reality (or at least with respect to what the law involves).[12] This is the first commitment entailed by Plunkett and Shapiro's account we want to point out. One quick point before proceeding: In what follows we'll use "legal reality" and "what the law involves" as interchangeable expressions.

Before moving on, it should be noticed that Plunkett and Shapiro do not commit to the view that there is actually something in the world that is "legal reality." They insist on leaving open the possibility that legal thought and talk might be about nothing. Given this, our observation above should be more cautiously formulated as follows: it follows from accepting that general jurisprudence is a part of the metanormative project that, if there is such a thing as legal reality, then norms are exhaustive with respect to it.

A consequence of accepting that legal reality is exhaustively made up of norms is that thought and talk about legal reality is thought and talk exclusively *about*

[12]A different way to formulate this claim is to say that by accepting that general jurisprudence belongs to the metanormative project, one is committed to the view that there is nothing that the law involves that is not normative in either robust or formal sense.

norms.[13] This is the second commitment we attribute to Plunkett and Shapiro. Sometimes through their article, Plunkett and Shapiro refer to thought and talk about norms as *normative* thought and talk. Once again, it is important to keep in mind that they explicitly reject a commitment to the view that normative thought and talk, and specifically legal thought and talk, are indeed about something. It could be the case that there is nothing normative thought and talk are about. Strictly speaking, our claim is that Plunkett and Shapiro's conception of general jurisprudence entails that legal thought and talk, if about anything, are exclusively about norms. Now that we have made explicit these two commitments entailed by Plunkett and Shapiro's account of general jurisprudence, we can move on to introduce our critical remarks.

The first objection we aim to advance against Plunkett and Shapiro's conception of general jurisprudence can be briefly stated as follows. Provided that for some legal philosophers the law is not normative (neither in a robust nor a formal sense), conceiving of general jurisprudence as part of the metanormative project commit us to either the problematic view that the works of those philosophers are not part of general jurisprudence, or, if we take such works to be part of general jurisprudence, it proves to be inadequate. In the next section, we develop this objection.

---

[13]In cashing out the sense of aboutness they endorse with respect to ethical thought and talk, Plunkett and Shapiro write:

> Now consider the idea of ethical thought and talk being about certain things. The sense of 'aboutness' we have in mind here is an intensional one: in the way that "Santa Claus lives at the North Pole" is about Santa Claus, that is, someone who might not exist. This notion of 'aboutness' is consistent with deflationary, minimalist, and quasi-realist readings of the representation involved here. At least at first blush, ethical thought and talk seem to be about things, at least in this intensional sense. Moreover, they seem to be about certain distinctively ethical things (e.g., ethical facts, properties, relations). For example, the thought that Bob has an ethical obligation to donate more of his money to charity is about (a) things that many nonethical thoughts are also about (e.g., Bob, his money, charity, donation) and (b) things that are distinctively ethical, namely, ethical obligation.[6]

And in footnote 6, the one that appears at the end of this paragraph, they add:

> We don't want to build it into our account that ethical thought and talk are in fact about anything distinctive at all, in even this razor-thin sense of 'about'. We remain agnostic here because certain views in metaethics deny this claim. Some metaethical expressivists maintain that ethical words or concepts are not the kinds of things that generate intensions, while other metaethical error theorists might think that they are simply too defective to produce intensions. In our account, then, it is the task of metaethics to explain how ethical things fit into reality only insofar as ethical thought and talk are about certain distinctive things (in the razor-thin sense of 'about' described in the text). Plunkett and Shapiro (2017), pp. 40–41.

We think Plunkett and Shapiro would endorse the very same sense of aboutness for the legal case.

3 Jurisprudes That Are Not Jurisprudes

3.1 American Legal Realism

To keep things manageable, and since Plunkett and Shapiro think that conceiving of general jurisprudence as a branch of the metanormative project is adequate even if it is not part of the narrow understanding, we will concentrate on the view that general jurisprudence is a branch of the wide understanding of metanormative inquiry. Plunkett and Shapiro's contention in this respect is that general jurisprudence is trivially classified as a branch of the metanormative project. We take issue with this contention. Let's elaborate.

When arguing for their view, Plunkett and Shapiro write:

> Consider the wide notion of the metanormative project. The law clearly involves norms in the weaker, formal sense of 'norm' identified above—namely, standards that can be used to measure conformity to themselves.[26] Thus, when one uses a wide notion of formal normativity, metalegal inquiry is trivially classified as a branch of metanormative inquiry.[14]

In footnote 26 (the one contained in this paragraph) they add: "One way to support this idea would be to hold the following: laws are norms in (at least) this formal sense of 'norm.'[15] We must acknowledge that, other than the one expressed in this passage, we failed to find in Plunkett and Shapiro's work any argument for why metalegal inquiry should be *trivially* classified as a branch of the metanormative project. Thus, it is important to highlight the limited scope of our objection—it targets (exclusively) Plunkett and Shapiro's argument as presented in the passage above.

As we pointed out earlier, Plunkett and Shapiro recognize that a philosopher may deny that the law involves robust normativity. A philosopher who denies that the law involves robust normativity also denies that general jurisprudence is a branch of the narrow understanding of metanormative inquiry. But, according to Plunkett and Shapiro, similar skepticism cannot arise with respect to the connection between the law and formal normativity. It is not clear to us why skepticism could not arise against the view that general jurisprudence is a part of the wide understanding of the metanormative project.

The claim that general jurisprudence is part of the wide understanding of the metanormative project is far from being obvious. Some story seems to be needed before we can accept it. As can be seen from the passage quoted, the reason for that claim offered by Plunkett and Shapiro is that the law *clearly* involves formal norms. Their argument seems to be very simple:

(1) if the law involves formal norms, then general jurisprudence is a branch of the project that aims to explain how thought, talk and reality that involves formal normativity fits into reality (the wide understanding of metanormative inquiry);

[14]Ibid., p. 50.

[15]Ibid., p. 50.

(2) the law clearly involves formal norms; therefore
(3) general jurisprudence is a branch of the project that aims to explain how thought talk and reality that involves formal normativity fits into reality (the wide understanding of metanormative inquiry.

This argument is unquestionably a valid one. However, it is not clear it is sound. It seems possible to cast doubt about the truth of premise (2). Plunkett and Shapiro take the claim that the law clearly involves formal norms to be a platitude. But it doesn't seem to be so. To be clear, our contention is not that (2) is false, but that it can be argued it is. Moreover, we take it that some relevant legal philosophers have explicitly contended that premise (2) is false. Skeptic views about the formal normativity of the law have long been part of the discussion about universal legal thought, talk, and reality. In what follows, we will present three examples of some legal philosophers who claim that (2) expresses a false thesis about the law.

For some legal philosophers, the law is not normative in either of the two senses identified by Plunkett and Shapiro. Take the case, for instance, of the movement that emerged in the United States in the 1920s and 1930s, usually referred to as "American legal realism."[16] According to a well-known interpretation,[17] American legal realists suggest that what we call legal norms are not properly norms but rather predictions of what the courts will do.[18] To say that all (so-called) norms that make up the law are predictions of future official behaviour is incompatible with saying that they are either formal or robust norms. More cautiously, if it is true that the law involves norms understood as predictions, then it is false that it involves norms understood in the formal (or robust) sense. Contrapositively, if it is true that the law involves formal (or robust) norms, then it is false that it involves norms understood as predictions. For the sake of exposition, let's make explicit that we understand the realist thesis as a universal claim: all (so-called) norms that make up the law are predictions of future official behavior. Similarly, it might be worth recalling that we have already argued for a universal reading of Plunkett and Shapiro's theory. If we understand American legal realism and Plunkett and Shapiro's view as making universal claims about the (so-called) norms that make up every legal system, then

[16]According to Brian Leiter, among American legal realists we can find Karl Llewellyn, Jerome Frank, Felix Cohen, Herman Oliphant, Walter Wheeler Cook, Underhill Moore, Hessel Yntema, Max Radin, and Holmes. See Llewellyn (1930, 1931), Frank (1930, 1931), Cohen (1935), Oliphant (1928), Cook (1937), Moore (1923), Moore and Callahan (1943), Moore and Hope (1929), Moore and Sussman (1931), Yntema (1941), Radin (1925, 1930) and Holmes (1897).

[17]Hart (1961).

[18]Brian Leiter has largely argued for a different interpretation of American legal realism. According to Leiter's interpretation American legal realism should be understood as advancing a new methodological approach towards the study of law, rather than a conceptual explanation of "law". See Leiter (2001, 2007, 2010, 2013) and Cohen (1935). It is not our purpose here to discuss what interpretation of American legal realism is more appropriate. We will stick to the interpretation suggested by Hart, as something like it has been explicitly defended at least for some American legal realists such as Cohen. See Ibid.

we seem to have found an example of some legal philosophers who explicitly deny (2).

But things might not be that simple. It might be argued that, correctly understood, American legal realists do not deny that the law contains proper norms, but rather hold a particular (and allegedly mistaken) conception of legal norms. It is commonly contended that conceiving of legal norms as predictions of the future behaviour of courts does not deny the existence of a connection between the law and *some* kind of normativity. What American legal realists fail to do, it is said, is to come up with an appropriate characterization of that connection. Legal realists seem to suggest that there is a third type of normativity that is neither formal nor informal but rather, say, predictive.

Finding premise (2) problematic in those terms (i.e., claiming that the law does not clearly involve formal norms because it involves norms understood as predictions), may not be sufficient to pose a serious problem for Plunkett and Shapiro's conception of general jurisprudence. It might simply be that their conception of normativity is under-inclusive. In other words, it might be that even if American legal realists deny that the law clearly involves formal or robust norms, they don't deny that there is *some* connection between the law and normativity. If so, the lesson to be taken from looking at American legal realism should not be that Plunkett and Shapiro's characterization of general jurisprudence is incorrect and has to be abandoned, but that it is incomplete and has to be modified. They didn't fail in thinking that legal thought, talk and reality is normative, they failed to offer an exhaustive characterization that covers all types of normativity. A charitable reading of their theory should fill the gap and find those further senses of normativity that Plunkett and Shapiro might have missed. By expanding their conception of normativity in order to include this new sense(s) of "normativity" and "norm," Plunkett and Shapiro could still be able to argue that general jurisprudence is a part of the metanormative project. The notion of normativity could be expanded to cover robust, formal and something we could call *predictive* normativity. Then, there would be three understandings of the metanormative project and general jurisprudence would belong to one of those.

We contend that to modify Plunkett and Shapiro's conception of normativity in that way is an unviable option. Put roughly, it seems to us that the notion of *predictive normativity* and *predictive norms* cannot be made to work. To build on this idea, Let's take a look at what *predictive normativity* and *predictive norms* would be like.

To begin, let's notice that those who think that American legal realists consider legal norms as bearing some kind of connection to normativity, conceive of normativity itself in slightly different (although not incompatible) terms to Plunkett and Shapiro. In their attempt to remain as neutral as possible with respect to different substantive views about what normativity is, Plunkett and Shapiro choose to not even mention the term "reasons for action."[19] This term, however, is central to the conception of normativity attributed to American legal realists. In this interpretation of legal realism, it is assumed that legal norms (aim to) provide agents with *reasons for acting* in certain ways. In the view of American legal realists, it is said, the reasons for action that legal norms purport to provide are the prudent concerns of those who seek to engage or avoid the power of the courts.[20] Put differently, according to American legal realism, when provided by a legal norm, a person's reason for doing a certain action is tantamount to the person's prudent desire to avoid the punishment that, according to that legal norm, a court is most likely to impose in case she fails to perform the action. If we look closely into this way of understanding normativity attributed to American legal realists, we will easily appreciate that it is implausible. Let's elaborate.

The debate around reasons for action is one of the largest and most full of controversy within philosophical discussion. However, there seems to be consensus (to the extent consensus among philosophers is possible) about a distinction between two kinds of reasons for action. A *normative reason*, on the one hand, is "a consideration that counts in favour of some action or attitude."[21] For María Alvarez:

> a reason is said to be a "normative reason" for acting because it favours someone's acting. But what does it mean to say that a reason "favours" an action? One way of understanding this claim is in terms of justification: a reason justifies or makes it right for someone to act in a certain way. This is why normative reasons are also called "justifying" reasons.[22]

Normative reasons are usually distinguished from *motivating reasons*. In describing motivating reasons, Alvarez says:

> A motivating reason is a reason for which someone does something, a reason that, in the agent's eyes, counts in favour of her acting in a certain way. When an agent acts motivated by a reason, she acts "in light of that reason" and the reason will be a premise in the practical reasoning, if any, that leads to the action. Motivating reasons can also figure in explanations of actions that cite agents' reasons, what are called "reason explanations" of actions. Because of that, they are sometimes called "explanatory" reasons. . .[23]

In the philosophical literature, arguing that the reasons for action provided by legal norms are normative reasons is highly uncontroversial. It is also highly uncontroversial that prudential desires of any class are not normative. Our contention is that even if we accept that predictions offer reasons for action, those reasons are better understood as motivating reasons, not normative reasons. Recall, legal norms

---

[19]There is a vast literature concerning the proper way to understand what reasons for action are. As it will become clear later, for our purpose in this paper, it is enough to provide the reader with a rough understanding of the distinction between normative and non-normative reasons for action. The distinction has been suggested by philosophers such as Raz, Smith, Parfit, and Dancy. See Raz (1975, 2011), Smith (1994), Parfit (1997) and Dancy (1995, 2000).

[20]Cohen (1935).

[21]Scanlon (2004), p. 231.

[22]Alvarez (2017).

[23]Ibid.

understood as predictions provide people with prudent desires to avoid certain consequences. Desires, it is usually maintained, lack the justificatory force distinctive of normative reasons. Desires do not justify actions but merely motivate them. Scanlon, for instance, argues that "when a person not only recognizes something as a reason but also is moved to act this is due to the presence of some further motivating element in addition to that recognition—something appropriately called a desire."[24] More evidence in this sense can be found in H. L. A. Hart's *The Concept of Law*. When arguing against the prediction theory, he writes:

> The fundamental objection is that the predictive interpretation obscures the fact that, where rules exist, deviations from them are not merely grounds for a prediction that hostile reactions will follow or that a court will apply sanctions to those who break them, but are also a reason or justification for such reaction and for applying the sanctions.[25]

It is not clear from this passage whether Hart thinks that predictions provide reasons for action. What seems clear is that he takes the prediction view to do a poor job at capturing the potential of legal norms to provide justificatory reasons for some actions. Our take on these observations is that legal norms conceived as predictions of future official behaviour do not provide normative reasons for action, and thus they are not normative in any sense Plunkett and Shapiro could embrace.[26] If we understand the normativity of legal norms in terms of providing some type of normative reasons for action, and we understand whatever we call legal norms as predictions of official behavior that provide motivating reasons for action, the notions of *predictive normativity* and *predictive norm* cannot be made to work. If, even in this interpretation, American legal realism fails to conceive of legal norms as *normative*, it seems that we have found a group of legal philosophers who deny that the law involves norms, either robust or formal (or something else).

---

[24]Scanlon (1998), p. 35.

[25]Hart (1961), p. 84.

[26]We agree with Enoch in recognizing that the discussions on the reason-giving force of the law are sometimes confused: "When Shapiro (2001, p. 176) introduces his 'practical difference thesis', for instance, he talks in motivational terms, though it seems to me what he has in mind is really that the law must be able to make a normative difference. And for a similar unclarity regarding the distinction between motivating and normative reasons, see Green (1999, p. 40)", See Enoch (2011). The articles cited by Enoch in this passage are Shapiro (2001) and Green (1999). We take it that, if Plunkett and Shapiro were to explain normativity in terms of reasons for action, then they would agree with Coleman and Enoch in saying that it is clear that the relevant question is whether the law gives *normative* reasons for action—and, if it does, what kind of *normative* reasons. See Coleman (2001), pp. 71–72; Enoch (2011).

3.2 Jurisprudes That Are Not Jurisprudes (II): The Imperative Theory of Law

In the following two subsections, we will briefly introduce two positions that, like American legal realism, seek to explain legal reality talk and thought while denying a relationship between the law and normativity.

Two of the main representatives of the Imperative theory of law—Bentham and Austin[27]—claim roughly that the law consists of coercive orders enacted by a de facto authority. We do not need to go very deep on Austin and Bentham's line of thought. It will be enough for our purposes here to give a couple of quotes of Hart's reconstruction of their imperative theory:

> A command for Bentham was a kind of assertion differing from others only because it was specifically an assertion about the speaker's volition concerning the conduct of others. He did not recognize it as a form of non-assertive discourse (. . .) Secondly, he considered that the ordinary imperative forms of language used for giving commands are essentially elliptical and when expressed at full length would display the fact that they were assertions about the speaker's will. Thus he says the imperative form 'Kill that robber' is an elliptical way of saying 'My will is that you kill the robber' and a law expressed as 'Export no corn' is an elliptical form of the assertion 'It is my pleasure that you do not export any corn.'[28]

And regarding Austin's conception, he noticed that:

> [coercive orders] are not, and could not be, the standard way in which law functions (. . .). Instead, such particularised forms of control are either exceptional or are ancillary accompaniments or reinforcements of general forms of directions which do not name, and are not addressed to, particular individuals, and do not indicate a particular act to be done.[29]

We believe that, understood in this way, Bentham and Austin's theories, alongside American legal realism, cannot welcome the stipulation of any relation between the law and normativity in any of the senses described above.

3.3 Jurisprudes That Are Not Jurisprudes (III): Genoese Legal Realism

Put roughly, the so-called Genoese-legal-realism claims that what the law is depends on what the meaning of legal texts turns out to be, but there are no objective criteria to adscript legal meaning to legal texts.[30] So the legal interpreter—the judge—determines the meaning of legal texts by adjusting her subjective (political or

---

[27]We could also include here some passages of Th. Hobbes' *Leviathan* Hobbes (1996), pp. 175–177.

[28]Hart (1982), p. 248.

[29]Hart (1961), p. 21.

[30]See Guastini (2011) and Barberis (2017).

moral) preferences to the meaning of a legal text. Thus, we should distinguish between legal texts—a legal provision or texts with no meaning—and legal norms or rules—a legal provision after an adscription of meaning on the interpreter's behalf. Notice, then, that ultimately legal rules and norms should be conceptually boiled down, according to Genoese-Legal-Realism, to the will of the interpreter.[31] And, what kind of normativity would be involved in the sheer will of a legal interpreter? Not any kind of normativity, according to Genoese legal realists.

When it comes to General Jurisprudence, Genoese legal realists claim, there is a fundamental dichotomy between those who see "law as a norm" and those jurisprudes that see "law as a fact." Genoese legal realists are among the latter. And, what type of fact is the law? As we said, it is the sheer will of the interpreter. In that sense, Genoese legal realists, similarly to Bentham and Austin's position, claim that legal authority is, at the end of the day, a de facto authority—that is, some sort of sovereign-interpreter.

In any case, that very social fact—the will of the interpreter—involves no normativity (as opposed to Hartian positivism, in which the complex facts that ground or make the law, a social practice constituted by an internal point of view of its participants, involve some kind of normativity). To know the law, for Genoese legal realists, is to have a particular kind of empirical knowledge (who is the sovereign, what is her will), not normative knowledge.[32]

It is worth noticing that we are not assessing the merits of the different positions introduced in the last three subsections. Our only purpose is to show that, regardless of their plausibility, there are some theories in general jurisprudence that see "law as a fact." Or, to put it differently, we are not disputing here that those positions are implausible or false general jurisprudence positions. The thesis about which we seek to cast some doubt is that they are *not* positions within general jurisprudence, which is, as we will see, what follows from Plunkett and Shapiro's argument.

Let us refer to legal philosophers who deny a connection between the law and normativity as "non-normativist."[33]

3.4 The Dilemma

We will explain now why we think that the works of philosophers who deny the relation between normativity and the law introduce a problem for Plunkett and Shapiro's conception of general jurisprudence. The problem these works pose can be presented in the form of the following dilemma: Either Plunkett and Shapiro

---

[31] See Chiassoni (2016), p. 349.

[32] Ibid., p. 408.

[33] Among the "non-normativists", we could easily add as well Scandinavian legal realists. For an excellent reconstruction of this position, one that shows that they were "non-normativists", see Hart (1983).

conception of general jurisprudence is adequate, in which case the works of non-normativists legal philosophers are not works on general jurisprudence; or those works are works on general jurisprudence, in which case Plunkett and Shapiro's characterization proves inadequate. Clearly, more has to be said before it becomes apparent that the dilemma is genuine and that it poses a serious problem for Plunkett and Shapiro's account of general jurisprudence. In order to do that, let us begin by analyzing the first disjunct.

To start things off, let's assume that Plunkett and Shapiro's characterization of general jurisprudence is adequate.[34] That is, let's assume that general jurisprudence is the part of metalegal inquiry that aims to explain how universal legal thought, talk—and what (if anything) such thought and talk are distinctively about—fit into reality overall. Keep in mind that metalegal inquiry is a part of metanormative inquiry. Accepting that general jurisprudence is a branch of the metanormative project entails that there is a relation between the law and some kind of normativity. More specifically, it entails that the law involves formal or robust norms (or another kind of norm if there is any).

As we observed, we can interpret the works of some legal philosophers as denying the thesis that the law involves formal or robust (or any other kind of) normativity. For them, legal (universal) thought, talk and reality are not (at least not necessarily) normative in character. For such philosophers, it follows, the descriptive explanation of the law does not require, nor entail, accepting a relation between the law and normativity. Since the works of anti-normativist philosophers reject that the law involves norms (robust or formal), Plunkett and Shapiro's conception of general jurisprudence suggests that those works belong to a different explanatory project. We find this conclusion problematic.

The conclusion strikes us as problematic for two reasons. First, the works of anti-normativists have been widely regarded by legal philosophers as part of general jurisprudence. They have been part of debates concerning legal reality, thought and talk, and how they fit into reality overall. Second, by excluding these works Plunkett and Shapiro seem to go against what they take to be two of the main reasons from which their view earns its keep, namely, its ability to accommodate a wide range of positions and debates within legal philosophy and to make room for future developments in general jurisprudence. Let us expand on these two ideas.

For years, American legal realism has been considered one important part of general jurisprudence. Hart's objection against the predictive view seemingly assumes that the works of American legal realists are part of the same theoretical enterprise as his own theory. Hart's objection against American legal realism itself is commonly regarded as part of a debate characteristic of general jurisprudence. It would be hard to make sense of the genuineness of such a debate, if American legal realism belonged to a different explanatory project. Our contention here is that Plunkett and Shapiro's conception of general jurisprudence, if adequate, would suggest that American legal realism belongs to a different explanatory project,

[34]It is important to keep in mind here the programmatic nature of Plunkett and Shapiros' proposal.

which seems to be in sharp contrast to what until now has been common ground among legal philosophers.[35]

In a similar vein, Hart thought that both Bentham and Austin were fundamentally wrong.[36] As we suggested before, for our purposes in this paper, whether Bentham and Austin were wrong is irrelevant. What is relevant is that Hart considered that the imperative theory of law—which cannot be accommodated in terms of formal or robust normativity—was indeed part of the same theoretical project in which he was engaged. Otherwise, it would be rather hard to explain why Hart treated imperativism as a rival theory of his. Nobody would deny that Hart's debate against Austin and Bentham is a debate within general jurisprudence.

Similarly, since the Genoese-legal-realists see "law as a fact", this theory cannot be illuminated by a conception of general jurisprudence according to which legal thought and talk are exclusively and exhaustively normative. It doesn't seem right to claim that Genoese legal realists are engaged in a different explanatory project about the law. Genoese-legal-realist aim at explaining legal thought, talk and reality. The takeaway from these observations is that, if we accept the characterization of general jurisprudence suggested by Plunkett and Shapiro, we will have to count a good deal of theories that have been long regarded as part of general jurisprudence as belonging to a different explanatory project. Since most legal philosophers (Hart, for instance) should agree that the works of non-normativist philosophers are part of general jurisprudence, Plunkett and Shapiro's account seems problematic.

The second reason to think that the conclusion that American legal realism, the imperative theories of law, and Genoese-Legal-Realism, are not part of general jurisprudence renders Plunkett and Shapiro's account problematic, pertains to some of the core motivations they say we have to take up their proposal. As observed by them, one of the reasons by which their account is supposed to earn its keep is that "it illuminates existing positions and debates within legal philosophy."[37] As we hopefully made clear, their account would fail to illuminate a number of important positions within legal philosophy, namely, American legal realism, the Imperative theory of law and Genoese-Legal-Realism.

Now, it's possible that, faced with our objection, Plunkett and Shapiro would emphasize that they try to illuminate *existing* positions within the most influential legal philosophy, and since both American legal realism and the Imperative theory of law are widely discredited, they don't qualify as *existing* positions in the relevant sense. As for Genoese-legal-realism, their counter-objection would continue, it's a position as vivid as parochial, in the sense that it has not penetrated in any debate with a wide, international audience and, in that sense, doesn't qualify either as an *existing* position within the most influential legal philosophy.

---

[35]Perhaps Brian Leiter's reconstruction of American legal realism understood mainly as a theory of legal adjudication would be an exception to this widely accepted belief.

[36]See Hart (1982), p. 249; Hart (1961), chap. 4.

[37]Plunkett and Shapiro (2017), p. 39.

Let's assume that something along these lines would be in fact Plunkett and Shapiro's counter-objection. Our response to them would be that it doesn't matter how popular those theories are. The main—if not the unique—thing that matters when trying to illuminate legal philosophy, is philosophical ideas defended with philosophical arguments.

Moreover, some of the intuitions and philosophical theses (or at least parts of them) on which "non-normativist" theories of general jurisprudence are based, have been lately rediscovered by legal philosophers who are among the most discussed ones, like F. Schauer, B. Leiter, B. Tamanaha or K. Himma. Plunkett and Shapiro's conception of general jurisprudence could hardly account for some fundamental parts of recent contributions of these legal philosophers. This would show that the debates generated by the "non-normativists" theories of law qualify as *existing* debates even if we take what we assume to be Plunkett and Shapiro's meaning of "existing."

Plunkett and Shapiro's account would also fail to illuminate emerging (possible and actual) debates in legal philosophy like the one recently suggested by Alice Schneider.[38] This debate revolves around the modal status of the connection between the law and any kind of normativity. Put roughly, she argues that the law is not necessarily normative, even in the thin (formal) sense of normativity. Her argument draws on a distinction between legal facts and thin norms, based on a description of laws as non-normative facts, but as what she calls "diagnostic categories." Beyond how persuasive we might find Schneider arguments, it seems to us that Plunkett and Shapiro's conception of general jurisprudence is unable to accommodate her proposal, and thus it is unable to accommodate the debate it may give rise to as part of general jurisprudence. If the law contains laws that are not normative but diagnostic categories, assuming Schneider's view is correct, then there is a part of legal reality that is not normative, and presumably legal non-normative thought and talk about it. To engage in a debate like this would not be a way to advance general jurisprudence if we were to adopt Plunkett and Shapiro's view. A conclusion like that seems undesirable to us.

Another possible reply Plunkett and Shapiro might offer against our observations is that even if we have always considered legal realism(s) and imperativism as theories in general jurisprudence, this consideration is wrong. It might be the case that excluding those theories, and others alike, from the scope of general jurisprudence is a theoretical cost worth paying.

It is hard for us to see the benefits Plunkett and Shapiro's conception of general jurisprudence could bring in order to compensate for leaving out theories that (would) endorse the non-normativity of law. Set aside for a moment the question of whether legal realism and imperativism are part of general jurisprudence. Suppose, for instance, that new developments in other disciplines (philosophy, cognitive science, etc.) were to point towards the thesis that the best way to explain (at least part of) legal reality, thought and talk (and how they fit into reality overall) implies

[38]Schneider A Law Without Rules: Disputing Legal Normativity [unpublished manuscript].

that (at least part of) legal reality thought and talk are not normative. In following the theoretical program suggested by Plunkett and Shapiro, legal theorists aiming to do general jurisprudence would miss out on such developments, as they would be committed to analyzing law as a normative phenomenon. Which benefit could Plunkett and Shapiro's understanding of general jurisprudence bring that pays back for missing the opportunity of advancing our knowledge of legal reality thought and talk in that way? We see none.

Plunkett and Shapiro's proposal does not illuminate anti-normativist positions in general jurisprudence and, in their article, such a restriction remains entirely unmotivated. Such a move comes at a theoretical cost, since, as we mentioned in the very beginning of our article, it can be said that the spirit of their article is ecumenical. Unfortunately, they go too quickly in implicitly discarding some general jurisprudence positions and, then, we could say, they frustrate its ecumenical spirit. On the other hand, Plunkett and Shapiro's account fails to offer a program for general jurisprudence that allows us to advance possible debates around legal thought, talk and reality.

The way in which the second disjunct of the dilemma introduces a problem for Plunkett and Shapiro's account of general jurisprudence is rather evident. If it is true that Legal Realism(s), the Imperative theory, Genoese-realism and raising arguments like Schneider's, are to be conceived of as belonging to the explanatory project of general jurisprudence, an account of general jurisprudence that exclude them cannot be useful. The uselessness of such a conception seems a good reason to reconsider whether general jurisprudence is an explicatory project that aims to explain how (universal) (normative) legal thought, talk, and what (if any) those thought, and talk are distinctively about fit into reality overall.

4 Not Everything Is Normativity: Detached Legal Statements

Let's recall that Plunkett and Shapiro conceive of general jurisprudence as the project that explains how legal thought and talk (and reality) fit into reality overall. In this section, we will leave aside other general jurisprudence positions and claim that there is at least one important kind of legal statements—statements that are part of legal thought and talk—that cannot be considered normative in either a robust or a formal sense (or any other way of normativity compatible with Plunkett and Shapiro's view). It is hard to us to see how a programmatic project that would require us not to focus on this part of legal thought and talk can be useful in advancing general jurisprudence.

According to Raz, there are two kinds of statements in legal discourse—committed and detached.[39] Committed statements are, roughly, statements in which the utterer accepts the rules in question—that is, she takes the rules as offering *all things considered* or *genuine* reasons for action.[40] Detached statements, by contrast, are statements in which the utterer adopts the point of view of someone who is committed to the normative system those statements are based on, without committing herself.

Before moving any further, it is worth noticing that although first introduced by Raz, up to this day, the notion of *detached statement* has been used for a good number of legal philosophers.[41] It is not our intention here to do an exegesis of Raz or anyone else's particular conception of detached statements. However, we will endorse two ideas that have been to some extent object of consensus in the literature about detached legal statements: first, the distinction between detached and committed legal statements is a matter of pragmatics rather than semantics;[42] second, detached legal statements are not normative. Let's elaborate on these ideas a little more.

In the literature, it is not clear what exactly is the difference between committed and detached statements. We adhere to the position according to which the distinction is drawn in virtue of the pragmatic features of legal statements rather than their logical or semantic features.[43] As Enoch claims, "[i]t is quite possible that the normative flavour of internal, committed legal statements is not a part of their semantic content, but rather a part of their pragmatic features."[44] If this is so, then all legal statements are pragmatically ambiguous—"L is legally valid" can be a detached or a committed statement. The disambiguation is not a matter of semantics, but a matter of how the normative language is used by speakers—that is, a matter of pragmatics.

[39]Raz (1980), pp. 234–238. There is a third kind of statement, external legal statements, that doesn't need to concern us in this article.

[40]See Raz (1998), p. 248. Raz explicitly declares that commitment here means moral commitment, that is, statements providing moral (or, simply, unqualified) reasons for action ("Committed statements, which are ordinary moral statements about what ought to be done, what rights and duties people have because of the law", p. 248), and that internal legal statements, in Hartian terms, are, despite Hart's theoretical qualms, morally committed statements ("Committed statements are essentially the same as Hart's internal statements", p. 248, and "I find it impossible to resist the conclusion that most internal or committed internal legal statements, at any rate those about the rights and duties of others, are moral claims", p. 249). In the same vein, see Vecchi (2017), pp. 96–97.

[41]See Enoch (2011), Mullins (2018), Duarte d'Almeida (2011) and Toh (2007).

[42]We understand the semantic features of a legal statement as the information part of that statement's communicative upshot—the information it communicates—that is linguistically encoded. On the other hand, we understand the pragmatic features of a legal statement as the information part of its communicative upshot that is encoded by certain facts about the user of that statement: her beliefs, intentions, dispositions, etc.

[43]Enoch (2011) and Mullins (2018).

[44]Enoch (2011), p. 23.

We hold that when the utterance of a legal statement is used by a speaker to give reasons for action to the hearer, that statement is a committed statement. On the other hand, when the utterance of a legal statement is proffered by the speaker to inform the hearer about a certain fact, that statement is a detached statement.

According to Mullins, the pragmatic approach to this distinction should be understood in the sense that there is a general implicature according to which when someone proffers a statement that contains a normative operator, like "You should do p," the utterer is committed to the rule.[45] Conversely, "detachment arises," Mullins claims, "because of the defeasibility of the implicature in question [...] Detached legal statements occur where, in the specific context of utterance, the implicature that arises to the effect that the speaker is committed to the [...] rules in question is *explicitly* or *contextually* cancelled."[46]

Now, when it comes to the law, committed statements are called—at least within a Hartian framework—internal legal statements. We accept that internal legal statements are capable of providing at least formal reasons for action. We do not need to explore the possibility of internal legal statements giving robust reasons for action because the project suggested by Plunkett and Shapiro can account for formal normativity, and internal legal statements involve at least formal normativity.

It is not obvious, though, that detached legal statements are normative statements, not even in the formal sense of normativity. If they are not normative statements, then Plunkett and Shapiro would face a dilemma that is somehow similar to the one presented above (see Sect. 3.4). Either detached legal statements are not part of legal thought, and talk or Plunkett and Shapiro's account of general jurisprudence leaves out of its explanatory reach any effort to explain a fundamental part of legal thought and talk.

In what follows, we will defend that detached legal statements are (1) an instance of legal thought and talk despite the fact that (2) they are not an instance of, strictly speaking, normative thought and talk.

We will start off by arguing that they are not normative. To see this point more clearly, let's take a look at a couple of non-legal situations. Let's suppose that one of us says to the other: "You shouldn't eat that salad—it has bacon in it." Let's also suppose that the hearer is vegetarian whereas the utterer is not. Is the utterer giving a normative reason not to eat the salad? Not exactly—the utterer is merely letting the hearer know that the salad has meat in it. The reason not to eat the salad was already there when the utterer said "You shouldn't eat that salad—it has bacon in it." The hearer had a reason not to eat the salad in virtue of her being a vegetarian, not in virtue of the utterer using a normative operator such as "Shouldn't."

---

[45]See Mullins (2018). According to a widely spread view, implicatures can be understood as the part of the content communicated by an utterance of a sentence P in context C that the speaker of that sentence P is committed to by her utterance, and both the speaker and the hearer are expected to know that the speaker is committed to. Grice (1991).

[46]Mullins (2018), p. 377 emphasis added.

Let's now suppose that you are in Mexico City for the first time. Someone has invited you to have tacos for lunch. When you get to the place, you order some tacos "al pastor [meat]" and ask some ketchup to put on them. One of us, a vegetarian, who is also attending the lunch, tells you: "You shouldn't put ketchup on the tacos—you should put chilli sauce." The utterer of this statement is not giving you a normative reason not to put ketchup on the tacos. He is merely informing you that, in Mexico City, it is considered wrong to put ketchup on tacos "al pastor." The existence of a normative reason not to put ketchup on tacos depends on a set of conventional rules widely accepted by taco eaters in Mexico City, not on one of us reporting the existence of such rules.

In both cases, what the utterer is doing is letting the hearer know something that she didn't know, at least at a time *t*, when the utterer uttered her statement. If the utterer is involved in some kind of reason-giving here, it's an epistemic reason-giving.[47] In the first case, the utterer is pointing out an empirical fact that the hearer hasn't noticed—the bacon in the salad. In the second case, the utterer is indicating the existence of a normative fact—the existence of a conventional rule in Mexico City among non-vegetarians.

They are detached statements in the sense that the utterer uses the statement, that contains a normative operator, with an epistemic purpose. The statement "You shouldn't eat that salad—it has bacon in it," proffered in the context of the first example, doesn't entail "You have a reason not to eat meat"—it merely illuminates a fact (the salad having bacon) that makes the situation a particular instance of the application of the rule that you are committed to. In this case, the reason-giving is epistemic, since the utterer is just illuminating a fact that was opaque to you. In the same vein, "You shouldn't put ketchup on those tacos—you should put chilli sauce," as it's proffered in the context of the second example, doesn't entail "You have a reason not to put ketchup on the tacos"—it merely points out the existence of a social rule. Or, to put it in terms of the pragmatic analysis, in both cases we can infer, from the context, that the general implicature of commitment on behalf of the utterer has been cancelled—and so detachment has arisen.

Now, let's turn to the legal case. Let's suppose that you go to a lawyer and you ask her whether you should pay a tax T, a tax that has been enacted by a legislature of a social-democratic majority. This is her answer: "I'm a libertarian, so I think that T is morally wrong. But T is legally valid according to the criteria of legal validity—you ought to pay T." Your lawyer is merely informing you of the fact that T is legally valid. But the existence of the legal obligation to pay T is independent of your lawyer proffering "You ought to pay T." The rule according to which "You ought to pay T" preexisted the conversation with your lawyer. Thus, when your lawyer concludes that "You ought to pay T," given what her commitments are, she is giving you a reason, but that giving here is epistemic, not normative. Since the utterer has explicitly declared that she is not committed, the general implicature has been cancelled and, again, detachment arises.

---

[47]Enoch (2011), p. 4.

The detached language is almost indispensable for lawyers. As Mullins says, "When lawyers, academics and jurists discuss the law, they very often do so in circumstances where they think it imperfect or unjust, or where they have yet to form a final view as to the law's worth."[48]

But what if it is not a lawyer advising you but a judge who proffers "You ought to pay T"? Would that be a legal detached statement or an internal statement? Here, again, it all depends on pragmatics—if the judge declares herself that she is a libertarian as well, or if the audience can infer from the context that she is, she would be using the statement detachedly;[49] if she explicitly states that she is a social-democrat, or if we can infer it from the context, she would be committed to T and then she would be using the statement to give normative (formal or robust, it doesn't matter now) reasons for you to behave in a certain way.

But we can hear an objection approaching. It is rather uncommon for judges, when adjudicating, to reveal their moral or political commitments, especially when they don't overlap with the content of the law. In this sense, the cancellation of the general implicature of commitment when judges are adjudicating would hardly be explicit. And to infer the cancellation from the context also seems problematic. It would be almost impossible to tell, the objection would conclude, when a judge is proffering a detached legal statement.

We agree on two things. It's highly infrequent that a judge, when adjudicating a particular case, explicitly cancels the mentioned general implicature. We also agree that the contextual evidence to infer that a judge is proffering a detached legal statement is normally weaker than in the case of lawyers, scholars or jurists. But we disagree on the claim that this evidence is always so weak as to completely (or almost completely) rule out the possibility of inferring the cancellation of the general implicature of commitment for some cases. Let's put an example. In Mexico City, voluntary interruption of pregnancy was prohibited before 2007. In 2007, the legislature of Mexico City—which has the same legislative powers of a state—passed a law allowing voluntary abortion within the first twelve weeks of pregnancy. It is not hard to imagine a judge proffering two incompatible legal statements in two different moments: "'Abortion is permitted' is legally not valid," before 2007; and "'Abortion is permitted' is legally valid," from 2007 onwards. Given that it's highly unlikely that this judge changed her mind, morally speaking, on abortion from the

[48]Mullins (2018), p. 384.

[49]Perhaps some would say that a judge that adjudicates against her own moral commitments is inconsistent. We think there is no inconsistency in claiming that "I *morally* ought to p" and "I *legally* ought to p". And this is not only a logical possibility—the fact that, for the most part, judges apply the law homogeneously could be explained in (at least) two different ways: either all (all!) judges think likewise in moral and political terms or they differ politically and morally but agree on what the criteria of legal validity are. The latter explanation seems more plausible and we take this as a signal that some judges, at least in some cases, adjudicate against their own moral and political commitments. But we admit that at the end of the day whether this means that they are inconsistent or not depends on whether somebody embraces positivism or some form of anti-positivism. We don't want to engage here, though, in the positivist vs. anti-positivism debate. The fact remains that some (or perhaps many) judges proffer detached legal statements in this sense.

final months of 2006 to the first months of 2007, it seems that we can infer that either her utterance of "'Abortion is permitted' is legally not valid" in 2006 or her utterance of "'Abortion is permitted' is legally valid" in 2007, is a detached legal statement. The diachronic context allows us to infer with some confidence that either in 2006 or 2007 the general implicature was cancelled. It's true that we cannot exactly tell whether the cancellation was made in 2006 or in 2007—and here it is where the weakness of the evidence pops up with force. But the only thing we need here in order to meet the objection aforementioned is to show that it's possible for judges to proffer detached legal statements. We believe we have just done that.

Hence, whether the statement "You ought to pay T" has any normative force—that is, if "You ought to pay T" provides you with any reasons for action—is a matter of how the utterer is using the statement. If the utterer doesn't do or say anything that allows us to infer that she has cancelled the general implicature, then "You ought to pay T" should be understood as an internal legal statement. An internal legal statement of that kind involves at least formally normative force. But, if she is using her statement to merely illuminate the existence of a legally valid norm, the statement has no normative force. Detached legal statements are, at the end of the day, descriptive statements.

Nothing said up to this point rules out the possibility of detached legal statements having motivational force (they have at least some motivational force many times, actually). But the relevant question is whether detached legal statements make any normative difference. And the answer, given their descriptive (pragmatic) status, is negative.[50]

However, we do not need the descriptivist interpretation of detached legal statements to be the case in a conclusive way. For our purposes here, that is, to show that there is an important part of legal talk that should be understood as not normative, it's enough to show that the descriptivist interpretation of detached legal statements is a plausible one. And we have argued that it is.

But are detached legal statements actually legal talk and thought? Are detached legal statements, in other words, statements *of* law?

We will defend now that the answer to both questions is on the affirmative.[51] Along the lines of this claim, Kevin Toh has said:

> Joseph Raz has argued that Hart's bipartite taxonomy [between internal and external legal statements] obscures from view a very significant class of internal statements and that there is a need to further distinguish among internal statements. The internal legal statements Hart had in mind are those that display a speaker's acceptance of, or commitment to, the norms of the legal system within he speaks. In addition to such *committed* internal statements as Raz

[50]Let's recall one more time that "You ought to pay T" is semantically ambiguous. So, the way to distinguish between its normative interpretation and its descriptive interpretation is by a means of a pragmatic analysis.

[51]According to Raz, Hart himself was bound to accept that "not all legal statements are internal". See Raz (1998), p. 249. Our conclusion, then, is congenial with Raz's reconstruction of the Hartian position.

> calls them, there are, he observes, *detached* internal statements. Detached internal legal statements, like their committed cousins, are assertions of law.[52]

That detached legal statements are assertions of law is hard to deny if we go back to the possibility of our libertarian judge (or, if you prefer, to the actual judge deciding about abortion in Mexico City). It's true that we—that are, ex hypothesis, in a privileged epistemic position, one that allows being aware that she sympathizes with libertarianism—know that the judge has cancelled the commitment to "You ought to pay T." But it's also true that when she adjudicates that "You ought to pay T," such a statement is an assertion of law. Detached legal statements are legal thought and talk, *descriptive* talk and thought, but *legal* though and talk nonetheless.

We are not sure, though, that detached legal statements are, strictly speaking, a kind of internal legal statements. If what makes the difference between internal legal statements and detached legal statements is the explicit or implicit attitude—of commitment or detachment—of the utterer, then the existence of a libertarian judge that adjudicates social-democratic taxes would mean that there can be assertions of law that are not internal legal statements.

What this would suggest, then, is that perhaps there are not exactly two levels of discourse at play here, but three: the general jurisprudence level, the legal level, and an intermediate level where detached legal statements lie.

However, this tripartite division would not modify our objection. General jurisprudence is about legal thought and talk. And detached legal statements—even if they lack the commitment feature—are legal thought and talk. But since general jurisprudence, as conceived by Plunkett and Shapiro, is a metanormative enterprise—that is, an enterprise about a specific kind of normative language—, it follows that theories that belong to general jurisprudence cannot account for an important (probably even decisive) part of legal thought and talk.

The dilemma for Plunkett and Shapiro kicks in again. Either detached legal statements are not legal thought and talk, or Plunkett and Shapiro's account of general jurisprudence requires us to do general jurisprudence leaving out of this explanatory project an important, probably decisive part of legal thought and talk. We see no reasonable way out from this dilemma for the account of general jurisprudence constructed by Plunkett and Shapiro.

Our own view—that we will not elaborate here—is that a useful account of general jurisprudence should illuminate legal thought and talk, regardless of such thought and talk being normative—internal legal statements—or descriptive—detached legal statements. This shouldn't sound peculiar at all. This is what most jurisprudes (including Shapiro[53]) do all the time.

---

[52]Toh (2011), pp. 109–110 citations omitted, and emphasis in the original.

[53]With some exaggeration, we could say that almost every single contemporary jurisprude in analytic philosophy of law has dealt at some point with detached legal statements. See for instance Shapiro (2001, 2011).

5 Conclusion

In this paper, we have argued for two main claims. First, that Plunkett and Shapiro's conception of general jurisprudence does a poor job at illuminating important positions and debates usually regarded as part of general jurisprudence. Second, that their conception requires us to leave unexplained an important part of legal thought and talk. If our observations are correct, it is hard to appreciate the programmatic appeal of Plunkett and Shapiro's proposal. Contrary to what they think, their account does not illuminate existing positions in general jurisprudence and cannot be used by legal scholars to advance the philosophical discussion in some important respects about legal thought, talk, and what, if any, such thought and talk are about.

References

Alvarez M (2017) Reasons for action: justification, motivation, explanation. In: Zalta EN (ed) The Stanford encyclopedia of philosophy, Winter 2017. Metaphysics Research Lab, Stanford University
Barberis M (2017) Genoese legal realism. In: Sellers M, Kirste S (eds) Encyclopedia of the philosophy of law and social philosophy. Springer Netherlands, Dordrecht, pp 1–6
Chiassoni P (2016) Da Bentham a Kelsen. Sei capitoli per una storia della filosofia analitica del diritto. Giappichelli, Torino
Cohen F (1935) Transcendental nonsense and the functional approach. Columbia Law Rev:809–849
Coleman J (2001) The practice of principle: in defense of a pragmatist approach to legal theory. Oxford University Press, Oxford
Cook WW (1937) 'Facts' and 'Statements of Fact'. Univ Chic Law Rev 4:233–246
Dancy J (1995) Why there is really no such thing as the theory of motivation. Proc Aristot Soc 95:1–18
Dancy J (2000) Practical reality. Clarendon Press, Oxford
Duarte d'Almeida L (2011) Legal statements and normative language. Law Philos 30:167–199
Enoch D (2011) Reason-giving and the law. In: Oxford studies in philosophy of law. Oxford University Press, Oxford, pp 1–38
Frank J (1930) Law and the modern mind. Brentano's, New York
Frank J (1931) Are judges human? Parts I and II. Univ Pa Law Rev 80:233–267
Green L (1999) Positivism and conventionalism. Can J Law Jurisprud 12:35–52
Grice P (1991) Studies in the way of words. Harvard University Press, Cambridge
Guastini R (2011) Rule-scepticism restated. In: Oxford studies in philosophy of law. Oxford University Press, Oxford, pp 138–162
Hart HLA (1961) The concept of law, third. Oxford University Press, Oxford
Hart HLA (1982) Essays on Bentham: jurisprudence and political philosophy. Oxford University Press, Oxford
Hart HLA (1983) Scandinavian legal realism. In: Essays in jurisprudence and philosophy. Clarendon Press, Oxford, pp 161–169
Hobbes T (1996) Leviathan, or the matter, form, & power of a common-wealth ecclesiasticall and civil (1651). Oxford University Press, Oxford
Holmes OW Jr (1897) The path of the law. Harv Law Rev 10:457–478
Leiter B (2001) Legal realism and legal positivism reconsidered. Ethics 111:278–301

Leiter B (2007) Naturalizing jurisprudence: essays on American legal realism and naturalism in legal philosophy. Oxford University Press, Oxford

Leiter B (2010) American legal realism. In: Patterson D (ed) A companion to philosophy of law and legal theory, second. Wiley-Blackwell, Singapore, pp 249–266

Leiter B (2013) Legal realisms, old and new. Valpso Law Rev 47:949–963

Llewellyn K (1930) The bramble bush. Oceana, New York

Llewellyn K (1931) Some realism about realism – responding to dean pound. Harv Law Rev 44:1222–1264

Marmor A (2011) Philosophy of law. Princeton University Press, Princeton

Moore U (1923) Rational basis of legal institutions. Columbia Law Rev:609–617

Moore U, Callahan C (1943) Law and learning theory: a study in legal control. Yale Law J 53:1–136

Moore U, Hope T (1929) An institutional approach to the law of commercial banking. Yale Law J 38:703–719

Moore U, Sussman G (1931) Legal and institutional methods applied to the debiting of direct discounts – I. Legal method: banker's set-off; II. Institutional method; VI. The decisions, the institutions, and the degree of deviation. Yale Law J 40:555–575, 1219–1250

Mullins R (2018) Detachment and deontic language in law. Law Philos 37:351–348

Oliphant H (1928) A return to stare decisis. Am Bar Assoc J 14:159–162

Parfit D (1997) Reasons and motivation. Proc Aristot Soc Suppl Vol 71:99–129

Plunkett D, Shapiro S (2017) Law, morality, and everything else: general jurisprudence as a branch of metanormative. Ethics 128:37–68

Radin M (1925) The theory of judicial decision: or how judges think. Am Bar Assoc J 11:357–362

Radin M (1930) Statutory interpretation. Harv Law Rev 43:863–885

Raz J (1975) Practical reason and norms. Oxford University Press, Oxford

Raz J (1980) Sources, normativity, and individuation. In: The concept of a legal system: an introduction to the theory of a legal system. Oxford University Press, Oxford

Raz J (1998) The purity of the pure theory of law. In: Paulson SL, Paulson BL (eds) Normativity and norms: critical perspectives on Kelsenian themes. Clarendon Press; Oxford University Press, Oxford, pp 195–220

Raz J (2002) The authority of law: essays on law and morality. Oxford University Press, Oxford

Raz J (2011) Reasons: explanatory and normative. In: From normativity to responsibility. Oxford University Press, Oxford, pp 13–35

Scanlon TM (1998) What we owe to each other. Belknap Press, Cambridge

Scanlon TM (2004) Reasons: a puzzling duality? In: Wallace RJ, Pettit P, Scheffler S, Smith M (eds) Reason and value: themes from the moral philosophy of Joseph Raz. Oxford University Press, Oxford

Shapiro S (2001) On Hart's way out. In: Coleman J (ed) Hart's postscript. Essays on the postscript to the concept of law. Oxford University Press, Oxford, pp 149–191

Shapiro S (2011) Legality. Belknap Press, Cambridge

Smith M (1994) The moral problem. Blackwell, Oxford

Toh K (2007) Raz on detachment, acceptance and describability. Oxf J Leg Stud 27:403–427

Toh K (2011) Legal judgments as plural acceptances of norms. In: Oxford studies in philosophy of law: volume 1. Oxford University Press, Oxford

Vecchi DD (2017) Enunciados no comprometidos y punto de vista jurídico: una perspectiva renovada. Crítica Rev Hispanoam Filos 49:91–121. https://doi.org/10.22201/iifs.18704905e.2017.118

Yntema HE (1941) Jurisprudence on parade. Mich Law Rev 39:1154–1181

Part V
New Theoretical Approaches

Law's Virtual Empires: Game Analogies and the Concept of Law

Jason Grant Allen

Abstract In this Chapter, I explore the future development of a well-worn tool in the elucidation of the concept of law: the analogy between law and games. In particular, I explore how the analogy might be extended in the context of complex, modern games that take place in a virtual environment: Massive Multiplayer Online Role-Playing Games ('MMORPGs'). Are these games jurisprudentially interesting, in the sense of shedding light on the concept of law? Or is nothing to be gained from them that cannot be taken from analogies with games like chess and baseball? I first trace out the traditional uses of the games analogy, and then I suggest some ways in which analogies between law and MMORPGs might be helpful. These include providing fresh insight answers into long-standing jurisprudential questions and posing new questions for jurisprudential enquiry.

1 Introduction

Legal theorists are increasingly called upon to engage with the implications of technologically-mediated social practices, from the interpretation of self-executing 'smart contracts' to the ownership of 'cryptoassets' to determining the situs of cyber-crime for the purpose of jurisdiction. How well equipped is contemporary legal theory to do this? What avenues suggest themselves for exploring the concept of law in the 'Information Age'? And what might an exploration of law in new technical contexts increase our understanding of the concept of law generally?

This chapter has benefitted immensely from the critical feedback of VAJ Kurki, Andrew Halpin, Iza Skoczen, Jeffrey Lipshaw, Martin Florian, the Editors, and an anonymous reviewer. A draft of this paper was presented at the Centre for Law, Language and Philosophy at the Jagellonian University, Krakow, on 14 May 2019. I am grateful to the participants for their feedback, particularly to Radosław Pałosz for his written comments. The text was finalised in early 2020. The usual disclaimer applies—all errors are my own.

J. G. Allen (✉)
Humboldt-Universität zu Berlin, Berlin, Germany
e-mail: jgallen@cantab.net

J. L. Fabra-Zamora, G. Villa Rosas (eds.), *Conceptual Jurisprudence*, Law and Philosophy Library 137, https://doi.org/10.1007/978-3-030-78803-2_15

Analogies between law and games are a well-worn tool for the explication of the concept of law.[1] For example, H.L.A. Hart used the games analogy to explain: (i) the difference between rules that tell you *what* to do and rules that tell you *how* to do things;[2] (ii) what it means for an action (such as passing legislation or creating a will) to be 'valid';[3] (iii) the difference between rule-following and habitual behaviour, the importance of the internal aspect of rule-following in distinguishing law from force, and the importance of rules in justifying and criticising action;[4] (iv) the continuity of rules through changes of sovereign and subject;[5] (v) the relationship between rules in a hierarchy of 'primary' and 'secondary' rules,[6] and (vi) the critical difference between the 'internal' and 'external' perspective which is, on Hart's account, generative of legal authority itself.[7] Express or implicit in these points were further points, for example: (vii) the notion of a power or ability to do a certain kind of act; (viii) the special role or status according to which an individual acts as an 'official' within a legal system; and (ix) the notion of a 'legal system' as a (hierarchical) set of rules deriving from an ultimate conventional 'rule of recognition'. Alf Ross also explored law and games,[8] as have contemporary legal theorists. Scott Shapiro uses the games analogy repeatedly to explain his 'planning theory' of law,[9] and Andrei Marmor asks how law is like chess to explore the nature of the 'master norm' that distinguishes law from *prima facie* similar social phenomena, elaborating a theory of 'deep conventionality' common to both law and games.[10]

Yet, despite the sophistication of these theories of law, recourse to the games analogy has often been *ad hoc* rather than systematic.[11] Further, it is probably fair to say that analogies have seldom been drawn between law and the rules constituting and governing complex game-worlds in connected virtual environments, despite emerging literature on the law of games.[12] In the spirit of exploring 'new directions' in the concept of law, this chapter explores what the games analogy might teach us if extended to cover Massive Multiplayer Online Role-Playing Games

[1]Definition of the concept 'game' itself is difficult; Lipshaw suggests a family resemblance approach, which in my view is sensible; some of the features that games share are: being rule-constituted, being played for fun, and forming a discrete context of social interaction in which very different rules may operate. Further features I assume will become clear throughout the course of the Chapter. See Lipshaw (2008), p. 620.

[2]In particular, how to do things like 'win' or 'vote': Hart (2012), pp. 9, 30, 34.

[3]Hart (2012), pp. 34, 40.

[4]Hart (2012), pp. 55, 136, 138.

[5]Hart (2012), pp. 58, 62.

[6]Hart (2012), p. 99.

[7]Hart (2012), p. 56.

[8]See Ross (2018), Ch 1 §3; see also Duarte (2018), p. 149.

[9]Shapiro (2012), pp. 11, 12, 184.

[10]Marmor (2007), pp. Ch. 6.

[11]Jackson (1991), p. 100.

[12]Most of this literature has been directed towards solving specific problems, such as the possibility of virtual crimes or the ownership of virtual property.

('MMORPGs').[13] This contribution is exploratory and programmatic; my intention is, first and foremost, to open new topics for discussion. In broad terms, the avenues I suggest entail a closer engagement with the ontology of law and games as social practices; this follows a neo-Hartian line of jurisprudence from Oxford language philosophy through the social ontology of John Searle and 'institutional' theories of law presented by scholars such as Neil MacCormick, Ota Weinberger, DWP Ruiter, Jaap Hage, Shapiro and Marmor.[14]

2 From Chess to MMORPGs

Chess is a game with a large set of possible game-states, which makes it such an interesting game of skill. These game-states are made possible by a fairly simple set of rules: There are 64 squares on a chessboard, half white and half black, on which two players play with 16 pieces each. There are six classes of pieces, each with different modes of movement (e.g., black/white squares only, straight/diagonal lines only). All pieces are vulnerable to being 'taken' by all other pieces, except for the 'king', who cannot be taken but only put in 'check', but he can be put in check by any class of piece. There are some quirks such as 'castling' and the 'promotion' of pawns. Besides that, there is not much to it.[15]

MMORPGs are complex and heterogenous phenomena in which social and technical elements are inextricably mixed.[16] In a MMORPG like *World of Warcraft*, one designs a character or avatar to play based on a number of starting options, such as the 'race' of a character and its type or class. Gameplay consists of completing in-game activities to obtain rewards, such as artefacts which equip or improve one's avatar. This enables one to complete a larger set of in-game activities, e.g., more challenging quests or defeating more powerful opponents. Play includes not only interactions with other characters, but actions over objects as well; characters can collect artefacts and things that act like money, trade them with other players, and deposit them in 'banks'. One's play in the game might extend over years on a continuous basis. The game-world might host millions of players interacting with each other at any given time.[17] Other games like *Second Life* simply provide a virtual

[13]For a discussion of MMORPGs, see Asbjørn Jøn (2010).

[14]See in particular MacCormick and Weinberger (1986) and Ruiter (2010).

[15]Chess is traditionally played on a two-dimensional board with figurines; the game-play of chess can, however, be replicated by a system of notation in which letters and numbers stand in for pieces and squares, and chess can be rendered graphically by computers in various ways. Both the latter options afford the option to play chess over long physical distances and with delays in time. On these forms of chess, see Johansson (2005).

[16]De Paoli and Kerr (2009), p. 1.

[17]Actually, these millions will be distributed over many servers, so only tens of thousands my actually interact with each other directly—but the 'game world' broadly defined provides a context for millions.

environment in which players engage, *via* their avatars, in more or less everyday interactions.[18]

Already here an important difference appears, which will trace through this investigation and inform its conclusions; it is that MMORPGs more closely approximate the great 'game of life' than do games like chess. In chess, there is always a 'right' procedure from any position; perhaps this is why intelligent machines have proved so good at winning such games in recent years. Real life, and games such as poker or boxing, consist of bluffing, deception, pre-emption and a sophisticated (and all too human) theory of the opponents' intentionality.[19] Further, games like chess have a clear 'winning' goal state, while MMORPGs (again like real life) are a more continuous, narrative format in which one completes tasks or 'quests' but is never really 'finished'. It is, however, on the conventional nature of games that I wish to focus here, namely the property of games that they are *constituted by rules*.

The intuitive departure point for exploring the relevance of MMORPGs to law is that so many legal transactions now occur in a technologically-mediated 'space' that is ontologically similar to MMORPGs. As Philip Brey notes, computer systems have become the site of objects, events and actions; while many are obvious simulations of their 'real world' counterparts, many are 'just as real' as their counterparts in the physical world: 'electronic money is, for all purposes, just as real as physical money, and electronic gambling can have the same devastating consequences as gambling in a physically real casino.'[20] Keith Culver and Michael Giudice have observed that the Internet has become so common-place since the widespread use of the World Wide Web in the 1990s that cyberspace—a non-geographical 'world' created by the structured exchange of information between networked devices—has become an everyday category, too:[21]

> Cyberspace, on this view, is a real world, but it is a world apart. What happens in the virtual world is not simply a simulacrum of the real world, mapping back to it by firm links, however temporary or long-lasting. Rather, virtual worlds construct separate, often purposely self-contained realities, perhaps most vividly illustrated by the rise of web-accessed, user-constructed worlds such as [*Second Life*] and [MMORPGs such as *World of Warcraft*].[22]

These virtual worlds subsist even when their players log off. A virtual-reality flight simulator, Tom Boellstorff argues, is not a 'virtual world' because it runs from a single, unconnected computer; it is not a 'space' that persists in time even when not being used. A virtual game-world, on the other hand, is a 'place in its own right' that

[18]It may not be accurate to call *Second Life* a MMORPG in strict terms, but I will include it in the discussion for the sake of convenience with a caveat.

[19]I think Jeffrey Lipshaw for his comments to this effect, and to his reference Jacob Bronowski's recollections of a conversation with John von Neumann about the nature of games in *The Ascent of Man* (1973).

[20]Brey (2003), p. 268.

[21]Culver and Giudice (2017), p. 181.

[22]Culver and Giudice (2017), p. 182.

persists and 'would exist even if no-one were currently "inworld"'.[23] On this view, virtual worlds are 'additional realities'. The importance of this will unfold throughout the chapter, but the initial point is that games create *sub-domains of socially constituted reality* that are distinct but interconnected and, at times, overlapping.

As more and more of conventional social (including legal and economic) reality moves 'online', describing the way that law operates in cyberspace will be one of the main challenges facing legal theory. This includes, among other things, describing the legal status of objects located in cyberspace and actions performed in cyberspace: Does a virtual sword constitute a 'virtual chattel'?[24] Does touching an avatar's breasts without (the player's? the avatar's?) permission constitute 'virtual sexual assault'?[25] These questions have a practical edge: A Japanese court recently held that bitcoins were not 'things' capable of ownership,[26] and an Australian court has held that indecent cartoons constituted child pornography.[27] Questions will arise, increasingly, in the context of interactions with governments, too; an example is Estonia's 'e-Residency' programme, by which users join 'a new digital nation for global citizens, powered by the Republic of Estonia'; once registered, they can access Estonian government and business services for the purposes of company formation, corporate compliance and taxation, and so forth. Estonian citizens use the same platform for the full suite of ordinary governmental services such as welfare as well.[28]

The notion of a 'digital nation'—the space in which a global community of e-Residents 'resides'—quite obviously shares some basic ontological features with a MMORPG; granted, there be no dragons here, but the entities that exist in such a space, and the space itself, are composed of structured information that is capable of visual representation to the human eye. Users can type a command or click a mouse to perform operations within the space such that its state changes—in both cases, such a state change might involve payment with commercial bank money, or transfer of real estate (real or virtual), for example. Increasingly, digital actions have real-world effects, and the ontic texture of the real world approximates the worlds of MMORPGs.

While lawyers have been interested in questions such as the status of virtual property, the civil liberties implications of algorithmic decision-making, or the possibility of sexual assault in a digital environment, the focus has mainly been at a practical level; *legal theorists* have been less concerned with the implications of new information and communications technology for thinking about the nature of

---

[23]Boellstorff (2016), pp. 394, 395.

[24]See Lastowka and Hunter (2004) and Fairfield (2005).

[25]See Dibble (2005); see Danaher (2018) for examples and discussion.

[26]A translation of the judgement is available here: https://www.law.ox.ac.uk/sites/files/oxlaw/mtgox_judgment_final.pdf.

[27]See e.g., *McEwen v Simmons* [2008] NSWSC 1292, which held that indecent cartoons involving characters from *The Simpsons* constituted child pornography.

[28]See https://e-resident.gov.ee/.

law and legal systems.[29] If the games analogy has been helpful to legal theorists' efforts to understand the concept of law, perhaps taking account of the richer ontic aspect of computer-based games could suggest some new directions in thinking about the concept of law in the Information Age? In the balance of this section, I explore four dimensions to the 'extended' games analogy that I think make it prima facie worth considering. This sets the stage in Sect. 3 to examine what light it might shed on one of the deeper, perennial questions in jurisprudence—the nature of legal normativity. I conclude in Sect. 4.

2.1 *Theorising the 'Digital Real'*

The first thing that an extended games analogy might contribute is an impetus to theorise what Boellstorff calls the 'digital real.'[30] Boellstorff's main contention is that we should not adopt a straightforward opposition between the 'digital' and the 'real', in which the real is assumed to be physical; conflating the physical with the real and the digital with the unreal, he argues, can have 'devastating consequences for addressing the reality of the digital.'[31] Digital demand deposits held with a commercial bank, for example, are certainly 'real' in a very important sense. Boellstorff explains that some anthropologists have pursued an 'ontological turn' in the last decades and reflects in this context on the nature of reality in digital environments. Although his discussion is focused on an internal conversation within anthropology, the notion of an ontological turn more broadly offers an exciting point of articulation with Oxford language philosophy, from which both Hartian legal positivism and social ontology (especially in the work of John Searle) have sprung.[32] These two disciplines, in turn, have merged in legal theory's own 'ontological turn'—'institutional' theories of law such as MacCormick's.

At the most basic level, law and games are capable of analogy because they are both *domains of social reality constituted by rules*. Searle has often used games to illustrate what he calls the logical structure of socially-constructed institutions (including legal institutions). Institutions are constituted by conventions, expressed linguistically in declarations,[33] that are analytic in the sense of giving definitions and conferring powers without necessary reference to pre-existing facts—they are almost tautological in character.[34] So-called 'constitutive rules' offer part of the definition of the institution of a 'checkmate' or a 'touchdown', for example: '[That] a checkmate in chess is achieved in such and such away can appear now as a rule, now as an

[29]Culver and Giudice (2017), p. 183. However, see e.g., Palka (2017).

[30]Boellstorff (2016).

[31]Boellstorff (2016), p. 387.

[32]See e.g., Kwak (2017).

[33]Not unlike JL Austin's performative utterances: see Austin (1962).

[34]Kwak (2017), p. 12.

analytic truth based on the meaning of 'checkmate in chess'.[35] In broad terms, this 'invisible ontology'[36] is created when social agents impose 'status functions' on objects (including persons and events) in the physical world of 'brute' reality; when we take a creek to 'count as' a boundary, for example, the creek *qua* boundary starts to emanate 'deontic powers' such as rights and obligations and thereby to perform a role it could not perform in virtue of its physical properties alone.[37] Law and games, along with other practices such as religion, are, in this sense, autonomous or self-generating conventional domains. It is possible to create a new game, and it is possible to create a new legal system, *ex nihilo*, apparently from nothing more than collective intentionality and language.

A novel feature is that MMORPGs have a layer of technological rules that 'analog' reality lacks, i.e., the code that creates the online environment and governs how entities behave in that environment. In Searleian terms, they involve the imposition of status functions on *digital* as well as *physical* 'brute facts'.[38] Exploring the ontology of cyberspace in the game context may therefore help us to understand situations where the law is technologically-mediated, for example in the context of digital payments, where a legal status is imposed on a digital artifact such as a bank's electronic ledger.[39]

2.2 *Modelling the Interaction Between Discrete Systems of Rules (or Rules in Discrete Systems)*

First, it is convenient to note the basic conceptual separation between games and 'real life'. We have already seen that the divide between the 'digital' and the 'real' is spurious; parts of the real *are* digital. But a separation from the 'real' is key to the definition of games, conventionally called the 'magic circle' that circumscribes game environments and separates them from real life.[40] Players routinely perform actions within MMORPG environments that would be illegal if they occurred in the real world, including killing (avatars) and stealing (virtual goods). These actions are not only *not wrongs* in the game-world; they are often central to game-play. It is this

[35] Searle (1969), p. 34.

[36] See Smith (2003), p. 12.

[37] See generally Searle (2010), pp. 6–11 for a brief presentation of the basic concepts.

[38] This has led to an interesting debate within social ontology which I am unable to engage with here.

[39] Indeed, electronic money is one of the phenomena that has generated serious debate between social ontologists.

[40] See Huizinga (1938); for a critical analysis, see Fairfield (2009). I have necessarily assumed much about the nature of games in this brief investigation. See further Caillois (2001) and the systematic review of definitions in Juul in Copier and Raessens (2003).

magic circle that is broken when in-game actions assume meaning in the outside world (or outside-world meaning 'bleeds' into the game-world[41]), such as the sale for US dollars of a *Second Life* house or in-game speech constituting hate-speech or a verbal assault.[42]

As Josh Fairfield has observed, the magic circle is often crossed.[43] Some lament this, while others celebrate it—I will not take an evaluative position here.[44] What interests me is the *interaction* between different sub-domains of reality and the normative orders that pertain to them. In the case of MMORPGs, End User License Agreements ('EULAs') are set out, on a take-it-or-leave-it basis, by 'game gods' and deal with matters ranging from offensive speech to the ownership of virtual goods and avatar identities.[45] While these EULAs have dominated legal analysis to date, Fairfield also identifies player consent, community-negotiated norms, and background laws as relevant normative sources for MMORPGs. Games generally are interesting because they require legal theorists to model the interactions between actions in one rule-governed 'world' and the law of another world, ultimately the 'real world'. For example, despite the general prohibition on battery, football tackles are legal and may result in injury that is not actionable under American law. An offside tackle that results in an injury will not sound in tort merely because it was offside, whereas a foul tackle that falls outside the consent-based carve out to the tort of battery will.[46] This is a complex interaction between national law and the rules of the game. MMORPGs are particularly interesting in this regard because they are larger than small states like Estonia, and routinely comprise interactions between subjects of different nation states;[47] their communities, therefore, have the ability to generate community norms and have a stronger *prima facie* claim to recognition than the players of any other kind of game.

While the notion of law as a system of rules is fundamental for many legal theorists, what exactly constitutes a 'legal system' and how discrete legal systems interact is not always clear; further, as Culver and Giudice have argued, legal systems have generally been taken to be *state-based* legal systems, and the

41 Castronova in Balkin and Noveck (2006), p. 74.

42 Jeffrey Lipshaw also draws a useful distinction between models and games—although both are 'constructs of rules', he argues, '[g]ames are real in ways that models are not'. Games have a property of 'thingness', an independent reality, while models have the property of 'aboutness', in that they map onto something else that is real. See Lipshaw (2008), p. 618.

43 Not only because in-game actions have real world consequences—sometimes, games form an important part of the broader religious and legal social order, for example the Meso-American ball games. See e.g., Scarborough and Wilcox (1993) and Auguet (1972). On trial by battle, which was only formally abolished in English law in the nineteenth century, see Russel (1980). A dystopic scenario of this type is explored in the young adult fiction franchise *The Hunger Games* by Suzanne Collins.

44 Compare e.g., the chapters by Castronova and Balkin, respectively, in Balkin and Noveck (2006).

45 See e.g., Abramovitch and Cummings (2007).

46 See Fairfield (2009), p. 832, citing the American *Restatement (Second) of Torts* (1965).

47 See e.g., https://mmo-population.com/ for indicative figures by game.

phenomenon of legality outside the nation state is now challenging conventional legal theory.[48] The rise of intra-state, trans-state, supra-state and super-state legality is pervasive, and any theory that fails to engage with them is not really a descriptive one.[49] This, they conclude, means that legal theory must engage with forms of legality that emerge in virtual sub-domains of social reality. Thus, for Fairfield, it is not the magic circle that is important but the legal system's posture towards consent, community self-regulation, and the official recognition of community norms: 'EULAs interact with community norms, individual consent, and background law to generate legal outcomes.'[50] In my view, the insulation and entanglement of MMORPGs with national law (directly and indirectly) provide a worthwhile site for exploration.

For legal theory, this presents MMORPG environments as an additional category of (more or less institutionalised) normative ordering that is worthy of interest—especially from a pluralist or non-statist perspective. Because of the inherent historical and geographical contingency of a legal system according to the positivist view, an extended games analogy may prove useful in exploring pluralist theories of legal positivism. Indeed, because their game-worlds are so persistent and complex, a further cluster of questions arises. As the techno-libertarian literature of the 1990s shows, it is possible to conceptualise cyberspace as a place in which non-state forms of legality emerge and (so it is argued) should be allowed to flourish.[51] Currently, a debate about national jurisdiction in cyberspace is occuring in earnest.[52] MMORPGs offer a rich source of hypotheticals and counterfactuals for this growing literature.

2.3 *Modern Agency (Are We All Avatars Now?)*

Another novel feature of MMORPGs is how the games mediate players' actions through an online avatar. Where a baseball player plays with his own physical body, and a chess player plays by moving pieces around a board,[53] a MMORPG player's actions are mediated in the game-world through the actions of an avatar who appears in the game-world as an acting subject. Its actions may ultimately be attributed to a player, who is generally a physical human being, in real life. But while the actions of (one of) my avatars might be attributable to me, in a meaningful sense they are the

[48]Culver and Giudice (2017).

[49]Culver and Giudice (2017), p. 23.

[50]Fairfield (2009), pp. 825, 834.

[51]See e.g., Johnson and Post (1996).

[52]See Post (2017), see Allen and Lastra (2020).

[53]Actually, it depends what kind of chess: the standard case involves two players and a physical board; players can also play chess by notation or, indeed, in a virtual environment: see Johansson (2005). It would also be possible for two avatars to sit down to a game of chess in *Second Life*.

acts of my avatar, and I could not perform them without the avatar and the virtual environment in which it 'lives'. While I am not my online avatar, my avatar may perform actions that have legal relevance for me in the offline world.

Two points of analogy are interesting in this context. The first is what the notion of an avatar can teach us about legal personality. Raph Koster has argued that our legal identities may eventually become so avatar-like that our decisions about the rights of avatars today will hold important ramifications: 'Some day it's gonna be your bank records and your grocery list and your credit report' in a 'very large, distributed server, anarchic, virtual world where it might be very *hard* to move to a different service provider'.[54] Now that scandals concerning social media are accumulating, concerns about the data use of monopoly digital platform providers are growing, and interactions between citizens *inter se* (and with officials) are moving into cyberspace, Koster's warning seems prescient.

But Koster's parallel between the avatar and legal personality is insightful on a deeper level, too. In law, one human being can be the referent of a number of legal 'avatars.' While we do not allow one human being to be two legal persons as such, we come close to it with one-man corporations, executors and personal representatives,[55] and even public offices.[56] One human being can occupy multiple legal *personae* for the purposes of a logic of action, i.e., her acting *qua* shareholder of a company and there acting *qua* director of the same company, for example. One human being can occupy different legal statuses in different legal systems.[57] And many legal systems already recognise non-human entities as persons who can act by a representative.[58] In the wake of systematic treatment of European Jews as objects rather than persons, Hannah Arendt famously explored the fate of 'human beings who, unprotected by any specific law or political convention, are nothing but human beings'.[59] Such a position is dangerous because 'we actually live in a world in which human beings as such have ceased to exist for quite a while.'[60] Arendt's line of thought has been developed in Giorgio Agamben's exploration of biological *versus*

---

[54]Koster in Balkin and Noveck (2006), p. 66.

[55]When I act as a personal representative, for example, my personality is 'split' to the extent that I act in some contexts in my own right and in other context on behalf of or even 'quasi' another person.

[56]Recall Hart's example of King Rex 'giving private orders to his mistress' as opposed to giving public orders to his subjects *qua* King: Hart (2012), p. 68. The British monarch is traditionally seen as occupying or constituting a 'corporation sole': see Allen (2018), p. 304.

[57]See e.g., *Charles Duke of Brunswick v The King of Hanover* (1842) 49 ER 724, which held that the King of Hanover was exempt from the jurisdiction of the English Courts for acts done by him as a sovereign prince, but was liable to be sued in those Courts in respect of matters done by him as an English subject.

[58]See e.g., *Bumper Development* Corporation v *Commissioner* of *Police* of the *Metropolis* [1991] 1 WLR 1362, in which the High Court of England and Wales recognised a Hindu temple as a litigant.

[59]Arendt (1943), pp. 76–77.

[60]Arendt (1943), pp. 76–77.

political existence, and the disjunction between the rights of 'man' and the rights of the 'citizen.'[61] For Arendt and her generation of refugees, documents such as passports and birth certificates had taken on a whole new importance. More of our existence as *Rechtssubjekte* (i.e., subjects of a legal system) today is a matter of entry in a digital database than we would perhaps like to admit.

This leads to the second point. Developments in machine learning and 'artificial intelligence' are challenging conventional notions of what it means to be an agent, i.e., an entity capable of acting or causing effects within the legal system. Traditionally, the actions of automata such as machines have only mediated effects in a legal system, i.e., *via* rules that attribute the action to a (human) agent. This is also an important frontier in the legal theory of personhood.[62] Combined with the ability to connect automata to complex sensor networks (including cameras) in the so-called 'Internet of Things', we can expect a further erosion of the border between online and offline worlds, with implications for legal theory.[63] If this is the case, then the games analogy may become less of an analogy and more of a description of contemporary reality itself.[64]

2.4 Technically-Mediated Acts-in-the-Law

One of Hart's central claims in *The Concept of Law* was that law does not only impose duties on subjects—it also empowers them to act in new ways. Hart posited a *summa divisio* between so-called 'primary' and 'secondary' rules, which tracks in broad terms with Searle's notion of 'regulative' and 'constitutive' rules:[65]

> Under rules of the one type, which may well be considered the basic or primary type, human beings are required to do or abstain from certain actions, whether they wish to or not. Rules of the other type are in a sense parasitic upon or secondary to the first; for they provide that human beings may by doing or saying certain things introduce new rules of the primary type, extinguish or modify old ones, or in various ways determine their incidence or control their operations. Rules of the first type impose duties; rules of the second type confer powers, public or private. Rules of the first type concern actions involving physical movement or changes; rules of the second type provide for operations which lead not merely to physical movement or change, but the creation or variation of duties or obligations.[66]

I wish to focus on this idea of 'operations' which lead to the creation or variation of invisible 'rights and obligations.' This is closely related to the notion of 'legal

[61] See Agamben (1995).

[62] See generally Kurki and Pietrzykowski (2017).

[63] See Culver and Giudice (2017), p. 205.

[64] Lord Hodge recently suggested the serious exploration of the legal personality of Artificially Intelligent automata by reference to the corporation sole: see Hodge (2019), pp. 16–17.

[65] See Zaibert and Smith in Tsohatzidis (2007).

[66] Hart (2012), p. 81.

power', 'legal ability', or 'competence.'[67] The notion of legal power I adopt here follows closely the scheme of 'competence' presented by VAJ Kurki, which incorporates the notion of 'acting-in-the-law'.[68] The notion of actions having invisible legal consequences implies that there is something more at play than the actor's physical abilities.[69] Raising my hand or signing a piece of paper can, depending on the context, result in 'voting' or assault, in creating a 'deed'[70] or a scrap of paper.[71] This highlights the need for a or logic of action as a central project in the theory of law—and one that was traditionally neglected among Anglophone legal theorists.[72] Hart again used examples taken from games to illustrate the ability to perform rule-constituted actions, the enactment of legislation to a move in chess.[73] I will return to the concept of validity in the next section. For now, I wish to ask whether looking at modes of action in virtual environments could enrich our consideration of the logic of action more generally.

The extended games analogy can perhaps help us to understand acting-in-the-law as the intentional exercise of a rule-based ability in digital environments. Familiar problems of action by non-human agents have arisen in the context of group agents such as corporations; the will of an individual office-holder, as an 'organ' of the corporation, is taken to animate the actions of the body as a whole. Our problem here is slightly different; even assuming straightforward action by an individual, what do we make of actions mediated by computers? Philip Brey draws a distinction between *epistemic* and the *ontic* functions of computers; the former include what has traditionally been called information processing functions, and are fairly intuitive. In their ontic role, 'computers simulate environments and tools to engage these environments' in ways that utilise their information processing capabilities but actually do much more.[74] Computers *simulate worlds* by digitally encoding sound, images, and motion and by presenting digital information in analogue, manipulable forms such as graphic user interfaces.[75] It is increasingly through these interfaces that we act both as individuals and as the organs of larger groups. For example, the Australian

[67]See Lindahl and Reidhav (2017) for an overview of the literature on power; Zaibert (2007).

[68]Although he did not use the Continental term, the act-in-the-law is also implicit in Hart's account. On Kurki's view, x holds a legal competence C to effect legal consequence r if and only if x can perform an act-in-the-law to bring about r. An act-in-the-law is defined as follows: An act a performed by x constitutes an act-in-the-law if and only if (i) x performs a with the intention of bringing about the legal consequence r, and (ii) the fact that x has performed the act a in order to bring about r is an element of a set of actually occurrent conditions minimally sufficient for r: Kurki in McBride (2017), p. 38.

[69]See Brinz (1873), p. 211; Lindahl (1977), p. 211.

[70]See e.g., *Edwards v Canada (AG)* [1930] AC 124.

[71]See Rubinstein (1965), p. 5.

[72]See Hart (1982), p. 195.

[73]'Conformity with the conditions specified by the rules conferring the legislative powers is a step which is like a "move" in a game such as chess': Hart (2012), pp. 30–32.

[74]Brey (2005), p. 384.

[75]Brey (2005), p. 394.

Migration Act 1958 (Commonwealth) s. 498A now provides that a Minister may arrange for the use, under the Minister's control, of computer programs for any purposes for which the Minister may, or must, make a decision, exercise a power, or comply with an obligation, and that the Minister is taken to have made the decision, exercised the power, or complied with the obligation that was made, exercised, complied with, or done by the operation of that computer program. This requires the law to explain the attribution of a software process to a legally cognisable decision-maker. Simply put, acting-in-the-law has become a *socio-technical* phenomenon in the sense that an act-in-the law involves an assemblage of both human elements (such as volition, speech, or physical movement) and technological elements.[76]

In theorizing digital acts-in-the-law, the games analogy might again be of assistance. Let us consider what kind of logical scheme would be necessary analyze a move in a game of chess by my avatar in *Second Life*. A legal system imposes meanings on actions—increasingly on digital actions, whether in a graphically rich user interface such as a game or a more mundane database. Here, as always, several layers of rules operate together, as explained above—the rules of chess, the technical rules of the game that govern how the avatar can move game-objects (e.g., using its virtual hands), the rules of the EULA that, e.g., restrict playing chess for real-world money, the law(s) of the land(s) in which the players are located.

While it is not possible to pursue such a project here, developing a logical scheme to analyze action in MMORPGs could provide a beneficial counterpoint to developments in legal deontic logic and the logic of legal action. As observed by theorists such as Hart, Ross, and Searle, rule-sets comprise both rules of competence and rules of conduct.[77] These rules stipulate (i) what actions I *can* and *may* do (e.g., perhaps I *can* hack my opponent's account, but I *may* not according to the EULA), (ii) what actions my avatar can and may do (e.g., perhaps it can touch its virtual opponent indecently, but it may not according to the community norms of the game), and (iii) what each kind of chess piece can and may do (I will return to this point below).[78]

[76]See De Paoli and Kerr (2009). A closely related question, which I cannot explore here, is the increasing inability of humans to understand the machines they are using, and, what may be the same thing, the intervenience of increasingly intelligent automata. While acting through a computer programme is, in many respects, just like acting through a lever or a mechanical device, the chain of cause and effect may be less direct; an official may use an algorithm the workings of which neither she nor its creators truly understand, for example, and which incorporates some element of expertise in the sense of rule-application with a greater degree of independence from human intention. While I cannot state a considered view here, it seems possible that the chain of attribution could become convoluted, if not broken, by increasingly intelligent automata in the future. While this introduces a number of legal policy questions (for example, should the owner of an autonomous vehicle be responsible for its 'actions' or should the programmer?), it is on the technical aspects that I wish to focus here. See e.g., Hacker (2018) on attribution and imputation in the context of machine learning and data driven agency.

[77]The nomenclature is taken from Ross (1959) and the dichotomy it postulates corresponds roughly to Hart's primary and secondary rules as well as Searle's regulative and constitutive rules.

[78]For example see Lindahl (2005).

Our logical scheme would need to distinguish between straightforward abilities (i.e., the ability actually to move the chess piece) and rule-based abilities (i.e., the 'ability' to move in a diagonal line and 'take' another chess piece); within the former category, it would need to distinguish between physical ability (i.e., the ability to operate a mouse) and 'virtual' physical ability (i.e., the ability of the avatar to actually move a chess piece).[79] Clearly distinguishing between these modes of action, keeping action straight from obligation, and keeping the relevant 'actor' in clear view, is essential to analyzing such complex activities.

Another interesting difference appears in this context: The rules that *constitute* an in-game action, such as 'castling' in chess, are generally co-extensive with the rules that *regulate* that action.[80] There is no difference between it being *possible* for me to castle and being *allowed* to castle. In other words, most conventional games are closed systems, self-contained little worlds in which the only actions regulated are those made possible by the game itself.[81] The richer game-states of MMORPGs, on the other hand, could open up a gap similar to the one we observe in real life. There is a prima facie case to be made that an avatar *may* do whatever *can* do; thus Edward Castronova has argued compellingly for defence of the magic circle.[82] I will return to this argument in Sect. 3, below. For now, it is pertinent to ask whether the subject of those restrictions is the avatar or the player. In the latter case, which I think is more

---

[79]For example, in the *Sims Online* game, there is no way for a 'Sim' to kill another Sim although the player can perform a number of actions to induce 'death' in a Sim character they control: see e.g. https://sims-online.com/sims-4-death-guide-killing-your-sims/.

[80]For a critical view of the classical distinction, and an account of regulative rules as a sub-species of constitutive rules that create 'deontic facts', see Hage in Araskiewicz (2015).

[81]Actually, the picture just painted of chess is a little simplistic, as chess must imply rules against cheating. Generally, legal obligations constrain game-play—while not a rule of chess *per se*, I am not allowed to punch my opponent for taking too long to move, for example. My point is simply that the relevant actions the law must now govern include 'virtual' actions. A second point of complication was pointed out to me in Krakow. There were disputes about the legality of castling and upgrading pawns in the 1950s, where the existing rules were silent. In MMORPGs, too, there may arise situations which 'break the physics of the game' in unanticipated ways. I am unable to develop this line of enquiry here. In general, however, it may point to the fact that from within the rule-set of a game, some kind of power-structure is always needed to interpret the rules and that this interpretation will occur by reference to norms outside the game. The rules of the game are never enough. Perhaps this explains the devilish, intractable nature of the relation between law and morality? A closely related point is the ever-present problem of cheating, or (to put it more neutrally) 'exploits'. Every rule-set will have gaps that can be used opportunistically to the advantage of the subject (whether or not to the detriment of any other subject). In law, we tend to operate on the presumption of freedom to exploit (hence the complexity of tax law) except in certain categories such as the law of fiduciary obligations. In games, we tend to presume the opposite.

[82]Castronova in Balkin and Noveck (2006), p. 68.

likely, we see the law of the real world invading the game—'[m]eaning has begun to bleed into synthetic worlds'—making them less game-like.[83]

Either way, in a world where Ministers exercise powers by means of computer programs, it is necessary for legal theory to analyze the Minister's physical abilities as well as her augmented 'virtual' abilities, e.g., to manipulate objects in digital information repositories. Granted, these abilities are not mediated by an avatar—although networked computing systems may come to look more like a video game and less like books in the future.[84] But if we allow ourselves to explore the analogy with a little imagination, there is a sense in which the Minister is acting 'outside herself' *qua* official already.[85] Perhaps the figure of the MMORPG avatar can shed some light on the concept of official agency generally.

3 Validity in Law and in Games

Despite considerable literature on the concept of legal validity, there is still a degree of ambiguity in the term, which can refer to the existence, bindingness, applicability, or efficacy, as well as its conformity with certain criteria or its membership in a valid set.[86] Validity can further be predicated of acts-in-the-law, legal rules, and legal systems themselves.[87] The classical accounts of validity often speak at cross purposes; Hart, Kelsen, and Ross, for example, all adopt different and incompatible conceptions of validity.[88] In this section, I focus on the notion of validity as predicated of actions, i.e., of (attempted) exercises of competence of the type discussed above.

Paolo Sandro describes validity as an 'artificial ontological status that supervenes on that of the existence of legal norms.'[89] I am less interested in the validity of norms than the validity of acts pursuant to norms. But here, too, the notion of an *artificial ontological status* is apposite. Hart, for example, used the games analogy to explain the nullity of an invalid exercise of a competence: In both law and games, 'valid' exercises of a competence create consequences that are invisible and intangible because they are simply the logical product of the application of the rules that enable them. An invalid move produces a 'nullity' in the sense that these invisible,

[83] See Castronova in Balkin and Noveck (2006), p. 64. This is evident in the example of a virtual sexual assault—in the case that a virtual breast is positioned, as a social object, the same as a physical one, meaning will have saturated the virtual environment. See also de Sousa Santos (1987), p. 287.

[84] Balkin and Noveck (2006), p. 3.

[85] See Fortes in Gluckman (1962), p. 57.

[86] See Sandro (2018), pp. 100–101.

[87] See Spaak (1994), p. 52.

[88] See Bulygin (2015), p. 30.

[89] Sandro (2018).

intangible legal effects are said to be absent. In this sense, the notion of 'validity' explains the result of an exercise of a rule-conferred power that complies with all of the necessary conditions: 'if you wish to do X, this is the way to do it.'[90] Lars Lindahl and David Reidhav explain that acts-in-the-law 'are not 'factual' actions; they are (to use the language of David Hume) artificial or (to use the language of Searle) institutional, in the sense of presupposing and becoming possible by a system of norms. In contrast to 'factual' actions, which either occur or not, acts-in-the-law are characterised as legally valid or invalid.'[91]

Games and law are both contexts in which the actions of recognised subjects have meanings and rule-based consequences such as validity. There are differences between games and law, however, some of which have important consequences for the concept of normativity that operates in game contexts and legal contexts, respectively. Most immediately, it is fair to say that games generally are characterised by *play*. The richness of MMORPG-based play, and the observed tendency for real life to 'bleed' into these games, make them an interesting and challenging context in which to examine normativity.

3.1 Law, Games, and Playing for Keeps

In a recent contribution, Brian Bix has used the games analogy to support the case that we should examine law as a normative system without getting bogged down in the connection between law and morality.[92] This is a project of which I broadly approve. Essentially, Bix puts the judgment of the consciously and intentionally dissenting subject into the foreground when determining whether any given set of structured social practices is 'normative': It is only through one's own recognition or acceptance that one can be said to be a subject of law—otherwise, one is an object of a foreign legal system. While one may be unable to escape the coercive power of a state, one can choose not to think of that entity's actions in a normative way.[93] Recall that, for Kelsen, the *Grundnorm* was a possible but not a necessary interpretation of the world; the anarchist, he recognised, would see the actions of officials as nothing but naked power, the proverbial gunman situation writ large. Bix supports his argument with an analogy to chess:[94]

> The general view of normativity underlying the present analysis is often explained in analogy to games. For example, one might say to people playing chess that they ought not (e.g.,) to move the bishop in a certain way. However, those same people could decide never

[90]Hart (2012), p. 28.

[91]Lindahl and Reidhav (2017), p. 161.

[92]Bix (2018), p. 8.

[93]Bix (2018), p. 4.

[94]Kelsen (1992), p. 36.

> to play chess, in which case these sort of prescriptions about how one ought to move the bishop would have no application.[95]

And he says of Hart's concept of legal normativity:

> [O]ne could read Hart as saying that for the person who accepts the law, the sort of reason the law gives is (simply) a legal reason [rather than, e.g., a moral one], just as in other contexts people might consider themselves as subject to chess reasons (while playing that game—e.g., reasons within the game for moving the bishop diagonally rather than otherwise, and to this square rather than another one), etiquette reasons, or fashion reasons.[96]

This allows Bix to account for the inherently normative nature of law, 'at least in a thin way', without extensive metaphysical assumptions or moral claims.

Andrew Halpin rejects Bix's proposal on the basis of the 'tigerish' nature of legal normativity.[97] The way that an individual subject thinks about law, i.e., as being or not being authoritative, does not change the quality of the law like it does for a game. Halpin distinguishes three senses in which a rule may have a quality of normativity: (i) in its membership in a system of rules that are said to be normative, (ii) in its acceptance as normative and enforcement by officials within that system, and (iii) in its application to a particular subject of law.[98] All of these qualities of normativity, he argues, can be observed in games and law. Halpin accepts that the individual subject may either accept or reject the normativity of the rule in question in both the law and game context. But, he argues, there is a difference. When an individual refuses to play chess, the other forms of normativity fall away, but when an individual rejects the type (iii) normativity of a *legal* rule as it applies to him, the other forms continue to operate regardless. The key for upholding all the forms of game normativity is individual acceptance, but not so for law; even if an individual rejects the normativity of a legal provision, the other qualities of normativity subsist.

In rural Western Australia where I grew up, school children had invented a fascinating concept for games like 'chasey': A player could call out the word *balees* if he did not want to play, and be immune from being chased and tagged 'it'.[99] We spoke about a person being *balees*, that is having the status of *balees* within the context of the game. I take Halpin's point to be that there are is no *balees* in the game of law; you have to play whether you like it or not. The difference of opinion could be stated, perhaps, as this: Halpin thinks that taking an internal point of view is constitutive of being part of a game, but not of being subject to a system of laws.[100] At the least, Halpin thinks that there are aspects to legal normativity that are more like a tiger—a creature with nature-given properties including redness in tooth and claw—than like golf, which is a wholly rule-based practice that imposes meaning on

---

[95]Bix (2018), p. 4.

[96]Bix (2018), p. 6.

[97]Halpin (2019).

[98]Halpin (2019), p. 13.

[99]The spelling is phonetic, I am not sure of any official spelling. Chasey, known by various names, is a game in which one child must chase the others until s/he can 'tag' one to make him or her 'it'.

[100]See Jackson (1991), p. 102.

arbitrary movements of a ball across a field, and is generally voluntary. Perhaps this is related to the point, made by Jeremy Bentham and famously developed by Clifford Geertz, that humans engage in 'deep play' in which the stakes are so high that it makes no utilitarian sense.[101] Perhaps these games are played out of a sense of compulsion, internal or external.

Taking tigerishness as a criterion, I am not sure that it is always possible to draw a line where games stop and law begins. Gambling games, for example, entail the loss of money, and gambling often subsists in extra-legal spaces in which the bookie's tigerish thugs enforce the rules. Traditional and religious law, on the other hand, may not be very tigerish at all. Indigenous law, for example, applies in some post-colonial contexts on an opt-out basis, but is more 'law-like' than game-like in my view.[102] Bix's bold essay, and Halpin's early reply, open a debate that I am only able to mention here.[103] In general, I would ask whether it is the *normativity of law* that is tigerish, or the *political nature of the human group* that creates a legal system and imposes it on dissenters.[104] I do not think that law is necessary tigerish in the sense Halpin argues. If I call *balees*, but the organised group still treats me as a player, the nature of the activity has fundamentally changed—from a game to a hunt, or at least from a shallow game to a deep one.

3.2 Law, Games, and the Shades of Normativity

Whatever we make of the 'tiger question', the suggestion that there are different types of normativity is an important one. Here, I explore how normativity might differ according to context, which approaches the question from a slightly different angle. People play games when they abide temporarily by a set of rules which constrain their behaviour in exchange for the benefits of taking part.[105] From certain theoretical perspectives, at least, something similar could be said of law. We have seen that games and legal orders both comprise systems of rules that constrain conduct and confer competence, and that, if theorists such as Searle are correct, the logical structure of these rules are fundamentally similar in both contexts.

Zaibert observes that Searle's ontology of social phenomena is, at base, an exegesis on his early analysis of the institution of promising, in which he claimed to have derived an 'ought' from the factual premise that 'A promises to give B five dollars'.[106] The 'ought' so derived, however, is (by Searle's own admission) not a

[101] See Geertz (1972), p. 15, developing a gloss on Bentham's notion of 'deep playing' i.e., gambling games that are against the utilitarian interests of the player.

[102] A young Aboriginal man, for example, may choose to leave an Aboriginal community in which traditional law is enforced. See Brennan (1994), p. 91.

[103] A direct contribution is also made by Spaak (2018).

[104] See also Marmor (2017), p. 20; Marmor (2011).

[105] Bartle in Balkin and Noveck (2006), p. 34.

[106] Zaibert (2007), p. 419; see Searle (1964).

'moral' ought;[107] it is a 'humbler', more contingent ought that is the creature of 'constitutive rules of phenomena which we ourselves create in this way or that way, but that we could have chosen to create differently.'[108] This, argues Zaibert, explains Searle's interest in games: Because he is only interested in non-moral normativity, the normativity he discusses—including legal normativity—is only ever on a par with the normativity of games. Indeed, it seems fair to say that positivist conceptions of legal validity are never absolute; they are always relative to a (posited) legal system, for example in relation to a 'master norm'.[109]

Hart and Kelsen occupy a central place in modern legal positivism because they both argued so compellingly for a middle way between natural law and traditional positivism; they presented a *descriptive* account of the existence of *genuinely normative* obligations. According to Smith and Zaibert:

> Hart's strategy—though he does not himself admit it—is to distinguish between two types of normativity. On the one hand is the robust normativity of the natural law theorist... On the other hand is Hart's own brand of normativity—what we might call soft normativity—which is what is necessary, in his view, for the existence of laws. Soft normativity is the sort of normativity that flows logically from the very nature of secondary rules... Hart himself appeals to the example of games in order to illustrate this point.[110]

If Smith and Zaibert are right, then the *prima facie* plausibility of the games analogy brings us to a cross-road: Either game normativity and legal normativity are one (what they call 'soft'), or there exists an *a priori* set of facts on which 'robust' normativity rests, i.e., non-conventional demands on our behaviour. This, in turn, brings us back to a theory of moral realism; Searle, they observe, avoids the discussion of realism as it pertains to moral normativity altogether, and attempts to replicate his 'ought' from 'is' derivation on a grand scale. But '[i]n tandem with the shunning of realism as it pertains to ethics... goes the shunning of precisely those types of normativity which are not soft.'[111] In their view, robust normativity is to be derived not from speech acts but from intentional states, which in turn rest in the fundamental biological nature of the human being.

This is a more ambitious project than I can do justice to here.[112] For my present purposes, however, it is perhaps sufficient to ask why 'soft' normativity is unsatisfactory for law, that is, why we need legal normativity to be 'robust'. Could it not be the case that law draws its own 'magic circle', inside which fairness, rationality, non-domination, and other values are preserved from the Hobbesian scrum of the brute reality that surrounds it? Does our search for absolute normativity obscure the value of the conventional normativity generated by law and games? Games are

---

[107]See Searle (1969), p. 176.

[108]Zaibert (2007), p. 420.

[109]See Navarro and Rodriguez (2014), p. 118.

[110]See Smith and Zaibert (2007), p. 158.

[111]Smith and Zaibert (2007), p. 170.

[112]It seems to me that such a project would seem to entail a realist phenomenology akin to that of Adolf Reinach: See Reinach (1913).

realms of normativity writ small: They show us that there is value in studying 'small n' normativity, and such normativity shows regular features across very different domains of life. MMORPGs, on the other hand, show us that these limited rule-constituted worlds can become both large and complex and important to their players' lives. Perhaps law is just *very* massive multi-player role-playing *deep game* whose players have forgotten that they are 'playing'?

3.3 Games and Law as Worlds of Fiction

This leads to a final, challenging notion; if this avenue of reasoning is followed, the games analogy suggests that law, along with games, is a world of fiction. There is support for this within the positivist tradition. Recall that, for Hart, a legal system is a system of rules that are hierarchically structured and comprise a system by common reference to a master rule, a 'rule of recognition'. Unlike the lower-order rules, which are derived from higher-order rules up to the 'master' rule, the existence of this rule can only be determined from the 'external perspective'. This rule is, at base, a matter of fact—a convention.[113] If a Searleian view of convention is taken, this rule would take the form that X 'counts as' Y, i.e., *as something that it is not.*[114] Likewise for Kelsen, law is a hierarchically structured system of rules that refers back to a master rule, a *Grundnorm.*[115] In his earlier theory, Kelsen described the *Grundnorm* as a 'cognitive hypothesis' that enabled an interpretation of certain facts of the world as a 'legal system' without recourse to meta-legal authorities.[116] But in the second edition of his *Reine Rechtslehre*, Kelsen began to refer to the *Grundnorm* as a fiction in the sense of Hans Vaihinger's 'as if' philosophy: For whatever reason, the later Kelsen became dissatisfied with the notion of the *Grundnorm* as a purely cognitive postulate, and became convinced that the *Grundnorm* must, after all, rest in the will of some founding authority.[117] However, Kelsen posited that this political authority, and/or its constituent will, was a fiction rather than a historical fact. A Vaihingerian fiction is a 'conceptual aid' that helps us square the circle; fictions help us to understand the world by making claims about the world which are in clear opposition to the facts: 'In a fiction we treat X as if it were a Y in order to better understand the world, even though we very well know that X actually is not Y or cannot be Y.'[118] If Searle is correct, something like a fictions actually helps us to *create* the social world, not just *understand* it; institutions are inherently a bit fictional. The basic logical operation, on which the whole of his account of social reality is based,

[113] Hart (2012), p. 110.

[114] Searle (2010), p. 96.

[115] See Paulson (2013).

[116] Kelsen (1960), p. 205.

[117] See Spaak (2005), pp. 405–406.

[118] Kletzer (2015), p. 24.

is to 'count' X 'as' Y in order that it should begin exuding invisible 'deontic powers' that are generated, in fact, in our own intentionality. Of course, X *is not* Y, and that is the whole point. There are shades of fictionalism in the Uppsala School of legal realism, too, for example in the work of Axel Hägerström.[119]

Marmor's conventionalist theory probably pushes the fictional nature of law the farthest. Take a proposition such as 'Sherlock Holmes lived in London'. London is a real city, whereas Sherlock Holmes is a fictional character. We are, therefore, dealing with a proposition about a world of fiction—about 'fiction facts' or 'truth in fiction',[120] in this case the facts of a fictional London'.[121] According to Marmor, fictions typically incorporate, by implication, factual assumptions about the world, which are then overlaid with 'fiction facts'. Mixing fictional and factual premises—for example about the city of London—can lead to wrong conclusions.[122] It is therefore necessary to keep things straight, with 'closed prefixes' whereby we preface any claim with the prefix 'according to fiction *F*...'. Closed prefixes, argues Marmor, are those in which a constitutive relation obtains between certain essential features of the world designated by the prefix, and the truths of the statements expressed in that world.[123] Besides fictional literature, Marmor identifies law and structured games as closed prefix contexts.

Law, on this view, is a kind of 'authoritative fiction', an intangible artefact created by communicative means that gives rise to closed prefixed contexts in which truths are constituted by performative speech acts.[124] Fiction, games, and law are all domains in which a class of facts are constituted by performative speech acts—in particular by declarations which Marmor calls 'institutional performatives'.[125] The truth value of any statement about the content of a legal premise depends on the specific jurisdictional prefix. As positivists insist, this feature distinguishes law from morality, which is generally taken to be universal and not to be alterable at will. According to Marmor, this shows law's self-constituting, reflexive, self-referential nature; it only makes sense to talk about legality within the framework of the law itself, i.e., on the pretext, presupposition, convention, or fiction, that all this really exists, even though we know it is a contrivance of our own making.[126] Both a new legal system and a new game would start with a catalogue of 'let's count this as that'.

In his seminal essay on the disciplinary relations between law and anthropology, Geertz noted the consternation that arises when one realises that 'legal facts are made

---

[119]See Sandström (2010).

[120]See Lewis (1978).

[121]See Marmor (2014), p. 77.

[122]For example, that (i) Sherlock Holmes lived at 221B Baker St and that (ii) the actual 221B Baker St was a bank in Sir Arthur Conan Doyle's London would lead to the false conclusion that (iii) Sherlock Holmes lived in a bank.

[123]Marmor (2017), p. 6.

[124]Marmor (2017), p. 1.

[125]Marmor (2017), p. 11.

[126]See also Kwak (2017), p. 19.

not born, are socially constructed, as an anthropologist would put it.'[127] That is, law is not a model of an antecedent social reality, but a game itself that constructs a domain of reality around it.[128] If law matches 'fact-configurations and norms', and if those fact configurations 'are not merely things found lying about in the world' but are instead 'but close-edited diagrams of reality the matching process itself produces', he argues, 'the whole thing looks a bit like sleight-of-hand.' Fiction it may be: a sham, however, it is not. Instead, it is an instance of a 'rather more fundamental phenomenon, the one in fact upon which all culture rests: namely, that of representation.' Law, he says, is 'part of a distinctive manner of imagining the real.'[129]

The conceptual role of fictions in legal theory remains underdeveloped. To say that something is a 'fiction' does not mean it is not genuine, or a lie—only that it is a social construction of a particular kind.[130] The existence of property rights, corporations, bank accounts, and nation-states are not immutable facts of the universe; they are fictions sustained by our shared beliefs and practices. The games analogy is instructive for legal theory because it can help to show us the role that fictions play in the construction of legal reality and the relation between this layer of reality and others including (ultimately) physical reality. A legal system imposes an artificial ontology on the world by positioning objects—both objects of physical reality and objects of other domains of social reality—as objects of law: This red lamp counts as a Stop Sign, this one does not; this woman counts as a President, this one does not; this religious ceremony counts as a Wedding, his one does not; this plan counts as a Scheduled Drug, this one does not; and so forth. 'Law' is just one layer of a complex, composite reality. Part of the value of MMORPGs is, perhaps, that they show us just how complex and sophisticated a world of fiction can be when it is instantiated and sustained by advanced technology.

4 Conclusion

In this chapter, I have explored an extension of the familiar games analogy to MMORPGs. Although this has been more of a programmatic exploration than a final, considered theory, a number of points have emerged which can be stated by way of conclusion.

First, I think it is fair to say that an extended games analogy is worthwhile. But I think it has also become clear that MMORPGs provide less a case of *analogy* than a category of jurisprudentially interesting normative social practice that is interesting in its own right. The games analogy may, therefore, work better (*qua* analogy) with games such as chess and baseball. However, MMORPGs do offer a rich and

[127] Geertz (1983), p. 173.

[128] I thank Jeffrey Lipshaw again for making this point clear.

[129] Geertz (1983), p. 173.

[130] See Johansson (2005).

challenging context for working out the structure of systems of rules and pose some important questions about the formalisation of modes of action and deontic modes as well as the interaction between rule-sets that nest within each other.

Secondly, it seems that MMORPGs may foreshadow developments in the digital real. This includes the manipulation of digital objects and technically mediated legal action. For example, questions about the ownership of in-game digital objects preceded disputes about the ownership of so-called 'cryptoassets' such as bitcoins, which are purely digital objects, by several years.[131] MMORPGs also provide substantive testing grounds for debates about speech and action in a digital environment that may prove to have broader relevance. They offer a novel perspective on old debates about legal personality and agency and perhaps provide a context in which legal theorists can start hashing out some of the issues of non-human agency that could quite possibly become more than academic in the coming years.

Thirdly, closely following on from the points above, my brief investigation of MMORPGs suggests two methodological priorities for legal theory in the coming decades. The first is the pursuit of an *ontological turn* in legal theory as the law increasingly regulates socio-technical phenomena. The increasing influence of social ontology on legal theorists over the past several years is evident; I have found the conceptual tools of social ontology helpful for explaining legal entities as varied as the British Crown and bitcoins, and I think that legal theorists more broadly will do well to incorporate—and adapt—the categories and methods of social ontology, especially those working in the neo-Hartian tradition. The second is a *pluralist turn.* MMORGPs, and online practices in general, are jurisprudentially interesting in large part because they provide an instance of non-state normativity. A rigid statist approach to the concept of law has little to say about them and will become, in my view, increasingly less relevant as time goes on. More interesting is an examination of the dynamics of interaction between states and other *loci* of political association and normative order—even if one thinks that the state will, and ought, to retain a dominant position, the landscape has changed and its new features are worthy of study.[132]

Finally, as MMORPGs suggest a blurring of the magic circle dividing 'play' from 'real life', perhaps they suggest a blurring of the line dividing game normativity from legal normativity, instead suggesting law and games as two species of *conventional normativity*. In my view, this would justify a partial shift in focus towards forms of 'soft' normativity independently of the search for 'robust' normativity. This would, perhaps, be consistent with the pluralist agenda suggested immediately above; if we divorce the concept of law from the concept of the state (and therefore of *one* system of 'law, properly so called'),[133] the need for legal normativity to be something other than 'soft' diminishes. In other words, if state law ceases to be the only game in town, the pretence that it is something other than game-like can be abandoned. There

---

[131]See Allen (2019).

[132]For example, see Allen and Lastra (2020).

[133]See Raz in Roughan and Halpin (2017).

can be laws within laws, games within games, some more and some less deep, some gaming communities more and some less tigerish. Questions of robust normativity—of moral normativity—can thus be bracketed out, as Hart wanted them to be, to provide an evaluative yardstick for the law.[134] Depending on one's view, these observations may render robust normativity irrelevant or more important than ever; either way, they certainly show the extent and complexity of social practices structured by conventional normativity and enrich long-standing debates in so doing.

References[135]

Abramovitch SH, Cummings DL (2007) Virtual property, real law: the regulation of property in video games. Can J Law Technol 6(2):73
Agamben G (1994) 'We Refugees' (1995). Symposium 49(2):114
Allen JG (2018) The Office of the Crown. Camb Law J 77(2):298
Allen JG (2019) Property in digital coins. Eur Prop Law J 5(1)
Allen JG, Lastra RM (2020) Border problems: mapping the third border. Mod Law Rev 505
Anscombe GEM (1958) On brute facts. Analysis 18(3):69
Arendt H (1943) We refugees. Menorah J 31(1):69
Asbjørn Jøn A (2010) The development of MMORPG culture and the guild. Aust Folklore 25:97
Auguet R (1972) Cruelty and Civilisation: The Roman Games
Austin JL (1962) How to do things with words. CUP, Cambridge
Balkin JM, Noveck BS (2006) The state of play: law, games, and virtual worlds. NYU Press, New York
Bentham J (1970) In: Burns JG, Hart HLA (eds) An introduction to the principles of morals and legislation. Athlone
Bix B (1972) Understanding the model of rules: toward a reconciliation of Dworkin and positivism. Yale Law J 81(5):912
Bix B (2018) Kelsen, Hart, and legal normativity. Revus 34:1
Boellstorff T (2016) For whom the ontology turns: theorizing the digital real. Curr Anthropol 57 (4):387
Brennan FSJ (1994) Constitutional possibilities for self-determination for Aborigines and Torres Strait Islanders. In: Fletcher C (ed) Aboriginal self-determination in Australia
Brey P (2003) The social ontology of virtual environments. Am J Econ Sociol 62(1):269
Brey P (2005) The epistemology and ontology of human-computer interaction. Minds Mach 15:383
Brinz A (1873) Lehrbuch der Pandekten Band I, 2nd edn
Bulygin E (2015) Essays in legal philosophy. OUP, Oxford
Caillois R (2001) Man, play and games (trans: Barash M). University of Illinois Press, Urbana
Cross K (2016) Sexual assault enters virtual reality. The Conversation, 10 November 2016. URL: http://theconversation.com/sexual-assault-enters-virtual-reality-67971
Culver K (2001) Leaving the Hart-Dworkin debate. Univ Tor Law J 51(4):367
Culver K, Giudice M (2017) The unsteady state: general jurisprudence for dynamic social phenomena. CUP, Cambridge
Danaher J (2018) The law and ethics of virtual sexual assault. In: Barfeild W, Blitz MC (eds) Research handbook on the law of virtual and augmented reality. Elgar, Chetalham

[134] Hart (1958).

[135] All URLs last accessed 3 March 2020.

De Paoli S, Kerr A (2009) The cheating assemblage in MMORPGs: toward a sociotechnical description of cheating. In: Proceedings of DiGRA 2009, p 1
de Sousa Santos B (1987) Law: a map of misreading. Toward a postmodern conception of law. J Law Soc 14(3):279
Dibble J (2005) A rape in cyberspace. Village Voice. URL: https://www.villagevoice.com/2005/10/18/a-rape-in-cyberspace/
Duarte D (2018) Norms on language and the regulativeness of constitutive rule. Diritto & Questioni Pubbliche 18(1):135
Dworkin R (1967a) The model of rules. Univ Chic Law Rev 35:14
Dworkin R (1967b) Law's empire. CUP, Cambridge
Dworkin R (1967c) Taking rights seriously. CUP, Cambridge
Fairfield J (2005) Virtual property. Boston Univ Law Rev 85:1047
Fairfield J (2009) The magic circle. Vanderbilt J Entertain Technol Law 11(4):823
Fortes M (1962) Ritual and office in tribal society. In: Gluckman M (ed) Essays on the ritual of social relations. MUP, Manchester
Geertz C (1972) Deep play: notes on the Balinese cock fight. Myth Symbol Cult 101(1):1
Geertz C (1983) Local knowledge: further essays in interpretive anthropology
Graveson RH (1941) The movement from status to contract. Mod Law Rev 4(4):261
Hacker P (2018) Verhaltens- und Wissenszurechnung beim Einsatz von Künstlicher Intelligenz. Rechtswissenschaft [2018]:243
Hage J (2015) Separating rules from normativity. In: Araszkiewicz M, Banaś P, Gizbert-Studnicki-T, Płeszka K (eds) Problems of normativity, rules and rule-following. Springer, Dordrecht
Halpin A (2019) The Tigerish nature of legal normativity. Revus 37:1
Hart HLA (1958) Positivism and the separation of law and morals. Harv Law Rev 71(4):593
Hart HLA (1982) Essays on Bentham. OUP, Oxford
Hart HLA (2012) The concept of law, 3rd edn. Clarendon Press, Oxford
Hildebrant M (2016) Law as information in the era of data-driven agency. Mod Law Rev 79(1):1
Hindriks FA (2003) The new role of the constitutive rule. Am J Econ Sociol 62(1):185
Hodge L (2019) The potential and perils of financial technology: can the law adapt to cope? University of Edinburgh, 14 March 2019. URL: https://www.supremecourt.uk/docs/speech-190314.pdf
House of Commons Science and Technology Committee (2018) Algorithms in decision-making: Fourth Report of Session 2017–19 (HC 351, 23 May 2018)
Huizinga J (1938) Homo Ludens. Wolters-Noordhoff, Groningen
Jackson BS (1991) Towards a semiotic model of the games analogy in jurisprudence. Droit et Société 17–18:99
Jellinek G (1892) System der subjektiven öffentlichen Rechte, Freiburg
Johansson I (2005) Money and fictions. In: Larsson F (ed) Kapten Mnemos Kolumbarium. Philosophical Communications, Gothenburg, Sweden
Johnson DR, Post DG (1996) Law and borders - the rise of law in cyberspace. Stanford Law Rev 48:1367
Juul J (2003) The game, the player, the world. In: Copier M, Raesens J (eds) Level Up: Digital Games Research Conference Proceedings
Kelsen H (1945) General theory of law and state (trans: Wedberg A). HUP, Cambridge
Kelsen H (1960) Reine Rechtslehre, 2nd edn. Franz Steiner
Kelsen H (1992) In: Paulson SL (ed) Introduction to the problems of legal theory (trans: Paulson BL). Clarendon Press, Oxford
Kleinberg J, Himabindu L, Leskovec J, Ludwig J, Mullainathan S (2018) Human decisions and machine predictions. Q J Econ 133(1):237
Kletzer C (2015) Kelsen on Vaihinger. In: Del Mar M, Twining W (eds) Legal fictions in theory and practice. Springer, Dordrecht
Kripke S (1971) Identity and necessity. In: Munitz MK (ed) Identity and individuation. New York University Press, New York

Kripke S (1980) Naming and necessity. HUP, Cambridge
Kurki VAJ, Pietrzykowski T (eds) (2017) Legal personhood: animals, artificial intelligence and the unborn. Springer, Dordrecht
Kwak AJ (2017) What's in a game? Law Method 1
Lastowka FG, Hunter D (2004) The laws of the virtual worlds. Calif Law Rev 92(1):1
Leiter B (2003) Beyond the Hart/Dworkin debate: the methodology problem in jurisprudence. Am J Jurisprud 48:17
Lewis D (1978) Truth in fiction. Am Philos Q 15(1):37
Lindahl L (1977) Position and change. Springer, Dordrecht
Lindahl L (2005) Hohfeld relations and spielraum for action. In: Dahlman C (ed) Studier i Rättsekonomi: Festskrift till Ingemar Ståhl, Studentlitteratur
Lindahl L, Reidhav D (2017) Legal power: the basic definition. Ratio Juris 30(2):158
Lipshaw J (2008) Models and games: the difference between explanation and understanding for lawyers and ethicists. Cleveland State Law Rev 56(3):613
MacCormick N (1997) Institutional normative order: a conception of law. Cornell Law Rev 82 (5):1051
MacCormick N (2007) Institutions of law. OUP, Oxford
MacCormick N, Weinberger O (1986) An institutional theory of law: new approaches to legal positivism. Springer, Dordrecht
Maine HS (1861) Ancient law. Holt and Company, New York
Marmor A (2007) Law in the age of pluralism. OUP, Oxford
Marmor A (2011) An institutional conception of authority. Philos Public Aff 39(2):238
Marmor A (2014) The language of the law. OUP, Oxford
Marmor A (2017) Law as authoritative fiction. Cornell Legal Studies Research Paper No. 17-10, 2017. URL: https://ssrn.com/abstract=2921943
Navarro PE, Rodriguez JL (2014) Deontic logic and legal systems. CUP, Cambridge
Palka P (2017) Virtual property: toward a general theory. PhD Thesis, European University Institute, 2017. URL: http://cadmus.eui.eu/handle/1814/49664
Paolo S (2018) Unlocking legal validity: some remarks on the artificial ontology of the law. In: Westerman P, Hage J, Kirste S, Mackor AR (eds) Legal validity and soft law. Springer, Dordrecht
Paulson SL (2013) How Merkl's Stufenbaulehre informs Kelsen's concept of law. Revus 21:29
Post DG (2017) How the Internet is making jurisdiction sexy (again). Int J Law Inf Technol 25:249
Pound R (1937) 50 years of jurisprudence. Harv Law Rev 50(4):558
Raz (2017) Why the State. In: Roughan N, Halpin A (eds) In pursuit of pluralist jurisprudence. CUP, Cambridge
Reinach A (1913) The a priori foundations of civil law (trans: Crosby JF) (1983) 3 Aletheia 1, originally published as Adolph Reinach, Die a priori Grundlagen des bürgerlichen Rechts, Niemayer
Ross A (1959) On law and justice. University of California Press
Ross A (2018) In: Holtermann JvH (ed) On law and justice (trans: Bindreiter U). University of California Press, Berkeley
Rubinstein A (1965) Jurisdiction and illegality. Clarendon Press, Oxford
Ruiter DWP (2010) Legal institutions. Springer
Russel MJ (1980) Trial by battle and the writ of right. J Leg Hist 1(2):111
Sandro P (2018) Unlocking legal validity: some remarks on the artificial ontology of the law. In: Westerman P, Hage J, Kirste S, Mackor AR (eds) Legal validity and soft law. Springer
Sandström M (2010) Fact, fiction or in between? Axel Hägerström's quest for legal realism. Scand Stud Law 48:329
Scarborough VL, Wilcox DR (1993) The Mesoamerican Ballgame. University of Arizona Press, Tucson
Searle J (1964) How to derive "ought" from "is". Philos Rev 73(1):43
Searle J (1969) Speech acts. OUP, Oxford

Searle J (1995) The social construction of reality. Simon and Schuster, New York
Searle J (2010) Making the social world. OUP, Oxford
Shapiro S (2012) In: Ripstein A, Dworkin R (eds) The Hart-Dworkin debate: a short guide for the perplexed. CUP, Cambridge
Siegel J (2016) Meatspace is cyberspace: the Pynchonian posthuman in bleeding edge. Orbit 4(2):1
Smith B (2003) John Searle. CUP, Cambridge
Spaak T (1994) The concept of legal competence. Dartmouth
Spaak T (2003) Norms that confer competence. Ratio Juris 16(1):89
Spaak T (2005) Kelsen and Hart on the normativity of law. In: Wahlgren P (ed) Perspectives on jurisprudence: essays in honour of Jes Bjarup
Spaak T (2018) A challenge to Bix's interpretation of Kelsen and Hart's views on the normativity of law. Revus Online
Stavropoulos N (2014) Legal interpretivism. In: Zalta EN (ed) The Stanford encyclopedia of philosophy (Summer 2014 Edition). URL: https://plato.stanford.edu/archives/sum2014/entries/law-interpretivist/
Twining W (2000) Globalisation and legal theory. CUP, Cambridge
Zaibert L (2007) On power, conventions, and the varieties of normativity. In: Kanzian C, Runggaldier E (eds) Publications of the Austrian Ludwig Wittgenstein Society Vol. 3: cultures—conflict, analysis, dialogue

The Foundations of Legal Constructivism

Enrique Cáceres Nieto

> *What is real? How do you define real? If you are talking about what you can feel, what you can smell, what you can taste and see, then what is real is just electrical signals interpreted by your brain.*
> *Morpheus (The Matrix)*

Abstract In this chapter, I develop foundations for what I call "legal constructivism," an epistemological, theoretical, and methodological approach that explains how positive law and legal theories actively participate in the construction of social reality as they are embodied in agents interacting both with other agents in institutions created by the law itself and with civil society. After outlining the bases and key theoretical building blocks of legal constructivism, I examine this approach from a legal philosophy standpoint.

1 Introduction

In this chapter, I develop foundations for what I call "legal constructivism" (LC), an epistemological, theoretical and methodological approach that explains how positive law and legal theories actively participate in the construction of social reality as they are embodied in agents interacting both with other agents in institutions created by the law itself and with civil society. While my conception of LC is based on the larger epistemological project of "radical constructivism" that has influenced contemporary sciences, it is adapted to explain law's distinctive characteristics, which differentiate it from the world of experience inherited from other sciences.

This chapter concisely and coherently compiles various research projects that, despite being conducted independently and at different levels of depth over several

E. Cáceres Nieto (✉)
Instituto de Investigaciones Jurídicas, Universidad Nacional Autónoma de México, Ciudad de México, Mexico

J. L. Fabra-Zamora, G. Villa Rosas (eds.), *Conceptual Jurisprudence*, Law and Philosophy Library 137, https://doi.org/10.1007/978-3-030-78803-2_16

years, all align with my main research object: the creation of an alternative concept of law.[1] This paper does not simply present an edited reconstruction of what has been written before. For the first time, I compare my proposal with other works to highlight its originality, among other philosophical achievements, and, ultimately, produce a constructivist approach to law and a constitutive vision of legal provisions. Likewise, for the first time, I move past the epistemic or metatheoretical considerations of my previous work and present the foundations of LC as a substantive theory of law.[2]

2 The Motivation: Law and Reality

Let us start by recalling the words of Kant:

> What may be the case with objects in themselves and abstracted from all this receptivity of our sensibility remains entirely unknown to us. We are acquainted with nothing except our way of perceiving them, which is peculiar to us, and which therefore does not necessarily pertain to every being, though to be sure it pertains to every human being.[3]

The idea of there being no "given" reality and of that which we refer to as such being the result of cognitively processing environmental information appears centuries later, with, significantly, the support of physics. According to Heinz von Foerster,

> [...] "out there" is no light and no color, there are only electromagnetic waves; "out there" there is no sound and no music, there are only periodic variations of the air pressure; "out there" there is no heat and no cold, there are only moving molecules with more or less mean kinetic energy, and so on. Finally, for sure, "out there" there is no pain.[4]

The different ways of organizing different versions of "reality" are linked to the biological properties of each species. The reality in which bees live is vastly different from ours because they can see ultraviolet light. Similarly, bats perceive the world differently as a result of echolocation.

Hence, belonging to the species *homo sapiens* might be thought to guarantee that all human beings can access the same reality. However, this is not true. For example,

---

[1]For previous developments of Legal Constructivism in English, see Cáceres Nieto (2007a, 2011, 2016c). For some formulations in Spanish, see Cáceres Nieto (2007b, 2012a, b, 2015, 2016a, b).

[2]Despite being a novel proposal, "legal constructivism" has gradually gained recognition in academic circles. Further development has been made possible by the support of the National Council of Science and Technology of México on two occasions (through the Frontiers of Science and the new Frontier Science projects). Its definition has been included in the Legal Dictionary of the National Autonomous University of Mexico Law School. A Laboratory of Legal Constructivism: Cognition, Complexity and Law was opened at the Institute for Legal Research at the National Autonomous University of Mexico, currently under my direction.

[3]Kant (2015), p. 59.

[4]Foerster (1984), pp. 293–294.

consider bubbles appearing on a computer screen in front of you. For most people, they are simply bubbles; for a physicist, they might be sub-nuclear processes waiting to be counted.

One might say this concerns not reality but different ways of perceiving reality, or distinguishing "seeing something" from "how something is seen". However, how can we recognize what we call "reality" without having some way of perceiving it? If we talk about processing information, it can be said that it is impossible to distinguish between what is real and what is considered real (for example, the existence of a god). Even if there are different ways of processing information and considering the perception of reality, not every way of processing information features the same epistemic justification. For example, although both religion and science try to account for the origins of humankind, only scientific explanations can be proven.

In contrast, given scientific explanations are highly objective, it is not possible to conclude that their results describe how the world is *per se*. If that were the case, there would be no need for scientific debates preceding the advance of science. Furthermore, scientific models about what is considered real are created by epistemic communities that do not share the same arsenal of epistemic, theoretical and methodological artefacts. Accordingly, different scientific explanations are provided for the same phenomenon, promoting what is known as the problem of inference to the best explanation.

3 Epistemic Constructivism

Metaphysical realism has dominated Western epistemology since the sixth century B.C. Its central tenet is the existence of an objective reality that stands independently of the cognizing subjects who persistently seek to discover it.

Since the mid-twentieth century, with the support from diverse disciplines (philosophy, physics, biology, etc.), the influential school of epistemic constructivism has challenged the dominance of metaphysical realism. For constructivists, reality does not exist and that which we consider the knowledge of reality is the product of the cognitive activity of agents, particularly scientists. This view has been advocated by scientists and writers from broadly diverse disciplines, represented by authors such as Gregory Bateson,[5] Niklas Luhmann,[6] Humberto Maturana,[7] Francisco

[5]Bateson (2000).

[6]Luhmann (1991, 1997).

[7]Maturana (2009a, b) and Maturana and Valera (2004).

Varela,[8] Edgar Morin,[9] Jean Piaget,[10] Lev Vygotsky,[11] Heinz von Foerster,[12] Ernst von Glasersfeld,[13] Paul Watzlawick,[14] Alexander Wendt,[15] and Gaston Bachelard.[16]

According to von Glasersfeld,

> Radical constructivism, thus, is *radical* because it breaks with convention and develops a theory of knowledge in which knowledge does not reflect an "objective" ontological reality, but exclusively an ordering and organization of a world constituted by our experience. The radical constructivist has relinquished "metaphysical realism" once and for all, and finds himself in complete agreement with Piaget, who says: "Intelligence organizes the world by organizing itself".[17]

Similarly, in his foundational text, *The Invented Reality*, Watzlawick writes,

> [. . .] the title of the book already seems less nonsensical. Indeed, if the *what* of knowledge is determined by the corresponding cognitive process (the *how*), our image of reality, therefore, does not depend on what is external to us, but inevitably depends on how we conceive that *what* [. . .] all reality is, in the most direct sense, the *construct* of those who *believe* they discover and investigate reality.[18]

Briefly, the central premises of epistemic constructivism are the following:

(1) there is no given, objective reality because what precedes the constructed reality is a world of experience that is organized by our cognitive attributes and biological limitations, just as occurs with any other species;
(2) the construction of reality does not take place in the cold mental space of individually considered subjects but is the product of interactions with our environment and even other species;
(3) the cognizing subject is not merely a contemplative actor confronting a given reality but plays an active role in constructing what they assume to be real;
(4) the constructs do not result from a correlation with reality but are the product of a functional adaptation process balancing the way we shape the world with its usefulness for our purposes.

This chapter's purpose is not to provide a detailed account or discussion of the central ideas of epistemic constructivism. Nevertheless, it is worth mentioning, albeit briefly, some misunderstandings that have given rise to unfounded objections.

---

8 Maturana and Valera (2004) and Varela et al. (2016).

9 Morin (2005).

10 Piaget and García (2008).

11 Vygotsky (1979, 1986).

12 Foerster (1960, 1984).

13 Glasersfeld (2003).

14 Watzlawick (1984).

15 Wendt (2003).

16 Bachelard (2000).

17 Glasersfeld (1984), p. 24.

18 Watzlawick (1984), pp. 9–10.

One of the most frequent criticisms of constructivism describes it as bordering on solipsism or extreme relativism. By suppressing the existence of what is outside, the difference between knowing and imagining becomes completely unsupportable.

In this sense, it should be noted that constructivism does not deny that we interact with a dimension that includes what is external to us; instead, it suggests only that what exists features a given and objective ontological structure unrelated to the cognizing subject.

Metaphysical realism is an extrapolation of how we have constructed what we assume is real based on results obtained from the classical mechanics scientific paradigm. In recent years, the limitations of this mode of "painting the world as it is" have provoked a crisis deriving from problems the approach cannot explain. The results obtained from complexity sciences promotes the emergence of new extrapolations towards metaphysical assumptions of the world as a complex system that admits embedded deterministic phenomena. In the constructivist view, these assumptions are mere epistemic artefacts that do not feign to fit with any given reality.

Another misguided objection is supposing that constructivism assumes an individual epistemology in which each subject can arbitrarily construct their own reality without any convergence with the reality of others. Although we constructivists assume that our understanding of the world is mediated by our cognitive life, this does not signify negating the possibility that organisms with the same resources can coherently organize the world "phenomenologically". What would not be admissible would be to suggest that any of those representations or models we use to organize experience correspond to a given and objective reality. Such an assumption would refute the evolutionary path of science.

One further source of confusion is of a semantic nature and concerns the use of the expression "reality", a term with a peculiar kind of polysemy by which it denotes both what is "out there" and knowledge about it. In the first sense, "reality" denotes different things depending on the epistemic assumptions taken as a starting point: whether the Kantian noumenon, the objective reality one seeks to discover or the world of experience organized by the cognizing subject. That is, in the first sense, "reality" is also polysemous depending on what "out there" is supposed to denote. In the second sense, "reality" denotes the knowledge we have from what is denoted by the starting point, which in turn presents new polysemies (the phenomenon, the discovered reality or the organization of the world). Constructivism wields epistemic reasons by which to assume that the relationship between the world of experience "reality" and the way we shape the key(s) that allow us to open the lock(s) regarding the ideas of an objective and given "reality" and a "reality" which is discovered.

One final misconception concerns supposing that, for constructivism, all constructs carry the same epistemic value because they cannot be contrasted with a given reality. The constructivist approach to this indicates that, despite the many ways of modelling the world, they do not all carry the same epistemic justification, a proposition that is compatible with the functional nature of our explanations about the world of experience. From this perspective, while being epistemically constructivist is not incompatible with adopting the methodology of empirical research, it does not assume that a result obtained "paints reality" as it is.

Although more an objection than a misunderstanding, a question also arises regarding how constructivism can explain the fact we have learned to manipulate and, to a certain extent, control the physical world by discovering how certain aspects of reality act similarly. This question is answered by von Glasersfeld's metaphor:

> [...] most scientists today still consider themselves "discoverers" who unveil nature's secrets and slowly but steadily expand the range of human knowledge; [...].[19]
>
> [...] the constructivism I am proposing differs *radically* from the traditional conceptualizations. This radical difference concerns the relation of knowledge and reality. Whereas in the traditional view of epistemology, as well as of cognitive psychology, this relation is always seen as a more or less picture-like (iconic) correspondence or match, radical constructivism sees it as an adaptation in the functional sense.[20]
>
> In everyday English, that conceptual opposition can be brought out quite clearly by pitting the words *match* and *fit* against one another in certain contexts. The metaphysical realist looks for knowledge that *matches* reality.[21]
>
> If, on the other hand, we say something *fits*, we have in mind a different relation. A key fits if it opens the lock. The fit describes a capacity of the key, not of the lock.[22]
>
> [...] From the radical constructivist point of view, all of us [...] face our environment as the burglar faces a lock that he has to unlock in order to get at the loot.[23]

As von Glasersfeld's metaphor suggests, we are able to both construct and manipulate the social world we construct.

4 From Epistemic Constructivism to Legal Constructivism

The idea of what we assume is reality arises from the way we process the information surrounding us. This is crucial for understanding not only science but also law. Let us consider some examples. Empirically speaking, the ocean can be seen as water moving in a continuous ebb and flow. However, jurists have established a difference between national and international waters. Given this apparent distinction, we can note the absence of visible boundaries. The definition of borders between countries is similarly hazy. In these examples, what is important for considering something as real is the mental models used to process information and their epistemic justification

[19] Glasersfeld (1984), p. 20.
[20] Glasersfeld (1984), p. 20.
[21] Glasersfeld (1984), p. 20.
[22] Glasersfeld (1984), p. 21.
[23] Glasersfeld (1984), p. 21.

rather than simple perception. Even then, it is essential to emphasize that the way information is organized promotes different behaviours.

Unfortunately, except for Nicholas Luhmann's work,[24] which belongs more within the realm of legal sociology than general theory of law, discussions of constructivism in the legal domain have been practically non-existent. Nonetheless, we should be careful when attempting to transpose the premises of classical radical constructivism to law. Law features its own distinctive characteristics, which differentiate it from the world of experience studied by sciences such as physics, chemistry and biology. In those areas, the world of experience being studied exists, to some extent, prior to the scientist's experience. In the case of law, legal scholars establish the conditions that enable the world to be organized. Through the constitutive role of legal provisions, legal scholars produce the cognitive constructs that distinguish national waters from international waters and categorize the same brute facts into murder, infanticide manslaughter, voluntary manslaughter, premeditated murder, etc. Similarly, these constructed notions can be deconstructed through reforms or partial repeals.

5 Legal Constructivism: Definition, Epistemic Foundations and Comparisons

It should be evident that LC was born as a response to the collapse of the epistemic paradigms supporting the main theoretical accounts of the law. These are, on the one hand, metaphysical realism, represented by essentialism, theological natural law and rationalist legal theories, and, on the other hand, the naïve empiricism maintained by contemporary forms of legal positivism.

The goal of LC is to position law on the same playing field as other disciplines, especially after the aforementioned collapse.

Despite the impact of constructivism on other areas of knowledge, consideration of the relationship between "constructivism" and "law" has been rather limited, if not practically non-existent, in the context of the general theory of law. Moreover, it has been used in a very different sense from the one I attribute to it. It has sometimes been attached to certain forms of economic analysis of law[25] or to the hermeneutic activity of legal operators, particularly judges, understood as a social practice, but without explicitly stating the meaning assigned to "constructivism".[26]

Within the scarce literature on the general theory of law, two authors stand out: Gunther Teubner[27] and Vittorio Villa.[28] Although I share their central idea that law

[24]Luhmann (1991, 1997).

[25]Ackerman (1988).

[26]Lifante Vidal (2020).

[27]Teubner (1989).

[28]Villa (1999, 2011).

does not refer to a given, independent and objective reality, we frame the relationship between constructivism and law differently, although not necessarily incompatibly.

Villa researches the metatheory of law, and his work introduces different concepts of constructivism in general, critically analyzing the descriptivist premises of various legal theories, including those of Kelsen, Dworkin and Ferrajoli. He also explains the relationship between constructivism, the theory of interpretation and value judgments in law. The main difference between our proposals is that this work presents metatheoretical considerations at the epistemic level without directly discussing any particular theory, although I also refute descriptivist assumptions of the dominant theories. Furthermore, while Villa's analysis is purely philosophical and analytical, my proposal emphasizes naturalization. For example, regarding what he calls systemic constructivism, Villa writes:[29]

> The fourth idea that I identified through the term "systemic constructivism" refers to a more varied constellation of concepts that are different from one another: let us think of a spectrum of positions that include Piaget's genetic epistemology, evolutionary epistemological concepts, those coming from the general theory of systems and, finally, theories of auto-poietic systems.
>
> I do not have either space or the ability to engage in a detailed examination of these concepts. I would like to point out, however, that these—although they sometimes assert specific positions that are not very different, from a strictly epistemological point of view, from the ones I propose here—operate, nonetheless, within a philosophical context that is profoundly different from the one underlying my work [. . .].[30]

As seen in the following, some of the foundations of my proposal are the theory of complex systems and cognitive sciences, which Villa considers incompatible with his approach.

Meanwhile, Teubner takes as a starting point assumptions of radical constructivism from the perspective of legal sociology and adopts a position more compatible with my theory:

1. Under a constructivist social epistemology, the reality perceptions of law cannot be matched to a somehow corresponding social reality "out there". Rather, it is law as an autonomous epistemic subject that constructs a social reality of its own.
2. It is not human individuals by their intentional actions that produce law as a cultural artefact. On the contrary, it is law as a communicative process that by its legal operations produces human actors as semantic artefacts.[31]

Our theories mainly converge in the first sentence of this quote. However, we fundamentally differ because Teubner, a faithful Luhmannian, does not centre his analysis on individual agents but on law as a communicative process. The price of this theoretical abstraction is evident in bizarre metaphorical expressions such as

---

[29]Translation mine.

[30]Villa (2011), p. 57.

[31]Teubner (1989), p. 730.

"law produces human actors as semantic artefacts", as if humans were mere linguistic entities.

In contrast with Teubner's position and the level of abstraction of his theory, my conception of LC positions individual agents and their cognitive properties at the centre of theoretical reflection. Notwithstanding, it does not embrace an individualistic position of cognition and nor does it consider reality the product of isolated minds. For LC, reality is an emergent property deriving from the processes of self-organizing interaction that take place between agents, their cognitive niches and institutions, which implies the need to consider these interactions on a sub-emerging scale prior to the social reality that emerges from their interaction. Including individual agents as a scale for a complex system enables linking LC to advances in cognitive sciences and naturalizing it experimentally, as well as enabling the creation of agent-based computer simulation models.

The central premises of my version of LC can be summarized as follows:

(1) an agent's cognition is embodied, and the mental models from which we organize the world (like keys) emerge from it at a more detailed scale than that of the subject;
(2) legal training, including both positive law and the theoretical artefacts generated by academics, influence the reconfiguration of an agent's mental models prior to their training as legal scholars, who are thus qualified to enter legal reality;
(3) as legal operators, agents participate in the production of legal reality and, therefore, social reality from a sub-emerging level of self-organizing interactions;
(4) if agents are considered nodes of a dynamic network, their interactions do not happen haphazardly because they participate in institutional structures created by law itself;
(5) positive law plays a fundamental role in the creation of an agent's mental models through their constitutive properties. However, this does not imply that given objective norms or fixed normative structures are generated: as they are incorporated into a legal operator's mental models, the beliefs derived from positive law and legal theory are co-dependently redefined with the rest of the elements that make up the cognitive life of agents.

Regarding the relationship between constructivism and law, it should be noted that, in the last decade, a small group of academics specializing in international law, either implicitly or explicitly, have been working towards a constructivist understanding of international law inspired by the work of constructivists in the field of international relations. However, unlike LC, their position is based on sociological and historical assumptions rather than cognitive or epistemic conceptions. Nonetheless, both approaches share an explanation of law as the result of social interactions based on both social and legal norms.[32]

[32]Brunée and Toope (2012).

6 The Central Elements of Legal Constructivism

My conception of LC draws on resources from the fields of cognitive sciences, complexity sciences and linguistic philosophy. This section expands upon its main elements.

6.1 Definition of Social Reality

In this chapter, the expression "social reality" denotes the set of social (re)-presentations that results from cognitive processes, including beliefs, thoughts, feelings, attitudes and perceptions of what is considered true in the world, and determines our institutionalized and intersubjective social interactions. Social reality can be constituted or emerge from the self-organizing activity of groups of individuals. Emerging social reality can be expressed as "X creates Y, in which X denotes a social group and Y denotes the created reality", as in the case of racism. Meanwhile, constituted social reality can be expressed by the formula "X constitutively creates Y" in which "constitutively" involves an act of will. One example of this is the court system. In the case of "natural reality", there is no "X" that creates "Y".

6.2 Concepts from Cognitive Sciences

(1) Agent: This refers to any entity whose dynamics presuppose cognitive properties. At different levels, it can denote individuals, systems, networks of individuals involved in group cognition processes, institutions or networks of institutions.[33]
(2) Embodied cognition: This thesis claims that cognition involves not only the brain but the entire organism. Substantial experimental work has demonstrated that many cognitive systematizations take place without conscious control.[34]
(3) Situated cognition: This thesis claims that embodied cognition is generated, operates and adapts according to the agent's interaction with the environment.[35]
(4) Legal mental models: The result of a legal operator's embodiment of legal and philosophical theories, as well as of doctrine and positive law. When integrated

[33]Coming from the theory of agency and the cognitive sciences, this is commonly associated with the works of Anscombe (1957) and Davidson (1963), the concept is adapted by me for the development of LC. For further reading, see Mele (1997), Moya (1990) and Roessler and Eilan (2003).

[34]Coming from the cognitive sciences, this is adapted by me for the development of LC. Further reading: Chipman (2016) and Frankish and Ramsey (2012).

[35]Further reading: Adams and Aizawa (2009); and especially: Smith (1999).

into a belief system, this becomes part of many cognitive processes, including attention, perception, evocation and adaptation. As noted, the role of mental models is not merely contemplative; instead, they play a fundamental role in the behaviour of legal operators.[36]

Although legal mental models comprise a nucleus of the aforementioned cognitive modules (i.e., philosophy of law, positive law, etc.), their dynamics also involve non-legal cognitive modules such as non-legal theories, implicit theories, prejudices, moral beliefs, cognitive biases and subjective experiences. All of these modules interact in an embodied, self-organizing manner from which the mental model that determines what we consider to be the case in the world emerges.

It is important to recognize that, in practice, all of these modules are triggered by situations and depend on many variables, including the type of legal case, the phase of the legal process phase, the general political context, the organizational culture and the philosophical-legal theories maintained. For instance, judges' different philosophical beliefs can promote different interpretations of the same positive law and, therefore, different judgments.

(5) Cognitive input: This is the information used for cognitive processing, usually originating from "outside" the agent. Examples include a case narrative, a counterargument and a statement of evidence.[37]
(6) Artefact: This refers to everything that has been created or adapted for particular goals.[38]
(7) Normative artefact: This is a norm or set of norms whose goal is to regulate human behaviour.[39]
(8) Constitutive artefact: This is a kind of speech act that creates the possibility of creating institutional facts.[40]
(9) Extended Mind: This thesis holds that if the brain's function can be enhanced or supplemented by external artefacts, these would also be part of the mind.[41]
(10) Cognitive niche: This refers to the environment in which an agent's situated cognition occurs.[42]

---

[36] I have developed this concept in several of my works, adapting it from Model Theory. The first use of the concept Mental Model is from Craik (1967), p. 57. For previous developments of LC in English, see Cáceres Nieto (2007a, b, 2011, 2012a, b).

[37] See note 34 on Embodied cognition.

[38] Further reading on the philosophical definition on artefacts see: Dipert (1993).

[39] See note 38 on artefacts.

[40] See note 38 on artefacts.

[41] This concept derives from the philosophy of mind, and it is also one from the four "E" in 4E cognition or 4E mind. Further reading: Newen et al. (2018) and Menary (2010).

[42] This term was originally proposed by Kinzey et al. (1987) and is adapted by me for the development of LC.

(11) Affordance: These are the satisfiers that agents can find in a cognitive niche depending on their biological or cognitive properties.[43]

6.3 Concepts from Complexity Sciences

(1) Complex system:[44] A dynamic and evolutionary system whose chief properties are:

A. Self-organization: The system's structure and dynamics result not from any central control unit but from the self-organizing interaction between its elements. For example, every ant is a stupid agent, but collective intelligence emerges from the self-organizing processes between colony members.[45]
B. Emergence: The phenomenon of a system (S2) that emerges from a self-organizing system (S1) with properties that cannot be traced to S1. For example, while chloride and sodium are toxic to human beings as individual elements, this toxicity ceases to exist when these elements are combined to constitute salt.[46]
C. Sub-emergence: Dynamics of a complex system (S1) during the process of self-organization before the emergence of a system.[47]
D. Phase space: A dimension in which the set of the possible states of a system can take place.
E. The transition of phase space: The passage from a phase space (F1) to another phase space (F2), generally resulting from emergence.
F. Turbulence: A state of imbalance in a system caused by a new factor interacting with that system. An example is using a blender to mix two different colours of paint.
G. Attractor: Generally speaking, the point at which the evolution of the states of a complex system tends to occur within its phase space, regardless of its initial conditions. An example is instant coffee dissolved in hot water.
H. Heterogeneity: This indicates that the system constitutes elements and even vastly different types of subsystems. Each subsystem features its own dynamics, time, and scale, interacting with the other elements in the global system, as in the case of the human body.

---

[43]This concept was originally presented by Gibson (1979), p. 127. It is adapted by me for the development of LC.

[44]Further reading: Waldrop (1993, 2009), Holland (2014), Floriani Neto et al. (2018) and Fabó et al. (2017).

[45]Further reading: Foerster (1960).

[46]The concept has a long history and has evolved over time. For a great study on the subject, see Caston (1997). Further reading: Bedau and Humphreys (2008) and Broad (1925).

[47]See note 46 on Emergence.

I. Coevolution: A property of two or more systems indicating that, upon interaction, transformations with a reciprocal influence follow. In the example of prey-predator models, the more predators, the less prey; however, when prey decreases, predators decrease, consequently increasing prey.
J. Oblique control: An intervention that produces one or more instances of turbulence in a system for the purpose of initiating a self-organizing process that leads to new desired emergent dynamics. An example is a vaccine.
K. Co-dependence or co-definition: This indicates that the properties of the elements in the system depend on global system dynamics and vice-versa.

(2) Complex networks: Complex systems comprising elements that are connected and interact with each other. Connected elements are known as "nodes", and the links between them are known as "edges".[48]

In social networks, nodes are referred to as "agents". In this work, different kinds of legal operators are considered legal agents, while legal norms used to justify a decision are the nodes of a legal network.

6.4 Concepts from Linguistic Philosophy

My conception of LC borrows several ideas from linguistic philosophy, including notions of regulatory rules and constitutive rules, brute facts and institutional facts, legal constitutive rules, and institutional legal tracts.

John Searle notably distinguishes between regulative rules and constitutive rules, brute facts, and institutional facts.[49] Regulatory rules are those that regulate behaviour whose existence does not depend on the rules. These behaviours or events are referred to with the term "brute fact". Constitutive rules are those that create the conditions for the existence of new forms of behaviour and specific facts, which are referred to by the term "institutional fact".[50] For example, chess moves are institutional facts that can only exist because of the chess rules that established them.

As in the case of the relationship between constructivism and law, despite its theoretical importance for the legal world, only a few legal philosophers have been interested in explaining legal norms as constitutive rules. Probably due to the prevalence of statutory law over jurisprudential law in the Romano-Germanic tradition, these works have been written by theoreticians of that tradition. For example, in Spanish legal philosophy, Gregorio Robles[51] has proposed a theoretical model of law based on comparative analysis of the rules of games and the rules of law, distinguishing between ontic rules (which create the conditions for the existence

[48]See note 44 on Complex Systems.

[49]Searle (1995), pp. 27–28.

[50]Searle (2010), p. 133.

[51]Robles Morchón (1988).

of action: spaces, times, competencies and subjects), deontic rules (which create behaviours) and conventional technical rules (which establish relations of logical necessity for operation in the legal world). The conjunction of these rules has been described as the "ontic-practical realms" to which both law and games belong, in contrast to moral laws, which are simply practical rules.

Interest in the role of constitutivity in law is also found in Italian legal philosophy, especially in the work of Gaetano Carcaterra,[52] who has devised a constitutive theory of law more closely connected to Austin's theory of speech acts[53] than Searle's concept of constitutive rules.[54] In his work, Carcaterra produces an evolutionary analysis of the main models of normativist theories, which he historically classifies as imperativist and prescriptivist, before then building a mixed theory for use as a starting point in the creation of a single theory that dismantles previous categories to propose a theory of law based only on performative norms. The works of Robles and Carcaterra share the characteristic of correspondence with the analytical approach to law, which I have also used in my conception of LC.[55]

Beyond the analytical philosophical tradition, and despite its author not having mentioned the term "constructivism", it is worth considering the Scandinavian realism work of Karl Olivecrona.[56] Drawing on Austin's theories[57] of performative acts (as does Carcaterra[58]), Olivecrona addresses an issue that has captured the attention of several contemporary legal philosophers due to the influence of empiricist epistemology on law: the determination of the epistemic status of fundamental legal concepts for which there has been no direct empirical reference; that is, nobody has ever directly observed the physical, real-world manifestation of subjective law – no one knows its color, its weight or shape. Olivecrona's response to this problem comprises affirming that while the language of law is not part of the world of acts perceptible through the senses, its origin is found in the language of magic and characterized by its function as a means of social control through its impact on the psychology of its users.

Importantly, while LC is compatible with analytical jurisprudence and Scandinavian legal realism, it avoids falling into methodical syncretism by considering legal norms as types of constitutive rules, as Searle does,[59] and, to some extent, institutional legal acts as psychological (not magical) processes, as Olivecrona does.[60] Compatibility is enabled by the thesis of embodied cognition and the mental

---

[52]Carcaterra (1979, 2014).

[53]Austin (1975).

[54]Searle (1995), pp. 27–28.

[55]Cáceres Nieto (2007b).

[56]Olivecrona (1971).

[57]Austin (1975).

[58]Carcaterra (1979, 2014).

[59]Searle (1995, 2010).

[60]Olivecrona (1971).

models of legal operators, by which both constitutive norms and ways of organizing legal reality into institutional legal acts comprise parts of an agent's cognitive life.

In contrast, and faithful to its rejection of metaphysical realism and the descriptivist assumptions of legal theory, LC assumes that legal provisions are not given objects but have potentially different meanings that trigger actions that materialize in social interaction through a cognitive behavioural duality.

7 Legal Constructivism as a Substantive Theory of Law

Based on the theoretical concepts presented in the previous section, LC strives to answer some of the leading research questions that recur in general theories of law and to provide alternative responses to prevalent ones. These questions are: (1) In which sense is law a matter of norms? (2) What is the structure of legal systems? (3) How does law relate to other normative systems? (4) What are the conditions for the effectiveness of law?

Contrasting with legal philosophy's traditional responses, LC suggests

(1) instead of the law consisting of a set of given objective norms, positive law is the "LEGO[61] of statements", with vast different potential structures and meanings for normative constructs that serve to support many possible behaviours;
(2) where the traditional view claims that normative systems feature a hierarchical and pyramidal structure, a connectionist model is possible instead;
(3) rather than dispositional decision-making that claims that legal operators can and should make cold, rational decisions, a modular theory of legal mental models should be considered;
(4) instead of understanding the effectiveness of laws as compliance with rules, institutional legal facts can be theorized as emerging dynamics.

7.1 The Connectionist Theory of the Legal System

For LC, the hierarchical and pyramidal model of normative systems does not adequately account for the cognitive processes that legal operators effectively conduct using their mental models, and nor does it provide an adequate concept of law when it is no longer linked to the concept of State.

One connectionist theory applied to law assumes that it is expressed through different types of legal discourses with both explicit (normative remissions) and implicit (associative memory) hypertextual connections. The kind of discourses and

[61]LEGO is a line of plastic toys that originated in Denmark and consists of interlocking pieces that allow the free construction and building of structures that can be replaced, deconstructed and reused.

hypertextual properties may differ depending on the specific legal tradition. The main discourses in the civil law tradition are legislation, case law, doctrine, legal philosophy and, complementarily, political and moral philosophy. When the resulting network of connections of this particular discourse is incorporated at a cognitive level, it constitutes technical modules, legal operators, mental models.

Exploratory results for experiments conducted at the Legal Constructivism Laboratory at the Institute for Legal Research at the National Autonomous University of Mexico apparently support the thesis that the technical legal module of legal mental models forms part of sub-emergent and self-organizing processes that incorporate deep cognitive and embodied processes, such as implicit theories, subjective experiences, cognitive biases, etc. All of these work unconsciously as part of a complex adaptive and heterogeneous system.[62]

In addition to explaining how legal operators actually work through their mental models, it is also possible to understand the role of law in today's legal globalization process. For LC, the different normative systems are connected in a complex heterogeneous adaptive network, the diversity of which implies the hypertextual connectivity of national legal systems and other cognitive inputs derived from non-State institutions such as NGOs, international organizations, soft law firms and other types of legal systems to solve similar cases.

Ultimately, the interaction of legal statements with the rest of the heterogeneous system nodes promotes the emergence of the structure and meaning of the law in the era of legal globalization.

7.2 *Theory of Normative Constructs*

According to contemporary legal theory, legal rules are "given objects" belonging to a particular legal system and determined by a rule of recognition. However, it is worth examining whether these allegedly "given" and "objective" legal rules are ready to be "recognized" as part of a system and, if they are, why lawyers discuss different interpretations of the same statement, why courts of a higher judicial hierarchy often feature different criteria and why litigation exists.

It is important to emphasize that the expression used to designate this theoretical construct includes the word "recognition", the noun form of the verb "recognize", which can refer to the act of identifying something as a member of a kind. According to this concept, a rule is recognized as a part of a specific legal system because it has accomplished a certain rule of recognition. For example, a rule is recognized as part of the English legal system because it was created by the English parliament.[63]

[62]Constructivismo jurídico, Cognición, Complejidad y Derecho (Proyecto Fronteras de la Ciencia CONACYT 541/2016).

[63]Hart (2012), p. 100.

For LC, "given" material is a fundamental part of what jurists process using their mental models, which are cognitively incorporated into the various types of discourse mentioned (positive law such as doctrinal law, legal philosophy and even political philosophy and moral philosophy).

The connections resulting from the cognitive processing of legal operators are the basis from which normative constructs emerge. Thus, for example, legal doctrine may contain the definition of a term referred to in legislation, but it can also connect norms belonging to different normative bodies, promoting a normative construct that has never been created by a legislator.

A legal operator's generation of associative connectionist networks is not limited to following or opting for explicit hypertext connections because the operator generates heuristic associations derived from the legal operator's own experience, associations which may differ from those that other legal operators might generate. Over time, the growth of this network of connections constitutes the operator's experiential base, which they use in and adapt to similar situations.

In conjunction with normative connectivity processes, assigning propositional content to normative constructs may require at least two types of processing: a semantic one and a hermeneutic one. Semantics implies the processing of the meaning of words, such as determining the spectrum of vagueness in which the meaning of a term will be located (for example, the time-lapse that can be signalled by "prompt and expeditious"). Hermeneutic processing, which presupposes semantics, corresponds to the so-called methods of interpretation (extensive, restrictive, analogical, etc.) and weighting.

It is important to emphasize that doctrine can reformulate positive law and, therefore, the propositional attribution of a normative construct.

Consequently, we can conclude that there are no given legal rules but a set of LEGO pieces that can be moulded and assembled into different structures and with different meanings according to the diverse mental models of legal operators.

Given each could constitute a normative construct following a long sequence of cognitive processes, legal rules are neither given nor recognized; instead, they are constructed.

7.3 *Theory of Legal Mental Models*

Mental models with a modular structure emerge from embodied states (sub-emergent and self-organizing processes) and can be one of the following types:

(1) The legal technical module: This includes (a) laws, (b) case law, (c) metalinguistics, (d) doctrine, and (e) philosophical-legal aspects of the positive law. All of these components interact according to the development of the reticular connectionist theory of the legal system and the theory of normative constructs.

(2) Complementary modules: These include non-legal constructs generated by operators based on their experiences of the world, experiences which are also organized in various ways and include subjective experiences, cognitive biases, personality traits, motivations, prejudices and implicit theories.

Legal operators' decisions are the result of the self-organizing processes that occur in these different modules as part of a complex adaptive system whose dynamics are ecologically determined by the cognitive niches that affect the permutation of states of embodied and situated cognition. From this perspective, it makes no sense to hold onto any of the reductionist theories of legal decisions.

7.4 Theory of Legal Effectiveness as Institutional Legal Facts of Emerging Dynamics

7.4.1 Legal Constructivism and Institutionalism

An individualistic explanation for how the mental models of legal operators operate is insufficient to explain the effectiveness (or ineffectiveness) of law in social life because their embodied cognition and behaviour are the result not of their cognitive processes but of their institutional cognitive niches.

As in the case of ant colonies, from whose self-organizing interaction intelligent collective behaviour emerges, or in the case of neurons, where each is a stupid agent from whose self-organizing interaction thought emerges, the dynamics of legal institutions emerge from the self-organizing processes derived from legal operators' mental models, which combine both technical and complementary modules, all within an embodied dimension.

Sometimes the very institutional design constituted by law can promote the emergence of counterproductive dynamics. One example is found in prisons, whose objective is social re-adaptation but where schools of crime often emerge.

In the context of the dynamics of the self-organizing interactions manifesting during a process, path dependence becomes apparent, determining the universe of possibilities for the subsequent dynamics in each phase's closure. For example, having the necessary evidence to "determine the truth" in a criminal case presupposes group cognition dynamics. However, the truth's final emergence depends on many variables: the proper preservation of the chain of custody; the quality of expert services, technical training and experience, the material resources available (i.e., the reagents needed to carry out DNA tests); the possibility that through due process important evidence has been admitted to solve the case; the progress of the hearing; the epistemic obstacles and/or discrepancies established in the law itself for determining the truth (and so on and so forth).

As demonstrated, the construction of what is considered real in law is an emerging property of a complex adaptive system in which both normative constructs and institutional legal facts are defined co-dependently from the self-organizing interaction of each of the parties, their embodied states, the modules activated in their mental models, communicative interaction, and so on.

Moving to a higher level from agents to institutions, the same theoretical framework can explain what happens when agents are not individual subjects but institutions that interact with other institutions. Just as the emerging dynamics of a trial depend on the self-organizing interaction between litigants, the dynamics of an institution emerge from the sub-emergent processes that take place in the series of trials and a specific dynamic corresponding to the objectives of the law may or may not emerge from the dynamics between networks of institutions. For example, the emergence of the state corresponding to the enjoyment of the human right to a healthy environment depends, among other things, on a country's healthcare system, the proper treatment of toxic waste, the food quality control, the pharmaceutical industry and the quality control of medical teaching. Each of these, in turn, comprises different legal codes, case law decisions, doctrinal principles, and so on.

That is, effective law emerges from an institutional environment that exerts pressure on agents and shapes particular mental models that are used for interacting with other agents in a self-organizing way.

When a diversity of cases presented to courts has achieved a state of equilibrium and a set of possible decisions to rule on them has emerged, we can speak of a "normative instantiation" in a modality.

The pressures exerted by institutional culture can lead to the emergence of correct or dyspraxic heuristics. These pressures can be diverse: the lack of expertise of other legal operators, excessive work, institutional pressure from other institutions, a lack of sufficient human or material resources to cope with the demand, etc. All of these affect the emergence of normative constructs by which law impacts the social construction of reality. In other words, the effectiveness of law, the law that affects social reality, is an emerging property of a highly sophisticated sub-emergent framework that has nothing to do with the claims of objectivity and rationality postulated by legal positivism.

Here, LC offers an alternative model based on the plurality of possible behaviours derived from different agents and their respective states of embodied cognition, mental models, situated cognition, extended mind, self-organizing interactions and emerging dynamics, the patterns of which can be modelled and analyzed to generate strategies to design institutions from which dynamics based on the objectives of the law emerge and, if necessary, to induce turbulences that lead to states of phase transitions of dyspraxic systems to adjust to the desired state.

7.4.2 The Role of Citizens (the Forgotten *Explanandum*)

One of the aspects least addressed by the dominant legal theory is the role of civil society in normative effectiveness. While some authors limit themselves to maintaining that a minimum degree of efficiency is a condition for the existence of the law, others construct their theory by illuminating the role of legal operators, leaving the role of citizens in the shadows. This defect of explanans has been the object of study of some of the few legal complexity theoreticians, including J.B. Ruhl and Thomas Webb.[64]

For Ruhl, law is a dynamic social system that occurs in the space of interaction determined by rules. For him, the dynamics of law satisfy some of the characteristic properties of a complex system: they behave by following one or more of the three main types of attractors (fixed, recursive and strange or chaotic), they promote emerging phenomena, and they are sensitive to initial conditions and demonstrate catastrophic behaviour.[65]

Ruhl exemplifies the presence of attractors using a simple example. Driving a car occurs within a space of interactions that corresponds to the urban infrastructure and necessarily involves following the traffic rules. Each driver begins from a starting point and aims to reach a destination (fixed point attractor). The relationship between the two points is usually repeated when a daily routine is followed (recursive attractor). However, the transit from the initial attractor to the destination is open to multiple possible trajectories (strange or chaotic attractor). Although Ruhl refers to a single person (John) in his example, the characterization of law as a complex system becomes more evident if one considers morning traffic when going to work or taking children to school. In these cases, the set of cars driving along an avenue represents the space of the social dimension. The same traffic regulations must govern each of the drivers (as occurs with each ant that follows a trail of pheromones), each driver starts from a set of initial conditions, and each driver has an endpoint. However, although each driver usually repeats the same routine, several drivers may experience incidents that affect the other cars (breakdowns, accidents, running out of gas, being pulled over by the police, etc.). These contingencies can produce unpredictable alterations in each driver's trajectory and force them to look for an alternative route that, in turn, provokes changes in the daily dynamics of traffic.[66]

If we consider a helicopter pilot who reports traffic conditions for radio and television stations to inform drivers and suggest alternative routes, we can observe different emerging dynamics on different days, each of which, although commensurable, will never be exactly the same (phase space). This is because the impact of daily incidents is not predictable.

Sometimes a small change in the legal system can lead to the loss of stability of a social system as a whole and even to its destruction. Ruhl exemplifies this phenomenon through consideration of the counterproductive consequences of rigid reforms to environmental legislation.

In addition to his theoretical considerations, Ruhl makes several suggestions regarding administrative law, recognizing that flexible regulation enables more significant system adaptation and, therefore, more efficiently avoids catastrophes than rigid and inflexible regulations do. In this way, Ruhl demonstrates the

[64]Ruhl (1996) and Webb (2014).

[65]Ruhl (1996), pp. 862–875.

[66]Ruhl (1996), pp. 862–866.

connections between positive law, public institutions and citizens as characteristic elements of the heterogeneity of law.

Webb uses Ruhl's ideas (among others)[67] as a starting point for a theoretical proposal of law from the perspective of complex theory that considers the similarities and differences of the concept of autopoiesis[68] proposed by Luhmann.[69]

For Webb, the properties of the complex system that characterizes law are self-organization, emergence, adaptability, memory and irreversibility.[70] Like Ruhl, he argues that the dynamics of law take place in a space. However, Webb specifies that this space is always situated and that contextual factors always limit the system's dynamics because no one has access to all of the information needed to understand the global functioning of the system. Its knowledge is distributed, contingent, local, specialized and contained within areas and sub-areas. Agents interact through groups of local interactions, make decisions with incomplete knowledge and always make choices that can produce changes in the system's global behaviour, unknowingly impacting its general dynamics.

System memory and learning are contained in texts such as books, codes, case law and precedents (hypertextual theory) and can operate through selective forgetting to make way for new information (e.g., precedents that are no longer used).

Concerning the boundaries of the system, while these exist, he admits that there are environments that are difficult to define (for instance, the distinction between law and morality), which makes legal systems adaptive and co-evolutionary according to the "external" attractors that mark the trend of their dynamics.

Regarding the system's balance, Webb warns that internal conflicts can be generated by contingent and local knowledge, which can promote "bad adaptations". Moreover, he suggests laws must promote a constant adaptation to the social environment, a feature of complex adaptive systems.

Finally, the previous states of a system determine the space of adaptive possibility of the subsequent stages, meaning that the system satisfies the property of path dependence.

The concepts of LC complement the ideas of Ruhl and Webb to recognize that the dynamics of systems are not solely a function of laws. These dynamics result from self-organizing interactions between legal operators, institutions, networks of institutions and agents not constituted by law (as in the case of non-legal professional networks), with these interactions corresponding to behaviours produced by states of embodied cognition and the mental models of all interacting agents.

---

[67] Webb (2014), p. 482.

[68] Webb (2014), pp. 483–484.

[69] Concept developed by Maturana and Valera (2004), p. 69, it is introduced to social systems by Luhmann (1991), p. 480; Luhmann (1997).

[70] Webb (2014), p. 485.

8 The Method of Legal Constructivism as Action-Research

The objective of LC is not limited to developing conceptual models. If this were so, nothing would differentiate it from speculative philosophy. Instead, LC also seeks to induce self-organizing processes in the embodied cognition of agents themselves, enabling the production of new forms of self-organizing interactions from which dynamics that conform to what is established by law can more substantially emerge.

To achieve this, LC uses methods employed by complexity science, including computational simulators, discrete mathematics, non-linear dynamic equations, agent-based models, complex adaptive networks and artificial intelligence.

Similarly, it makes use of neuropsychological methods, including electroencephalography and electrodermal activity registers, to identify brain activity during the cognitive and emotional processes of legal operators. In the near future, it is expected that LC will also utilize both functional magnetic resonance equipment and transcranial magnetic stimulation to analyze the subcortical activity of these same operators.

In the Laboratory of Legal Constructivism at the Institute for Legal Research of the National Autonomous University of Mexico, we are conducting research based on these methodologies with promising results, elaboration of which is beyond this work's scope.

9 The Concept of Law Revisited

I do not intend to define necessary and sufficient properties of the word "law" but to make a theoretical stipulation that must be understood, considering everything discussed in this chapter.

For LC, "law" denotes a complex system comprising a set of constitutive texts or constituted by agents and institutions created by texts belonging to the same set. These texts can be connected through a hypertextual relationship with texts other than positive law (legal doctrine, legal philosophy, etc.) and produce diverse normative constructs. When the aforementioned texts have been embodied, they promote the mental models that determine what is considered to be the case in the legal world and how to behave in it. The self-organizing behaviour that occurs between legal operators and civil society plays an important role in the emergence of institutional legal facts and social dynamics.

Based on this definition, law features the following properties: it is a *complex*, *dynamic*, *evolutionary*, and *multi-scale* (both functionally and temporally) system because different agents and institutions (networks) operate at different times and produce effects at different hierarchical levels; it is heterogeneous because it consists of several types of agents; it is a multiplexer because each agent can substitute states of embodied cognition in a situated manner; it is adaptive because it can adapt to changes in its environment; it is resilient because it can absorb the turbulence of the environment and maintain its identity; it is propagative because it socializes the agents incorporated in it; it is redundant because the socialized agents become socializing agents; it is recursive because the emerging properties of the system influence agents' behaviour, which, in turn, influences the emerging dynamics of the system whose identity will persist as long as there is no turbulence that produces a change in its state, space or system phases.

References

Ackerman B (1988) Del realismo al constructivismo jurídico. Ariel S.A.

Adams F, Aizawa K (2009) Why the mind is still in the head. In: Robbins P, Aydede M (eds) The Cambridge handbook of situated cognition. Cambridge University Press, pp 78–95

Anscombe GEM (1957) Intention. Basil Blackwell, Oxford

Austin JL (1975) How to do things with words, 2nd edn. Harvard University Press

Bachelard G (2000) La formación del espíritu científico. Siglo XXI editores S.A. de C.V.

Bateson G (2000) Steps to an ecology of mind: collected essays in anthropology, psychiatry, evolution, and epistemology. The University of Chicago Press

Bedau MA, Humphreys P (2008) Emergence. Contemporary readings in philosophy and science. The MIT Press

Broad CD (1925) The mind and its place in nature. Routledge & Kegan Paul

Brunée J, Toope SJ (eds) (2012) Constructivist approaches to international law. In: Dunoff JL, Pollack MA (eds) Interdisciplinary perspectives on international law and international relations: the state of art. Cambridge University Press, pp 119–145

Cáceres Nieto E (2007a) A constructivist model for the judicial determination of facts. In: ICAIL '07: Proceedings of the 11th international conference on artificial intelligence and law. Association for Computing Machinery, pp 285–286

Cáceres Nieto E (2007b) Constructivismo jurídico y metateoría del derecho. IIJ-UNAM. URL = <https://biblio.juridicas.unam.mx/bjv/detalle-libro/2518-constructivismo-juridico-y-metateoria-del-derecho>

Cáceres Nieto E (2011) Steps toward a constructivist and coherentist theory of judicial reasoning in civil law tradition. In: Law and neuroscience: current legal issues, vol 13. Oxford Scholarship Online, pp 459–482

Cáceres Nieto E (2012a) Complejidad y derecho. Un ensayo de constructivismo jurídico institucional con base en la teoría de los sistemas complejos. In: Corona J (ed) Complejidad: la encrucijada del pensamiento. Universidad de Guanajuato, Porrúa

Cáceres Nieto E (2012b) Dispraxis jurídica. Modelos mentales y constructivismo jurídico complejo. In: Cano Valle F et al (eds) Dispraxis. IIJ-UNAM. pp 191–212. URL = <https://archivos.juridicas.unam.mx/www/bjv/libros/7/3138/13.pdf>

Cáceres Nieto E (2015) La Constitución emergente: un ensayo de metateoría constitucional desde el constructivismo jurídico. In: Trueba Buenfil F (ed) Contribuciones al derecho constitucional. IIJ-UNAM, pp 139–157. URL = <https://archivos.juridicas.unam.mx/www/bjv/libros/8/3980/10.pdf>

Cáceres Nieto E (2016a) Constructivismo jurídico, entropía y neguentropía en el constitucionalismo contemporáneo. In: Serna de la Garza JM, Santos Olivo I (eds) La dinámica del cambio constitucional. IIJ-UNAM, pp 63–90. URL = <https://archivos.juridicas.unam.mx/www/bjv/libros/10/4828/5.pdf>

Cáceres Nieto E (2016b) Constructivismo jurídico, sociedad civil, turbulencias autoorganizativas y combate a la corrupción. In: Salazar P et al (eds) ¿Cómo combatir la corrupción? IIJ-UNAM, pp 41–51. URL = <https://archivos.juridicas.unam.mx/www/bjv/libros/9/4315/7.pdf>

Cáceres Nieto E (2016c) Legal constructivism: law, cognition and complexity. In: Fabó E et al (eds) Systemic actions in complex scenarios. Cambridge University Scholars, pp 103–120
Carcaterra G (1979) La forza costitutiva delle norme. Bluzoni
Carcaterra G (2014) Le norme constitutive. G. Giappichelli Editore
Caston V (1997) Epiphenomenalisms, ancient and modern. Philos Rev 106(3):309–363. https://doi.org/10.2307/2998397
Chipman SEF (ed) (2016) The Oxford handbook of cognitive science. Oxford University Press
Craik KJW (1967) The nature of explanation. Cambridge University Press
Davidson D (1963) Actions, reasons, and causes. J Philos 60(23):685–700. https://doi.org/10.2307/2023177
Dipert RR (1993) Artefacts, art works, and agency. Temple University Press
Fabó E, Ferone E, Ming Chen J (2017) Systemic actions in complex scenarios. Cambridge University Press
Floriani Neto AB, Cáceres Nieto E, Chiodi G, Petroccia S (eds) (2018) Governing turbulence, risk and opportunities in the complexity age. Cambridge Scholars Publishing
Foerster H (1960) On self-organizing systems and their environments. In: Yovits MC, Cameron S (eds) Self-organizing systems. Pergamon Press, pp 31–50
Foerster H (1984) Observing systems, 2nd edn. Intersystems Publications
Frankish K, Ramsey WM (eds) (2012) The Cambridge handbook of cognitive science. Cambridge University Press
Gibson JJ (1979) The ecological approach to visual perception. Houghton Mifflin Harcourt
Glasersfeld E (1984) An introduction to radical constructivism. In: Watzlawick P (ed) The invented reality. How do we know what we believe we know? (contributions to constructivism). W. W. Norton & Company, pp 17–40
Glasersfeld E (2003) Radical constructivism: a way of knowing and learning. RoutledgeFalmer
Hart HLA (2012) The concept of law, 3rd edn. Oxford University Press
Holland JH (2014) Complexity: a very short introduction. Oxford University Press
Kant I (2015) Crítica de la razón pura, 16th edn. (trans: Morente MG, Fernández Nuñez M). Porrúa
Kinzey WG, Tooby J, DeVore I (1987) The reconstruction of hominid evolution through strategic modeling. In: Kinzey WG (ed) The evolution of human behavior: primate models. SUNY Press, pp 182–237
Lifante Vidal I (2020) In defence of a constructivist conception of legal interpretation. REVUS, J Constitut Philos Law 40:63–83
Luhmann N (1991) Sociología del riesgo, 3rd edn. Universidad Iberoamericana
Luhmann N (1997) Organización y decisión. Autopoiesis, acción y entendimiento comunicativo. Anthropos
Maturana H (2009a) La realidad: ¿objetiva o construida? Vol. I: Fundamentos biológicos de la realidad. Anthropos, Universidad Iberoamericana, Instituto Tecnológico y de Estudios Superiores de Occidente
Maturana H (2009b) La realidad: ¿objetiva o construida? Vol. II: Fundamentos biológicos del conocimiento. Anthropos, Universidad Iberoamericana, Instituto Tecnológico y de Estudios Superiores de Occidente
Maturana H, Valera F (2004) De máquinas y seres vivos. Autopoiesis: la organización de lo vivo, 6th edn. Editorial Universitaria Lumen
Mele AR (ed) (1997) The philosophy of action. Oxford University Press
Menary R (ed) (2010) The extended mind. The MIT Press, Cambridge
Morin E (2005) Introduction à la pensée complexe. Éditions du Seuil
Moya CJ (1990) The philosophy of action: an introduction. Polity Press, Cambridge
Newen A, De Bruin L, Gallagher S (eds) (2018) The Oxford handbook of 4E cognition. Oxford University Press
Olivecrona K (1971) Law as fact, 2nd edn. Stevens & Sons
Piaget J, García R (2008) Psicogénesis e historia de la ciencia. Siglo XXI editores S.A. de C.V.

Robles Morchón G (1988) Las reglas del derecho y las reglas de los juegos. Ensayo de teoría analítica del derecho, 2nd edn. UNAM
Roessler J, Eilan N (eds) (2003) Agency and self-awareness. Oxford University Press
Ruhl JB (1996) Complexity theory as a paradigm for the dynamical law-and-society system: a wake-up call for legal reductionism and the modern administrative state. Duke Law J 45 (5):849–928. https://doi.org/10.2307/1372975
Searle J (1995) The construction of social reality. Penguin Press
Searle J (2010) Making the social world: the structure of human civilization. Oxford University Press
Smith BC (1999) Situatedness/Embeddedness. In: Wilson RA, Keil FC (eds) The MIT encyclopedia of the cognitive sciences. The MIT Press, pp 769–770
Teubner G (1989) How the law thinks: towards a constructivist epistemology of law. Law Soc Rev 23(5):727–757. https://doi.org/10.2307/3053760
Varela FJ, Thompson E, Rosch E (2016) The embodied mind. cognitive science and human experience. The MIT Press
Villa V (1999) Costruttivismo e teorie del diritto. G. Giappichelli, Torino
Villa V (2011) Constructivismo y teorías del derecho. IIJ-UNAM
Vygotsky LS (1979) Mind in society. The development of higher psychological processes. Harvard University Press
Vygotsky LS (1986) Thought and language. The MIT Press
Waldrop MM (1993) Complexity: the emerging science at the edge of order and chaos. Simon & Schuster
Waldrop MM (2009) Complexity: a guided tour. Oxford University Press
Watzlawick P (1984) Forewood. In: Watzlawick P (ed) The invented reality. How do we know what we believe we know? (contributions to constructivism). W. W. Norton & Company, pp 9–11
Webb TE (2014) Tracing an outline of legal complexity. Ratio Juris 27(4):477–495. https://doi.org/10.1111/raju.12056
Wendt A (2003) Social theory of international politics. Cambridge University Press

www.ingramcontent.com/pod-product-compliance
Ingram Content Group UK Ltd.
Pitfield, Milton Keynes, MK11 3LW, UK
UKHW021315130926
15127UKWH00002B/17
* 9 7 8 3 0 3 0 7 8 8 0 2 5 *